BRITISH OPIUM POLICY

IN

CHINA AND INDIA

BY

DAVID EDWARD OWEN

ARCHON BOOKS
1968

17371

SBN: 208 00676 1
LIBRARY OF CONGRESS CATALOG CARD NUMBER: 68-8024
PRINTED IN THE UNITED STATES OF AMERICA

TO
THE MEMORY OF
ERNEST JONES OWEN

PREFACE

THE Indo-British opium trade to China forms one of the most curious chapters in the annals of European expansion. That roughly one-seventh of the revenue of British India should have been drawn from the subjects of another state as payment for a habit-forming drug is, in the words of a British official, "one of the most unique facts that the history of finance affords." And when it is recalled that a large share of the opium sent to China was produced under the aegis of a state-administered monopoly which existed principally for supplying that market, the picture appears still more grotesque. Yet this was the situation that existed in the Far East during the nineteenth century. On the one hand was the East India Company, and later the crown, holding a monopoly of the production of opium in Bengal and controlling the export trade from the native states by means of transit duties. On the other was the Middle Kingdom into which enormous quantities of the drug were introduced, illicitly before 1858, legally thereafter. Plying between the field of production and the market were merchants or their agents, who bought Bengal opium from the East India Company or the Indian government, and carried it to China. That the trade proved a grievous source of friction in Anglo-Chinese relationships is a commonplace scarcely to be repeated.

Such a state of affairs invites explanations, and, indeed, it has already been explained by a host of pens. With few exceptions books on the drug trade have been *ex parte* statements, products of confirmed pro- or anti-

opium views. Defenders of the trade have tended to lay
all of the blame at the door of the Chinese, whose undeniable taste for the narcotic and whose ineptitude in
enforcing their contraband laws laid them open to condemnation. The opposition has also been prone to distort
the facts and to see in opium the sole or chief issue at
stake between Great Britain and China in the nineteenth
century. But beyond the field occupied by the pamphleteers are other works, such as H. B. Morse, *International
Relations of the Chinese Empire,* comprehensive in subject matter and scholarly in method, which are invaluable
to a student of British opium policy. Where, as in the
years immediately preceding and following the first
Anglo-Chinese war, Morse has marked the path with special thoroughness, I have not scrupled to follow his
guideposts.

My own purpose, however, has been to describe British
policy in both India and China, the source and the chief
market. It is a fundamental assumption of these chapters
that an appreciation of the opium system in India is essential to an understanding of the situation as it developed in China. Since this study professes to deal only
with the trade from India to China and with British policy towards it, I have remained fairly strictly within the
limits implied by the subject. Thus I have made no attempt to explain excise arrangements in India and Burma
or to give an account of the trade to China in non-Indian
opium, save where the latter affected British interests.
Irrelevant also would be a consideration of opium as an
international problem. Before the Hague conferences
met, an Anglo-Chinese agreement had doomed the Indian
trade to China, and before the Geneva conferences were
summoned, it had come to an end.

In the interest of simplicity but at the sacrifice of strict
accuracy, I have ventured to omit diacritical marks and

the hyphen in rendering the names of Chinese individuals. Thus T'ang Shao-yi is written Tang Shao Yi. Except where otherwise noted, the word ''dollar'' refers to the Spanish dollar. I have given approximate exchange values for both dollars and taels in a ''Note on Currency, Weights, and Statistics.''

I must acknowledge, although I cannot adequately repay, my debt to those who have assisted in bringing this volume to completion. A Sterling fellowship, awarded to me by the graduate school of Yale University, to which this study was originally submitted as a doctoral dissertation, enabled me to examine the records at the India Office. I must testify also to the unfailing courtesy of Mr. W. T. Ottewill, superintendent of records, and his staff. The late Professor Frederick Wells Williams not only gave generously of his counsel but allowed me to draw freely on the resources of his incomparable library. Professor Kenneth Scott Latourette, to whom I owe my initial interest in Far Eastern history, and Professor Charles Seymour made helpful criticisms of the manuscript in an earlier form. I am much indebted to Professor Charles M. Andrews and Professor Leonard W. Labaree for their editorial supervision. Their corrections in the manuscript resulted in the excision of many, though I fear not all, inconsistencies of statement and infelicities of style.

D. E. O.

New Haven, December, 1933.

CONTENTS

CHAPTER I

A HISTORICAL INTRODUCTION

O PIUM, asserted Galen in the second century A.D.,
is the strongest of the drugs that stupefy the sense
and induce sleep.[1] Greek physicians, predecessors
of Galen, introduced the juice of *papaver somniferum* into
the annals of medical science, but its diffusion into the
East was the work of other hands.[2] To gifted Arab doctors eventually fell the medical legacy of the classical
world, and with the inheritance came knowledge of the
drug opium, whose Greek name *opion* the Arabs appropriated, calling it *afyun*. For transmitting the drug to the
East the Arabs were perhaps the best fitted of all the ancient peoples. Long before the golden age of Moslem civilization at Bagdad, Sabean seamen were piloting their
lateen-rigged craft into remote corners of the eastern
seas, making regular calls at ports along the Malabar
Coast, and as early as 300 A.D., a colony of Arab traders
seems to have been established at Canton.[3] Some three
centuries later began the brilliant expansion of Arabian,
now Mohammedan, arms, which resulted in the conquest
of Sind in the eighth century. Roughly coincident with
the arrival of the Moslems in force appear the first no-
tices of opium in Sanskrit medical works.[4] It was presum-

[1] *De Compositione Medicamentorum*, in Kuhn, *Medicorum Graecorum
Opera*, XIII, 273.

[2] See J. Edkins, *Opium: Historical Note*, pp. 3-4; Sir G. Birdwood and
W. Foster, *First Letter Book of the East India Company*, pp. liv-lv; Sir
G. Watt, *Return of an Article on Opium, Parliamentary Papers*, 1890-1891.

[3] F. Hirth and W. W. Rockhill, *Chau Ju-kua*, p. 4.

[4] *Report of the Royal Commission on Opium*, IV, 1894, Q. 26,628-26,631,
26,680-26,689; II, 1894, App. XXVII.

ably, then, the Arabs, early intermediaries between the East and the West, who supplied the Orient with its once distinctive vice.

However hazy may be the early career of opium in the East, when Portuguese navigators first sought the Orient ''for Christians and for spices,'' not only the cultivation of the poppy but trade in the drug itself was well established. Arab and Indian merchants were marketing opium in Burma, the Malay Peninsula, China, and the East Indies, and it was not for Europeans to leave unmolested a profitable commerce. When Cabral returned to Lisbon from his voyage to the East, opium was an item in his cargo, and Don Affonso de Albuquerque, writing from Canaor in 1513, witnessed to the impression made by the trade upon the early empire builders. ''If your Highness would believe me, I would order poppies . . . to be sown in all the fields of Portugal and command afyam to be made, which is the best merchandise that obtains in these places . . . and the labourers would gain much also, and the people of India are lost without it, if they do not eat it; and set this fact in order, for I do not write your Highness an insignificant thing.''[5]

The eager notebooks of other travelers contribute details, fragmentary, it is true, but full enough to establish the currency of opium in Moghul India. Van Linschoten, the Dutch globe-trotter who visited the East late in the sixteenth century, pictures in quaint and graphic language the effects of indulgence in the drug. Part of the supply, he remarks, comes from Cairo and Aden, but the larger share from Cambay and the Deccan; Indians, especially along the Malabar Coast, consume large quantities. ''Amfion is made of sleepe balls or poppie and is the gumme which cometh forth from the same, to ye which end it is cut up and opened. He that useth to eate it must

[5] F. C. Danvers, *The Portuguese in India*, I, 73-74, 290-291.

eate it daylie, otherwise he dieth and consumeth himself.
. . . . Such as use it go as if they were alwaies halfe a
sleepe, they eate much of it because they would not feele
any great labour or unquietness when they are at work
but they use it most for lecherie.''[6]

In official circles of Moghul India the poppy and its
derivative seem to have had their uses. The emperors
themselves discovered in the seeds a subtle means of
dealing with political enemies, "whose heads the monarch is deterred by prudential reasons from taking off.''
An infusion of poppy seeds in water, explains Bernier,
"is brought to them early in the morning, and they are
not permitted to eat until it be swallowed. This drink
emaciates the wretched victims; who lose their strength
by slow degrees, become torpid and at length die.''[7] Mohammedan records indicate that as early as the year
1000, opium was used by the rulers of India as an indulgence. One is said to have drunk a beverage containing
the drug, while another, of a later period, "ate opium like
cheese out of the hands of his mother.''[8] The governor of
Surat was characterized by the English factor as "an
olde, corrupte, perverse, and cunning fox, though seldom
free from his ophium intoxications.''[9]

To a credulous Portuguese who accompanied Magellan
we are indebted for a curious account of the use of opium
as a homeopathic protection against poison. The king of
Cambay, it appears, desired to render his heir immune
from the poisonous attacks of rivals. Beginning with in-

[6] J. H. van Linschoten, *Voyage to the East Indies*, II, 112-114. Most of
the evidence on the early history of the poppy in India is summarized, with
ample quotations from the sources, in J. B. Lyall, "Historical Note," *Report of the Royal Commission*, VII, 1895, App. A, and R. M. Dane, "Historical Memorandum," *ibid.*, App. B.

[7] F. Bernier, *Voyage to the East Indies*, I, 120-121.

[8] H. Blochmann and H. S. Jarrett, *Ain-I-Akbari*, I, 378, 384, note.

[9] W. Foster, *English Factories in India, 1646-50*, p. 239. See also J. T.
Wheeler, *Early Records*, p. 26.

considerable doses and gradually increasing the amount, he so thoroughly immunized the young prince against the assassin's potion that, like the Mithradates of A. E. Housman,

First a little, thence to more,
He sampled all their killing store

without disaster to himself. So completely had he been fortified that, according to the gullible Barbosa, as soon as "a fly reached his flesh, it died and swelled up."[10]

For the common people opium served a multitude of purposes. It was a standard household remedy then, as it is to-day. Wrestlers used it to enable them to perform feats beyond their strength.[11] Soldiers, too, discovered virtue in a drug that would inspire them "to run up on any Enterprise with a raging resolution to die or be victorious."[12] The Rajputs in the service of the king of Siam were remarked for their courage, "though it be only the effect of Opium." Travelers testify to the employment of the drug as an aphrodisiac, though estimates of its efficacy vary widely. And Indian women, according to one chronicler, found in opium a convenient means of escape from the tyranny of a masculine world. "They drink it dissolved in a little oil and die in their sleep without perception of death."[13]

The early opium trade drew its supplies from two principal areas, the Near East and India.[14] Of the Indian product the chief sources were the Ganges Valley and the native states which form the hinterland of the northwest

10 D. Barbosa, *Description of the Coasts of East Africa and Malabar*, I, 122-123.

11 J. Fryer, *New Account of the East Indies and Persia*, I, 279.

12 *Ibid.*, II, 106.

13 Barbosa, *Description of the Coasts of East Africa and Malabar*, I, 123.

14 The poppy was also cultivated in China, as will appear presently, but the manufactured drug was consumed locally.

coast, states which now compose the Rajputana and Central India agencies. Opium from these native principalities has been known traditionally as Malwa opium, from the region where its output is the largest. It is impossible, with any show of precision, to date the beginnings of poppy cultivation in India, but we may infer from descriptions written in the sixteenth century that the industry was already of years' standing. During the reign of Akbar (1556-1605), poppy land was accounted a regular source of revenue to the Moghul state, and in the *Institutes of Akbar* the areas of production, comprising practically all of northern India, are listed with some degree of particularity.[15] The local dynasty of Gujarat had found, before the time of Akbar, that the trade in opium could be regulated for the profit of the government. In the capital city of Ahmedabad Rs. 5000 were annually realized from stalls for the sale of the drug.[16] Cultivation in the Malwa section appears to have been unrestricted, the peasant receiving advances on his crop from a merchant or village money-lender in the conventional Indian fashion. Much of the foreign trade seems to have been the preserve of the Arabs. Their representatives were residing at Canton and other ports of China, and they had access to both the Indian and the Near Eastern

[15] Sir William Hunter in his standard *History of British India*, I, 172-173, assumes that opium was not produced in India before the appearance of the Portuguese. His evidence is Albuquerque's letter of 1513, which refers to the stoppage of opium shipments from the Persian Gulf, "owing to the thrashing which we gave Aden." This opinion seems to be amply refuted by sixteenth-century travelers—Linschoten, Barbosa, Garcia d'Orta, Caesar Fredericke, and Ralph Fitch, who comment on Malwa under the usual name of Cambay opium. Fitch also speaks of trade in the Patna drug. Conservative as is the Indian peasant in adopting new crops, it is incredible that poppy cultivation could have sprung up between the time of Albuquerque and that of the chroniclers who have been cited. Still less is it likely that the industry could have reached the dimensions described in the *Ain-I-Akbari*. Blochmann and Jarrett, *Ain-I-Akbari*, II, 70 ff.

[16] E. C. Bayley, *Muhammedan Kingdom of Gujarat*, p. 7.

sources of supply. Chinese merchants also appear to have taken some part in transporting the drug on the last stage of its journey. Barbosa, Magellan's cousin, observed Chinese junks carrying it as return cargo from Malacca.[17]

Opium, as we have seen, attracted the attention of the Portuguese when they established themselves on the west coast of India at the dawn of the sixteenth century. Where formerly the trade had been the property of Oriental merchants, the assertive European now proceeded to capture the major share. With brutal abandon, the Portuguese set out to ruin the commerce of Arab and Indian, and in a large measure their efforts were successful.[18] From their factories in India, the Portuguese exported opium mainly to China, where they were granted the right to settle at Macao.[19] Their reception on the mainland was not cordial, for Chinese prejudices had been aroused by Mohammedan residents as well as by the reckless actions of Europeans.[20]

Relying upon papal fiat, which had assigned the entire eastern world to their exploitation, and upon their own naval strength, the Portuguese vigorously sought to exclude Dutch and English interlopers from the lucrative commerce. But without avail, for monopoly was not to be complaisantly admitted by the newcomers, to whom ruthlessness was no stranger. The Portuguese lost their hegemony in the East to the Dutch, then in the first flush of independence, and to the English, full of zeal "for the

[17] Barbosa, *Description of the Coasts of East Africa and Malabar*, I, 241.

[18] See Danvers, *Portuguese in India*, I, *passim*, and Hunter, *History of British India*, I, Chapters III and IV, for discussions of Portuguese policy towards native commerce. Incidentally the first European notice of opium in Indian waters describes the capture of "8 Guzzarate ships" laden with "arfiun" and other merchandise. Sir G. Birdwood and W. Foster, *First Letter Book of the East India Company*, p. lv.

[19] The precise date of the Portuguese settlement at Macao is unknown.

[20] Edkins, *Opium: Historical Note*, p. 39.

honour of our native land, and for the advancement of trade of merchandise within this realm of England." Before 1612 the Dutch had established a factory on the west coast of India. Like other Europeans, they found opium to be a desirable article of trade because of the generally constant demand for it in regions farther to the east. It could be obtained in exchange for specie and European goods, transported to the islands of the East or to Malacca, and there bartered for pepper or other spices.[21] There is no evidence that China was an important market for Dutch opium. On the contrary, all other aims were subordinated to that of monopolizing commerce with the East Indies. It was pepper that lured them. "Where wouldn't they go for pepper! For a bag of pepper they would cut each other's throats without hesitation, and would foreswear their souls, of which they were otherwise so careful." And opium proved an admirable medium of barter for the coveted spice. By treaties with native princes the Dutch sought to monopolize the importing business into Java and Malacca. Illegal opium might be seized "and so bring a Clamour and Noise about one's Ears, not easily quieted," the buyer subject to capital punishment and the seller seriously embarrassed.[22]

The trade of the Dutch in Malwa opium was insignificant in comparison with their later achievements in Bengal. In the Ganges Valley the Portuguese never dominated matters as they did on the west coast, and it was the Hollanders who here appropriated the fruits of exploration. In their zeal they are said to have fallen on the expedient of training Ceylon elephants and trading

21 J. B. Tavernier, *Voyages*, Part II, p. 132.

22 C. Lockyer, *Account of the Trade in India*, p. 68; Danvers, "Memorandum on Dutch Trade in Opium during the 17th Century principally compiled from Dutch East India Records at The Hague," *Report of the Royal Commission*, VII, 1895, App. B.

them to Bengal merchants for opium and other merchandise.[23] It was in 1659 that they began to procure their supply from Bengal, and when the trade reached its height a century later, they were shipping more than one hundred tons to Batavia alone.[24] Thereafter the opium business of the Dutch declined, partly because of the persistent intrusion of interlopers and partly because of chaotic political conditions in Bengal.

The English reached the west coast of India a century after the Portuguese pioneers.[25] To the newcomers, as to other Europeans, opium was revealed as a useful article of commerce, both for export to Europe and for barter in lands farther east. On the sixth voyage of the company (1609), five hundred pounds were included in the list of commodities for the London market.[26] Shipments to Europe remained small, but Malwa opium was sent in larger quantities to various ports in the East Indies.[27] With China the East India Company established direct commercial relations as early as 1637. There is no evidence to show that opium was represented in the official cargoes, although the drug was certainly introduced by servants of the company as individuals and by private adventurers. Thus the intrepid Robinson Crusoe made two profitable voyages to the coast of China with opium,

23 T. Bowrey, *Countries around the Bay of Bengal*, p. 181.

24 Danvers, ''Memorandum on Dutch Trade.''

25 The English seem to have been only slightly less implacable than their predecessors towards native commerce. On one occasion the factor at Surat alludes to the capture of two Malabar junks off the coast of Arabia by one Captain Quayl, apparently an interloper, ''out of which he got some smale quantity of offim.'' Foster, *English Factories in India, 1630-33*, p. 180. See also Foster, *English Factories, 1622-23*, p. 264.

26 Birdwood and Foster, *First Letter Book of the East India Company*, p. 328.

27 Foster, *English Factories in India, 1618-21*, pp. 7-8, 65; Foster, *Letters from the East India Company's Servants*, IV, 293; V, 60-64; *Cal. State Papers, East Indies, 1513-1616*, §792.

which, he had heard, "bears a great Price among the Chinese."[28] The English, however, exerted little influence on the trade from the west coast until in the nineteenth century the growth of Malwa opium exports made restrictive measures necessary to protect their Bengal monopoly.

But in Bengal the English became commercially as well as politically dominant, and it was opium from this source that was to dictate British policy. The area of production comprised Bengal, Bihar, Orissa, and Benares, the best varieties being manufactured in Bihar and secondarily in Benares. Patna was the center of the industry. Early travelers leave one in no doubt of the preeminence of the Patna drug or of the high development of the industry in the Ganges Basin.[29] Ralph Fitch properly described Patna as "a very long and great town" with "a trade of very much opium and other commodities."[30] More than a century later Captain Hamilton testified, inaccurately to be sure, that the city supplied all the rest of India.[31] Calicut and other ports on the Malabar Coast were important entrepôts for the interior. An English observer commented upon the war between the Dutch and the samorin of Calicut as having cost the latter "a good milk cow, for the chiefs . . . for many years had vended between five hundred and a thousand chests of Bengal ophium yearly up in the inland countries where it is very much used. The water carriage up the river being cheap and secure, the Price of Ophium high, and the Price of Pepper low, so that their profits were great both ways."[32]

[28] Oxford edition, pp. 473, 502.

[29] See Bowrey, *Geographical Account of the Countries around the Bay of Bengal*, p. 134, note. There is also some evidence of opium production along the Coromandel Coast, but little is known of it.

[30] *The Voyage of M. Ralph Fitch*, II, 388. See also *ibid.*, p. 386.

[31] *New Account of the East Indies*, II, 22.   [32] *Ibid.*, I, 315.

That the Patna industry was deemed important by the natives themselves is indicated by the monopoly which the Moghuls established over it. To a group of merchants in the city was granted the sole right of purchasing the produce of peasants in the vicinity, in return for an annual payment to the government.[33] The fortunate monopolists, on the one hand, could depress the price paid to cultivators for their raw opium, and on the other, could raise the selling price, thus doing handsomely for themselves and for the royal treasury. Poppy culture around Patna seems to have been free, but the peasants were permitted to sell only to state contractors, who manufactured the opium and sold it for export or for local consumption.[34] This old Moghul monopoly, though its footprints now are dim, is of more than passing significance, for in it is to be found the lineal ancestor of the British opium system of to-day.

India as the source, China as the destination, is the theme of this study. But although the rôle assigned to China is chiefly that of a market for the Indian drug, opium was no novelty when Europeans began to import it.[35] Centuries before had come the poppy itself, probably

[33] Since there is no mention of the Patna monopoly in the *Ain-I-Akbari*, it is inferred that the system was established in the seventeenth century after the death of Akbar. Europeans tended to adopt similar schemes. Witness, for example, the Dutch monopolies in Java and the Spanish tobacco *régie* in the Philippines. See *Fifth Report from the Select Committee*, 1812, p. 23.

[34] In 1683 opium was first sent to England from Bengal on the company's account, but for more than a century the imports were inconsequential. Before 1765 none was sent officially to the other factories in the East save a small quantity to Sumatra. It was only as the China market developed that the British opium trade from Bengal expanded. Sir G. Birdwood, *Report on the Miscellaneous Old Records at the India Office*, p. 22; Hinchman's evidence, *Ninth Report from the Select Committee*, 1783, App. 59B.

[35] The following section is based primarily upon Edkins, *Opium: Historical Note*, the most painstaking and credible account of the early days of the

introduced into the venerable empire by the Arabs, who had established themselves at Canton perhaps two or three centuries before the Hegira.[36] According to Chinese chroniclers, Islam was preached to the colony between 618 and 636, and by the eighth century the Moslems had so increased in number that they were able to sack and burn the city.[37] As early as the fourth century, jasmine and henna, plants that appear to have come in with Arabian commerce, were growing in China. And when Chinese writers begin to refer to opium, the word used is *ya-pien,* probably derived from the Arabic *afyun.*

Prior to the first half of the eighth century there is no positive evidence that the poppy was known in China. But in the reign of Tang Ming Huang it finds indubitable identification at the hands of one who quotes from a still earlier work. A poet of the same dynasty in stanzas ''On leaving a winding Valley and approaching my Western Home'' establishes the fact of poppy cultivation in West China.

Passing the dangerous staircase
I issued from the winding defile of the Pao valley . . .
I am now near my home.
The sadness of the traveler in his journey
Of ten thousand li
Is today dissipated.
Before my horse I see
The *mi-nang* flower.[38]

As in India, a beverage made from the seeds seems to have been the first form in which the poppy was used.

poppy in China. Except where otherwise credited, statements of fact are taken from this monograph.

[36] S. W. Williams, *Middle Kingdom,* II, 373, thinks it possible that the poppy was indigenous to China.

[37] F. Hirth and W. W. Rockhill, *Chau Ju-kua,* p. 14.

[38] Poppy heads, because the seeds were similar in shape to millet, were called *mi-nang,* millet bags.

In the latter part of the tenth century, it entered the official pharmacopoeia—the Herbalist's Treasury—as an antidote for mercury, "the stone that confers immortality," by which the Chinese of the time were seeking to repel the advance of old age. Thereafter the seeds of the opium poppy appear frequently in Chinese prescriptions —curious mixtures of shrewd empiricism and superstition. The chief use of the poppy was clearly medicinal, but the Chinese seem not to have been unaware of its other properties. Thus in poetic rhapsody a Chinese De-Quincey reveals the ecstasy of those who seek refreshment from the brilliantly colored flower. After describing the method of cultivation and the preparation of the drink, the poet continues:

> I see here the Hermit of the Shade,
> And the long-robed Buddhist priest.
> When they sit opposite I forget to speak.
> Then I have but to drink a cup of this poppy-seed drink.
>   I laugh,
>   I am happy,
>   I have come to Ying-chuan,
> And am wandering on the banks of its river.
> I seem to be climbing the slopes of the Lu Mountain
> In the far west.[39]

In the twelfth century the use of poppy seeds was supplanted, in part, by the more potent capsule.[40] The drug extracted by grinding the capsule contained true opium, but with it were mixed impurities of the pulp. As a remedy for dysentery, its power was regarded as almost

[39] Despite the exhilarating dreams which the poet enjoyed, his chief argument for the drink is its therapeutic value. "Old men whose powers have decayed . . . who when they eat meat cannot digest it . . . should take this drink."

[40] The seed sac, which measures, on the average, about two inches in length.

magical. But Chinese doctors were alive to its dangers as well as to its virtues. "Though its effects are quick," said one, "great care must be taken in using it, because it kills like a knife."[41]

Three centuries after the capsule derivative became common appears the first notice of genuine opium, prepared not by pulverizing the head but by scoring the capsule and dehydrating the juice which exudes. During the period of the Mings, the connection between China and the Near East became more intimate. Armed with the mariner's compass, Chinese seamen steered their uncouth junks to Malacca, to India, and even to the Persian Gulf. On several occasions diplomatic representatives were sent, who visited most of the large seaports between Canton and Aden. Thus the natives of the usually aloof empire had ample opportunity to learn the secrets of Mohammedan civilization.

The first mention of true opium in China further strengthens the presumption that not only the poppy but the drug itself reached the Far East through the agency of the Arabs. A writer who lived in the middle of the fourteenth century describes with some care the preparation and uses of the narcotic, prefacing his instructions with the remark, "Opium is produced in Arabia from a poppy with a red flower."[42] The author, for twenty years in charge of the province of Kansu, had been in close contact with a large Mohammedan population. To his testimony must be added that of three other independent witnesses who lived during Ming times, one of whom re-

[41] Dr. J. Dudgeon in a pamphlet, *Statistics and Resolutions of the Evils of the Use of Opium,* asserts that evidence is lacking to show that the poppy grown in China in the early days was the opium poppy. Some of the older allusions to the flower may be arguable, but the statement cited above indicates that no later than the twelfth century *papaver somniferum* was being used by Chinese who were aware of its properties.

[42] The typical Bengal poppy was white.

fers to opium as *a-fu-yung,* a term plainly derived from the Arabic *afyun,* but whose directions for manufacture clearly have to do with the native Chinese drug. During the lifetime of this writer, all foreign commerce was placed under imperial interdict, owing to the intemperate conduct of Japanese raiding parties.[43] The supply of medicines from abroad ceased. Opium was at best difficult to obtain, and Chinese doctors sought, therefore, to meet the need by including in their pharmacopoeias instructions for its manufacture. In short, there is good ground for concluding, first, that the drug was introduced by the Arabs, and secondly, that it has been produced in China for something over four centuries.

If Europeans may be acquitted of having first brought opium to the Middle Kingdom, they were, nevertheless, indirectly responsible for providing the Chinese with their characteristic vice—opium smoking. Hitherto the drug had been taken internally, broadly speaking, for medicinal purposes. It was only through contact with the West that the natives of China came to realize the virtues of opium as an indulgence, pure and simple. When the Spanish conquistadores established themselves in the Philippine Islands, they brought with them the tobacco plant, one of the first gifts from the New World to the Old. Thence it was carried to the coast of China, probably by Fukien sailors trading to Manila. The "smoke-plant," as it was called, seems to have met with almost instant popularity, for the last of the Mings issued a severe proscription against its use. But the habit was not to be checked by the empty fiat of a waning dynasty, and even the early Manchus had to acknowledge their inability to exterminate what they regarded as a moral evil. The first of the line promulgated an explosive edict addressed to the princes and high officials—an Oriental analogue to

[43] The prohibition of foreign trade went into effect in 1523.

the "Counterblaste to Tobacco"—which reveals the universality of smoking among the nobility. It had even, the Manchu monarch asserted, corrupted the military system. "Why do you not lead the soldiers yourselves in the practice of archery? . . . To smoke tobacco is a fault, but not so great a fault as to neglect bow exercise. As to the prohibition of tobacco-smoking, it became impossible to maintain it, because you princes and others smoked privately, though not publicly; but as to the use of the bow, this must not be neglected."[44]

Gradually the practice of mixing drugs with tobacco developed, first apparently in the East Indies. Engelberg Kaempfer, who visited Java in 1689, inspected primitive opium dens, where tobacco mixed with the narcotic was dispensed.[45] From the East Indies the habit appears to have spread to Formosa, between 1624 and 1662 under the rule of the Dutch. Here the malaria-tainted jungle made opium an esteemed addition to the rudimentary *materia medica*. Opium divans soon appeared and with them confirmed addicts, who, in the words of a Chinese writer, unless they "be killed will not cease smoking." Once in Formosa the new vice easily found its way to the mainland. In the days of Koxinga, the picturesque half-patriot, half-pirate, who wrested Formosa from the Dutch, groups of Chinese colonists established themselves on the island. Among these the habit became entrenched, thence spreading to the province of Fukien. But its diffusion seems not to have been as rapid as that

44 The promulgator of this edict did not actually become emperor of the Chinese until three years later, when his forces captured Peking. A curious sequel to the prohibition is the following: "The extensive use of tobacco, and the introduction of the Hookah into China, even to his Majesty's residence at Jehol, has called forth from him a general order to forbid the culture of tobacco, which is prepared for the Hookah, in every province of China." *Indo-Chinese Gleaner*, no. 6, October, 1818.

45 *Amoenitates Exoticae*, pp. 642-645.

of its forerunner, tobacco smoking. When the great Kang Hsi pacified Formosa in 1683, with his base of operations at Amoy, he was in the heart of the opium-smoking area. Yet there is no record of prohibitory edicts directed against the vice.[46]

Not until 1729 did the first of a long line of anti-opium laws find place in the Chinese statute book. Word had reached Peking of the ravages of the drug, and the emperor now stepped in to meet the problem. The unique feature of this early edict was that all parties to the transaction were to be punished severely save only the buyer, who himself had prepared his doom. Keepers of opium shops, like "propagators of depraved doctrines," were to be strangled after a short imprisonment, while assistants might expect a hundred blows with the bamboo and banishment a thousand miles from their homes. Even boatmen, bailiffs, soldiers, customs officials, and magistrates were included in this sweeping edict. In the following year another edict condemned certain doubtful practices among the colonists in Formosa, such as robbery, enticing the aborigines to commit murder, and vending opium.

It should be emphasized that the Chinese government in this first anti-opium law was not moved by fear that the vice would engulf the empire. Opium smoking was apparently still confined to Formosa and Fukien. The edict was merely meant to fumigate a plague spot in a section remote from Peking, where, it was felt, a pernicious habit had produced an epidemic of lawlessness. Smoking the drug was not yet the national vice of China. Indeed no allusion whatever is made to it in the writings of the Jesuit missionaries, who from 1580 to the beginning of the nineteenth century enlightened the West about the East. And Staunton's account of the Macartney mission

46 H. B. Morse, *Trade and Administration*, p. 328.

of 1793 has little to say of the habit.[47] Until well along in the eighteenth century and probably later, the smoking of opium was a localized phenomenon and was not regarded as a critical problem in Peking. But with the passing of the years and with the increasingly insistent pressure of the West, the new vice came to assume the dignity of a national menace. In its changing status European as well as Chinese played his part.

In the succeeding pages we shall explore this development. We shall observe, on the one hand, a sincere but impotent government at Peking, beset by smugglers and hampered by corrupt officials, waging a losing and humiliating battle against opium. On the other, we shall see the English in Bengal declaring a monopoly over the opium industry and themselves providing the supply for China. This step, taken with true Anglo-Saxon concern for the immediate necessity, involved the East India Company and later the crown almost inextricably in the drug business and provided a revenue which, as the traffic grew, came to appear quite indispensable.

[47] Sir G. L. Staunton, *An Authentic Account of an Embassy . . . to the Emperor of China*, I, 174; Williams, *Middle Kingdom*, II, 377; Edkins, *Opium: Historical Note*, p. 37.

CHAPTER II

THE ESTABLISHMENT OF THE MONOPOLY IN BENGAL

ALTHOUGH the use of opium had existed in the Far East from remote times, it was left to the European to organize the industry on a large scale. As we have seen, he had no part in introducing the drug into the Orient, but it was his talent for organization that made of it a world problem. Opium appeared as an irritant in international affairs simultaneously with the expansion of British arms in India and British trade in China, and its progress represents one of the less savory aspects of the westernization of the East. Conceivably, of course, the traffic from India might have developed to its nineteenth-century proportions under the aegis of native rulers, but it could never have received the careful nurture and the minute attention bestowed upon it by the East India Company. The British, when they conquered Bengal, found an industry badly organized and presumably incapable of great evil. At the close of Warren Hastings' administration there existed a state monopoly of opium, productive of revenue and increasingly an essential feature of the Indian fiscal system. An excellent and convincing rationale, to be sure, can be offered for every step by which the company became involved in the opium business. Each seemed inevitable. But, however extenuating the circumstances, the fact remains that it was the European who raised the drug trade to its nineteenth-century stature.

When disintegration finally overtook the old Moghul state early in the eighteenth century, its formal monopoly in opium disappeared. Unofficial engrossing continued in the hands of a group of Patna merchants, who through collective action and financial power were able to assure their own preëminence, though petty traders called "pykars" also took some part.[1] They made the customary cash advances to cultivators, and, when the manufacturing process was completed, offered the opium to European purchasers. Prices fluctuated violently, depending upon political conditions as well as upon the amount and quality of the drug.

The hegemony of the Patna merchants was of relatively short duration, for the transformation of European trading companies into empire builders led inexorably to the collapse of the native monopoly. When, during the war with Siraj-ud-daula, the English were forced to leave Calcutta, only the Dutch remained as purchasers of opium. Professing their complete indifference to the drug, they were able to buy at prices ruinous to the dealers of Patna.[2] In 1757 the English returned not merely as traders but as the dominant political power in Bengal. With puppet nawabs in nominal control, the path to empire opened before the company.

This change in the status of the British was mirrored almost immediately in the opium industry. Opportunities for the aggrandizement of the company's servants were immeasurably enhanced. Private trading operations were the rule, and the members of the provincial council at Patna, as meagerly paid as their fellows, awoke to find

[1] Letter from the president [Warren Hastings], Proc. President and Council, 15 Oct. 1773, *Ninth Report from the Select Committee*, 1783, App. 59A. (Hereafter this report will be cited as *Ninth Report*, 1783.) See also the reply of Ram Chandar Pandit to a questionnaire from Earl Cornwallis in A. Shakespear, *Duncan Records*, II, 160-162.

[2] *Duncan Records*, II, 162-163.

themselves in possession of an incipient monopoly. The high prices which had prevailed since the battle of Plassey stimulated cultivation, and the various Europeans— English, French, and Dutch—sent their agents to make advances and later to collect the crop.[3] In the competitive struggle for the opium of Bihar, the British, represented by the company's servants at Patna, seem to have been the most active. With the French and the Dutch, who were loath to relinquish their share in the profitable business, rivalry was keen. But as early as 1761 conditions approaching monopoly were established.[4] On at least two occasions the Dutch officially complained of the engrossing tendencies of the Patna council, and the court of directors, with customary sensitiveness to the opprobrium of monopoly, expressed dissatisfaction with the enterprise of its agents.[5]

Competition with the Dutch and French continued amid incessant quarrels, which led occasionally to bloodshed and loss of life. But a solution was in sight. In 1765 the hands of the English were strengthened when Clive assumed the diwanni of Bengal, that is, the right of collecting the revenues of the nawab. To the commercial supremacy of the company's servants was thus added an official status. As the select committee of Parliament put it, they "appeared as magistrates in the markets in which they dealt as traders."[6] The alert Patna council immediately took steps to realize on its new position.

---

[3] *Ibid.* See also Van Sittart's minute, Bengal Revenue Consultations, 23 Nov. 1773, *Ninth Report*, 1783, App. 59A; Hinchman's evidence, *ibid.*, App. 59B.

[4] "I have personal knowledge of its having existed so long ago as 1761." Letter from the president, Proc. President and Council, 15 Oct. 1773, *Ninth Report*, 1783, App. 59A.

[5] Henry Van Sittart to Peter Amyatt, 13 Jan. 1763, *Third Report from the Select Committee*, 1773, App. 36; company's letter to Bengal, 22 Feb. 1764, *Fourth Report from the Select Committee*, 1773, App. 1.

[6] *Ninth Report*, 1783, p. 61.

Native merchants had been virtually excluded from the opium business, and only the Dutch and the French remained. To quiet the persistent complaints of European traders, the English at Patna declared a monopoly of Bihar opium, compounding the claims of the Dutch and the French with a specified number of chests annually.[7] Thereafter the council exercised a monopoly for the personal profit of its members, providing a small quantity on the company's account for export and selling the remainder to private merchants. For practical purposes the control of the council was absolute, although some of the independent traders continued to make advances to ryots.[8] Thus the opium trade of Bihar had fallen into the hands of an irresponsible body, a group of the company's servants who administered it for their own emolument.

The situation was patently anomalous, unsatisfactory alike to the company, to private traders, and to peasants. Here was a source of revenue diverted into the pockets of a few men, whereas it might have served the interests of the company. Great annoyance was felt by independent merchants, whose attempts to participate in the trade met with violent opposition from the Patna contractor. Their exclusion was "exclaimed against as a grievous oppression; everyone conceiving himself to be equally entitled to the benefits of a Trade from which they are not excluded by an authentic act of Government.'"[9] Charges of mismanagement and oppression practised upon the ryots were too common to be ignored. Indeed the extraordinary increase in production strengthened the presumption against the Patna monopolists.[10] The unique position

[7] *Duncan Records*, II, 163.

[8] "Ryot" is the common term for an Indian peasant.

[9] Letter from the president, Proc. President and Council, 15 Oct. 1773, *Ninth Report*, 1783, App. 59A.

[10] Before the agreement with the other Europeans the total purchases of the English, French, and Dutch had fallen to about 500 chests. In 1770-1771

of the contractor as representative of both trader and magistrate created a splendid opportunity for injustice in the interest of profit, since the peasant had little appeal from any exaction that might be laid upon him.

No less painful to the company was the loss of revenue. The "Gentlemen at Patna" were appropriating funds always needed by the official treasury. When in April, 1772, Warren Hastings was made governor of Bengal with a mandate to reorganize the entire governmental structure, the time was ripe for action on the opium question. During the following year he addressed himself to the troublesome Patna monopoly. Hastings clearly regarded some form of monopoly as inevitable despite the lip-service which he paid to free trade in the abstract. In a long letter to the Bengal council he passed in review the three possible schemes for dealing with the production of opium.[11] In the first place, the company might grant an exclusive concession to some individual or group, in other words, monopoly by contract. A second possibility was to take the entire production, manufacture, and sale of opium into the hands of the company itself, monopoly by agency. Finally, every restriction might be removed and the trade laid open to all merchants indiscriminately.

The first two proposals, Hastings reflected, were liable to all the conventional objections levied against monopolies. The natural growth of the industry would be handicapped, and the drug would not sell at its true value, "beside the detestation in which the word [monopoly] itself is universally held, even by those who do not understand

the yield rose to 1400 and in the following year to 1800. Henry Van Sittart to Peter Amyatt, 13 Jan. 1763, *Third Report from the Select Committee*, 1773, App. 36; Van Sittart's minute, Bengal Revenue Consultations, 23 Nov. 1773, *Ninth Report*, 1783, App. 59A.

11 Letter from the president, Proc. President and Council, 15 Oct. 1773, *Ninth Report*, 1783, App. 59A.

the meaning of it." As between contract and agency, the former, he felt, could be more easily administered and would probably prove more profitable.

With the question of free trade in opium the governor felt compelled to deal at greater length, in deference perhaps to the rising *laissez faire* sentiment in England. In the course of his argument he enunciated the principles that remained, by and large, the opium policy of the East India Company through the first two decades of the nineteenth century. Having admitted the strength of the free-trade position in general, he sought to prove it inapplicable to the drug trade. Ordinary commerce, "which always languishes under confinement," might prosper best without governmental restraint, but to increase the production of an article not necessary for life would be no advantage. And opium "is not a necessary of life, but a pernicious article of luxury, which ought not to be permitted but for purposes of foreign commerce only." The drug market was a highly limited one, and a profitable trade therefore depended upon a restricted output. The interests of nobody, Hastings urged, would be injured by monopoly, since opium was a unique commodity having no connection with the general trade.

The governor's opposition to a free trade in opium evoked no dissenting voice in the Bengal council. This unanimity was reflected in a resolution passed on November 23, 1773, which formally terminated the control of the Patna council and established a monopoly under the Bengal government.[12] The exclusive privilege of supplying opium was awarded to one Meer Muneer, a native who had acted as contractor for the Patna council.[13] He was to

[12] Bengal Revenue Consultations, 23 Nov. 1773, *Ninth Report*, 1783, App. 59A.

[13] The contract between Meer Muneer and the company, dated 2 Dec. 1773, reveals the fact that Ram Chandar Pandit was associated in the enterprise. For the text see *Ninth Report*, 1783, App. 61. The Dutch were to be

provide all of the opium produced in Bihar, together with all that he might obtain in Ghazipur or other territory belonging to Oudh.[14] Meer Muneer engaged to deliver the drug at the factory in Calcutta, where it was to be sold at public auction. To protect the cultivator from the contractor, the council included in the agreement a clause which forbade him to compel a reluctant ryot to sow the poppy.

The Bengal administrators had thus chosen the path that they and their successors were to follow. Free trade in opium they regarded as quite unthinkable. Opium, after all, was peculiarly susceptible to monopoly control, for as a trade it was highly speculative in character and subject to sharp fluctuations in price. To withdraw the restraining hand of the government, it was felt, would produce anarchy in Bengal, when order was at best precarious. If every merchant, including European interlopers, were given the right to make advances to cultivators, the latter would receive money in abundance, would squander part of it, and at harvest time would default on their engagements. The violent scenes of the Patna monopoly in its early days would be reënacted, with the peasants, as usual, the chief sufferers. Ryots, when they found themselves unable to deliver the quantity of opium for which they had received advances, would resort to adulteration, to the immense detriment of their product.

allowed 500 chests per annum. Neither the French nor the Danes are mentioned in the contract, but subsequent records indicate that they received 300 and 200 chests respectively. India Office Bengal Public Consultations, 13 July 1795; Dane, ''Historical Memorandum,'' *Report of the Royal Commission*, VII, 1895, App. B, p. 38.

14 The company agreed to pay 320 sicca rupees per maund for Bihar opium. A Bengal maund is about eighty pounds, and a chest of Bengal opium ordinarily weighs two maunds. The term ''sicca'' refers to a newly coined rupee, which bore a somewhat higher premium than the ordinary rupee. The contractor was to receive Rs. 350 per maund for any opium that he was able to buy in the possessions of Oudh.

In any case, free trade would probably prove not only a dubious but an impossible policy, for the history of the opium industry had been one of monopoly, either private or official. It would be exceedingly difficult for the company, with its tenuous hold on India, to prevent engrossing and to insure a genuinely free trade.

Warren Hastings, at least, recognized opium to be a harmful drug, and he wished to discourage its consumption in Bengal. Clearly this could be more easily accomplished by monopolizing the supply than by attempting to regulate a free trade. But more convincing perhaps than any of these arguments was that of revenue. The addition of political responsibilities to its ordinary commercial activities had thrown the company's finances into more than usual chaos. It was the task of Warren Hastings to effect every reasonable economy and to canvass new sources of income. In the opium trade appeared a possible field for development and one which, before the recall of Hastings, was to net the company more than a half million sterling.[15]

In 1773 these considerations seemed decisive. Politically the establishment of the monopoly was quite defensible. It produced revenue where none had existed and a relative degree of order in an industry where confusion had prevailed. The practical issue, to repeat, was between monopoly and free trade. Prohibition was never seriously considered, nor can we be surprised that it was not. To blame the company for having refused to embark on such a course would be to impute to the eighteenth century a standard of social ethics utterly foreign to it. The free traders in the court of directors and elsewhere were

---

[15] Hastings had planned to use the opium revenue to pay the allowances of the board of revenue, in lieu of the privilege of private trade. Revenue letter from Bengal, 31 Dec. 1773, *Ninth Report*, 1783, App. 30; M. E. M. Jones, *Warren Hastings*, pp. 252-253; Hastings to Laurence Sulivan, 10 March 1774, G. R. Gleig, *Warren Hastings*, I, 382.

moved by no desire to suppress the sale of opium. Their
argument, on the contrary, was that monopoly was a
stupid and unjustifiable barrier to the normal expansion
of trade. And, had the Indian administrators sought to
forbid poppy cultivation, it is doubtful whether success
could have been achieved. There were many more important things to be done, and the company's position in
Bengal was too uncertain to have made of prohibition
anything but a utopian experiment.

However explicable his motives, Hastings still must
answer for having involved the company in the opium
business, and it proved to be a business which was easier
to enter than to abandon. During the first years of its
existence the monopoly was comparatively innocuous,
since only a small supply was provided. But, when the
company discovered that the potential demand in China
was infinitely greater than the normal Indian production
and as the revenue began to mount the character of the
monopoly changed. What had been in part a device for
controlling cultivation then became equally effective for
expanding it. Warren Hastings could scarcely foresee the
year when nearly fifty thousand chests of Bengal opium
would be shipped to China. In 1773 all arguments seemed
to favor the step that he took, but it was this same step
that established the company in its unedifying business
of opium vending.

The method of conducting the enterprise during the
régime of Meer Muneer (1773-1774) varied little, if at
all, from the procedure during the monopoly of the Patna
council. The entire process, from preparing the ground
for seed, to the final auction sale at Calcutta, was based
upon an elaborate system of advance payments. The contractor himself received them from the company and in
turn made engagements with the ryots on the basis of
advances. These early payments enabled the peasant to

manure the ground and to carry on the plowing and har-
rowing so vital to poppy cultivation. When the juice was
collected in March, April, and May, and delivered to the
contractor, it still had to undergo a refining process
which required about six months. At the conclusion of the
whole operation, the drug had cost the contractor about
Rs. 100 per maund. Profits were ample, but the position
of the contractor was withal a trying one. He must be
prepared to suffer from dishonest cultivators who absconded with his advances or who disposed of their yield
clandestinely to interlopers, while a failure of the poppy
crop might well mean the loss of most of his capital.[16]

At Calcutta the entire provision was sold at public auction for export. With the fall of the auctioneer's hammer
the participation of the East India Company in the
opium trade was brought to an end. It is plain from the
deliberations of the council that no interference with the
export trade was contemplated. The intention was merely
to substitute for the unofficial engrossing of the Patna
factory an avowed monopoly under the Bengal government. With the exception of one disastrous venture to
China and some inconsiderable shipments to London and
the East Indies, the company concerned itself only with
the production, manufacture, and sale of the drug in
India. Distribution was left to the purchasers at the Calcutta sales. They might export the opium wherever they
chose, with no questions asked by the company. It was,
nevertheless, with an eye upon the taste of the foreign
consumer that the monopoly policy was adopted.[17] If gold
were to flow steadily into the coffers of the company, a
drug of the required standard must be produced, and the

[16] Letter from the provincial council at Patna, 27 March 1775, Bengal
Revenue Consultations, 3 May 1775, *Ninth Report*, App. 59A.

[17] It is perhaps worth noting that the Malay, not the China, opium trade
was mentioned in the resolution which brought the monopoly into existence.

best means of insuring that quality was an official monopoly.

The opium industry of Bengal was thus taken under the wing of the East India Company. First the preserve of the Moghul emperors and then of private merchants, it had fallen into the hands of the company's officials at Patna, who administered it as a personal monopoly. From this status to public monopoly was but a short distance, and this distance was traversed at the suggestion of Warren Hastings. The monopoly was still directed by a private contractor who sold the opium to the company. It was then purchased by merchants for export. The policy thus embarked upon, of controlling the production of opium and preserving an official attitude of indifference as to its final destination, forms the foundation stone of the British opium system, the superstructure of which was still to be erected.

In 1774, under Lord North's regulating act of the previous year, a new council of five members was created with Hastings as governor-general of India. Three of its members were sent out from England, General Clavering and Colonel Monson, politicians of mediocre ability, and Philip Francis, whose pen had lost little of the mordant touch that made him the reputed author of the *Letters of Junius* and who was to find in Hastings a congenial target for his invective. Save for a few years that Colonel Monson had served in the south of India, the three were utterly lacking in Indian experience, but they had come fortified with invincible prejudices against the company and strongly influenced by their free-trade prepossessions. The governor-general found himself unable to control his own council, for his only consistent supporter was Richard Barwell, a civil servant of Bengal.

In the spring of 1775 the new council was brought face to face with the problem of the opium monopoly. The contract with Meer Muneer, which had run for nearly two years, was about to expire, and the questions of monopoly versus free trade and contract versus agency were raised once more. To the late contractors the enterprise had apparently proved remunerative, at least sufficiently so to arouse the interest of the Patna council, whose members begged that they be allowed to act as the company's agent in the business. Their letter was full of large promises, among them "to secure annually to the amount of 33,000 chests of genuine unadulterated Ophium.'"[18] While the governor-general appears not to have taken this amazing offer at its face value, his ideas had undergone a change since the first contract had been awarded. He was now inclining strongly towards an agency managed by servants of the company. Barwell, who ordinarily saw eye to eye with his chief, also favored the agency system.

The other three members of the council were temperamentally opposed to all monopolies. But despite their free-trade formulae, they were inclined to make some slight allowance for the peculiar character of the opium industry. Philip Francis, more uncompromising than his colleagues, took occasion to register his belief that the trade might be laid open without unhappy results.[19] If monopoly were to be the plan, he agreed that it should be by contract rather than agency. The decision, three to two, was for continuing the award of contracts, with the

---

[18] Letter from the provincial council at Patna, 27 March 1775, Bengal Revenue Consultations, 3 May 1775, *Ninth Report*, 1783, App. 59A. It is obvious that the estimate of the Patna factory was many times the normal yield. In 1773-1774, 3311 chests had been provided, or about one-tenth of what the optimistic council suggested. G. W. Forrest, *Selections from the State Papers, 1772-1785*, II, 483. The figure 33,000 may, of course, be an error on the part of an eighteenth-century printer.

[19] For Francis' plan, see *Sixth Report from the Select Committee*, 1782, App. 14, and his *Letter to Lord North*, pp. 78-79. See also S. Weitzman, *Warren Hastings and Philip Francis*, p. 299.

additional proviso that manufacture should take place at Patna under the supervision of the provincial council.[20] When proposals were received, it was discovered that four Englishmen and eight natives had responded.[21] All twelve, however, were passed over in favor of an unofficial bid submitted by Barwell for one Richard Griffith, whose offer was clearly the most advantageous to the company, since he had apparently been informed by Barwell of the terms submitted by his competitors.[22] To another contractor was granted the right to supply opium from Bengal proper.[23]

Henceforth during the Hastings administration, opium contracts were let without the formality of soliciting bids. At the request of the contractors the arrangement of 1775 was extended another twelve months, not without some discussion in the council. On this occasion the monopoly itself narrowly escaped the *coup de grâce*. Philip Francis, whose lance was always poised to slay the dragons of monopoly, especially if the monsters acknowledged Hastings as their master, launched into a condemnation of all monopolies, public and private. But at the crucial point, when the continuance of the company's opium system was hanging in the balance, he was deserted by his usually staunch supporter, General Clavering. As long as

---

[20] Governor-general and council to the court of directors (revenue), 3 Aug. 1775, *Ninth Report*, 1783, App. 61.

[21] For the advertisement for tenders, see *Ninth Report*, 1783, App. 62.

[22] Bengal Revenue Consultations, 1 Aug. 1775, *Ninth Report*, 1783, App. 64.

[23] The term ''Bengal opium'' is a generic one applied to the produce of the Ganges Basin. The best opium came from Bihar and later from Benares also. The drug produced in Bengal proper was of an inferior grade. The new contracts differed in some respects from the earlier one. They provided for the delivery of a fixed number of chests, 2980 from Bihar and 1000 from Bengal proper. The Bihar contractor was to receive only Rs. 190 per chest but was to enjoy a commission of two and one-half per cent on the proceeds of the Calcutta sales.

there was a factory at Patna, the general observed with
more than a modicum of truth, there would be a monopoly, and far better one frankly proclaimed, carefully
managed, and aggrandizing the company than the private
engrossing that would inevitably occur, whatever measures were taken to prevent it.[24]

At the expiration of Griffith's contract, the council,
now reduced to four members by the death of Colonel
Monson, adopted a new policy, one which drew criticism
both from the court of directors and from the committee
of Parliament which investigated the company's affairs.
The right to provide opium for a period of three years
was awarded arbitrarily to John Mackenzie, a friend of
Philip Francis.[25] Although the agreement was more favorable to the company than previous arrangements had
been, the council placed itself in a dangerous position in
two respects: first, there was no advertisement for bids;
and secondly, the contract was to hold for three years.[26]
Indeed, in the debates within the council, opposition to
the monopoly itself seems to have subsided, and it was
the triennial feature that provoked discussion. To commit
the company to a contract of that kind was doubtful, for
the court of directors, none too benevolently disposed
towards the monopoly, might order its abandonment at
any time. A compromise was finally reached by which the
award was made unconditional for one year and would be
continued for two more unless the monopoly were legis-
lated out of existence. In 1780, when Mackenzie's three-

[24] Bengal Revenue Consultations, 3 Sept. 1776, *Ninth Report*, 1783,
App. 63.

[25] See ''A Summary Abstract of Mr. Hastings' Government and Present
Situation,'' Dodwell, *Warren Hastings' Letters to Sir John Macpherson*,
p. 69.

[26] Proc. Governor General and Council (revenue), 16 May 1777, *Ninth
Report*, 1783, App. 67. The contractor agreed to pay Rs. 10,000 annually to
the company. Otherwise the terms were identical with those of the preceding
contract.

year term expired, his contract was renewed for another
year in spite of protests lodged by the court of directors.[27]

Following the precedent established in 1777, Hastings,
by this time supreme in the council, again granted the
opium contract without calling for bids.[28] This transaction was not without its element of scandal, for the recipi-
ent was Stephen Sulivan, who was the son of the chairman of the court of directors, an intimate friend of Hastings. The young man had come to India to recoup the
finances of his family, which had suffered as a result of
the struggle between the elder Sulivan and Clive for control of the company.[29] Sulivan's contract held for four
years regardless of the directors' opinion, and the safeguarding conditions imposed upon the previous contractor were omitted.[30] In short, the council made the rough
ways exceedingly smooth for the new contractor. Still
more discreditable appeared the arrangement when, after
holding his rights for a few days, Sulivan disposed of
them at a large profit to a purchaser who in turn resold
them.[31] The stake of the original contractor became

[27] Bengal Revenue Consultations, 11 April 1780, *India Courier Extraordinary, . . . Appendix . . . relative to W. Hastings,* VI, 82. (This collection will be cited hereafter as *Warren Hastings Documents.*)

[28] Bengal Revenue Consultations, 16 March 1781, *Ninth Report,* 1783,
App. 71; 22 May 1781, *ibid.,* App. 72; general letter from Bengal, 5 May
1781, *ibid.,* App. 85B.

[29] *Cambridge History of India,* V, 175. "I think he [Stephen Sulivan]
may be of the Supreme Council if it be enlarged. But profit more than station must of necessity be our object. . . . By your affectionate friendship
much more may be done for him out of council; and, too true it is, that
much is wanted." H. H. Dodwell, *Warren Hastings' Letters to Sir John
Macpherson,* p. 84.

[30] The penalty for non-fulfillment was reduced, and the inspectorship of
opium at Patna was abolished. This office had been created in 1775. Its
abolition formed the subject of ironic attack by the prosecution during the
Hastings trial. *History of the Trial of Warren Hastings,* Part II, p. 64.

[31] At the impeachment of Hastings it was proved that Sulivan had received £40,000 when he sold the contract and that the purchaser had received

merely that of speculator. "He is a Contractor of a new Species," pointedly remarked the committee of Parliament, "who employs no capital whatsoever of his own, and has the market of Compulsion at his entire command."[32]

The Sulivan episode forms the last chapter in the history of opium contracts under the administration of Warren Hastings. While the system was developing in Bengal, the court of directors in London was reluctantly reconciling its free-trade professions with the unpleasant fact of governmental monopolies. Officially the directors were committed to an open commerce, and all of their despatches reflect a genuine desire to see it established. On one occasion they deplored the fact "that we see in every page of your consultations, restrictions, limitations, and prohibitions, affecting various articles of trade."[33] In 1764 the directors had entered a futile protest against the activities of their servants at Patna. When, therefore, the Bengal council determined to introduce a genuine monopoly, the plan appeared rather as a relief. The servants of "John Company" were inclined to be intractable, their salaries were niggardly, and after all, the opium trade had been usually monopolized by some-one. The Hastings proposal was, to the court, far from ideal but doubtless superior to what had gone on before. Although the monopoly could not be praised, it might be tolerated.

The Mackenzie contract provoked a violent protest from the court because of the way in which it had been awarded.[34] In Calcutta the censure was jauntily ignored, and when the contract was again granted, the procedure

£70,000 when he resold it. *Ibid.*, pp. 70, 73, 93; see also Higginson's evidence, *Ninth Report*, 1783, App. 75.

[32] *Ninth Report*, 1783, p. 72.

[33] Company's general letter to Bengal, 30 June 1769, *ibid.*, App. 27.

[34] Company's letter to Bengal, 23 Dec. 1778, *ibid.*, App. 70.

was precisely the same, award by special favor. To the directors, the Sulivan affair was nothing short of outrageous. That a new contract should have been concluded in this fashion after their condemnation of the former one appeared to be nothing more nor less than "contempt for our authority."[35] But the directors, far removed from the scene of action, were impotent, especially when dealing with a governor-general like Warren Hastings. They might dethrone him, but they could not alter his policy.

The point of view expressed by the court of directors was reflected by the committee of Parliament which published its *Ninth Report* in 1783. This document was the work of Edmund Burke, who made it the vehicle not only for his zeal for purging the Indian administration but for his own antipathy towards Hastings. The evils of the opium system were reviewed at some length. There was evidence, for example, that cultivators had been the victims of oppression, and there had been rumors of trouble between the agents of the contractor and the subordinate revenue collectors, so that "the Plowman, flying from the Tax Gatherer is obliged to take refuge under the wings of the Monopolist."[36] The subject could not be dismissed without a eulogy of free trade by the committee, whose ignorance of the opium industry was exceeded only by its penchant for applying doctrinaire economics indiscriminately. No ethical questions were raised in regard to the opium trade itself. On the contrary, the blows of the investigators were showered upon the restraint of commerce practised by the company. To defend the opium monopoly was, to the committee, fatuity itself. The possible evils of an open trade—a debased product, litigation, and violence—were dismissed as purely imagi-

[35] Company's general letter to Bengal, 12 July 1782, *Ninth Report*, 1873, App. 86. When this reproof was issued, Laurence Sulivan was no longer chairman of the court of directors.

[36] *Ibid.*, p. 71.

nary or, if real, to be corrected by the sovereign remedy of competition. There seemed to have been a conspiracy on the part of the company's servants to deny the cultivator the full return from his labor. In short, ''upon whatever Reasons or Pretences the Monopoly of Opium was supported, the real Motive appears to have been the Profit of those who were to be concerned in it.''

If the opium monopoly had drawn only censures from the court of directors and a bludgeoning from the select committee, its reputation was to be cleared in some degree by the high court of Parliament itself. On April 4, 1786, Edmund Burke rose in the House of Commons to charge Warren Hastings, Esq., with high crimes and misdemeanors. Among the articles which he presented was one dealing with corrupt contracts, a part of ''the prodigal and corrupt system which Mr. Hastings had introduced into the finances of India.''[37] In the almost interminable proceedings that followed, this charge received due emphasis, though neither Burke, Fox, nor Sheridan spent their sonorities upon it. The prosecution on the charge of corrupt contracts was chiefly in the hands of St. Andrew St. John, Michael Angelo Taylor, and Sir James St. Clair Erskine.

Their attack centered upon the admittedly irregular procedure in the Sulivan contract.[38] No crime was imputed to Hastings in the creation of the monopoly system, but the furtive gift of the contractor's privilege in 1781 and the omission of the usual safeguarding clauses

[37] Speech of St. Andrew St. John, 23 May 1791, *History of the Trial of Warren Hastings*, Part IV, p. 63. Eleven, out of a total of twenty-two charges, were presented on this occasion.

[38] The charge was that Hastings ''had granted a Contract for the Provision of opium for four years to Stephen Sulivan, Esq., without advertising for the same, on terms glaringly extravagant and wantonly profuse, for the purpose of creating an instant fortune to the said Stephen Sulivan.'' *Ibid.*, Part VIII, p. 269.

were a quite sufficient basis for the corruption argument of the prosecution. The sale of the contract by Sulivan and its subsequent resale were established beyond doubt.[39] Clearly the governor-general had disobeyed his instructions. He had granted the opium contract privately and as a mark of special favor. Sulivan was the son of Hastings' good friend, who had earnestly solicited the governor-general's patronage. He was inexperienced and palpably ignorant of the opium business. It was a dubious transaction, but that the contract "was given him for the express purpose of sale" proved to be a thought sired by the virtuous wish of the prosecution.[40]

Edward Law, later Lord Ellenborough, bore the brunt of the defense. Since it was impossible to clear his client of disobedience, he resorted to the familiar method of counter-attack. Why, he inquired, should all the emphasis be laid upon the Sulivan contract when nearly the same arrangement had been made with Mackenzie four years before? Obviously because the latter was a friend of Philip Francis. Moreover, the opium system was the unique creation of the defendant, and any revenue from that source was his gift to the company.

In defending himself, both in the Commons and in the Lords, Warren Hastings rested his case on pragmatic grounds. He had struck the barren rock, and streams of revenue had gushed forth. When the English acquired Bengal, the trade was nominally free, and, in the words of one of his adherents, "the Opium became so debased, that many people were ruined by the sophisticated stuff which they bought for Opium, and the Trade in Opium from Bengal was almost lost."[41] But through the system established by the late governor-general, "the Opium re-

---

[39] E. A. Bond, *Speeches in the Trial of Warren Hastings*, IV, 271.
[40] Speech of Michael Angelo Taylor, 23 May 1794, *ibid.*, p. 269.
[41] J. Price, *Letter to Fox*, p. 7.

covered its primitive goodness,'' and an important branch of the revenue was created. The crux of Hastings' defense is to be found in the profits which his monopoly brought to the company's treasury.[42]

Admitting that the contracts of 1777 and 1781 had not been awarded competitively, he sought to explain his motives in disobeying instructions. Why were the contracts not put up at auction? Because it was not to the company's advantage to grant them on too favorable terms, for the contractor, in order to make his profit, would be driven to debasing and adulterating the drug. In the first instance the man who received the privilege was a friend of Francis, in the second of Hastings, but in both cases the aim was ''to have a man of credit, honour, and property, upon whom we could rely for the faithful and just performance of his engagement.''[43]

On April 23, 1795, the charge was finally brought to vote. The decision of the Lords, however much a verdict by ennui, was conclusively in favor of acquittal, nineteen to five.

While the trial of Warren Hastings was running its weary course at Westminster, the monopoly which he had bequeathed to the company was gradually assuming

[42] *The Minutes of what was offered*, p. 176. The yield to the company during Hastings' administration was as follows:

Year	£ sterling	Year	£ sterling	Year	£ sterling
1773-74	39,837	1777-78	22,149	1781-82	68,912
1774-75	14,256	1778-79	49,572	1782-83	43,470
1775-76	56,255	1779-80	57,527	1783-84	78,300
1776-77	21,908	1780-81	8,475	1784-85	53,348

Total   534,009

—*Warren Hastings Documents*, II, 15.

[43] Bond, *Speeches in the Trial of Warren Hastings*, II, 504. This statement seems disingenuous in the light of the use to which Sulivan put the contract. Hastings, however, protested that he knew nothing of its sale, and the prosecution failed to disprove his assertion.

its final form. Two major questions, at least, were still regarded as open. In the first place, should the monopoly itself be continued or should some other system be devised for raising a revenue from opium? Secondly, if the monopoly were to survive, should it be administered by contract as hitherto or should it be an agency managed by servants of the company? In 1785, during the inglorious interim administration of Sir John Macpherson, the future of the opium system was debated anew. Aversion to it had been expressed by both the court of directors and the committee of Parliament, and the council prudently decided to give further scrutiny. In a long minute the governor-general suggested several possible substitutes for monopoly control.[44] One was the imposition of an increased land tax on areas under poppy cultivation and another a heavy export duty on the drug.[45] Dismissing both as impracticable, however compatible with the wishes of the directors, Macpherson was obliged to echo the views of his predecessor. He emphatically disclaimed any secret admiration for monopolies and admitted that the results of the opium system thus far were not all that could have been hoped for.[46] But he nevertheless regarded the Hastings plan as the only sound one. He suavely reminded the directors of the fact that "it was upon the principle of monopolies that foreign Companies were first admitted in these Provinces and protected in particular branches of trade." All things considered, it was only through some sort of state control that a productive revenue could be assured.

[44] Minute by the governor-general, Bengal Revenue Consultations, 11 July 1785, *Warren Hastings Documents*, VI, 119-122.

[45] Macpherson also proposed that production and export be vested in an association of merchants.

[46] "I entertain my share of the general prejudices which prevail at home against every system that bears the appearance of monopoly."

The opium system then should be continued, presumably as a contract for four years. The governor-general determined not to lay himself open to the criticism that had fallen upon Warren Hastings but to advertise for bids. The contract was therefore granted to the lowest applicants for a period of four years.[47] No objection was raised by the directors, although they were still disturbed by the company's connection with a monopolistic enterprise. "Any evidence," they reminded their representatives in India, "tending to prove that it was not a free and open Trade under the actual Government of the Mahomedan Princes, should be entered upon your Consultations, to be employed as arguments to defend our rights, in any discussion which may arise in Europe."[48]

Despite the fact that the contract in 1785 was let competitively, its terms left something to be desired. Of this Earl Cornwallis, the new governor-general, was acutely aware, and it was to be his work to carry the opium system another step towards the inevitable government-operated monopoly. Before he attacked the problem of a new contract, Cornwallis made a painstaking effort to ascertain the real state of affairs. A questionnaire was sent to the collectors of revenue and other informed persons.[49] On three principal questions the governor-general sought enlightenment: the condition of the cultivators, the possible abandonment of the monopoly, and the relative merits of the contract and agency systems, if the monopoly were continued. As was to be expected, the answers revealed a variety of opinion, but in respect to the condition of the ryots, there was quite enough evidence to convince Cornwallis that something must be done for their

---

[47] Bengal Revenue Consultations, 11 July 1785, *Warren Hastings Documents*, VI, 127. The contractors were William Young and Patrick Heatley.

[48] Court of Directors to the governor-general in council (revenue), 27 March 1787, I. O. Despatches to Bengal, XVI.

[49] Dated 9 April 1788, *Duncan Records*, II, 157-158.

relief.[50] The testimony was clear that in some sections the poppy was grown under compulsion and that the ryots were not permitted by the contractor to relinquish cultivation.

On the issue of whether to continue the monopoly, again the council debated, and again, as if anticipating many subsequent discussions, decided to leave well-enough alone. The same fears that had withheld his predecessor now restrained the hand of Cornwallis. Fundamentally it was the threatened loss of revenue that saved the monopoly.[51] The governor-general and his council would not abolish it, nor would they change its structure. While recognizing the virtues of the agency plan, Cornwallis was unwilling to burden his officials with another responsibility. Furthermore, profit under the contract system was a certainty, while agency would be wholly experimental. In the deliberations of 1789 was forecast the theme which runs throughout British opium history, "Don't tamper with the opium revenue." And indeed the monopoly was never altered in any thorough fashion save under conditions of palpable necessity.

Notwithstanding the government's decision to persist in the contract plan, Cornwallis was genuinely distressed by reports that the peasants were being victimized. But rather than change the form of the monopoly, he chose to palliate its admitted evils by issuing new protective regulations. With these safeguards, the council artlessly prophesied, "the Cultivation of the Poppy may be rendered equally advantageous to the Ryots as any other article of Produce." The arrangements under which con-

[50] The replies are contained in I. O. Bengal Revenue Consultations, 29 July 1789.

[51] The loss, Cornwallis concluded, would be both direct and indirect. Not only would opening the trade mean a sacrifice of monopoly profits but it would probably lead to such deterioration in the quality of the Bengal drug as would impair its position in China and the East Indies.

tracts were let in 1789 and again in 1793 were curious, to say the least.[52] As purchaser of the provision,[53] the council was interested in keeping the price paid to cultivators as low as possible. Just as evidently it was to the advantage of the government to maintain a rate that would not discourage cultivation. The problem of keeping the ryot secure and contented, of ensuring profit to the contractor and revenue to the company was met by prescribing in detail the price which the contractor must pay the peasant for his poppy juice, as well as that which the company was to pay the contractor. In some districts the rate at which the contractor must buy opium was actually above that which he received from the company.[54] Further to alleviate the condition of the peasant, the government forced the contractor to cease levying certain additional charges, which had hitherto deprived the ryot of his full rate.

In other words, Cornwallis, attempting to reconcile the contract system with the welfare of the peasants, had come dangerously near a state-administered monopoly. He had prescribed the price at which the contractor must buy and had otherwise limited his field for initiative. It was an arrangement which would lead almost certainly to an agency managed by servants of the company.[55]

[52] Sir J. E. Colebrooke, *Digest of the Regulations . . . of Bengal*, III, *Supplement*, pp. 405 ff.

[53] "Provision opium" is technically the portion of the crop sold at Calcutta for export. In later years, when an excise system was set up, opium for home consumption was known as "abkari opium."

[54] I. O. Bengal Board of Revenue (Misc.) Proc. (opium), 21 Sept. 1789.

[55] The parliamentary committee of 1812 referred to this contract as one "wherein the government, on contracting for the price at which they were to receive opium, at the same time prescribed the price at which it should be purchased by the contractor; more especially when it appears, that as the latter was to exceed the former, it might be supposed that the contractor agreed to supply opium for the East India Company at a lower rate than he could purchase it himself." *Fifth Report from the Select Committee, 1812*, pp. 24-25.

While Cornwallis' compromise was receiving a trial in Bihar and Bengal proper, another stone was being laid in the structure of the monopoly. Thus far only these two areas had been comprehended within the company's opium system, though the contractor was free to purchase such quantities as he chose in the territory of Oudh. In 1775 over the protests of Warren Hastings a treaty was forced upon Oudh by which the estate of the raja of Benares was ceded to the British. No definite steps were taken to integrate the Benares industry into the Bengal system until early in 1787 when the company decided to extend its monopoly to that fertile district.[56] Handled for a few months as a contract, the enterprise was changed to an agency by Jonathan Duncan, newly appointed as British resident at Benares.[57] With the approval of the titular raja, he issued instructions for extending the cultivation "wherever there may be land and water for the growth of the poppy, to cause the same as far as may be consistent with the means and conformable to the fair and free goodwill of the cultivators."[58]

Duncan's agency survived for only a year, when Cornwallis, following his policy in Bihar and Bengal, instituted a four-year contract.[59] The new plan proved, if anything, even less of a triumph in Benares than in Bihar. There were complaints from the contractor that European interlopers were handicapping his work, and the council was obliged to order the deportation of British subjects convicted of meddling and to impose heavy fines

[56] I. O. Bengal Political and Secret Consultations, 20 Feb. 1787.

[57] J. A. Grant, resident at Benares, to the governor-general in council, I. O. Bengal Political and Secret Consultations, 9 March 1787, and Jonathan Duncan to the governor-general in council, I. O. Bengal Revenue Consultations, 7 Dec. 1787.

[58] Resident's Proc., 17 July 1788, *Duncan Records*, II, 167.

[59] Governor-general in council to the court of directors (revenue), 10 Aug. 1789, I. O. Letters from Bengal, XXVIII; C. Ross, *Cornwallis Correspondence*, I, 547; *Duncan Records*, II, 168-169.

on native culprits.[60] Unprotected by the Bengal regulations, the contractor found himself without redress for his grievances against the peasants. His position was somewhat strengthened by the council's decision to extend to Benares the regulations governing the monopoly in Bihar and Bengal.[61]

Meanwhile the contract system in the older districts was gradually discrediting itself.[62] It was scarcely to be expected that Cornwallis' singular arrangement would solve the problem of opium provision. The contractor, hedged about by restrictions, found his margin of profit becoming more and more attenuated. The consequence was that the drug was adulterated, and the revenue, although it held its own for a time, ultimately declined in an alarming fashion.[63] Not only was adulteration practised on a large scale, but so varied were the methods that there was not even a uniform standard of impurity.[64] Rumors from the China coast were ominous. Formerly, traders reported, the Chinese and Malays had accepted the company's mark on the outside of the chest as a guarantee of the quality of its contents. But now prospective purchasers, made wary by recent experience, insisted on opening each chest.[65] That the opium was of poorer grade than in the early days of the monopoly seems to have been beyond question.

The obvious remedy was that originally proposed by

[60] *Ibid.*, p. 170.   [61] *Ibid.*, pp. 173-174.

[62] For the contract of 1793 see I. O. Bengal Public Consultations, 26 April, 11 June, 28 June 1793; governor-general in council to the court of directors (commercial), 12 Aug. 1793, I. O. Letters from Bengal, XXXIII; Colebrooke, *Digest of the Regulations . . . of Bengal*, II, 594-597.

[63] The declaration of war between France and Great Britain and the presence of French men-of-war in the waters between India and China doubtless contributed to the decline in price after 1793.

[64] Letter from John Fleming, inspector of drugs, 12 June 1794, I. O. Bengal Public Consultations, 1 June 1795.

[65] Proc. Board of Trade, 21 and 28 May 1794, *ibid.*

Hastings, the abandonment of the farming system and the substitution of an opium agency under a covenanted servant of the company. In 1795 Sir John Shore, later Lord Teignmouth, who two years before had succeeded Cornwallis, virtually decided to abolish the contract, if the directors would consent.[66] Here the conclusive argument was the loss of caste which the Indian drug had undergone among merchants and exporters. Production was increasing, apparently with a corresponding deterioration in quality, and the market was flooded with unsalable opium. These conditions were registered in an almost unbelievable decrease in the revenue, from over nineteen lakhs[67] of rupees in 1793-1794 to something over three lakhs in 1796-1797.[68] The directors were much impressed, but, recalling the study that previous governors-general had given the problem, they were reluctant to authorize hasty steps.[69] There might be hesitancy in London, but in Calcutta there was conviction that the opium monopoly could be saved only by vigorous action. In 1797, "with a view of restoring and improving this important branch of the public revenues," the Bengal government decided to adopt the agency system. To this step the court of directors gave its assent.[70]

The monopoly was left in the hands of the board of trade which administered it through an agent in Bihar,[71]

[66] Governor-general in council to the court of directors (separate revenue), 30 May 1795, I. O. Letters from Bengal, XXXIV.

[67] An Indian term meaning one hundred thousand, usually written 1,00,000.

[68] Court of directors to the governor-general in council (separate revenue), 5 May 1799, I. O. Despatches to Bengal, XXXIII.

[69] Court of directors to the governor-general in council (separate revenue), 6 April 1796, ibid., XXX.

[70] Court of directors to the governor-general in council (separate revenue), 5 May 1799, ibid., XXXIII. The change was written into the law of Bengal as Regulation VI of 1799.

[71] For the first seven years of the monopoly's existence it was under the

while the Benares field was committed to the care of the commercial resident.[72] From the point of view of revenue the new plan justified itself almost immediately. Prices rose markedly in 1797-1798, and in the following year they were nearly three times as high as the rate at which opium had sold during the last months of the contract system.[73] This rise was reflected in the net revenue, which in 1798-1799 exceeded twenty-three lakhs, as compared with less than four lakhs in 1796-1797.[74] Reports from Eastern markets were again reassuring.[75]

Simultaneously with the setting up of the agency system, the council enunciated another policy, one that was to govern the production of opium for the next twenty-

general supervision of the board of trade. In 1780 it was transferred to an official called preparer of reports and superintendent of opium sales, who was responsible to the board of revenue. Thirteen years later the pendulum again moved towards the commercial branch of the company. The office of superintendent was abolished, and management was again vested in the board of trade. This arrangement continued until 1819, when a reorganization of the Bengal revenue establishment took place. The administration of the customs, salt, and opium revenues was then centered in a new body known as the board of revenue in the customs, salt, and opium departments. Revenue letter from Bengal, 25 Nov. 1780, *Ninth Report*, 1783, App. 78; I. O. Bengal Public Consultations, 29 March 1793; minute by the governor-general, 11 Feb. 1793, *Second Report from the Select Committee*, 1810, App. 9A; *Report of a Commission . . . to Enquire into the Working of the Opium Department*, 1883, p. 9.

[72] Governor-general in council to the court of directors (separate revenue), 15 Aug. 1797, I. O. Letters from Bengal, XXXVII. In 1835 the commercial residency at Benares was abolished and a full-time opium agent appointed. Although the agency was known as the Benares agency, the factory was at Ghazipur and the opium administration centered there. *Report of a Commission . . . to Enquire into the Working of the Opium Department*, 1883, p. 11.

[73] The price in 1796-1797 averaged Rs. 264 per chest, in 1797-1798 Rs. 426, and in 1798-1799 Rs. 750. After 1801-1802 it maintained an annual average of better than Rs. 1000 until 1840.

[74] Governor-general in council to the court of directors (separate revenue), 1 March 1804, I. O. Letters from Bengal, XLIV.

[75] Court of directors to the governor-general in council (separate revenue), 11 June 1800, I. O. Despatches to Bengal, XXXIV.

five years. This was the principle of restricting the output to a fixed amount of known quality and thus deriving the maximum revenue from as small a provision as possible. Five thousand chests was the quantity agreed upon.[76] The plan involved, among other things, limiting cultivation to the most favorable areas. The drug from Bengal proper had never been altogether satisfactory, for its quality was vastly inferior to the Bihar and Benares product, and the lower prices at which it sold tended to depreciate the value of the entire provision. In the spring of 1797, for example, a lot of Bengal opium was put up for sale, but the highest offer was Rs. 50 a chest.[77] In the end nearly two thousand chests were burned in order to relieve the market.[78] For these reasons the council resolved to discontinue cultivation in Bengal proper.[79] Notwithstanding the prohibitory edict, which seems to have been enforced rather stringently, much illicit manufacture certainly persisted.[80]

As the opium monopoly established itself as a permanent feature of the Indo-British revenue system, Parliament was gradually becoming tolerant of its existence.

[76] Governor-general in council to the court of directors (separate revenue), 15 Aug. 1797, I. O. Letters from Bengal, XXXVII; governor-general in council to the court of directors (political), 17 Dec. 1799, ibid., XL.

[77] Governor-general in council to the court of directors (separate revenue), 2 March 1797, ibid., XXXVII.

[78] Governor-general in council to the court of directors (separate revenue), 29 Sept. 1798, ibid., XXXVIII.

[79] Governor-general in council to the court of directors (separate revenue), 16 May 1798, Second Report from the Select Committee, 1810, App. 19. The decision of the council was embodied in Regulation I of 1797. The proscription was also extended to include the zillah of Boglepur in Bihar, which had traditionally been under the Bengal contractor.

[80] Governor-general in council to the court of directors (separate revenue), 10 Jan. 1810, I. O. Letters from Bengal, LVII; court of directors to the governor-general in council (separate revenue), 29 Jan. 1813, I. O. Despatches to Bengal, LX. In at least one place the poppy crop was uprooted in the winter of 1797-1798 and compensation paid. Hunter, Bengal Records, II, §§7053, 7424, 7425.

The select committee which reported in 1810 and 1812 was much more favorably disposed than its predecessor of 1783. The agency plan, observed the committee, was commendable and much superior to the now discredited contract. To be sure, the opium revenue was a staff which should not be called upon to bear much weight, for it was liable to severe strain from both ''adverse seasons and the state of the markets to the eastward.''[81] Two years later the investigators again praised the system, certain that it ''has answered the expectations formed of it, in every particular.''[82]

The structure of the British opium monopoly in Bengal had thus been reared and pronounced good to behold, though not too stable, by a committee of Parliament. This form it was to retain substantially unchanged throughout the nineteenth century. Warren Hastings, for reasons that are at least intelligible, had sluiced a stream of revenue into the treasury of the company. The plan which the first governor-general originated underwent modification at the hands of his successors. Steps were taken to curtail the area of cultivation, and the business was more completely absorbed by the state when the contract system was abolished and management vested in salaried servants of the company.

The fundamental principle of the Bengal monopoly was that cultivation could be undertaken only with the government's permission. Unlicensed cultivation was considered illicit, and a heavy fine was imposed upon those convicted of it. A ryot who desired to plant the poppy received advances from the government and obligated himself to sell his product only to the official agency and at a stated price. The opium was then subjected to a refining process and finally sold at auction in Calcutta.

81 *Second Report from the Select Committee*, 1810, p. 54.
82 *Fifth Report from the Select Committee*, 1812, p. 30.

After the drug had been once purchased for export, no further cognizance of it was taken by the company. The difference between the price paid to the ryots for their raw opium and that received at the auction sales, less the cost of manufacturing and overhead, represented the government's profit, a margin materially increased by the monopolistic conditions governing the industry.

During the eighteenth century few uncomfortable questions about the ethics of the company's opium policy were raised by the court of directors, by committees of Parliament, or by private critics. None was wholly favorable towards the monopoly, but all were incensed at the restraint of trade that was being practised, not at the unseemly spectacle of the government's fostering the opium traffic. Only in the mind of Warren Hastings, that "captain of iniquity—tyrant—thief—robber,"[83] there may have lurked disquieting premonitions. To him opium was "a pernicious article of luxury, which ought not to be permitted but for purposes of foreign commerce." But even Hastings was not sufficiently farsighted to perceive that in the foreign commerce which he encouraged was to lie the crux of the opium question.

[83] The words are Burke's. *History of the Trial of Warren Hastings*, Part VII, p. 154.

CHAPTER III

THE EARLY TRADE AT CANTON

THE China that was revealed to the West in the eighteenth and early nineteenth centuries seemed a curious anachronism. Traditionally isolated, its contacts with occidental peoples had been sporadic and, in general, unsought by the Chinese. It was the expansion of Europe that began the long process of beating down the barriers of the Middle Kingdom, and it was trade that provided the motive power. China, officially contemptuous of the mart and counting-house, found itself the possessor of commodities that lured the merchants of the West. And although Chinese authorities might profess supreme indifference to trade, they nevertheless took an active and frequently an oppressive interest in its continuance.

Indeed the whole policy of the Chinese state towards the West is filled with apparent paradoxes. The old system of administration, in form an absolute monarchy but with a large degree of provincial and local autonomy, was showing signs of decay. The strong hand of the great Manchu emperors had been removed before the turn of the century, and control was left to the futilities who were their successors.[1] Provincial self-government, however congenial in the days of China's isolation, now

[1] The last distinguished Manchu ruler, Chien Lung, died in 1796. Despite his unfamiliarity with the West, one of his ability might possibly have brought China through the period of adjustment. But the ignorance of western ways of even a Chien Lung was appalling. See his letter to George III in H. B. Morse, *Chronicles of the East India Company* (cited hereafter as Morse, *Chronicles*), II, App. J.

showed itself in a bad light. Peking, as the Chinese poet would express it, was ten thousand *li* from the ports frequented by foreigners. The result was that opportunities for "squeeze" through the commerce of Europeans excited the greed of all officialdom, from the lowest runner to the viceroy himself. In other words, the connection between Canton and the capital was so tenuous and the inflexible administration so ignorant of the West, that the Chinese government in dealing with Europeans appeared more inept than it was in reality.

The policy of the Chinese state towards foreign trade was to accept it but to control it in the interest of the revenue and, too frequently, of the private purse of officialdom. After 1757 commerce was confined to Canton, where it was carried on under annoying restrictions. Business could be transacted only with an official gild of merchants called the cohong, chartered by the Chinese government. To the commercial privileges of the hong merchants were added duties of a quasi-political nature. Indeed, while in Canton, foreigners were virtually their wards. A member of the cohong was required to act as "security merchant" for each incoming ship, that is, to guarantee that the barbarians would conduct themselves with decorum and would pay the assessed duties. The hong merchants always served as intermediaries between foreigners and the Chinese authorities, for no mere European trader could communicate directly with an official of the Middle Kingdom. A position in the cohong, with all its advantages, was no sinecure, for members were subject to all sorts of exactions, illegal as well as legitimate.[2]

On the other side of the counter was also a monopoly, and the monopolist, the Honourable East India Company.

[2] For the origin of the cohong see H. B. Morse, *International Relations of the Chinese Empire* (cited hereafter as Morse, *International Relations*), I, 66.

Trade between Great Britain and China was its exclusive preserve, while between India and China licensed vessels belonging to private traders were permitted. The latter were known as "country ships." Like the cohong the company's supercargoes were magistrates as well as merchants. No Englishman could land in China without the company's passport, and, should he become troublesome, that might be revoked. By the Chinese authorities the representatives of the company were regarded as the governing power in the foreign community, to be relied upon to restrain the turbulent barbarians. On the whole, relations between the two monopolies proceeded fairly placidly, save when officials presumed to interfere. The hong merchants had confidence in the company, and the supercargoes found a high degree of business integrity and often of generosity in the Chinese traders.[3]

In the almost perennial friction that marked Anglo-Chinese relations during the nineteenth century opium must be assigned an important but by no means a pre-eminent part. As we have seen, the drug had been known in China for centuries, but its adaptation to Chinese taste had been a comparatively recent development. The attitude of the Chinese government towards opium smoking had been stated emphatically in the edict of Yung Cheng (1729), which proscribed the importation and sale for smoking.[4] But the vermilion pencil of Yung Cheng was no

[3] See Morse, *Chronicles*, II, 88; W. C. Hunter, *Fan Kwae*, p. 44. On the other side of the question may be mentioned the penchant of hong merchants for accumulating debts and going into bankruptcy.

[4] Despite this prohibition opium appeared in the tariff of 1753 paying a duty of three taels per chest. F. Hirth, "The Hoppo Book of 1753," *Journal of the North China Branch of the Royal Asiatic Society*, 1882, p. 225. From this fact Edkins (*Opium: A Historical Note*, p. 20) has drawn the inference that opium could be legally imported as a foreign medicine (*ya-p'ien*) but not as a drug for smoking (*ya-p'ien-yen*). The inclusion of opium in the schedule of 1753 may be merely an example of carelessness in Chinese tariff making rather than an attempt to draw a nice distinction between the

more able to check the spread of the vice than were those of his successors.

During the early part of the eighteenth century imports were small.[5] Then with the diffusion of the opium habit in China, the quantity increased until in 1767, it was reported, a thousand chests were entering Macao alone.[6] The drug was carried by country ships, either English or "Moors," as well as by vessels of other nationalities.[7] The supercargoes, however, were convinced that opium was contraband and that to import it would compromise their own and the company's position.[8] As early as 1733 the company's ships *Windlesham* and *Compton*, sailing from Fort St. George, were forbidden to bring opium, "it having been the usual thing heretofore, for shipps bound from Fort St. George to carry

uses of the drug, especially when its value was listed at the ridiculous figure of only 100 taels. The current opinion among foreigners at Canton was that the opium trade was contrary to law.

[5] Statistics for this period are meager and generally untrustworthy. The usual statement for the trade early in the century is that, in 1729, 200 chests were being imported into Macao. Citations of this figure all seem to rest directly or indirectly on the *Bombay Gazette*, 20 Aug. 1820, quoted in J. Phipps, *China Trade*, p. 208.

[6] *Dalrymple's Oriental Repertory*, II, 289.

[7] Morse, *Chronicles*, II, 216. As frequently stated, the first English venture took place in 1773, though details are never given. The source seems to be the unreliable R. M. Martin, *British Relations with the Chinese Empire*, who gives no authority for his statement. There is little question that the British had been participating in the trade for years. In 1767, for example, the supercargoes wrote to Madras, "The Cuddalore Captain Boswall we have been told had some Chests of Ophium which were sold at Macao: but so has almost every Country Vessel that comes here, & We imagine they will continue to bring it, while no order [from the company] subsists to the contrary." *Chronicles*, V, 129.

[8] "We beg leave to observe that the use of Ophium is prohibited in this Country under the severest Penalties. . . . We therefore beg you will positively forbid any of our Commanders or others receiving it or sending it on board for this place." Morse, *Chronicles*, V, 154. See also the letter from Thomas Fitzhugh, a former supercargo, dated 7 July 1782, *Ninth Report*, 1783, App. 77.

ophium with them for sale in China.'"⁹ Henceforth opium
was a prohibited commodity on the vessels of the East
India Company, and the trade was left wholly to country
and non-British ships. The policy of the company is clear
enough, and with a single lapse it was maintained
throughout the existence of the China monopoly. The
exclusive right to manufacture and sell opium for export
had been assumed by the East India Company with its
eye upon markets farther to the east. But the Bengal
administrators were content to extract their profit from
the sale of the drug to private exporters. There the company's complicity ceased. No stigma of participating in a
smuggling trade to China should be attached to its name.

In 1781 the masterful hand of Warren Hastings forced
the company to a temporary breach of its self-denying
ordinance. The state of the Bengal opium industry was
undeniably bad. Two years' stocks were lying unsold, and
what was worse, no purchasers were in prospect. The
wars with the Spanish, French, and Dutch, and with
Hyder Ali and the Marathas had caused a scarcity of
specie in India, and the seas Chinaward, especially the
Straits, were infested by enemy cruisers.¹⁰ At the same
time the company's supercargoes at Canton were suffering from a lack of treasure with which to complete their
investment.¹¹

It was imperative that the China factory be placed in
possession of purchasing power. The Canton trade had
always been a one-sided affair, for there existed little
demand in the East for European goods, whereas the
West eagerly sought Chinese teas and silks. Conse-

---

⁹ Morse, *Chronicles*, I, 215.

¹⁰ Governor-general and council to the court of directors, 5 April 1783,
Warren Hastings Documents, VI, 105.

¹¹ The term ''investment'' denotes the resources of the China factory for
the purchase of the season's return cargoes. It implies no fixed allocation of
capital.

quently the factory was financed by large shipments of specie from England and India. If for any reason that supply were cut off, the trade must inevitably decline.[12] This was the problem that confronted Warren Hastings in 1781. For the preceding two years not an ounce of silver had been sent from London.[13] And it was impossible to relieve the wants of the supercargoes from the depleted stock of specie in Bengal.[14]

As a way out of the difficulty the governor-general embarked upon the opium trade on the company's account. Proposals by one Colonel Henry Watson and Cudbert Thornhill pointed the way.[15] The former suggested that the company consign the whole opium produce of Bengal directly to Canton, declaring a monopoly of the drug in the China market. The consumption of opium in the southwestern provinces alone, he asserted, amounted to twelve hundred chests, which at five hundred Spanish dollars per chest would provide amply for the investment.[16] The enterprising colonel offered his new ship the *Nonsuch* for the venture. Thornhill's plan was similar.

[12] The supercargoes were later to develop a new means of adjusting the trade balance. This device, which involved receiving the proceeds from country shipping into the Canton treasury in exchange for bills on London, will be described in the course of the present chapter.

[13] The English, being at war with Spain, no longer had access to the specie supplies of the Americas. Morse, ''The Provision of Funds for the East India Company's Trade,'' *Journal of the Royal Asiatic Society*, April, 1922, p. 242.

[14] Small quantities were shipped in 1779-1780. Lord Macartney wrote from Madras, ''Our distress for Money has rather increased than diminished & we cannot therefore flatter you even with the most distant hope of any supply from hence.'' Morse, *Chronicles*, II, 76.

[15] Colonel Watson to the governor-general in council, 27 March 1781, Bengal General Consultations, 17 Sept. 1781, *Ninth Report*, 1783, App. 80; Thornhill to the governor-general in council, 28 July 1781, Bengal General Consultations, 30 July 1781, *ibid.*, App. 76.

[16] The colonel's estimate of prices was excessively hopeful. In neither 1780 nor 1781, according to the supercargoes, did the rate rise above 300 dollars per chest. Morse, *Chronicles*, II, 140.

His armored sloop *Betsy* would stop first at Rhio,[17] where some seven hundred chests might be sold, the proceeds to be paid into the Canton treasury. The position of the governor-general was trying. Opium in Bengal was almost unsalable, and there seemed little chance that the trade could be revived while war continued.[18] But the work of the Canton factory must not be endangered, and London must have its tea. The council therefore decided to adopt the plan that had been suggested.[19] The attitude of the Chinese government appears not to have been considered in the discussions. As Hastings put it—perhaps more accurately than he knew—the Chinese prohibition was understood to be no obstacle to importing opium, and the supercargoes had never cited it as an objection.[20]

By the summer of 1781 the *Betsy* was ready to sail.[21] But she was never to see Canton. In March, while lying in the river at Rhio, she was captured by a French privateer, the *St. Thérèse,* after her captain had disposed of some 59,600 Spanish dollars' worth of opium.[22] Captain Geddes himself escaped, and upon reaching Canton, paid the proceeds into the company's treasury. The first chapter of Warren Hastings' smuggling venture thus resulted in a loss of more than five lakhs of rupees to the Honourable Company.[23]

[17] Also written Riouw or Bintang, an island just south of the Malay peninsula.

[18] No bidder had appeared to claim the opium even at Rs. 400 per chest. Governor-general and council to the court of directors, 29 Dec. 1781, *Ninth Report*, 1783, App. 82.

[19] Bengal General Consultations, 30 July 1781, *ibid.*, App. 76.

[20] Hastings seems not to have investigated the matter too carefully. The supercargoes had in fact cited it as an objection in 1770.

[21] The expeditions were financed by two loans of ten lakhs of rupees each. Bengal General Consultations, 30 July 1781, *Ninth Report*, 1783, App. 12.

[22] The Spanish dollar was invoiced by the company at five shillings. Morse, *Chronicles*, I, 47.

[23] This approximate figure is merely the difference between the invoice

The story of the *Nonsuch* is more involved. Early in 1782 preparations for her departure were completed. She was loaded with 1601 chests of Patna opium. Taking a circuitous route and flying French and Spanish colors at various stages of the voyage, she reached Macao Roads in July.[24] The arrival of a vessel carrying opium on the company's account, was, to say the least, embarrassing to the supercargoes. The trade was clearly regarded as contraband both by the council in Calcutta and the representatives of the company in Canton, who were rightly jealous of the company's good name with the hong merchants and with the Chinese government. Indeed their record had been most exemplary, despite an occasional small shipment of opium by individual servants of the company.[25] But the *Nonsuch* expedition was a smuggling venture pure and simple and was so conceived both in Canton and Calcutta.[26]

If the supercargoes found themselves unwilling opium smugglers, the hong merchants were no less reluctant to be involved. None would "have his name made use of in the affair in any shape whatever."[27] Finally a newly ap-

price (Rs. 709,108) and the sale price. The invoice also included some miscellaneous expenses incurred in Calcutta.

24 Court of directors to the governor-general in council, 28 Dec. 1782, *Warren Hastings Documents*, VI, 93. A foreign ship was required to go first to Macao, where her captain arranged for a pilot and an interpreter. At the Bocca Tigris or Bogue, measurage and other fees were paid. Then the vessel was allowed to proceed up the river to Whampoa, below the native city of Canton, which was the official anchorage for foreign shipping.

25 For examples see Morse, *Chronicles*, III, 142, 356; IV, 17-18.

26 In a letter explaining the consignment the council suggested that, since opium was contraband, the *Nonsuch* had best enter the river as an armed ship. The supercargoes, remembering previous experiences with armed vessels in the river, determined upon a bolder course and brought the *Nonsuch* to Whampoa, having paid the usual measurage dues. Bengal General Consultations, 2 Jan. 1782, *Ninth Report*, 1783, App. 81. For a controversy with regard to an armed ship in the river see Morse, *Chronicles*, V, 127 ff.

27 *Ibid.*, II, 78. The hong merchants, in general, abstained from opium dealings as scrupulously as did the supercargoes of the company. During the

pointed member of the gild named Sinqua, a former opium dealer who was well acquainted with contraband technique, was interested in the shipment. With himself he sought to associate Puankhequa, an older merchant. But the latter, though lavish with advice, would have nothing to do with the business, and, as a way out of the difficulty, four reputable merchants were prevailed upon to secure the ship corporately.[28]

Sinqua's offer of 210 head dollars[29] per chest was not one to bring delight to the sponsors of the expedition, but it was the best that was received during the three months the *Nonsuch* lay at Whampoa.[30] The supercargoes could not afford to hold the opium longer in the hope of more favorable terms. They admitted themselves tyros at the smuggling trade, having neither taste for nor experience in it. The market, they asserted, was already glutted. With maledictions on the governor-general and council, the company's agents took the only way out and sold the entire consignment to Sinqua on long credit at 210 head dollars per chest instead of the 500 Spanish dollars that Colonel Watson had so rosily visualized for the Indian administrators. Even then the Chinese merchant had the greatest difficulty in disposing of his purchase.

The balance sheet of the enterprise did not redound to the glory of its promoters. Rather was it a tribute to the ineptitude of the Honourable East India Company as smuggler. The opium was sold in Canton at a figure be-

following three or four decades they sometimes acted as securities for opium ships at Whampoa, but they do not appear to have dealt in the drug.

[28] General letter from Canton, 28 Dec. 1782, *Warren Hastings Documents*, VI, 94; Morse, *Chronicles*, II, 78.

[29] Head dollars were at a discount of two per cent. They were a recently coined Spanish dollar which contained only ninety per cent of fine silver as compared with the ninety-two per cent of the old milled Mexico dollar. *Ibid.*, p. 41.

[30] General letter from Canton, 28 Dec. 1782, *Warren Hastings Documents*, VI, 95.

low its invoice price in Calcutta, with other charges left
out of the reckoning.[31] The company lost more than eighteen per cent on the speculation, and with the account of
the *Betsy* included, the loss in dollars was well over
250,000.[32] But profit or loss, the directors would have no
more contraband trade on company ships. They did not
hesitate to provide goods for smuggling and to encourage
private merchants to transport these goods to China.
Yet their stoutly ethical souls revolted at the thought of
the company's actually participating in an illegal trade.
There was no objection, they told Hastings, to disposing
of the drug at Rhio and paying the proceeds into the Canton treasury, but "under any circumstances, it is beneath
the company to engage in . . . a clandestine Trade; we
therefore hereby positively prohibit more Ophium being
sent to China on the company's account."[33]

The East India Company's lone smuggling voyage to
China received a further airing at the Hastings trial.
The indictment, a part of the general charge relating to
corrupt contracts, was that Warren Hastings had "bor-
rowed money at a large interest for advancing the same
to the Contractor for Opium, and engaging the East
India Company in a Smuggling Adventure to China."[34]
In pressing this charge the prosecution was plainly in a
less favorable position than in attacking the Sulivan con-

[31] Morse, *Chronicles*, II, 77.

[32] In the search for a scapegoat blame was laid upon Captain Richardson
of the *Nonsuch*, who, it was urged, had loitered at Malacca to dispose of
his owner's opium, thus permitting private merchants to glut the China
market. In reply Richardson charged the supercargoes with negligence,
pointedly observing that he had sold Watson's opium for 340 Spanish dollars per chest. General letter from Canton, 28 Dec. 1782, *Warren Hastings
Documents*, VI, 95; Captain Richardson to the court of directors, 7 May
1786, *ibid.*, pp. 123-125.

[33] Company's general letter to Bengal, 12 July 1782, *Ninth Report*, 1783,
App. 87.

[34] *History of the Trial of Warren Hastings*, Part VIII, p. 269.

tract. The attempt to show that the loans had been floated with corrupt motives collapsed with scarcely a shred of proof.[35] Lord Thurlow, Hastings' staunchest supporter in the Lords, reduced the issue to its lowest terms when he questioned whether it was a crime for the governor-general in an emergency "to make the Company do that Act publicly, which the Directors and the Board of Controul have urged the Government of Bengal, by every possible means, to every possible extent, to get done by individual merchants." The Lords unanimously agreed that no high crime or misdemeanor on Hastings' part was involved.[36]

Despite the failure of the *Betsy-Nonsuch* undertaking dreams of using the opium trade for the benefit of the China investment continued to haunt the governors in Bengal. As long as the Calcutta treasury was being drained of its specie to supply the China factory, the council found itself searching for means of placing credits at the disposal of the supercargoes. One obvious method was to require that the price of opium purchased in Bengal be paid into the Canton treasury. In 1785 Sir John Macpherson adopted the plan, and by the end of the year arrangements had been made for the remittance of more than eight lakhs of rupees.[37]

The fallacy of the new scheme was quickly demonstrated.[38] For some years the Canton factory had added to its commercial activities a banking business by accepting from country merchants specie which their cargoes

[35] *Ibid.*, p. 245.

[36] This charge was one of the two on which the defendant was unanimously acquitted.

[37] Governor-general and council to the court of directors, 29 April 1785, *Warren Hastings Documents*, VI, 118-119; paragraphs from a letter proposed by the court of directors to be sent to the governor-general and council, *ibid.*, pp. 125-127.

[38] Morse, *Chronicles*, II, 121, 125. In the *Journals of Samuel Shaw*, p. 265, the operation of the plan is noticed.

from India had yielded and issuing bills on London in return. Money received by private merchants in China would thus be paid into the company's treasury and would go towards the investment. Country ships usually brought from India cargoes of far greater value than those which they bore on the return voyage, and for their surplus treasure merchants were glad to accept the company's bills. This method of remittance appeared superior to that which the council in Bengal had adopted, for it was less subject to uncertainty. As the supercargoes pointed out, it was probable that in the season 1786-1787 little more than three-quarters of the purchase price of Calcutta opium would actually find its way into the Canton treasury. The experiment proved a costly one and was abandoned.[39] Payment was received in the old way, the company trusting to the efficacy of its Canton banking service.

The peculiar character of Far Eastern commerce invested the opium trade with an economic significance that it might not otherwise have assumed. Shorn of statistical detail, the situation was this: China—and her statesmen were never reluctant to emphasize the unpalatable truth —had little need and less desire for British manufactures, while the tea and silk of the Middle Kingdom were the foundations on which the barbarians' Canton factory had been erected. During the first century and a half of the East India Company's existence vast quantities of bullion were sent to the Far East for the purchase of these luxuries. But during the latter part of the eighteenth century, partly because of the wars in Europe, the

---

[39] The same plan was proposed again in 1799-1800. On this occasion the directors ordered that the most substantial security be required ''in order to prevent a repetition of those losses and disappointments which we experienced under former transactions of this nature.'' Court of directors to the governor-general in council (separate revenue), 11 June 1800, I. O. Despatches to Bengal, XXXIV.

company encountered great difficulty in obtaining the necessary specie. In the years 1792-1793 to 1808-1809, for example, the trade in goods from China to England was more than double that from England to China. Even with shipments of specie from Great Britain amounting to nearly £2,500,000, the balance for the seventeen years was in favor of Canton by more than eight million.[40] In only three of these years were English goods sold at a profit in China.[41]

But if the Chinese would have little to do with Manchester and Leeds, their prejudices by no means extended to Indian cotton and opium. Increasingly, then, it was to the country trade that the supercargoes looked for their supply of treasure. Commerce from India to China exceeded that from China to India—by nearly a million sterling each year from 1802 to 1806.[42] A surplus was thus created, a considerable portion of which found its way into the Canton treasury of the company in return for bills of exchange.

The country ships, in whose holds were carried most of the cotton and all of the opium, sailed under a license issued by the East India Company. By this instrument the vessel was placed under the authority of the supercargoes while at Canton and its freedom otherwise restricted.[43] As early as 1787 the country trade was supply-

---

[40] Goods shipped by the company from England to China.. £16,602,338
Goods shipped by the company from China to England.. £27,157,006

Balance in favor of China............................ £10,554,668

This amount does not include expenses at Canton, which, if they were considered, would throw the balance still more heavily against Europe. W. Milburn, *Oriental Commerce* (1813 edit.), II, 475-478.

[41] *Ibid.*, p. 478.   [42] *Ibid.*, p. 483.

[43] From 1816 on, a clause in the license provided that it should be void if any opium were carried other than that sold at the company's sales in Calcutta. Governor-general in council to the court of directors, 11 Oct. 1816, *Third Report from the Select Committee*, 1831, App. IV, p. 3.

ing more than half of the China investment, and, although
the percentage was not always maintained, its prosperity
was a vital matter. Until 1823 opium was subsidiary to
raw cotton.[44] But there is ample evidence to show that
even before the great expansion of the opium trade after
1821, the company relied upon the drug as a means of
remittance to Canton. It was even suggested by the directors that the provision of opium be increased in order to
avoid shipping bullion from Europe.[45] Conversely, the
ease with which merchants could remit their opium profits to India contributed to a rise in price at the Calcutta
sales.[46] The Canton banking arrangements were an undoubted advantage both to the company and to private
traders.

Meanwhile the imports of opium into China were
slowly increasing. The trade at the Chinese end was carried on under the auspices of the Portuguese, whose position at Macao facilitated their leadership.[47] In 1799 about
two thousand chests of monopoly opium were being imported into Macao, but in previous years, before the Bengal supply had been restricted, annual shipments had

[44] Morse, ''The Provision of Funds for the East India Company's
Trade,'' *Journal of the Royal Asiatic Society*, April, 1922, p. 251.

[45] Court of directors to the governor-general in council (public), 26 March
1801, I. O. Despatches to Bengal, XXXV.

[46] Governor-general in council to the court of directors (political), 17
Dec. 1799, I. O. Letters from Bengal, XL.

[47] The status of the Portuguese at Macao was anomalous. They professed
to regard themselves as sovereign, but the Chinese authorities never admitted the tenure to be more than that of a leasehold. In point of fact, although the colony enjoyed virtual self-government, the Portuguese acknowledged the overlordship of the Chinese by the payment of 500 taels
annually. Two custom houses were maintained, one for the Spanish and
Portuguese trading from Manila and one for other Europeans and Chinese.
Illicit trade, even for the English, was rather simpler at Macao than at
Canton, for while the former was under the hoppo of Canton, regulations
were more difficult to enforce. Cordier, *Histoire générale de la Chine*, III,
132.

occasionally exceeded four thousand.[48] The first mention
of actual trading in opium at Canton appears in 1779,
when one Fergusson "bought a small vessel and brought
her to Whampoa to manage an Ophium concern."[49] By
1780 a depot had been established by British traders at
Lark's Bay, near Macao, an anchorage removed alike
from the exactions of Chinese officialdom and the surveillance of the Portuguese.[50] This opium base seems to have
continued operations on a modest scale until 1793, when
the attention of the authorities was drawn to it, probably
by the Portuguese who were distressed at the loss of
revenue to Macao.[51] The supercargoes, when called upon
by the hoppo[52] to investigate, expressed surprise that
Lark's Bay, for years well known to Chinese officials and
Europeans as a smuggling haven, should be made the
subject of action. There were no opium ships loitering in
the bay at the time, but the company's representatives
soothed the Chinese by admitting the practice to be a
bad one.

Opium ships were also coming to Whampoa and disposing of their cargoes under the benevolent patronage
of the local authorities. In 1798, however, Canton rumor
had it that measures were about to be taken against the
drug as "pernicious to the Health and Morals of the
Chinese."[53] The supercargoes, although confident that
the hoppo would never endanger his own contraband
profits, were insistent that the skirts of the company be
kept clean, and they requested that a peremptory order
be issued against the carriage of opium on company

---

[48] Morse, *Chronicles*, II, 325, 365. Statistics on the opium trade in this
period should be treated with great caution. For an analysis of the principal sources and routes see Morse, *International Relations*, I, 174.

[49] Morse, *Chronicles*, II, 51.   [50] See Phipps, *China Trade*, p. 208.

[51] Morse, *Chronicles*, II, 199-200.

[52] The official in charge of foreign customs at Canton.

[53] *Ibid.*, p. 316.

ships.[54] Rumor became reality a year later when, in December, 1799, the Canton administration placed itself definitely on record. Goaded into action by a chop from his superior, the hoppo addressed an edict to the hong merchants prohibiting them from dealing in opium or securing ships that carried it. The terms of this proscription indicate a suspicious familiarity with the mechanism of the contraband trade, which, the hoppo admitted, was carried on through the connivance of officials.[55]

Neither the supercargoes nor the Chinese dealers were greatly exercised over this display of energy.[56] As had been anticipated, the prohibition of 1799 ruffled the placid waters of the opium trade but slightly. It became evident at once that, although the trade within the Bogue might be somewhat embarrassed, at Macao it flourished with augmented vigor. By 1804 the supercargoes had satisfied themselves that the edict indicated no real change of policy.[57] The effects of the prohibition vanished with its author, and the trade was resumed at Whampoa with as little obstruction as before. The supercargoes apologized for their tardiness in communicating the reassuring news to Bengal. With a naïveté characteristic of the company's attitude, they reflected upon the questionable taste of "any public sanction of the British Govt. to its importation" and judged it more "advisable to avoid any public communication and merely apprizing the Traders be-

[54] They asserted "that no Edict has lately been issued." This statement, Morse thinks, relegates the edict of 1796, frequently cited, to the limbo of mythology. The assumption that there was such a document seems to rest on a memorial to the emperor, October, 1836, in *Correspondence relating to China, Parliamentary Papers*, 1840, incl. 5 in no. 90. For the form prohibiting the carriage of opium on company ships see Morse, *Chronicles*, II, 282, 327.

[55] For the text see Morse, *Chronicles*, II, App. M. This edict appears to have received imperial sanction. See also the text of the hoppo's edict of 1808, *ibid.*, III, App. S.

[56] *Ibid.*, II, 365.　　　　　　　　　　[57] *Ibid.*, p. 430.

tween this & Bengal that we perceived no impropriety in their bringing the Article to Market.'' This precaution was of course wholly unnecessary. Opium merchants were like weather-vanes in their sensitiveness to the winds of official opinion.

Despite the fact that the edict of 1799 was stillborn, opium was indubitably an illicit commodity thereafter. Any lingering doubts about the edict of 1729 were removed. The seventy years intervening had seen the gradual spread of the habit and the gradual expansion of the trade. Both Macao and, in a lesser degree, Whampoa, were frequented by opium merchants. Save for Warren Hastings' untoward venture in 1781-1782 and a few instances when junior officers had acted as agents for private houses in India, neither the East India Company nor the hong merchants participated in the trade. Nevertheless the company was vitally interested, first, because of its stake in the Bengal opium industry, and second, because the country trade in opium and raw cotton helped to supply the Canton factory with specie. Early in the new century, as will be indicated presently, the country trade so increased in value that the supercargoes were enabled not only to provide for their investment but also to remit treasure to India and England. Meanwhile Chinese officials were supplementing their incomes by tolls levied on the illicit drug.

China, however, was developing an anti-opium policy, at least on paper. The edict of 1799 was followed nine years later by another, the work of a new hoppo acting presumably under instructions from Peking.[58] In the following year this was reinforced by an edict from the viceroy himself.[59] After paying his respects to the depraved foreigners who thus seduced the Middle Kingdom

[58] *Ibid.*, III, App. S.
[59] *Ibid.*, App. U.

and to the "wicked people who buy and sell it backwards and forwards and thus diffuse a public mischief," he laid a large share of the blame on the always handy shoulders of the hong merchants. But the new law proved as futile as the old. Indeed it is a question whether it was intended to be more than a pretext for further exactions. Although the hong merchants were henceforth required to give bonds against the carriage of opium on ships secured by them, that need prove no obstacle as long as the trade was protected by a complaisant magistracy.

More interesting was the companion edict which forbade the export of "this countrys Silver and Gold."[60] Here curiously enough appears the converse of the question that had plagued the supercargoes and the Bengal government but a few years before. Formerly the company had been faced with the problem of getting specie to Canton; now the Chinese were fearful that not only the European money that they had received in past years but also their own sycee[61] was about to depart. Had there been a definitive shift in the balance of trade?[62] As far as British commerce alone was concerned, the anxiety of the Chinese was not groundless. The growth of the country trade and the success of the supercargoes' banking operations had made it no novelty for them to provide for their own investment and to remit specie to Calcutta and London. In the three seasons before the prohibitory edict nearly seven million dollars had been sent from Canton to India, where the treasury was seriously em-

[60] Morse, *Chronicles,* III, App. U.

[61] Uncoined native silver. The supercargoes inferred that, as formerly, the edict would apply only to gold and sycee, not to foreign dollars. It was therefore no new piece of legislation, but the reassertion of the principle at this particular time was not without significance.

[62] See *Ninth Report,* 1783, p. 55. Staunton, *An Authentic Account of an Embassy . . . to the Emperor of China* (2d edit.), II, 496, refers to the increase in prices caused by the influx of silver from Europe.

barrassed.[63] There were also clandestine shipments by both the company and private merchants.[64]

This apparent drain of treasure was intimately connected in the Chinese mind with the opium trade. The edicts of 1809, the one prohibiting opium, the other the export of specie, were issued simultaneously. Future expansion of the traffic was to relate them even more closely. But in the period now under consideration (to 1821) the loss of silver was not real nor was the assumed loss due solely to opium.[65] In 1818, for example, consignments to Canton of British and Indian goods and American specie exceeded the exports from China by six million dollars.[66] Included in the Indian trade to China was opium worth four and a half million dollars. It is therefore true that without the drug trade foreigners could have exported only one-fourth of the six million in silver that they actually shipped out. But the six million was more than covered by the seven million brought by Americans, who continued to supply the China market with specie.[67] When the total known volume of the foreign trade of Canton—English, Indian, and American—

[63] Morse, *Chronicles*, III, 56, 80, 100, 102. In 1810 also the supercargoes were instructed to send silver to London. The directors, finding it difficult to reconcile their law-abiding professions with a contraband necessity, offered their ''solicitude that no offence be given to the Chinese Govt. from the export of Bullion.''

[64] No specie whatever was brought to China by the company between 1809 and 1815. *Ibid.*, IV, 388.

[65] *Ibid.*, III, 337.

[66]
Indian produce	14,000,000
British goods and American specie	12,000,000
Total imports into China	26,000,000
Reported exports of goods	20,000,000

—*Ibid.*, p. 336.

[67] See K. S. Latourette, *Early Relations between the United States and China, 1785-1844*, p. 27. They imported specie until 1827, when they began the practice of bringing bills of exchange on London.

is considered, it will be seen that the balance was still in favor of China.

It was not only the edicts of over-zealous officials that distressed the company's representatives in Canton. Another cloud had appeared on the horizon of the British opium trade. This shadow, which the supercargoes viewed with apprehension, was the presence in the China market of Turkey and Malwa opium, non-monopoly products. The less serious of the two was the American trade in Turkey opium from Smyrna, first reported to the directors in 1807. The situation was one of great delicacy, and the letter which the supercargoes despatched to London was as remarkable for its curious coding of significant words as for its purport. Previously, they observed, some shipments had been made from Smyrna by way of America, but in the summer of 1806 the Americans developed the habit of bringing opium directly to China, where it was used only to adulterate the more costly Bengal product. There was, however, no occasion for undue alarm, for, although the market might be temporarily injured, only small quantities of Turkey could find sale at profitable prices. "It is to be hoped," the supercargoes piously concluded, "that the length of the voyage from any part of *Europe* will tend to render the danger of so dreadful a Calamity taking place as the introduction of the *seeds* of the *Plague* by the *importation* of this Drug into *China,* not so great as apprehended."[68] The forebodings of the company proved baseless as far as direct voyages from Smyrna were concerned, for the practice was soon dropped.[69] But with a lapse during the War of 1812, the American trade persisted, to the discomfiture of the Brit-

[68] In the supercargoes' letter the italicized words were in code. Morse, *Chronicles*, III, 73.

[69] T. Dennett, *Americans in Eastern Asia*, p. 116.

ish at Canton.[70] Although the quantities imported were probably larger than have been inferred, the drug was of such inferior quality that it never seriously challenged the position of Bengal opium.[71]

Far more threatening was the trade in Malwa opium, which was exported to China from Bombay and the Portuguese ports on the west coast of India. It was the product of the native states of Central India and Rajputana, and with its cultivation and manufacture the East India Company had no concern. The invasion of the Chinese market by the Malwa drug was to lead to the exclusion of British opium dealers from Macao and the concentration of their illicit trade at Whampoa. Shipments from the west coast of India to Macao, although scarcely a novelty, seem not to have drawn the attention of the company's supercargoes prior to the season of 1804, when one of the Macao authorities informed them that one hundred piculs had been brought by the *Lowjee Family,* apparently from Goa.[72] This official professed great solicitude for the company's monopoly and the Bengal trade, but what really disturbed him was the fact that the consignment had been sold at Whampoa rather than at Macao, the usual destination of Malwa. The company's representatives in turn expressed their apprehen-

---

[70] Morse, *Chronicles,* III, 179.

[71] The general impression has been that the imports of Turkey opium into China were extremely small. See the table in Morse, *International Relations,* I, 208, and in the *Report from the Select Committee* (Lords), 1821, p. 70. Morse's later researches at the India office have served to correct these estimates. The supercargoes, who should have been informed, stated that the importation in 1816 amounted to 600 piculs; in 1817, 300 to 400; in 1818, 1900; and in the following year "still further enlarged." *Chronicles,* III, 323, 339. A picul is equal to 100 catties, each weighing roughly one and one-third pounds. Malwa was packed in chests containing about 140 pounds, while a chest of Bengal weighed 120 catties (160 pounds).

[72] *Ibid.,* II, 429-431.

sion to the governor-general in India, urging that no pains be spared to exterminate this "illicit" commerce.

If no definitive measures could be taken to stop the trade, at least one of its ports of egress could be blocked. In 1805, therefore, the export of non-monopoly opium from Bombay was prohibited. Representations were also made to the viceroy of Goa, who generously agreed to forbid shipments from Goa and to instruct his subordinates at Daman and Diu to take similar action.[73] It is doubtful whether these steps met with complete success, for smuggling opportunities were large, and the Portuguese could not be expected vigorously to enforce a regulation from which they derived so little real benefit. For the next decade, at any rate, whatever Malwa trade there was, escaped the eyes of the supercargoes. But in 1815, when they learned that about three hundred chests had been brought to Macao and more than two hundred to Whampoa and that the profit to be gained from trading in "illicit" opium was about twice its prime cost, the supercargoes opened negotiations with the senate of Macao.[74] The Portuguese remained unimpressed, and, instead of prohibiting the trade, served notice that they were about to encourage it.[75] To spite the British the senate placed the knife to its own nose by reviving a set of

[73] Governor-general in council to the court of directors (separate revenue), 1 March 1804, I. O. Letters from Bengal, XLIV; governor-general in council to the court of directors (public general), 7 June 1806, *ibid.*, XLIX. The measures taken in India to protect Bengal opium from Malwa competition will be described in Chapter IV.

[74] In the previous year they had been urged to protest by the Bengal authorities but had declined to act. Governor-general in council to the court of directors (separate revenue), 7 Oct. 1815, *ibid.*, LXXII; Morse, *Chronicles*, III, 238-239, 250.

[75] The Macao authorities contended that the promise made by the viceroy of Goa in 1805 had been scrupulously adhered to, but that Malwa opium had been brought by British traders. I. O. Bengal Political Consultations, 17 Dec. 1816. The supercargoes' reply is in I. O. Canton Diary, 16 Dec. 1816.

moribund regulations, the net effect of which was to restrict the opium market of Macao to Portuguese subjects.[76]

The company's agents were naturally annoyed at the exclusion of British traders from the principal opium depot in China. Macao, to be sure, was less than ideal. Officials could not protect the stocks from Chinese raids, and the policy of the Portuguese of levying a huge slush fund to bribe Chinese magistrates seemed to the supercargoes merely an invitation to further exactions.[77] On the other hand, Whampoa could not be relied upon as a port for contraband goods. A fit of administrative integrity on the part of viceroy or hoppo might mean enforcement of the law, with devastating consequences to British opium dealers. In the season of 1818 the supercargoes observed with dismay that nearly two thousand chests of Malwa were imported into Macao.[78] From two unpleasant facts there was no appeal: British opium traders were excluded from Macao, and shipments of non-monopoly opium to that port were increasing with great rapidity.

The prospect seemed a gloomy one. Malwa opium was still inferior to Bengal and brought a much lower price

[76] The senate was apparently nettled by the fact that many opium ships had preferred Whampoa to Macao as an anchorage, by the high prices which governed the Bengal sales, and by the double duties imposed both in Bengal and England on Portuguese ships from China. Morse, *Chronicles*, III, 250-251.

[77] The supercargoes were justly irritated also at the conduct of one of the high officials of the colony, who in 1813-14 attempted to corner the stock of Bengal opium. To this ephemeral monopoly they ascribed the high prices asked for the company's drug and thus indirectly the growth of the competing trade. This inference was only partly correct, for the Malwa trade was the result of stimuli in the area of production as well as in the market. Note by J. Molony, 12 Aug. 1817, I. O. Canton Secret Diary, 1817; Morse, *Chronicles*, III, 323.

[78] Morse, *Chronicles*, III, 344.

in the Canton market.[79] In the decade 1811-1821, only about half as much had been sent from Malwa as from Calcutta. But if, as the supercargoes dismally foresaw, the quality of Malwa should continue to improve and its imports increase, the safety of the monopoly itself would be jeopardized. Only a Chinese strongly attached to the Bengal drug would pay the huge monopoly profit which the East India Company extracted. The supercargoes were correct in their prophecy. Competition from Malwa persisted as the *bête noire* of the Indian monopolists until the problem was finally solved not in China but in India. The solution, to anticipate what follows, served only to secure the opium revenue of British India and to intensify Anglo-Chinese antagonism.

Barred from Macao, British opium traders turned to their new contraband station at Whampoa and discovered it to be not without merit. "Nothing was more simple," testified one opium merchant, "than to sell the drug there."[80] When a vessel reached port, it made the usual customs declaration, listing only its legitimate cargo. The purchaser of Bengal opium was assured of its quality by the standard set by the East India Company. Other opium was sold on muster. As soon as shroffs had tested the money—for except in rare cases opium was a cash transaction—an order on the ship's officer was issued to the buyer.[81] The latter then presented his order and re-

---

[79] *Ibid.*, p. 339. The prices at Canton were:

For Bengal opium, 1817, per chest	1300 dollars
For Bengal opium, 1818, per chest	840
For Malwa opium, 1818, per chest	680

[80] Evidence of W. S. Davidson, *Report from the Select Committee* (Commons), 1830, Q. 2536. In 1819 at least one vessel was serving as an opium depot, secured by a member of the cohong. Morse, *Chronicles*, III, 358.

[81] Shroffs were Chinese assayers. By striking a coin against a fingernail allowed to grow long for the purpose, they were able to estimate its purity with a high degree of accuracy.

ceived his drug. Before transferring the opium to his own boat, the purchaser or his agent removed it from the chests and stowed it away in bags. Only a few minutes were required to place it in the smuggling boat, which then put off with all possible speed, outdistancing or defying any government craft on preventive duty.[82]

In all probability connivance of the mandarin boats had been previously arranged. That in fact was one of the responsibilities of the Chinese buyer. The preventive service appointed to watch opium ships rarely made objection to landing the drug, save when no satisfactory understanding with regard to "squeeze" had been reached.[83] None the less the life of an opium trader at Whampoa was not wholly tranquil. Whatever the usual attitude of the authorities, the traffic was legally contraband and therefore defenseless. Occasionally, when the price of connivance was set too high, no purchasers could be found. Or after a sale had been made, buyers would be unable to make the necessary arrangements for safe delivery and would demand a refund of their purchase money.[84] As long as the trade was centered at Whampoa, it suffered from too close proximity to officials, who in an excess of either venality or honesty might ruin it at any time.

If Portuguese authorities drove British contraband trade from Macao to Whampoa, Chinese officials were responsible for its expulsion from the Canton River. Between the edict of 1809 and 1821, when the opium vessels were evicted from Whampoa, there was intermittent conflict with the Canton authorities. But with the exception of two serious controversies, the attention which officials

[82] Evidence of John Aken, *Report from the Select Committee* (Commons), 1830, Q. 2000.

[83] Evidence of W. S. Davidson, *ibid.*, Q. 2525, 2532.

[84] *Ibid.*, Q. 2534-2535, 2547.

bestowed upon the trade was fitful and in general quite formal in character.[85] In 1815 occurred the first important anti-opium offensive. The attack centered at Macao, where six of the principal native dealers were taken into custody. New trade regulations were issued which required that Portuguese ships in the future should undergo search by Chinese officers.[86] At both Macao and Whampoa native traders grew wary. As for the English, the gesture came as an ominous augury at what might befall the company, hitherto immune from search. The supercargoes determined to resist any such innovation.[87]

In 1817 the latent trouble was aggravated by an act of piracy committed on the American ship *Wabash* carrying opium and specie.[88] The offenders were duly punished, but the fact that the ship had opium on board afforded convenient ground for refusing compensation. This incident proved to be something more than another ephemeral conflict with the Chinese authorities, for it raised anew the question of search.[89] The viceroy first applied pressure to the hong merchants, the senior of

---

[85] In 1811, for example, the new viceroy took occasion to deliver a homily on the evils of the opium traffic to the select committee of supercargoes. He had received special orders from the emperor, he said, to stamp out the trade and he sought the coöperation of the supercargoes, ''since the opium imported was chiefly the produce of the British colonies.'' His audience remained unimpressed. Morse, *Chronicles*, III, 164.

[86] Previously goods had been landed and stored, and duties paid only at the time of sale. For at least a century it had been an unwritten canon of Canton trade that goods could be smuggled only when they had been landed. In the future incoming ships were to report their cargoes to the hoppo immediately upon their arrival and allow themselves to be examined for contraband.

[87] Morse, *Chronicles*, III, 237-238. The records for 1816, as summarized by Morse, make no reference to the immediate outcome of the controversy. All available evidence indicates that, although there may have been difficulty in making deliveries, imports rose rather than fell off.

[88] J. F. Davis, *The Chinese*, I, 385; Morse, *Chronicles*, III, 318.

[89] It appears that in the previous year (1816) an edict had been received from Peking ''rendering the Hong merchants responsible for the ascertain-

whom was fined 160,000 taels and the three next in rank compelled to subscribe to "some Public service." Their state of mind may be imagined. They were being held responsible for a trade in which as a rule they had no part and which they deplored as a barrier to legitimate commerce. To protect themselves the merchants decided to secure no ship whose commander had not signed a bond affirming the legal character of his cargo, a declaration that was to be required of company ships as well as those of private traders. The threat of the cohong was successfully resisted by the supercargoes, but in the following month the authorities again evinced an intention of searching ships as they reached Whampoa. This course, the supercargoes reflected, would be proper enough in a civilized community where treaty rights guaranteed the position of foreigners. In China, where immemorial custom was pointed to as law, Europeans as well as natives must protect their traditional privileges. To reënforce their stand they invited H. M. S. *Orlando* to anchor off Chuenpi and to proceed, if required, to Whampoa. The gesture proved sufficient. Intimidated both by the presence of the *Orlando* and the unequivocal resolution of the supercargoes, the viceroy retreated for the time being.[90]

In their resistance to the Chinese demands the company's agents incurred the disapproval of the directors, who seem to have found the summoning of the *Orlando* peculiarly offensive. With all their tender solicitude for the opium system in Bengal, they had given the trade

ment of the question, whether or not any foreign vessel imports opium.'' This edict was exhumed by Commissioner Lin during the crisis of 1839. See *Correspondence relating to China, Parliamentary Papers*, 1840, incl. 2 in no. 145.

[90] Select committee of supercargoes to the court of directors (public), 8 Dec. 1817, *Third Report from the Select Committee*, 1831, App. II, p. 100; Morse, *Chronicles*, III, 321.

little stimulus at the Chinese end. They had rigidly prohibited their supercargoes from dealing in the drug and
the ships of the company from carrying it. In 1787 when
Lieutenant Colonel Charles Cathcart was sent on an embassy to Peking, his instructions directed him to state, if
necessary, that the company would prohibit the export
of Indian opium to China. The same paragraph appeared
in the instructions issued to Lord Macartney in 1792.[91]
Useful as the opium revenue was to British India, it was
less to be desired than the China trade monopoly, which
had been threatened by the stubbornness of the country
ships and the aid and comfort given them by the supercargoes. The directors urged their representatives to
concede the bond rather than to compromise themselves
with the authorities. In London the Chinese case might
seem reasonable but to the supercargoes in Canton it was
preposterous. Chinese authorities, they charged, ''are
never sincere in their declared intentions of suppressing
illicit traffic . . . as it has ever been considered one of the
principal advantages of their situations.'' As long as officials were issuing prohibitory edicts with one hand and
extending the other to receive bribes from illegal trade,
it would be disastrous to allow them more control over
British property.[92]

The harried supercargoes enjoyed only a short period
of calm, for in the autumn of 1821 the Chinese initiated
a series of measures destined finally to drive the traffic
from Whampoa to the outer anchorages.[93] Events which

[91] *Ibid.*, III, App. B and App. G. The Cathcart embassy was lost at sea
before it reached the coast of China.

[92] I. O. Canton Diary, 25 July 1819; court of directors to the select committee of supercargoes, 8 May 1818, in Dane, ''Circumstances that Preceded . . . the First Chinese War,'' *Report of the Royal Commission*, VII,
1895, App. C.

[93] In the spring and summer of 1820 two edicts from the viceroy and
hoppo were served on the supercargoes. The occasion seems to have been

could not be decently ignored thrust the contraband trade under the eyes of the provincial authorities. Accused by a native of "acts of public delinquency," they were moved to an incredible display of energy to clear themselves, as well perhaps as to extort more revenue from the long suffering cohong.[94] Whatever the motives of the viceroy, his acts and his pronunciamentos left little to be desired for picturesque vigor. Four ships—three country and one American—were under official disapproval for having brought opium to Whampoa. With the exception of one of the country ships the charge was admittedly true. At the outset the viceroy proposed to deal severely with the guilty craft, but a fortnight late, having found "that the Merchants roar out, as under the agonies of a head-ache," he moderated his demands.[95] The vessels were still forbidden to load export cargoes and were to leave port within five days.

Matters now took a turn which excluded the supercargoes from the rôle of mildly interested spectators. From two angles they were drawn into the affair. First of all, James Matheson, consignee of two of the vessels, requested instructions. For the supercargoes to order opium shipping out of port would be disloyal to the Indian revenue, but to support smugglers would implicate the company in an illicit trade. The advice which they gave—that Matheson might do as he pleased but must

another edict from Peking. No immediate action resulted, however. See Morse, *Chronicles*, III, App. W; *Chinese Repository*, April, 1837, pp. 548-549; *Indo-Chinese Gleaner*, Oct., 1820.

[94] A Chinese, formerly a go-between of the opium dealers and the Macao authorities, had been apprehended in an assault upon another native. To strengthen his case, he had charged officials with conniving at contraband trade. The relevant documents are in Morse, *Chronicles*, IV, App. Z.

[95] It had been ordered originally that half the import cargoes already landed should be confiscated, but the later edict specified only half the *profits* on the import cargoes. As a matter of fact, all of the goods except the opium were already in the hands of Chinese purchasers.

under no conditions involve the company—was a master-piece of neutrality. As a result, he removed his ships under a chop permitting them to leave port but never again to enter. The vessels went only as far as Lintin, where their presence continued to worry the hong merchants.

When the viceroy turned his attention to preventive arrangements for the future, the supercargoes were unwillingly thrust into the front line of the battle. Foreign ships including those of the company were, he ordered, to be secured only by the four senior hong merchants, who in rotation would give bond that incoming vessels carried no opium and would in turn be protected by a counter-bond from the ship's captain. The supercargoes, who had no intention of receding from the stand they had taken in the *Wabash* affair, were clear that the plan was dangerous. Of however honest intent, a captain could rarely if ever affirm positively that none of the drug had been brought into port on his ship, while the hong merchants who had given bond would be mulcted unmercifully.[96] The exasperation of the company's agents became all the greater when they received the text of the proposed bond. That a foreigner would sign such a document —assenting to confiscation of his property and expulsion from port if any opium were found on his ship—seemed inconceivable. To the company, traditionally acquitted of any charge of carrying opium, it was a direct insult. The authorities in the end proved amenable to the supercar-

[96] An incident which occurred during the crisis gave point to the supercargoes' objections. A Chinese servant from the company's ship *Atlas* was seized while in the possession of opium said to belong to the captain's steward. The security merchant ultimately was able to satisfy the authorities at the cost of 6000 dollars to himself. This episode was almost a repetition of one that had occurred in 1819, when a parcel of opium was taken from a boat belonging to the company's ship *Essex*. As in 1821, the security merchant was obliged to pay 6000 dollars. Morse, *Chronicles*, III, 356-357; IV, 17-18, 51.

goes' logic and the requirement was relaxed for company ships.[97]

The company had won its case, but the Chinese authorities, threatened with disgrace at the capital, had forced the trade from Whampoa and discouraged it at Macao. Henceforth the opium business was to be conducted not at the port but at the outer anchorages, where officials were usually content to ignore it. Lintin became the principal base of operations. There incoming country and American vessels would discharge their drug cargoes before moving up to Whampoa, where their commanders would solemnly sign the bond still in force for non-company ships.[98]

[97] The question was especially urgent because two of the company's ships had come into port and could not discharge their cargoes until an agreement was reached.

[98] "This ship commanded by me has come to Canton with a cargo of . . . With it no opium is brought in the vessel. Should any at a future day be discovered, I will willingly await legal trial and punishment. As is reasonable, I give this bond to be held in testimony hereof." J. R. Morrison, *Chinese Commercial Guide*, 1834, p. 16.

CHAPTER IV

THE MONOPOLY UNDER THE COMPANY

IN the period between the exclusion of opium shipping from Whampoa and the Anglo-Chinese war the trade was to experience phenomenal growth. The fourth decade of the century saw it multiplied about five-fold over its proportions in the second.[1] This extraordinary increase was produced not only by changing conditions in the China market but also by the expansion of the traffic in non-monopoly opium and by a new policy on the part of the company, a policy dictated by non-monopoly competition. Since 1797 the ideal of the Bengal administration had been to provide a fixed and relatively small supply of opium for its Calcutta sales, the government deriving an enormous profit upon each chest. Such a plan, however, presupposed absolute control of the market. As long as that was maintained, no change of policy was required. The company's revenues were secure, and the Chinese were debauched no more than was necessary.

This state of affairs obtained as long as monopoly opium dominated the China trade. But with the rise of a traffic in Malwa opium from the native states of India, the situation rapidly changed. When cries of distress began to echo from the supercargoes of Canton that "il-

[1] The average annual importation in the two periods may be summarized as follows:

	1811-1821	1829-1839
Bengal opium (chests)	3053	11,373
Malwa opium (chests)	1479	14,014
Total of Bengal and Malwa	4532	25,387

licit'' opium was proving a dangerous rival, the Bengal drug had to enter the struggle on a competitive basis. To command the Chinese market was the determinant in British opium policy throughout the century, and in this instance the guardians of the revenue acted vigorously to save the position of their product. The attempt which they made to extend the monopoly system to Malwa, a project managed with singular ineptitude, seems only to have stimulated the cultivation they had hoped to discourage. In the end, they were obliged to fight the native-state drug chiefly with commercial weapons. The output in Bengal was largely augmented, and the company contented itself with a somewhat smaller return on each unit.[2] This departure involved it in the drug business more inextricably than ever. The Canton market, where conditions were favorable for smuggling on a grand scale, was inundated with opium from both Malwa and Bengal. An incredible orgy of contraband trade resulted, one that became a scandal to Peking. When an imperial commissioner was sent to suppress the illicit commerce, there was precipitated a state of affairs from which emerged the Opium War.[3]

The early Portuguese travelers and empire-builders had observed a trade in opium from the west coast of India. This drug, commonly known as Cambay opium, was produced in the native states of Central India and Rajputana. During the eighteenth century the trade in Malwa opium, as the drug was later called, is wrapped in

[2] The average price per chest did not decline as much as might have been expected, principally because the absorptive power of the Chinese market had been underestimated.

[3] I am not, of course, suggesting that the opium trade was the chief issue at stake in that war. But it was a crisis in the traffic that brought on the conflict between Great Britain and China. I am further contending that an interpretation of that crisis must take account not only of events in China but also of conditions surrounding the Malwa industry and the adoption of a new policy in Bengal.

obscurity. Not until 1803 did the governor-general learn of its existence, and in the following year the supercargoes noted the arrival of a consignment at Whampoa.[4] Marquis Wellesley at once sought information from local officials in the Bombay area. The trade, it appeared, was of unknown antiquity. "The merchants of Surat," reported the custom master, "have traded in opium since it became a place of trade, and from the information of some of its oldest traders they believe it has not increased or decreased in any considerable degree until within the last 18 or 20 years, when it increased a little."[5] In Malwa the principal center was the city of Ujjain, to which opium was brought in a semi-manufactured state and where the refining process was completed. The purchasers were native merchants who bought the drug either on their own account or as agents for firms located in a port city.[6] Native governments had never sought to lay restrictions on cultivation, although they did impose transit duties on the opium as it was carried to the sea-

[4] Morse, *Chronicles*, II, 429.

[5] Custom master at Surat to the government of Bombay, 27 Aug. 1803, I. O. Bengal Public Consultations, 3 Nov. 1803. Statistics for the importation of Malwa opium into China are even less reliable than for Bengal opium. It seems probable, however, that shipments during the first fifteen years of the century were smaller than has been assumed. The surprise with which the supercargoes announced their discovery of a small quantity in 1804 may be taken as negative evidence, although it is not decisive because Malwa was usually consigned to Macao and the company's representatives were not always conversant with events at that port. The custom master at Bombay (to the government of Bombay, 22 Nov. 1803, I. O. Bengal Public Consultations, 22 Dec. 1803) thought that the quantity annually bought and sold at Ujjain, the chief opium market in Malwa, would total about fifteen lakhs of rupees. At the current prices this sum would represent between 3000 and 3500 chests, only a fraction of which would reach China.

[6] *Ibid.* See also a minute by Secretary Warden, Bombay, 20 April 1823, I. O. Bengal Board of Revenue (Misc.) Proc. (opium), 20 June 1823. A convenient assembling of the evidence on Malwa opium will be found in Dane, "Historical Memorandum," *Report of the Royal Commission*, VII, 1895, App. B.

coast. Cultivators produced as much as they desired and sold their product to whomever they chose.[7] The Malwa industry had never felt the hand of monopoly.

In the freedom under which the trade was conducted lay, therefore, the crux of the problem. Subjected to no monopoly restraint, the drug could sell for something like its intrinsic value. On the other hand, the maintenance of the Bengal system depended on the government's ability to control all other sources of opium, at least such as might offer competition in the China market. Measures must be devised which would either exclude Malwa opium from China or bring it under British control. During the next quarter of a century the company was to engage in diverse experiments before it finally developed an effective solution to the Malwa problem.

From the moment that Wellesley, the governor-general, received the Bombay government's report on native-state opium, he was clear that steps must be taken "for the prevention of further growth of that commerce, and for its ultimate annihilation."[8] But there was little that could be done. Cultivation could be prohibited in territory under the immediate authority of Bombay, together with shipments of opium from that port.[9] This might do well enough were Bombay the only point of export. Unfortunately the Portuguese ports, especially

[7] This statement ought perhaps to be qualified by noting that the peasant was often wholly in the power of middlemen and money-lenders, to whom he was obliged to turn over all or most of his crop.

[8] Governor-general in council to the government of Bombay, 30 June 1803, I. O. Bengal Public Consultations, 30 June 1803.

[9] Governor-general in council to the court of directors (separate revenue), 1 March 1804, I. O. Letters from Bengal, XLIV. See also Bombay Regulation 1 of 1805, §9. The British also sought to extend the prohibition to native states in Gujarat with whom political relations had been established. The court of directors was opposed to the plan, which consequently was abandoned.

Daman, as well as several native cities, were nearly as accessible and would serve as fairly satisfactory entrepôts. To prevent opium from the interior reaching them became a primary concern of the government's policy. The effort was doomed to failure, for insufficient territory was under British influence to obstruct all routes to the "illicit" ports.[10]

As a means of stopping this most serious leak in the system, the governor-general of Bombay opened negotiations with the Portuguese. A complaisant viceroy of Goa yielded to the pleas of the British envoy and agreed to prohibit the trade from that port. He also professed his willingness to write to the governors of Daman and Diu. The British received the news with ill-advised optimism, the governor-general indulging in "a confident hope that no Malwa Opium will henceforward find its way to the China Market.'"[11] But there is no evidence to show that the viceroy's mandate had the slightest effect upon the flow of non-monopoly opium, although both supercargoes and officials in India were easy in their assurance that all was well.[12] Ten years later it became apparent that the agreement was being violated, and, what was worse, that the Goa government was not disposed to coöperate further.[13] Another method more effective than the philan-

[10] The Mahi Kantha states in Gujarat in 1812 were obliged to prohibit the transit of opium through their dominions without a sealed permit from the government, and Baroda was also persuaded to forbid the sale of opium for export. These states produced little opium save for local consumption. Aitchison, *Treaties*, VI, no. 120.

[11] Governor-general in council to the court of directors (public general), 7 June 1806, I. O. Letters from Bengal, XLIX.

[12] The usual statistics show no diminution in imports of Malwa into China. It is certain that shipments continued to be made from Daman and other ports, whatever orders may have been issued from Goa.

[13] Governor-general in council to the court of directors, 7 Oct. 1815, I. O. Abstracts of Separate Revenue Letters from Bengal and India, I; letters between Major Schuyler, envoy at Goa, and the government of Bombay, I. O. Bengal Political Consultations, 11 July and 8 Dec. 1815. The original

thropy of the Portuguese or the signatures of a few native princes must be adopted.[14]

The fight against Malwa opium thus far had resulted only in defeat. Cultivation might be forbidden in the Bombay presidency, export prohibited through the port of Bombay, and treaties negotiated with local chieftains. But though British seaports might be controlled, the flow of opium through Portuguese cities continued to plague the monopolists in Calcutta and their supercargoes in Canton. Between 1814 and 1818 the competition in China became critical. Malwa was reported to be improving in quality; to the irritation of the company's representatives.[15] Since 1814 the growth of the native-state trade had been reflected in a progressive decline in the company's opium revenue.[16]

Moreover, political conditions in the Malwa area promised an increase in the competing traffic. The country had been overrun by lawless freebooters, the Pindaris, and ravaged by bands of Maratha soldiers. "Never had there been such intense and general suffering in India . . . armed forces existed only to plunder, torture and mutiny; government had ceased to exist; there remained only oppression and misery."[17] Late in 1817 Lord Hastings had begun military operations against the Pindaris and al-

agreement can perhaps be explained by the *entente* between Great Britain and Portugal in Europe. It was wholly one-sided as far as India was concerned.

[14] An attempt was also made, through the British resident at Poona, to close the Maratha ports to Malwa opium. Court of directors to the governor-general in council (separate revenue), 24 Oct. 1817, I. O. Despatches to Bengal, LXXVII.

[15] Morse, *Chronicles*, III, 339-340.

[16] A contributory cause was the notoriously bad quality of the provision in 1817 and 1818. Court of directors to the governor-general in council, 30 Jan. 1822, *Third Report from the Select Committee*, 1831, App. IV, p. 13. Hereafter this document will be cited as *Third Report*, 1831.

[17] Quoted in the *Cambridge History of India*, V, 376-377.

most simultaneously against the remnants of Maratha power. By the spring of 1818 both had been utterly annihilated. British intervention brought to the district a stability that it had not known for years. If poppy cultivation had managed to survive the troublous times of the Pindaris, it might flourish alarmingly under the suzerainty of the British raj, now acknowledged by the native states in the area.

The solution must be sought along two main lines of policy. Either the British must use their political hegemony to control the opium industry of the native states or they must increase the supply of the monopoly drug to the capacity of the Chinese market, cheerfully accepting a lower rate of return upon each chest. In the end the course adopted proved to be a curious mixture of the two, but it was the second that received most emphasis in the deliberations of the Calcutta council. The monopoly was now returning such huge profits as literally to beckon for competition. Since 1797-1798 the average revenue had more than tripled, with no appreciable increase in the quantity of opium produced.[18] The provision had not been enlarged since 1801-1802, when 4800 chests had been decided upon, and even then it had fallen short by several hundred chests annually. While the output in India was stationary, the market in China was expanding and a magnificent opportunity for interlopers was created. If the amount of opium sold on the company's account were increased and the price accordingly reduced, then traders in Malwa and Turkey opium would have a steep path to tread.

This was the view taken by the board of trade in Calcutta. The root of the difficulty, it was felt, lay in the enormously high prices that Bengal opium had been

[18] Board of trade to the governor-general in council, 23 April 1819, I. O. Bengal Revenue Consultations (salt and opium), 23 July 1819.

bringing at the Calcutta sales. Let the provision be therefore increased to the estimated demand of the China market, even if the company were obliged to be content with the same profit from two chests as it had formerly received from one. If the Bengal field could not supply what was required, Malwa might be used to supplement the provision. The board was careful to point out that "the comprehensive Policy aforementioned will not tend to increase the consumption of the deleterious Drug nor to extend it's baneful effects in Society—the sole and exclusive object of it is to secure to ourselves the whole Supply by preventing Foreigners from participating in a Trade of which they at present enjoy no inconsiderable share—for it is evident that the Chinese, as well as the Malays, cannot exist without the use of Opium, and if we do not supply their necessary wants, Foreigners will."

This policy the governor-general determined to adopt. It was obvious that the opium business could no longer be administered on the basis of a monopoly of the export trade. Malwa and Turkey must be fought commercially, since the Bombay government had by no means succeeded in blocking the routes to the coast for the former, and trade in the latter was wholly unrestrained. Henceforth the company's aim was "to endeavour to secure the command of the Market by furnishing a Supply on so enlarged a scale and on such reasonable terms as shall prevent competition, and as shall make up for the depreciation of the Article by the Aggregate profit on an extended Scale."[19] From what area could the additional supply be obtained? The total consumption of the China market was estimated roughly at eight thousand chests, or between three and four thousand more than the normal

[19] Governor-general in council to the court of directors (territorial: salt and opium), 30 July 1819, I. O. Letters from Bengal, LXXXI.

monopoly provision.[20] A fraction of the difference could be produced in Bengal, but for the present it seemed desirable to call upon Malwa, both to augment the Bengal yield and to reduce the amount of competing opium in China. It was therefore decided to purchase annually some four thousand chests of Malwa opium, and at the same time, to make a strenuous effort to suppress surplus cultivation.[21]

The new policy towards Malwa opium was thus to be composed of four strands. First, enough of that drug should be purchased to satisfy, when added to the regular Bengal provision, the entire body of Chinese consumers. Secondly, surplus cultivation in the native states should be suppressed. (This part of the plan was abandoned temporarily.) Again, the provision in Bengal should be materially increased.[22] And finally, the Bombay government was to press with renewed vigor its measures against the transport of opium through Gujarat and ports on the west coast.

This last item may be readily dismissed. For until 1824, when the British became frankly monopolistic in Malwa, little success was achieved. Meanwhile the Bombay government was able to negotiate restrictive agreements with enough states to block the direct route to Daman and Diu.[23] But other ways remained. None of the

[20] The supercargoes were not inclined to favor an enlarged supply, but they stated that conditions in the opium market had been so chaotic since 1814 that even persons long familiar with the trade disagreed "respecting an increase having taken place in the aggregate Consumption of China." Select committee of supercargoes to the governor-general in council, 20 Feb. 1819, I. O. Bengal Revenue Consultations (salt and opium), 23 July 1819.

[21] Resolution of the governor-general in council, 12 Nov. 1819, Abstracts on Malwa Opium, *Third Report*, 1831, App. IV, p. 27.

[22] The Bengal aspect of the new policy will be reserved for discussion later in the present chapter.

[23] Aitchison, *Treaties*, VI, nos. 29, 58, 104, 129, 139, 141, relating to Baroda, Kathiawar, Palanpur, Chota Udaipur, Rajpipla, and Mahi Kantha.

strategic states in what are now the Rajputana and Central India agencies was included, nor was Sind, though arrangements with Gwalior, Indore, and Jaisalmer seem to have been contemplated.[24] The route usually taken by Malwa opium henceforth was circuitous and expensive but still profitable. It left Malwa by way of Mandasor and proceeded to Pali. There it was transferred to camels and in this fashion taken to Jaisalmer. Another month was required before the opium reached Karachi, at the mouth of the Indus, whence it was shipped by boat to Daman. The whole journey required some two months and was a laborious undertaking for any trader. But the danger from British agents was slight, for at no time during the long trip did the forbidden drug touch British territory.[25]

Hardly more successful was the plan of purchasing for the company in the Malwa market. By buying some four thousand chests annually the Bengal administrators hopefully thought not only to discourage private traders but also to net a tidy profit for the company.[26] For the first year, 1820-1821, the company's opium interests in Malwa were left to the political agents already at their various stations. The results were discouraging. Some of the political agents took their new responsibilities lightly, and little opium seems to have been purchased.[27] The next inspiration of the Bombay government proved no happier. A special opium agent was appointed to live in the producing area, where he could observe the fortunes of

[24] Government of Bombay to the governor-general in council, 29 Dec. 1821, Abstracts on Malwa Opium, *Third Report*, 1831, App. IV, p. 27.

[25] Samuel Swinton to the board of customs, salt, and opium, 17 Feb. 1824, I. O. Bengal Board of Revenue (Misc.) Proc. (opium), 9 March 1824.

[26] The Bombay government estimated that the annual net profit would be more than twenty-five lakhs of rupees. Government of Bombay to the governor-general in council, 4 Sept. 1819, I. O. Bengal Revenue Consultations (salt and opium), 12 Nov. 1819.

[27] Governor-general in council to the court of directors (territorial: salt and opium), 23 March 1821, I. O. Letters from Bengal, LXXXV.

the industry at first hand and where he could make his purchases from the cultivators themselves, not from speculating middlemen.[28] The work of this individual left much to be desired. Not only did he fall short of the quantity he was to provide, but he paid outrageously high prices, recklessly drawing bills on the Bengal treasury.[29] When word got abroad that the government was planning to buy the entire crop, the acreage under poppy increased phenomenally. Furthermore the unfortunate agent seems to have played fast and loose in proposing indemnities for local princes.[30] In short, the sole result of the company's meddling with Malwa opium was to stimulate the cultivation which it had aimed above all things to prevent. The venture returned no considerable profit, and the trade through Daman was flourishing as never before.[31] In order both to effect a reformation in the Malwa agency and to coördinate it more closely with the Bengal monopoly, the management of the company's opium affairs in the native states was transferred from the hands of the Bombay government to those of the board of customs, salt, and opium in Calcutta.[32] The new

[28] Sir John Malcolm to the government of Bombay, 26 April 1821, I. O. Bengal Separate Consultations, 15 June 1821.

[29] It was calculated that each chest of opium cost the company Rs. 1500 instead of the modest Rs. 700 that had been anticipated. In a little over a year Taylor drew bills on Bengal for nearly one hundred lakhs. Memorandum from the examiner's office, Papers relating to Malwa Opium, 1821-24, I. O. Home Miscellaneous, DCCLXII; I. O. Bengal Political Consultations, 21 March 1823.

[30] Samuel Swinton to the board of customs, salt, and opium, 17 Feb. 1824, I. O. Bengal Board of Revenue (Misc.) Proc. (opium), 9 March 1824; Bengal Political Consultations, 25 Oct. 1822, Abstracts on Malwa Opium, *Third Report*, App. IV, p. 28.

[31] The quantity of opium which entered Daman between 1822 and 1824 was estimated at more than ten thousand chests. Samuel Swinton to the board of customs, salt, and opium, 19 June 1827, I. O. Bengal Separate Consultations, 12 Sept. 1827.

[32] Annoyance was felt by the Bombay government at having received

agent, who took up the work in 1823, conducted it with greater discretion. By announcing that he had no orders to "make purchases, and certainly would not think of making any until it [opium] fell considerably under 60 Rupees," he was able to complete his provision at a reasonable figure.[33]

It had become only too apparent that the plan of purchasing opium, combined with the blockading of routes to the sea, was not justifying the hopes of its authors. Cultivation was left undisturbed, and since the agent had been ordered to buy only four thousand chests, any surplus that remained might be exported to China by private merchants, if it could be brought to the sea. As has been indicated, the route from Pali to Daman was still open and was the greatest opium thoroughfare in western India. The Malwa agent might argue that this was the only passage left unstopped, but for all his optimism, the illicit trade was still breathing freely.[34] In its failure to deal effectively with this surplus the company's scheme stood self-condemned. As a prominent Bengal official asserted, "If some arrangement for shackling the trade in Malwa opium be not adopted, I confess I see little chance of our being able to prevent such a fall in price as will render the possession of the monopoly in Behar and Be-

blame for the high prices paid by the Malwa agent. The trouble had all started, the Bombay secretary insisted, when Calcutta urged that a sale be held in 1821. Few preparations had been made, and the opium had to be obtained at high rates. The Bombay government also protested against the decision that most of the Malwa yield was to be sold at Calcutta. The supreme government eventually was obliged to allot fifteen hundred chests to the western port. I. O. Bengal Board of Revenue (Misc.) Proc. (opium), 20 June 1823 and 10 Feb. 1824.

[33] Samuel Swinton to the board of customs, salt, and opium, 4 March 1824, I. O. Bengal Board of Revenue (Misc.) Proc. (opium), 23 March 1824.

[34] Samuel Swinton to the board of customs, salt, and opium, 4 Aug. 1824, I. O. Bengal Separate Consultations, 3 Sept. 1824.

nares of little value.''[35] To confine cultivation to the desired level, he urged, native chiefs must be given an economic stake in the enterprise. In other words, the native states must be drawn into the orbit of the British opium system.

When, in 1824, the government decided to monopolize the entire yield of Malwa, it was merely accepting the implications of its earlier decision. Since 1818 British policy had called for a reduction of the poppy area to the size required by the official monopoly. But for one reason and another, this aspect of the program had gone by default. Now, the council in Calcutta felt, it was all or nothing. A new attack must be made upon local princes, both those whose territory occupied strategic locations on the way to the coast, and still more important, those ruling states which produced the drug. And it must be made worth their while to coöperate.

Fundamental to the success of these designs was an arrangement with Udaipur (Mewar), a state lying to the northwest of Malwa and on the direct route to Sind. In the summer of 1824 the assistant to the Malwa agent requested permission to negotiate a treaty with the maharana. Perhaps suspicious of his proposal to arm himself with ''a good stock of Brandy and some Cherry Brandy by which more is sometimes to be effected than any other art of persuasion,'' the supreme government in Calcutta allotted the task to the regular political agent.[36] For the price of Rs. 40,000 the maharana agreed to prohibit the sale and transit of any opium other than that authorized by the British government. Unlicensed opium was to be confiscated and delivered to the agent at the current price in Malwa, one-half of the value to be paid to the in-

[35] Note by Holt Mackenzie, 10 July 1823, Abstracts on Malwa Opium, *Third Report*, 1831, App. IV, p. 28.
[36] I. O. Bengal Separate Consultations, 15 Oct. 1824.

former.[37] With Bundi a similar treaty was concluded.[38] Other states, such as Kotah, Indore, Dhar, and Dewas, all producing areas, contracted to limit cultivation as well as to prevent illegal transport. Holkar of Indore, whose agreement is typical of all, engaged to restrict the poppy area to such an extent as would yield no more than six thousand maunds, of which a thousand might be retained for local consumption, the remainder to be delivered to the company's godowns in Indore or Mahidpur. He also bound himself to prohibit contraband export.[39]

Notwithstanding this apparent success, the agreements concluded with Indore and the others represented only a portion of the states whose coöperation was essential. Some of the most crucial links in the chain which was to enclose illicit opium, the British raj found itself unable to forge. Jaipur, Kishengurh, and Gwalior, among others, remained intransigent. Routes to Daman by way of Karachi were still clear, and private traders were not slow to shift their operations to territories where no restrictions interfered.[40]

From the first the Malwa program had been put into force not without dissenting opinions, among them the influential voice of Sir John Malcolm.[41] As early as 1821 he wrote, "That our extension of the monopoly to Central India, will be attended with considerable trouble . . . is not to be doubted. It will, and indeed has already made,

[37] This payment, at least in theory, was made as commutation for transit dues and other taxes from which the maharana had formerly derived revenue. Abstracts on Malwa Opium, *Third Report*, 1831, App. IV, p. 29.

[38] *Ibid.*, p. 33.

[39] Aitchison, *Treaties*, IV, no. 48; also reprinted in Dane, "Historical Memorandum," *Report of the Royal Commission*, VII, 1895, App. B, pp. 56-57.

[40] Abstracts on Malwa Opium, *Third Report*, App. IV, p. 33.

[41] It was Sir John Malcolm who undertook the reconstruction of Malwa after the Pindari war. His knowledge of the region was probably more intimate than was that of any other Englishman.

an impression not favorable to our interests.''[42] When the restrictive system was tightened by means of the treaties negotiated after 1824, the opposition became more outspoken. Scarcely had the new scheme been launched—the treaties, in fact, had not yet been confirmed—when rumblings of discontent began to reach the reluctant ears of the government.[43] Sir Charles Metcalfe, resident at Delhi, forwarded a protest from the Kotah government, to which he added some unpalatable views of his own. The treaties, he charged, in some cases extorted by undue pressure and ''our irresistible influence,'' were likely to be detrimental to the native states and ultimately to the British conquerors themselves. The company's move towards a monopoly of opium in Rajputana was held in universal horror, and ''complete success can only be attained by such a mass of evil as must make every good and wise man shudder.''[44] According to the durbar of Kotah, his signature had cost his state some Rs. 60,000 loss in revenue, had crippled its commerce, and had worked general hardship. Altogether it was tolerably clear that at least one native state resented the new arrangement. The outraged despatches of Sir Charles Metcalfe fell on uneasy ears in Calcutta, but the official conscience was soothed by contemplating the prosperity which British pacification had brought to the country.[45] The treaties were therefore confirmed, and orders were issued for negotiating others which would bring the

[42] Malcolm to Secretary Warden, 26 April 1821, *Third Report*, 1831, App. IV, p. 19.

[43] Strictly speaking, the new scheme was never formally launched. It took several years to negotiate the treaties, and even then, as we have seen, the system was never complete.

[44] Abstracts on Malwa Opium, *Third Report*, 1831, App. IV, pp. 30-31. See also Sutherland, *Sketches*, p. 87.

[45] Colonel James Tod, author of a standard account of Rajputana, took a different view of the state of the region under British rule. See his *Annals and Antiquities of Rajasthan*, II, 1110.

remaining sources of the drug and routes to the sea under British control.

The existence of the Malwa monopoly, instituted as a last resort, was a tempestuous one. In London the court of directors felt no optimism for its future, holding it even less likely to succeed "than the other expedients which have so imperfectly answered your expectations."[46] And in Calcutta, Sir Charles Metcalfe, recently appointed to the council, was not inclined to still his protests. His opportunity came on the receipt of a despatch from the political agent at Udaipur, who, expressing satisfaction at the success of the monopoly, in the same breath requested an enlarged preventive establishment.[47] To this suggestion Metcalfe objected vigorously. It was a lamentable commentary on British rule, he observed, that "those officers who ought to be the Instruments of protection and the representatives of a paternal supremacy become the mere subaltern agents of an opium monopoly, searchers and confiscators."[48] Early in the following year, 1828, rumors of disorder in the native states again spurred him to action. In Bundi, it was reported,

[46] Court of directors to the governor-general in council, 11 July 1827, *Third Report*, 1831, App. IV, p. 19.

[47] Udaipur, it may be said, had ample reason to be satisfied with its status under the monopoly. As an important state on the principal road to the coast, it received a larger commutation for transit dues than some of the others. In fact, the receipts of the government of Udaipur under the new system were greater than under the old, while additional revenue was drawn from opium confiscations. Whatever the rulers of Udaipur may have thought of the monopoly, there were certainly other subjects of the state who could have found fault. Between December, 1824, and April, 1827, there were more than 250 seizures, although the quantity in most cases was small. J. Sutherland, *Sketches*, p. 86; I. O. Bengal Separate Consultations, 20 Sept. 1827.

[48] Minute by Sir C. Metcalfe, 10 Oct. 1827, I. O. Bengal Political Consultations, 21 March 1828. For the reply of the governor-general see his minutes of 10 Oct., 28 Nov., 1 Dec. 1827, Abstracts on Malwa Opium, *Third Report*, 1831, App. IV, p. 32.

a huge convoy of mountaineers had been formed to protect illicit opium that was to be carried into Jaipur and that two affrays had taken place with the maharaja's troops. In one of these encounters a near relative of the prince had been killed. Metcalfe implored the government "to revise the present system, which is so destructive of human life, and thus check the feeling of dissatisfaction, which exists in consequence of our Opium restrictions."[49]

Three months later, during the interim administration of William Bayley, an investigation was got under way. Reports from political officers in the Malwa and Rajputana fields left little doubt that the whole experiment had been an egregious failure.[50] Sir Edward Colebrooke, Metcalfe's successor at Delhi, asserted the monopoly to be both injudicious and futile. The price paid to cultivators was unremunerative, and the mercantile interests were dissatisfied at losing their principal article of export,

[49] Lieut. Hislop to G. Wellesley, 27 Jan. 1828, I. O. Bengal Political Consultations, 21 March 1828; minute by Sir C. Metcalfe, 16 Feb. 1828, *ibid.* For criticism in a similar vein see Sutherland, *Sketches,* p. 86. Henry St. George Tucker, one of the company's most distinguished servants in India, went to even greater lengths in his condemnation. "We have undertaken to pay Holkar [of Indore] the sum of six lacs of rupees annually; we are anxious that Scindia [of Gwalior] should be induced to accept a subsidy of the same description. . . . And for what purpose are these pecuniary engagements contracted? Are they intended as an indemnification to the chiefs and their subjects for suppressing the cultivation of the poppy? Quite the contrary. These burdensome contributions bear a rateable proportion to the quantity of opium supposed to be produced; and they therefore operate as a direct and powerful stimulant to the production of the article." This statement has been frequently cited by members of the anti-opium group as proof of the company's deliberate policy of stimulating poppy cultivation in the native states. It is true that the government's measures in Malwa resulted in increased production, but its intention was otherwise. Expansion had occurred chiefly when the company was buying opium with little attempt to limit cultivation. This much was freely admitted by the government. But the increase in production testified to the failure, not to the success, of its policy. Tucker, *Memorials,* pp. 155-156.

[50] Material dealing with these reports is printed in the *Third Report,* 1831, App. IV, as "Abstract of Correspondence regarding Malwa Opium."

now sold to the government perforce, while smuggling continued to prosper. The agent at Jaipur, a state which had repelled the advances of British gift-bearers, reported that the maharaja's court "exult and triumph in being exempt from opium engagements which are considered to have been enforced on neighboring states in violation of their independence." The rulers of Jodhpur and Jaisalmer complained of the scarcity and dearness of the drug, while Kishengurh, also outside the system, was gratified that the state had become a grand opium emporium. Kotah recorded dissatisfaction "from every individual high or low." Ryots were injured, revenue had declined, and the prince had lost caste in the eyes of his subjects. Neither Bundi nor Kotah, it was stated, had contracted their engagements voluntarily. The grim dilemma of the friendship or enmity of the conqueror had been presented to them, and of necessity they had elected the former. The wisest policy, said one agent, would be to absolve all states from their commitments, "even though it means the utter ruin of the Bengal monopoly."

With the exception of those officers who had had a part in making the odious treaties, the tenor of the evidence was unfavorable to the monopoly. The agreements, it was charged, had been forced upon native rulers and had humiliated them before their subjects. Ryots had been wronged by the limitation on the quantity of poppy land and by the excessively low price prescribed for crude opium. The general commercial life of the states concerned had been crippled, and the preventive system was onerous and vexatious. Moreover, the coöperation of the obdurate Sindhia of Gwalior was essential, and that, it appeared from the report of the political agent, was not likely to be forthcoming.[51] Finally, the scheme had utterly failed to achieve its original purpose, for the smuggling

[51] Abstracts on Malwa Opium, *Third Report*, 1831, App. IV, p. 37.

trade was enjoying even more than its usual prosperity. While the opium agent was having difficulty in providing 3500 chests, it was estimated by Sir John Malcolm that at least ten thousand were leaving through Daman.[52]

Lord William Bentinck, who had now become governor-general, was convinced "that evils of a very serious nature are inflicted by our monopoly system in Central India on all who fall within the sphere of its operation."[53] The only course left open was to leave the ryots and merchants of Malwa to their own devices and to abstain from active interference with the growth and transit of the drug. In this decision the court of directors heartily concurred.[54] But the decision of Bentinck's council, far from being a solution of the problem, was merely an acknowledgment of failure.

The monopoly in the native states had thus reached the end of its inglorious career, but no new means of protecting the Bengal revenue had been disclosed. The years 1829-1831 may therefore be regarded as a critical period in the government's connection with a disreputable industry.[55] Unless new measures were devised, the value of the Bengal drug must inevitably decline and the income from the monopoly be materially reduced. Never would the Indian government find a better time to withdraw bag and baggage. It had fallen heir to the monopoly and had retained it as a convenient source of revenue. On the whole, the company's opium business had been adminis-

[52] I. O. Bengal Board of Revenue (Misc.) Proc. (opium), 31 March 1829; governor-general and council to the court of directors, 21 Sept. 1830; Third Report, 1831, App. IV, p. 56.

[53] Resolution of the governor-general in council, 19 June 1829, ibid., pp. 42-43.

[54] Court of directors to the governor-general in council (separate revenue), 19 Oct. 1831, I. O. Despatches to Bengal, CXVIII.

[55] The importance of this period seems first to have been pointed out by Sir J. B. Lyall in a "Note on the History of Opium in India," Report of the Royal Commission, VII, 1895, App. A.

tered in as innocuous a fashion as was possible. But now that the revenue was in jeopardy a new policy must be developed. The government, in fact, must choose between two lines of action. The first was to make a virtue of necessity by abolishing the Bengal monopoly and prohibiting poppy cultivation in British India. The alternative was to lay whatever restrictions were practicable upon the native-state traffic, such as a transit duty on the route to Bombay, but at the same time to augment the provision and to reduce the price per chest in Bengal—in other words, to manage the monopoly in such a way that its product could compete commercially with that of Malwa. A compromise course would have been to substitute for the monopoly an export tax on opium.

Prohibition was a possibility but a purely theoretical one. It was never proposed in the meetings of the council, nor does any consideration seem to have been given it by officials of the company. Had such an experiment been tried, the subsequent history of the opium trade would have been vastly different. To pursue the speculation, the traffic to China would certainly have survived, but probably in less staggering proportions. One may admit that, even though British subjects had been forbidden to carry the drug, much would have been brought to China by Portuguese and by natives of states not under British jurisdiction. Still the quantity could scarcely have approached what was produced in Bengal after the program of expansion was under way and in Malwa after the system of transit passes was put into effect. Moreover, the Chinese had been relatively successful in browbeating the Portuguese. The trade would not have had the force of the British state behind it; and, of greatest importance at this stage, abolishing the monopoly would have cleared the company once and for all of complicity in an unsavory business. Chinese taste, it is true, would have remained unaltered. The capacity of the Chinese market was far from exhausted, and this could certainly have caused an increase in the Malwa trade. Yet, when all allowances have been made, it is impossible to believe that the flood of opium from both Malwa and Bengal which deluged the coast of China in the eighteen-thirties was without effect in diffusing the habit. This inordinate expansion, it seems probable, helped to crystallize the hostility of the Chinese government and to prepare the way for the Anglo-Chinese war.

It was in the logic of events that sooner or later the government should fall back upon the plan of imposing a transit duty on the direct route to Bombay and increasing the Bengal provision. But this decision was taken only after another year of futile experiment. The monopoly in the native states had been definitely terminated. Treaties relating merely to restrictions on transit were abrogated at once, although states which had contracted to limit their poppy area were still required to deliver the stipulated number of chests to the British agent. Yet instead of taking the obvious course, the council elected for another year to act the rôle of opium buyer, entering into competition with private merchants in Malwa.[56] One year's trial was sufficient. The agent was unable to deliver the quantity ordered by the Bombay government, and even then a part of his provision was drawn from old stores. As soon as it was learned that the restrictive clauses in the old native-state treaties had been abrogated, the price of crude opium rose, so that it was un-

[56] The plan of purchasing on the company's account was not quite so preposterous as might at first appear. It must be recalled that such opium could be brought to Bombay, while that of private merchants was transported by a much more expensive route to Daman. The Bombay government computed the cost of shipping a chest from Malwa to Daman at Rs. 340 and from Malwa to Bombay at only Rs. 40. I. O. Bengal Board of Revenue (Misc.) Proc. (opium), 10 Feb. 1824.

obtainable at the maximum price allowed the British agent. Some of the states bound by treaty to deliver fixed amounts defaulted their engagements, and all but two insignificant ones gave notice of their intention to have done with them.[57]

The only way out for the government was to issue passes for transit to Bombay.[58] The company was aware of the asset it possessed in its control of the best route from Malwa to the seacoast. Properly to evaluate that asset was the question—to impose the maximum transit duty that could be collected without driving the trade to the "illicit" route to Daman. Bombay estimated its value at Rs. 250 per chest, while Calcutta, a little less hopeful, thought that Rs. 175 to Rs. 200 could be safely imposed. The pass system was accordingly put into operation, with the rate set at Rs. 175 for a standard chest of about 140 pounds.[59] The results of the first year were disappointing, with the net yield only slightly more than eight lakhs of rupees. Success was not long delayed, however, for in the following year the Bombay opium revenue more than doubled, while not more than a tenth of the Malwa produce, it was estimated, left by Portuguese ports.[60] The original rate of duty was maintained until 1835, when it appeared that the trade through non-British entrepôts was on the increase.[61] This dangerous tendency necessitated a reduction in the price of transit passes to Rs. 125.

[57] Governor-general in council to the court of directors, 3 Aug. 1830, *Third Report*, 1831, App. IV, pp. 45-46.

[58] I. O. Bengal Separate Consultations, 13 July 1830.

[59] It was agreed that the profits from transit passes should go to the Bombay government, which for the past ten years had learned to count upon a revenue from opium.

[60] *Report from the Select Committee*, 1832, p. 71; evidence of Sir Charles Forbes, *ibid.*, Q. 2928.

[61] It was estimated that 5600 chests were exported from Daman in 1834-1835, as compared with the 7000 that left via Bombay. Government of Bombay to the court of directors, 2 July 1835, I. O. Letters from Bombay, LXI.

For eight years the new system pursued an even course. The net revenue showed a normal gain, and the reduced duty resulted in a striking advance in the quantities exported through Bombay.

Greater good luck was still in store for the company. In 1843 the fortunes of war deposited in the Bombay treasury a windfall which dwarfed previous increments. Trouble had been anticipated with the amirs of Sind, whose domains were an important link in the smuggling chain.[62] Sir Charles Napier, who was ordered there in 1842, had already convinced himself that annexation was inevitable, and he was determined to miss no opportunity for decisive action. An occasion was soon presented. In the battle of Miani, with his meager force of less than three thousand pitted against the thirty thousand placed in the field by the Baluchis, Napier won a brilliant victory. In the following month, March, 1843, the army of the amirs was utterly annihilated, and Sind was thus brought under the authority of the British raj. For the opium revenue of Bombay the accession was a godsend. With Sind numbered among the company's possessions the road to Portuguese ports was safely blocked. The Bombay government was enabled to charge as high transit duties as it pleased, its only restraint being the danger of smuggling. To the Bengal monopoly, as well, the new development brought a sense of security. The entire opium supply of India had virtually become the exclusive possession of the conquering British.

Bombay lost no time in realizing on its good fortune. Within two years the price of transit passes was more than doubled. The revenue between 1840 and 1843 from this source had slightly exceeded £225,000 annually. After the transit duty was raised, profits soared to £350,-

---

[62] Private merchants, it will be recalled, were now taking the roundabout way to Karachi in Sind and thence by sea to Daman.

000, to £600,000, and in 1848-1849 to more than £887,000. By degrees the pass rate was advanced until in 1879 it reached the peak, Rs. 750 per chest.[63]

While Malwa opium was being transmuted from a liability into a tangible asset, parallel changes were taking place in the Bengal monopoly. The corollary to a pass system in the west of India—especially before the annexation of Sind—was a radical alteration in the administration of the Bengal industry. From the establishment of the opium agency to the time when competition from the native states was felt, the annual provision had been small and fairly constant.[64] On this policy there was general agreement. The directors, though partly reconciled to the monopoly, were aware of the company's duty towards a subject population. In 1817 when their permission was obtained for creating a new agency to supply opium for local consumption, they said, "After all, we must observe that it is our wish not to encourage the consumption of Opium, but rather to lessen the use, or, more properly speaking, the abuse of the drug; and for this end, as well as for purposes of revenue, to make the price to the public both in our own and in foreign dominions, as high as possible. . . . Were it possible to prevent the use of the drug altogether, except strictly for the purpose of medicine, we would gladly do it in compassion to mankind; but this being absolutely impracticable, we can only endeavour to regulate and palliate an evil which cannot be eradicated."[65]

This statement represents something more than a protective coloring of altruism. On the contrary, it seems the

[63] *Report of the Royal Commission*, VI, 1895, p. 30.

[64] Statistics show a considerable variation in the annual yield during the period, but the discrepancy was the result of seasonal conditions rather than of any change in policy.

[65] Court of directors to the governor-general in council, 24 Oct. 1817, *Third Report*, 1831, App. IV, p. 11.

expression of a sincere desire on the part of the court to reduce the consumption of opium to its lowest possible minimum. But the company was quite willing to profit by what it could not prevent. A nice harmony was made to prevail between social morality and revenue. As an eighteenth-century divine put it,

> Thus God and Nature planned the general frame,
> And bade self-love and social be the same.[66]

It was impracticable to prohibit the consumption of what the directors professed to regard as a "pernicious drug." Accepting this as an impossibility, the best means of controlling its ravages was a monopoly in the hands of the government. But that system, in turn, would enable the monopolist to impose what prices he pleased. The plan worked as though magically conceived. Into the treasury would fall the opium revenue, while the people were being protected from over-indulgence in a dangerous narcotic.

This then was the official opium policy of the East India Company at the time when Malwa competition first became apparent—to monopolize the China market for Bengal opium, and with that assured to restrict the shipments to as low a point as was consistent with the revenue. There is evidence that this ideal owed something to a genuine, though not highly logical, concern for the welfare of the Chinese. In 1818, when Malwa was beginning to make the position of Bengal opium at Canton precarious, the vice-president in council reëmphasized this traditional policy, suggesting that, if the monopoly drug were sure of its supremacy in China, the provision might be gradually reduced.[67] It was precisely this condition that was lacking. And in the struggle for possession of the

[66] Quoted in R. H. Tawney, *The Acquisitive Society*, p. 14.
[67] Morse, *Chronicles*, III, 338.

market that ensued, no timorous scruples for Chinese well-being could be allowed to figure.

While Bengal opium stood unchallenged, the company could afford to be virtuous. In 1822, however, when "illicit" opium was causing much uneasiness, the directors applauded their servants for having considered "whether the Eastern market cannot be commanded . . . by supplying its entire demand at a price which would make competition unprofitable."[68] The government was not yet ready to go the whole way in expanding the Bengal industry but chose rather to follow its policy of interfering with Malwa cultivation and transit. Yet certain rather half-hearted attempts were made to increase monopoly production as well as to control Malwa trade. In 1822, for example, the collectors of three districts were appointed as deputy opium agents and awarded a commission on the opium that they delivered in excess of former years.[69] The donation granted to zamindars who urged poppy cultivation on their ryots was liberally increased, and the rate of payment to cultivators for their opium was raised.[70] These measures, taken while the government was still whistling to keep up its courage in Malwa, added significantly to the yield, but they were merely a forecast of what was to come.

It was in 1830 that the issue presented itself to the company in decisive form. Not only were conditions in the west of India such as to require a large augmentation in the Bengal supply, but it was becoming apparent that

[68] Court of directors to the governor-general in council, 30 Jan. 1822, *Third Report*, 1831, App. IV, p. 13.

[69] I. O. Bengal Separate Consultations, 9 May 1822.

[70] *Ibid.*, 27 Jan. 1825 and 28 Feb. 1828. The precise meaning of the term "zamindar" has given students of Indian history a good deal of trouble. For our purpose it will be sufficient to indicate that Bengal zamindars acted both as landlords, although their land was not held in fee simple, and as hereditary tax collectors. See *Cambridge History of India*, V, 409-410.

the capacity of the Chinese market was much greater than had been thought. No longer were the monopolists to restrict themselves to a modest four or six thousand chests. They were now talking of twelve, sixteen, and even twenty thousand.[71] Thus might the opium revenue be maintained at its former figure, although the governor-general was not hopeful of anything more.[72] If anything, London was even more dubious than Calcutta had been. The directors had no suggestions, but they felt obliged to deliver a warning to their servants. "Upon the whole, we cannot but consider your Opium revenue as in great hazard: and we think it of importance to warn you against placing implicit reliance upon a resource which may fail you."[73]

Hazard or no hazard, expansion was the course on which the Bengal administrators were compelled to embark, if the revenue was to be saved. The governor-general chose to open new districts rather than to force cultivation into the less favorable soil of "Countries already white with Poppy."[74] He at once sought the opinions of the two opium agents and of revenue collectors.[75] On his tour of the provinces in the upper Ganges the governor-general, Lord William Bentinck, was accompanied by members of the board of revenue, who were to study the area as potential poppy land.[76] In its eagerness to dis-

[71] Civil finance commissioner to the governor-general in council, 28 June 1830, I. O. Bengal Separate Consultations, 13 July 1830.

[72] Governor-general in council to the court of directors (separate revenue), 8 Feb. 1831, I. O. Letters from Bengal, CXIV.

[73] Court of directors to the governor-general in council (separate revenue), 19 Oct. 1831, I. O. Despatches to Bengal, CXVIII.

[74] Governor-general in council to the court of directors (separate revenue), 8 Feb. 1831, I. O. Letters from Bengal, CXIV.

[75] I. O. Bengal Board of Revenue (Misc.) Proc. (opium), 22 June and 20 July 1830.

[76] Governor-general in council to the court of directors (separate revenue), 8 Feb. 1831, I. O. Letters from Bengal, CXIV.

cover new fields, the government made appropriations
for experimental culture in at least six different districts,
one of which returned a product utterly unfit for use.[77]

It would be footless and next to impossible to enter
into the details of this expansionist movement, for during
these years the opium-producing area was constantly
fluctuating. In the upper Ganges, for example, a good
deal of money was expended through revenue collectors
for advances to ryots. The result was a complete fiasco.[78]
In northeast Rangpur, a district lying to the east of
Patna, it soon became clear that the peasants had no desire to grow the poppy and that the project must be
abandoned. By 1834 another district was conceded to be
hopeless.[79] Despite these failures the government persisted, encouraged by success achieved in other districts.
Altogether, between 1830 and 1839, about fifteen new districts were opened to the poppy, exclusive of several
others where the effort had come to nothing.[80]

The fourth decade of the century thus was an exceedingly busy one in the opium monopoly. Not only was a
vast amount of energy spent in forcing the poppy into
new areas, but other devices for increasing the provision
were also tried. Permission was given the board of customs, salt, and opium to buy opium from Oudh and
Nepal.[81] Several thousand rupees were advanced to enable poppy ryots in the Allahabad district to dig wells.[82]

[77] Governor-general in council to the court of directors (separate revenue), 10 April 1832, I. O. Letters from Bengal, CXVIII.

[78] *Report of a Commission . . . to Enquire into the Working of the
Opium Department*, 1883, p. 23.

[79] I. O. Bengal Board of Revenue (Misc.) Proc. (opium), 16 July 1833
and 11 Nov. 1834.

[80] *Supra*, note 78.

[81] Governor-general in council to the court of directors (separate revenue), 8 Feb. 1831, I. O. Letters from Bengal, CXIV; I. O. Bengal Separate
Consultations, 15 May 1832.

[82] I. O. Bengal Board of Revenue (Misc.) Proc. (opium), 3 Aug. 1830.

A scale of rewards was formulated for the benefit of ambitious underlings in the opium department, who thus might be inspired to put forth exceptional efforts.[83] The price paid to ryots for their opium had been substantially increased between 1827 and 1830, and in 1833 the rate was again raised for certain districts and an additional premium paid for excess produce.[84] Finally, in 1836, the office of sub-deputy opium agent, the most distinctive official in the opium department, was created.[85]

In this furor of expansion, when a larger provision was conceived to be a matter of life and death for the monopoly, there are hints that some degree of coercion was practised on ryots. One official wrote, "I feel it my duty to state that I think the impetus given of late years to the increased production of opium has caused a good deal of injury to private rights."[86] It was admitted by the board of customs, salt, and opium that many zamindars and ryots in Benares were not eager to grow the poppy. But the benefits which British rule conferred upon the people of Benares justified the government in expecting the coöperation of zamindars in the "apportioning of a suitable quantity of land for the advancement of the opium revenue."[87] These are only minor incidents, and it is perhaps to the credit of the British raj that the recorded indictment is so slight. There was almost certainly more forcible cultivation than the records show, for, with the strong pressure to increase the area under poppy

[83] *Ibid.*, 4 Dec. 1832.

[84] *Ibid.*, 23 July 1833; *Report of a Commission . . . to Enquire into the Working of the Opium Department*, 1883, p. 37.

[85] I. O. Bengal Separate Consultations, 6 April 1836. The revenue collector of the district acted as deputy opium agent *ex officio*. The sub-deputies were immediately responsible for the production of opium in the areas of which they had charge. They were full-time employees of the opium department.

[86] I. O. Bengal Board of Revenue (Misc.) Proc. (opium), 26 Oct. 1830.

[87] *Ibid.*, 20 June 1830.

which issued from Calcutta, and with the perennial difficulty of controlling native subordinates, some demonstrations of earnest but not too scrupulous zeal were inevitable.

The council's decision to supply cheaper opium to the
Chinese was to exert a profound effect upon Anglo-Chinese relationships. The results of the new policy appeared almost immediately. In the year 1831-1832 the
production as compared with the average of the previous
decade was nearly doubled, and in five years, when the
program of expansion was well under way, it had tripled.[88] With the increase in output, prices declined, at
first gradually but later, when the China market began
to show signs of glut, much more abruptly. For the whole
decade 1830-1839 they averaged less than half as much as
during the previous ten years, although the difference is
to be ascribed to the preventive efforts of the Chinese as
well as to the additional supply of opium.[89] These were
the statistical fruits that the company harvested.

All this, of course, had its influence upon the Chinese
market. The government departed from its earlier policy
chiefly because of its conviction that a transit duty on
native-state opium was insufficient to protect the monopoly. Malwa was more expensive to produce, but the huge
monopoly profit carried by the Bengal drug more than
compensated for the difference.[90] The unknown quantity
in the equation that the Indian authorities were solving

---

[88] *Return of Opium Exported to China . . . and the Selling Price in
Each Year*, (*Parliamentary Papers*), 1865.

[89] About Rs. 2000 in 1820-1829 and about Rs. 990 in 1830-1839. Even
with this reduction in price, the total revenue showed a gain of approximately thirty-five per cent.

[90] A chest of opium which normally sold in Calcutta for Rs. 1200 or
Rs. 1400 cost the company only Rs. 300. The select committee which reported
in 1832 concluded that the duty thus imposed was 301¾ per cent. *Report
from the Select Committee*, 1832, p. 70; evidence of W. B. Bayley, *ibid.*,
Q. 1695.

was the capacity of the Chinese to absorb opium. Calcutta
was persuaded that the market had by no means reached
its limit, a view that was of course wholly justified. But
there was little idea that it was as elastic as later proved
to be the case. The Indian government had expected that
Bengal might compete on equal terms with Malwa, that a
crisis in the trade might occur, and the native-state drug
be obliged to leave the field, or perhaps that both varieties might maintain their hold in China on a less profitable basis than hitherto.[91] The outcome was otherwise.
During the eighteen-thirties the Chinese market bought
opium on a scale that, a few years before, would have
been incredible, though at lower prices and with frequent
evidences of glut.

It may be granted then that the field for the sale of
opium in China was much larger than had been imagined.
Yet the Indian council was still guilty of forcing the market and of supplying the Chinese with a huge quantity of
relatively cheap drug. Malwa set the pace, and in the
period from 1828-1829 until the Anglo-Chinese war, imports of that variety into China exceeded shipments from
Bengal. Even here the company cannot be exculpated.
The policy of purchase on over-generous terms and the
mismanagement of the Malwa monopoly resulted in an
enormous expansion of that trade. These two currents—
the unsought increase in Malwa and the conscious extension in Bengal—converged about 1835-1836 to swell the
stream of China-bound opium to the greatest volume yet
reached, more than thirty thousand chests. The flood of
opium encouraged reckless smuggling in the Canton
River, which in turn intensified the already strained relations between Chinese and foreigners. All this, it may be
suggested, tended to confirm the frequently proclaimed
opposition of Peking to the traffic and finally to goad the

[91] I. O. Bengal Board of Revenue (Misc.) Proc. (opium), 2 Oct. 1832.

government into vigorous, if indiscreet, action against it.[92] Here then was a critical period in the early development of the traffic, and here too lies a partial explanation of the crisis of 1839.

Obviously the moral responsibility of the company may be easily over-emphasized. The opium question had scarcely assumed the dignity of a moral issue.[93] Protests from China had been fitful, and her sincerity, in the eyes of the British, was far from impeccable. Neither British nor Chinese merchants were much impressed by the preventive activity of officials. It was all a kind of oriental *opéra bouffe*, in which authorities no less than opium smugglers played their announced rôles. But when all allowances have been made, the fact remains that the Indian government missed a magnificent opportunity for withdrawing once and for all from the position of drug merchant. After its policy of expansion was launched and the revenue began to mount, the company became much less sensitive to the moral argument. It was later to appear to the Indian official, in his effort to rationalize an unpalatable fact, that the evils of opium had been grossly exaggerated and that the drug was actually a blessing to the industrious celestial—indeed that it was the only ray of light in the monotonous existence of over-burdened coolies. In short, the expansion carried out during the eighteen-thirties served to reveal the unexplored possibilities of the opium revenue and to commit the company more decisively than ever to its development.

While the results of the new policy were only dimly visible, the monopoly was again examined by a committee

[92] There is no certain evidence to prove a connection between the company's policy of expansion in India and the growing concern over the illicit opium trade felt by the Chinese authorities. The basis for the inference will be suggested in the following chapter.

[93] Opium was, however, recognized as a dangerous drug by the company with far more candor than was true of officials later in the century.

of Parliament. Officials of the company and of the opium department itself were summoned, who left behind them a massive body of evidence. The report which was submitted to Parliament in 1832 betrayed no sentimental attachment to the opium monopoly. But the revenue of nearly a million sterling annually, most of which was supplied by the remote Chinese consumer, proved the conclusive argument. After canvassing several methods of drawing revenue from opium, the committee concluded that it was monopoly or nothing. But the subject could not be dismissed without words of caution. The company must regard the income from opium as only a temporary expedient, since it no longer maintained exclusive control of either production or the market. In the light of this disturbing reality, it would "be highly imprudent to rely upon the opium revenue as a permanent source of revenue."[94] Yet temporize with the system as it would, Parliament had given official sanction to the continuance of the monopoly. In the future, individual opium traders could absolve themselves, as they were to do, by pointing to the complicity of the company. The defense of the latter was no less clear, for had not Parliament itself given the monopoly its blessing?

[94] *Report from the Select Committee*, 1832, p. 70.

CHAPTER V

THE TRADE AT THE OUTER ANCHORAGES

IF the opium trade was encouraged at its Indian source by the rise of Malwa and by the change of policy in Bengal, conditions in China were no less favorable to its prosperity. The chief effect of the hostile measures that had been undertaken by the Canton government in 1821-1822 was to remove the trade from the official control either of the supercargoes or of the Chinese authorities and to launch it upon a period of unprecedented growth. Politically the years 1821-1839 were marked by the termination of the East India Company's monopoly in China. For the semi-responsible hand of the supercargoes were substituted British officers vested with ill-defined and inadequate powers, who were known as superintendents of trade. Both before and after the company lost its hold at Canton, the mercantile community was growing more self-conscious and more restive under port restrictions.

To the issues dividing Westerner from Oriental the opium trade made its contribution. When imports began to increase so enormously, the court at Peking became exercised over the twin questions, the opium trade and the drain of silver to India. Two parties within the Chinese state, advocating different policies, fought for the ear of the emperor. On the one hand were the opportunists, who advocated legalizing the importation of the drug under certain conditions; on the other, the absolutists, who opposed any compromise with a moral evil such as opium was admitted to be by both sides. In the end the

Son of Heaven threw his weight with the latter party. The mission of Lin Tse Hsu to Canton and the Anglo-Chinese war were the results.

Economically the period was no less confused. Into Canton were imported rapidly increasing quantities of opium to be sold at decreasing prices. When imports exceeded the consuming power of the Canton area, new markets on the coast had to be opened. The years 1835-1839 saw the smuggling system reach its apogee.[1] In India the Malwa trade prospered under the transit-duty plan, while in Bengal the government was realizing its aim of a larger provision. In China, at the same time, agitation for legalizing the traffic, accompanied by uncertainty on the part of both authorities and dealers, created a matchless opportunity for foreign traders. Whereas, in the earlier years of the period, Indian ships had discharged their opium cargoes at the outer anchorages and left the smuggling to Chinese dealers, now the barbarian frequently brought his merchandise directly to Whampoa, to the embarrassment of both native officials and the better class of foreigners.

As we have seen, the attacks of the Canton government served to shift the base of smuggling operations from Whampoa to the outer anchorages, chiefly to Lintin.[2] The new center proved to have unsuspected advantages. Port charges and bonds could be completely evaded, while the exactions of Chinese officials, who took only casual notice of events at Lintin, Kumsingmoon, and Hongkong could be more easily held within reason. Unpleasant interference by the supercargoes, now eager to keep their skirts

[1] I refer only to the period before the first Anglo-Chinese war. After the treaty of Nanking the contraband trade was developed on an even more elaborate scale.

[2] Lintin became popular not only with opium ships but with others, especially Americans, who found it a haven free from the port charges exacted at Whampoa. Davis, *The Chinese*, II, 428; Morse, *Chronicles*, IV, 133-134.

free from pollution by the Lintin trade, could be minimized. The anti-opium demonstration of 1821-1822 thus
proved a godsend to the smuggling profession.[3]

During the eighteen-twenties, the community of free
merchants—English, Parsi, and American—included a
number of substantial houses, to whom the bulk of the
opium business fell, as well as several individual traders.
Of the English firms in 1830, the chief were perhaps Mag-
niac and Company (predecessors of Jardine, Matheson
and Company) and Dent and Company, while the Parsis
were represented by the Cowasjees of Calcutta, along
with others. The principal American house was Russell
and Company. These firms established their floating
warehouses at the island of Lintin, some forty miles from
Canton. There, during the winter months, was stationed a
fleet of receiving ships, whose stores were periodically re-
plenished by fast-sailing clippers from India, as well as
by more prosaic vessels.[4] The clippers, owned by firms,
individuals, or *ad hoc* partnerships, were small vessels,
constructed for speed and destined to carry cargoes of
little bulk but large value. Their swift keels set records,
unapproached by the unwieldy East Indiamen, for the
passage to China.[5]

To illustrate the method of conducting the trade during
the eighteen-thirties we may follow the course of an
opium shipment from Calcutta to the Chinese consumer.
The clipper, say the *Sylph,* would receive a cargo of perhaps a thousand chests of Patna and Benares opium, her

[3] In 1823 the Portuguese attempted to lure opium shipping back to
Macao, but the fleet was not inclined to relinquish its new freedom. *Canton
Register,* 19 Feb. 1831.

[4] Clippers first appeared in numbers during the fourth decade of the
century.

[5] The Cowasjee clipper *Sylph,* aided by the favorable monsoon, once made
the passage from Calcutta to Macao in seventeen days, seventeen hours.
Phipps, *China Trade,* p. 210. A more detailed discussion of the clippers will
be found in Chapter VII.

owners having purchased it at government auction. It was packed in chests containing forty balls each, each ball encased in a shell made of poppy petals and inferior juice called "lewah." Inside the shell was treacle-like juice, the crude opium.[6] If the clipper were a fast one and the weather propitious, the voyage to China might not require more than twenty-five days. Instead of moving up the river to Whampoa, she would go directly to Lintin. The Chinese pilot, who may have been taken on board, would clear himself by reporting that "the Captain was villainous and wicked and . . . refused to give his reasons for anchoring.'"[7] Reaching Lintin, the clipper would merely join the squadron of receiving ships, frequently superannuated East Indiamen, and would transfer her cargo to the hulk belonging to her owners.[8] She received in return specie that had accumulated from the sale of other cargoes. Once aboard the receiving ship, the opium would be stowed away to await the appearance of the Chinese smuggler.

Officials seem never to have interfered with the transshipment, and had they been inclined to, they would only have courted disaster, for the hulks were thoroughly armed. In general the connection of the authorities with foreign opium merchants was confined to periodic proclamations ordering vessels " 'loitering at the outer anchorage' either to come into port or sail away to their own countries, lest the 'dragons of war' should be opened, and with their fiery discharges annihilate all who oppose this, a 'special edict.' '"[9] Though fearsome in phrase, the proc-

[6] The term "crude opium" refers to the drug after it had undergone the preliminary manufacturing process but before it had been boiled and prepared for the pipe.

[7] Morse, *Chronicles*, IV, 93.

[8] The size of the Lintin fleet naturally varied. In 1834 the normal number of ships was perhaps ten or twelve. Phipps, *China Trade*, p. 210.

[9] Hunter, *Fan Kwae*, p. 66.

lamations of the hoppo became little more than official bulletins announcing the arrival of each new opium ship.

The *Sylph* might reach Lintin during the southwest monsoon, when other business was stagnant and opium occupied the center of the stage. Her consignees in Canton would arrange with a broker for the sale of the cargo and would issue to him an order on the captain of the receiving ship. Payment, except in rare instances with brokers of established reputation, was made upon receipt of the order.[10] To many British merchants the opium trade was "the safest trade in China, because you got your money before you gave your order."[11] From that point on, responsibility lay with the Chinese buyer.

Sometimes the actual landing of the drug was attended to by the broker or his agents. On other occasions the order passed through several hands before it was finally presented at the receiving ship. There was no difficulty in obtaining boats for smuggling purposes. Rates were quoted in the *Chinese Commercial Guide* for 1834 as twenty dollars for not more than fifty chests of opium.[12] The boats themselves deserve passing notice. The "fast crabs" or "scrambling dragons," as Chinese edicts usually called them, were built for both speed and defense. They were from fifty to ninety feet long, often carrying a crew of sixty or seventy men, who pulled the oars from benches on both sides of the deck. Power from the oars was supplemented by a mainsail and a foresail of mats, bamboos, and rattans. Abaft, the "smug boats" were broad of beam to accommodate the broker's agents. They carried ample armament, perhaps a large gun in the bow,

[10] Where the drug was the company's opium, examination was waived. Malwa, as already indicated, was usually sold on muster, and when delivered, each parcel was examined separately.

[11] Evidence of William Jardine, *Report from the Select Committee*, 1840, Q. 1431.

[12] Phipps, *China Trade*, p. 211.

two or three swivels, pikes, spears, and the all-important weapon of Chinese warfare—a supply of round stones.

When a smuggling boat drew alongside a receiving hulk, its order was immediately filled. The chests of opium were opened and the balls transferred to mat bags, each marked with the owner's private sign.[13] Occasionally one fast crab would carry as much as the contents of a hundred chests. The whole operation of unpacking, weighing, and packing required only a few hours. "From daylight to sunset you see alongside of the vessels [receiving ships] the smuggling boats which carry away the opium. . . . Step on board the opium vessels, and there again the evidences of an active and lucrative trade are everywhere around you. On one side of the deck you see ranges of chests of Patna and Benares,—the other strewed with the contents of the chests of Malwa. . . . Turn your eyes after, and you see . . . the Chinese employed for the purpose, emptying bags of dollars, and shroffing or examining them."[14]

In general, little attempt was made to throw a cloak of secrecy around opium transactions. Fast crabs would proceed up the river past government forts and cruisers in broad daylight, often engaging the pleasure craft of the barbarians in friendly races.[15] The *Canton Price Current* regularly listed market rates, and the supercargoes as regularly sent to India detailed information on the progress of the trade. After the abolition of the company's monopoly, the Canton chamber of commerce openly handed down decisions in opium cases.[16] The whole smuggling operation was frequently carried on

[13] Evidence of C. Marjoribanks, *Report from the Select Committee*, 1830 (Commons), Q. 711.

[14] *Calcutta Englishman*, 30 Jan. 1837, quoted in J. E. Bingham, *Expedition to China*, p. 39.

[15] H. H. Lindsay, *Is the War Just?*, p. 10.

[16] *Canton Register*, 7 Nov. 1837.

under the benevolent eye of a Chinese admiral, who sometimes so far forgot his official dignity as to pay a visit to
the purveyors of "foreign mud," while minor function-
aries were occasionally entertained at dinner on board
the receiving ships.[17] For stipulated payments the authorities allowed the trade to go on without molestation,
providing reasonable decorum was preserved. During
most of the period 1821-1839 the fee for the connivance of
the preventive fleet at Lintin seems to have been one dollar per chest. When, on one occasion, the smugglers grew
lax in their payments, the admiral, instead of invoking
force, merely requested that as a special favor the foreigners collect the "squeeze" and turn it over to him
monthly. This, we are informed, was actually done.[18]

Temporary interruptions in the trade were not unknown, usually occurring on the installation of a new
magistrate or at the expiration of the old agreement between opium brokers and officials. Ordinarily the matter
was soon arranged, "unless the newcomer was exorbitant
in his demands, or, as a broker would express it, 'too
muchee foolo'—i.e., 'the man is crazy.' "[19] When, for one
reason or another, the authorities set forth on an anti-
opium crusade, it was done with such a fanfare of edicts
that one unused to the methods of Chinese officialdom
might have believed that "cruizers are collecting like
clouds" and that disaster was about to overtake the
trade. Boats on preventive service would often inform
the higher officers that the seas had been swept of opium
craft. Most of this was simply part of a recognized ritual.

[17] Evidence of William Jardine, *Report from the Select Committee*, 1840,
Q. 1787.

[18] Lindsay, *Is the War Just?*, p. 10. Jardine, *antea*, Q. 1785, and Phipps,
China Trade, p. 210, repeat what is evidently the same story in terms a little
less damaging to the admiral's integrity. This fee did not include the
larger sums paid by opium brokers to the higher magistrates.

[19] Hunter, *Fan Kwae*, p. 66.

When seizures were made, great to-do was made over destroying the contraband. The popular view in Canton, however, was that little opium ever found its funeral pyre and that the real drug, more often than not, was returned to the smuggler—after he had paid his "smart money."[20] Yet the opium trade knew its vicissitudes. An exceptionally honest or an exceptionally greedy official might readily make trouble, or the Peking government, never a party to the scandalous proceedings at Canton, might exert pressure on local authorities. Chinese officialdom was extremely sensitive to "loss of face," and anything was preferable to discredit in the eyes of the Son of Heaven. But as a rule, official zeal would soon be exhausted, the effect of imperial reproofs would wear off, and all would be forgiven and forgotten.

On three occasions between 1821 and the ending of the company's monopoly in 1833 the opium trade felt the hand of the Chinese authorities. The first was a continuation of the assault that drove the drug fleet to Lintin. Although the hoppo imposed an embargo on legal commerce which lasted for several months, his reforming enthusiasm ultimately spent itself.[21] Again in 1826 a new viceroy sent ships to Lintin to drive away the opium vessels, which prudently moved to other anchorages. But an arrangement seems to have been made with the earnest official, for the trade soon resumed its accustomed course.[22] In the summer of 1831 an imperial communication was received in Canton, which outlined with accuracy and

[20] In June, 1838, when an opium ship lying in the river was boarded by men from a customs cruiser, the latter were beaten for their temerity on the ground that "they were sent to watch *native boats*, and to prevent them from smuggling; to interfere with those foreigners, and create a disturbance was an extreme of audacity never to be allowed." *Chinese Repository*, July, 1838, p. 143, note.

[21] Select committee of supercargoes to the court of directors, 6 Feb. 1824, *Third Report*, 1831, App. II, pp. 137-138; Morse, *Chronicles*, IV, 77.

[22] Morse, *Chronicles*, IV, 133.

great detail the smuggling system. This order from the emperor was essentially different from the blueprints which the hoppo had sent to the hong merchants several times a season, and in the proceedings of the viceroy Chinese dealers recognized a new note. Several brokers were thrown into prison, while others retired until conditions became more stable. The energy of the Canton government persisted until February, when a chop was issued that proved to be little more than the conventional anti-opium formula. This was taken as evidence that matters had been adjusted with the drug dealers. Meanwhile, "business as usual" calmed the lately troubled waters of illicit trade.[23]

Not infrequently it was the indiscretion of opium vessels themselves that caused trouble with the authorities. On one occasion an affray between a boat from the American storeship *Lintin* and a revenue cutter, in the course of which a Chinese was killed, led to a series of edicts.[24] In 1833 the supercargoes were distressed by an incident which occurred at Kumsingmoon where a brawl between men from the receiving fleet and Chinese villagers nearly developed into a pitched battle. Pressed by the Chinese officials, they were obliged to intervene, for country shipping had grown so headstrong and so defiant of their authority that they could no longer assume an attitude of indifference.[25] Such riots endangered the company's position and compromised legal trade. Suiting the word to the audience, they disclaimed for the benefit of

[23] *Ibid.*, App. AA; Phipps, *China Trade*, pp. 218-219; *Canton Register*, 9 Sept., 1 and 15 Oct. 1831.

[24] Morse, *Chronicles*, IV, 267-269.

[25] Private vessels were making habitual use of the outer anchorages. In the season of 1831 nearly half the country ships and a third of the American went no farther than Lintin. Captains were proving reluctant to submit their licenses for inspection, and they were usually supported by their owners. *Ibid.*, pp. 254, 356.

the Chinese any control over opium ships. But they threatened to revoke the license of the truculent captain of the *Hercules,* who had been chiefly responsible for the military operations.[26]

One other aspect of the opium traffic as it existed in China at the close of the company's monopoly remains to be noticed. The ease of trading at Lintin and the increased quantities of the drug coming from India encouraged merchants to seek their fortunes in ports above Canton. If the hinterland of the south was eager for the drug, why should not Chinese along the coast have it brought to them directly? During the eighteen-thirties, furthermore, it was often impossible to sell opium profitably at Lintin. A new market had to be found for the surplus stocks.

The beginnings of the opium traffic to the north and east occurred in the early twenties, although its principal development was not until the next decade. During 1822-1823 small vessels were reported to be experimenting with the new market, and in 1823, the *Merope* and the *Eugenia,* ships that had figured in the exile from Whampoa to Lintin, made voyages.[27] The *Merope* stopped at Namoa, an island off the coast of Kwangtung and Fukien, where some small sales were made, and then, proceeding to Amoy, attempted to open trade relations there. The voyage, on the whole, was a complete failure. Undeterred by the *Merope's* experience, other vessels followed her into the uncharted waters of the coast.[28] A Spanish

---

26 The sources for this incident are contained in *Papers . . . on the Subject of Hostilities between Chinese and British Subjects engaged in the Opium Trade, 1830-33,* in the *Parliamentary Papers,* 1840, and in Morse, *Chronicles,* IV, 350-351, 361-368.

27 Morse, *Chronicles,* IV, 93.

28 C. Gutzlaff, *Sketch,* II, 215; Morse, *Chronicles,* IV, 150; R. B. Forbes, *China Trade,* p. 111. The *Merope,* it should be added, made other and more profitable trips.

opium ship touched at every port between Canton and
Amoy, receiving prices far above the Canton level and
bringing back from its second voyage 132,000 Spanish
dollars. Its relations were most amicable with the authorities, who, it was understood, received twenty dollars
for every chest of opium landed.[29]

By 1830 the new market was well established. The
Sylph, the *Valetta,* the *Jamesina,* and the *Dhaule* schooner,
as well as vessels of foreign registries, were all making
more or less regular trips to Namoa and the Fukien
coast.[30] In the following year, Jardine, Matheson and
Company posted a permanent receiving ship above Canton, with a tender running to Lintin to replenish her
stock.[31] The search for northern markets was carried
even as far as the Liaotung peninsula, which was visited
by the *Sylph,* carrying an incongruous cargo of opium
and the eccentric Prussian missionary, Charles Gutzlaff.[32]

An intimate view of the procedure followed on the
coast is supplied by an observer who accompanied the
American ship *Rose* on a trip to Namoa.[33] The *Rose* an-
chored close to two English brigs belonging to Dent and
Company and Jardine, Matheson and Company. Soon a
Chinese magistrate appeared, accompanied by his reti-
nue. Given to understand that the *Rose* had put into
Namoa for supplies, he announced that, once they were
on board, not a moment must be lost in weighing anchor
for Whampoa. Then he solemnly pulled from his boot an
imperial edict prohibiting foreign trade at ports other

---

[29] Evidence of Captain John Mackie, *Report from the Select Committee,*
1830 (Commons), Q. 4437, 4448, 4450, 4473.

[30] *Ibid.,* Q. 4493.   [31] Hunter, *Fan Kwae,* p. 70.

[32] The east coast proved illusory as an outlet for British manufactures.
A small quantity could sometimes be sold when carried as a minor item in
an opium cargo. P. Auber, *China,* pp. 359-361; Davis, *The Chinese,* I, 116-
117; *Chinese Repository,* Feb., 1834, p. 474.

[33] Hunter, *Fan Kwae,* pp. 67-69.

than Canton. This part of the ceremony over, the attend-
ants returned to their boat, while his excellency went into
the cabin, where the discussion at once got down to reality. ''The Mandarin opened with the direct questions,
'How many chests have you on board? Are they all for
Namao? Do you go farther up the coast?' intimating at
the same time that *there* the officers were uncommonly
strict . . . but our answers were equally clear and
prompt, that the vessel was not going north of Namao,
that her cargo consisted of about 200 chests. Then came
the question of 'Cumsha,' and that was settled on the
good old Chinese principle of 'all same custom.' Everything thus being comfortably arranged, wine drunk and
cheroots smoked, his Excellency said, 'Kaou-tsze' ('I announce my departure')." As soon as the official visit was
concluded, Chinese buyers came on board. A day or two
later merchant junks appeared, flying a private signal at
their mastheads. These were purchasers who had paid
for their opium in Canton to be delivered at Namoa.
Here, it will be observed, the importer was responsible
for delivering the drug and for administering solace to
the official palm. To a much greater degree than at Lintin, the initiative lay with the foreigner.

Because, on the east coast, opium was almost invariably sold for cash, the impression was created that parts
of China were being drained of their silver by the depraved barbarians.[34] There were no exports to counter-
balance drug imports, with the result that quantities of
specie were carried away to Canton to provide teas for
the London market or to be shipped to India. During its
declining days the company became increasingly dependent upon opium proceeds for its investment, and as a
rule, few apprehensions were felt on this score.[35] But the

34 Morse, *International Relations*, I, 181.
35 Morse, *Chronicles*, IV, 151, 260.

fact that much of the specie brought from the east coast went into the coffers of the hong merchants at Canton in payment for return cargoes did not allay Chinese fears.

The attention of the higher authorities of the coast provinces was, of course, attracted by the smuggling trade on their shores. Here connivance was less simple than at Canton, for all foreign trade was forbidden.[36] Opium could not be screened by legal commerce. In 1834 the governor of Fukien made a report to the emperor concerning smuggling boats on the coast, describing the measures that had been taken to prevent law-breaking.[37] The Son of Heaven seems to have been unimpressed, for he curtly reminded the governor that provincial officials were responsible for order in their bailiwicks. Succeeding years record other enactments, which, like their prototypes in Canton, usually remained unenforced.[38]

Meanwhile the monopoly of the East India Company had run its course, and in 1833 it was formally abolished.[39] In China private merchants were becoming impatient under the restraints imposed by the company's representatives, while at home the rising sentiment for free trade could no longer tolerate such an acknowledged monopoly, especially when that monopoly seemed to obstruct the full development of the Chinese market for British manufactures. The superintendents of trade, who were appointed in place of the company's supercargoes, were neither representatives of a trading company nor regularly accredited envoys from one power to another. In that anomalous position lay one of their principal weaknesses. Lord Napier, the first to hold the office of chief superintendent, was instructed to act "with all pos-

---

[36] Davis, *The Chinese*, I, 116.   [37] *Canton Register*, 7 Jan. 1834.

[38] *Chinese Repository*, Nov., 1837, pp. 341 ff.; *Canton Register*, 10 Oct. 1837; *Correspondence relating to China, 1834-39*, 1840, incl. 3 in no. 76. (Hereafter this collection will be cited as *China Corr.*, 1840.)

[39] Effective 22 April 1834. 3 & 4 Wm. IV, c. 93.

sible moderation . . . and to abstain from the use of menacing language'' in dealing with Chinese authorities.[40] He was enjoined constantly to impress upon British subjects the duty of observing Chinese law. The superintendents were to make no appeal to the military and naval forces of Great Britain save in cases of urgent necessity. Their jurisdiction originally included only the port of Canton—that is, the river within the Bocca Tigris —but in 1836 it was extended to Macao and Lintin.[41] It is unnecessary here to relate the curious and unpleasant incidents which followed the appointment of Lord Napier. But it is essential to point out that the hold of any authority upon British traders was not palpably strengthened. Almost immediately the foreign office began to remind the chief superintendent of his limited power in dealing with British ships trading above Canton. "It is not desirable,'' Palmerston observed, ''that you should encourage such adventures; but you must never lose sight of the fact, that you have no authority to interfere with or prevent them.''[42] In this statement the foreign secretary unconsciously epitomized much of British policy towards the opium trade between 1834 and 1839.[43] Little was left to the superintendents but pious remonstrance, or at worst, abandonment of a malefactor to the mercies of the Chinese legal process.[44]

The concluding years of the Lintin period, then, were

[40] *China Corr.*, 1840, incl. 2 in no. 1.

[41] Palmerston to Robinson, 28 May 1836, *ibid.*, no. 52.

[42] Palmerston to Napier, 25 Jan. 1834, *ibid.*, no. 2.

[43] A license was no longer required for private merchants trading in China, and the superintendents could not threaten to revoke them as the supercargoes had done.

[44] In the superintendent's instructions provision was made for the establishing of a court of justice, but in January, 1834, Palmerston informed Napier that such proceedings were not to be commenced without thorough consideration. In 1839 the sentence of one such court was disallowed insofar as it affected the life and liberty of British subjects. *China Corr.*, 1840,

marked by the impotence of British officials and by rest-
lessness on the part of the foreign community, which was
now attracting to itself turbulent spirits from all over
the East. To add to the confusion, agitation for legalizing the opium trade was started by Chinese officials. The
legalization movement was a fact even before the flood
of memorials made of it a burning issue. As early as 1832
a paper from the governor and lieutenant governor of
Kwangtung had hinted at that solution.[45] The opening
shot in the battle of memorials was a document written
by Hsu Nai Tsi, a member of the sacrificial court at Peking.[46] Hsu Nai Tsi was a realist. Aware of the evils of
opium and of the corruption in the Chinese magistracy,
he insisted that the only way to control the drug was to
admit it upon the payment of a moderate duty. It was the
economic aspect that interested him most. As a result of
imports of opium and exports of specie, the price of silver was rising, for the tael, formerly worth not quite a
thousand copper cash, now brought twelve or thirteen
hundred. The inference, Hsu Nai Tsi argued, was that
opium should carry only a moderate duty and should be
sold only by barter. In June, 1836, the emperor's vermilion pencil ordered an inquiry by the Canton officials,
who, on the whole, reënforced the stand taken by the
memorialist.[47]

incl. 2 in no. 1, no. 2; *Chinese Repository*, Aug., 1839, pp. 180-194; Morse,
International Relations, I, 238, note 114.

[45] Phipps, *China Trade*, p. 221.

[46] For the text of the memorials and other relevant documents see *China
Corr.*, 1840, incls. in no. 90.

[47] When this instruction was issued, the foreign community regarded the
legalization question as settled. But the barbarians were skeptical both of
Chinese motives and of whether the new policy, if adopted, would really
throw the trade into legal channels. The smuggling trade was conducted on
a cash basis, while the proposed plan required that goods be exported instead of specie. The hong merchants, when asked to report, stated that they
felt barter to be impracticable. *Chinese Repository*, July, 1836, p. 138;

The issue was thus joined between the possibilists and the absolutists. Hsu Nai Tsi and the Canton government could see no remedy other than compromise, but another group soon appeared to demand no quarter for the drug. Two memorials, one from Chu Tsun, a sub-censor, and the other from Hsu Kiu, a councillor and member of the board of rites, stated the other position clearly and vigorously. In contrast to the arguments for legalization, in which the drain of silver always bulked large, Chu Tsun rested his case frankly on grounds of morality and national welfare.[48] The whole tone of the memorial affords eloquent proof that the situation, in Chinese eyes, was critical. Cultivation of the poppy, though nominally prohibited, had already evoked memorials from six provinces.[49] Consumption of opium was spreading and had even wrought its havoc in the army, that bulwark of Manchu power. How indeed could the march of the drug be stopped save by utter prohibition? But Chu Tsun's only proposal was one that China would neither accept nor employ effectively. To hold officialdom to its duties and to call local officers to repentance demanded a hierarchy of more lofty integrity than China possessed. As long as the remuneration of officials depended upon their ability as private financiers—they received no stated salaries—the way to thoroughgoing reform in the civil service was effectively blocked.[50]

Elliot to the foreign office, 27 July 1836, *China Corr.*, 1840, no. 82; Elliot to Palmerston, 2 Feb. 1837, *ibid.*, no. 90.

[48] As to the suggestion that opium be made a barter transaction, both Chu Tsun and Hsu Kiu observed with some acuteness that it would be as easy to prevent the import of opium as the export of specie.

[49] Yunnan, with which the memorialist was intimately acquainted, was producing several thousand chests annually.

[50] The temptation is all but irresistible to be over-ironic at the expense of the rapacious and corrupt officials of China. The experience of certain western nations, however, in enforcing their sumptuary laws offers a sobering analogy. In the United States, for example, the state of affairs under

From the memorials emerge the two principal objections of the Chinese government to the opium traffic.[51] These were held by both parties, the advocates of legalization along with the prohibitionists. The memorialists asserted, in the first place, that opium smoking was a moral evil and was debasing the Chinese people, and secondly, that the trade was causing a drain of specie and thus impoverishing the empire. With both was bound up the fear of the foreigner and his aggressive designs. When the Chinese had been sufficiently enfeebled by foreign dirt and their silver taken away from them, then they might fall prey to the despised barbarians.

The first objection may be readily admitted and dismissed. Despite the rationale for the trade supplied by British merchants and officials, opium smoking was a vice.[52] Although, throughout the nineteenth century and even into the twentieth, there has arisen a host of official apologists to proclaim it a harmless diversion, and although the royal commission spent much time in 1893-1894 eliciting evidence to demonstrate its relatively innocuous character, enlightened opinion has come to agree with the views of the Chinese. Their experience with opium was becoming increasingly painful. It was no stranger in the court of Peking, and outlying provinces were returning news of widespread demoralization.[53] As

the Volstead Act bore a more than superficial resemblance to conditions in China during the eighteen-thirties.

[51] In Morse, *International Relations*, I, 185-191, and in J. B. Eames, *The English in China*, pp. 254-264, will be found detailed analyses of the memorials. I have drawn heavily on Morse for the pages immediately following.

[52] It is not to be implied, of course, that opium smoking is comparable in its effects to the high-tension drugs, morphine, cocaine, and heroin, against which recent anti-narcotic agitation has been chiefly directed.

[53] In 1838 an officer of the sacrificial court reported that opium was smoked generally throughout Shensi, Shansi, and Kansu by both sexes. He

long as the controversy had to do with ethics, the Chinese case was invincible.

When economics is substituted for ethics, the issue becomes clouded. Silver was scarce, said the Chinese, and the shortage produced by imports of opium. Two bits of evidence were adduced. First, the tael of silver, as measured by copper cash, had increased in value. Secondly, the salt trade was reported to be in a desperate condition, because the commodity was sold for copper cash, while the duties were paid in silver. Certain contemporary observers also remarked upon the apparent scarcity of specie. One who visited Foochow in the summer of 1837, after noting the high price of silver, said, "The limited circulation of the precious metals is throughout the Empire very keenly felt."[54]

The question raised by the Chinese memorialists is an intricate one, which can be answered only in the most general terms. Any attempt to estimate the precise balance of the China trade is doomed to inaccuracy, for two of its most important items, opium and native silver, were nominally contraband. We have already seen that, during the entire span of trade between China and the West, the movement of the precious metals had been towards China, and that Europe had become increasingly dependent upon Indian opium and cotton to pay its debts to the Chinese. In 1817, for example, the value of the country trade represented more than three-fourths of the total imports into China, and in only two years between 1818 and 1833 did it fall below that proportion.[55] Through

pointed also to the high price of foreign dollars. *Canton Register*, 2 Oct. 1838.

[54] "Notes by Mr. Gutzlaff upon a Voyage to Fuhchoo," *China Corr.*, 1840, incl. 3 in no. 107.

[55] The import figures include the trade from non-Indian ports in the East, such as the Straits, etc. Except where otherwise credited, the statistics upon which these conclusions are based will be found in Morse, *Chronicles*. For

the growth of this Sino-Indian commerce the character of the Canton trade was altered, and it ceased to be concerned primarily with exports. By 1817 the tea and silk shipped to London and America was approximately balanced by cotton and opium from India and manufactures from the West. Nine years later, China's total imports exceeded her exports by more than 5,000,000 Spanish dollars.

The expansion of the opium trade, the memorialists assumed correctly, was the chief factor in shifting the balance. Whereas, in 1817, shipments of opium from India were valued at less than 4,000,000 dollars, by 1832 they exceeded 14,000,000.[56] During the years 1826-1833 more than 40,000,000 dollars were shipped out of China as against the 23,000,000 in specie and credits that foreigners brought in.[57] The following seasons saw the balance turn still more heavily against the Chinese. It is also certain that considerable quantities of specie, carried away in payment for opium, failed to find place in the statistical column.[58]

each year between 1817 and 1833 the author has appended a statistical summary of the season's business.

[56]	1817-1821 (annual average)	6,630,378
	1822-1826	8,327,825
	1826-1831	13,006,856

[57] To say that London paid for its tea with opium is more than a pleasant generalization. In 1836-1837, for example, teas to the value of 20,225,065 dollars were shipped out, while 19,746,759 dollars' worth of opium was imported. In 1837-1838, when the Canton government succeeded in checking deliveries of opium the two articles remained about equal in value. *Chinese Repository*, Dec., 1851, pp. 554-555.

[58] From 1826 on, aided by the opium trade and their own growing exports to Great Britain, American merchants tended to substitute bills on London for the treasure they had previously brought. The decisive influence in creating a shortage of specie at Canton was not, of course, the fact that Americans were no longer replenishing the Chinese supply. Opium had reversed the flow of silver and enabled Americans to sell their bills in Canton. But it does not seem improbable that the *visible* reduction in the influx of

Yet the shipments of silver from China to India seem insignificant when placed beside the amounts imported by Europeans in the past.[59] Some of the coast provinces may well have felt pressure, but there was still much foreign money in the country, which was regarded as indispensable by the port cities. As for the appreciation of silver, adduced by the memorialists as evidence of its scarcity, that may be accounted for by the debasing of the copper coinage practised during the last two reigns.[60]

On the other hand, China may have experienced more hardship than would seem probable to a western student. Oriental countries have long shown a talent for absorbing precious metals and withdrawing them from circulation. To say that the Chinese Empire had drawn no less than £90,000,000 (net) from the West is not to prove that such an amount remained in circulation. This silver presumably had been diffused through the empire and a part of it had certainly been consumed by the arts. When, in short, the balance turned against the Chinese, the amount of silver in actual use may have been relatively small. But the specie with which China bought its opium was taken out of the circulating medium. Thus a drain of treasure comparatively minute in proportion to previous imports would affect the supply of mobile silver, especially along the coast, more than would at first seem likely. Obviously such speculations raise difficult and unanswerable questions. It is clear, however, that silver was leaving China in payment for opium, that the net drain had been a fact for at least a decade before the memorials

American specie may have increased the alarm of Chinese mercantilists. See C. F. Remer, *Foreign Trade of China*, pp. 25-26.

[59] During the 130 years of the company's factory at Canton there had been imported into China no less than £90,000,000 in specie. Morse, *International Relations*, I, 202, note 93.

[60] In this paragraph I have attempted to suggest the line of argument taken by Morse, *International Relations*, I, 201-204.

appeared,[61] and that clandestine exports may have made the real loss greater than the records indicate.

Whatever the economic facts, the change in the flow of specie served to focus Chinese eyes upon the opium trade. During the three years from the presentation of the memorials to the outbreak of war in 1839, the situation grew steadily more tense. Several factors conspired to make the period 1836-1839 one of crisis and chaos. In the first place, the vacillation of the imperial court was a serious tactical error. Uncertainty and doubt as to its ultimate policy inspired, on the one hand, foreigners to a reckless campaign of smuggling, and on the other, the Canton administration to a captious attitude, ruthlessness alternating with indulgent connivance. Again, affairs within the foreign community were at ins and outs during the régime of the superintendents of trade. With the cessation of the company's monopoly, large numbers of private traders flocked to China, who represented, on the whole, a less desirable class than those of the earlier period. It was they who, when the preventive measures of the Canton government ruined the Chinese smuggling trade, brought their opium to Whampoa itself. Finally, the increase in the Bengal provision, together with the normal growth of the Malwa trade, resulted in annual imports averaging more than thirty-five thousand chests. This enlarged supply and the diminished prices which it brought resulted in feverish speculative activity on the part of opium merchants, so that the state of the Canton market would have been precarious even without the government's growing disapproval.[62]

It was a devious path that the Canton authorities fol-

---

[61] The statistics in Morse, *Chronicles*, III and IV, prove conclusively that the balance shifted no later than 1826.

[62] Court of directors to the governor-general in council (India financial), 25 May 1841, I. O. Despatches to Bengal and India, XXVII. In 1831 the

lowed during the three years. The opium trade was not viewed with the easy tolerance of previous days, and yet the viceroy's attempts to suppress it were by no means wholehearted. During most of 1837—to anticipate what is to follow—the campaign was waged on paper, though the edicts were more resolute in tone than the formal declarations of the past. In the autumn of 1837, the authorities turned their attention to native smugglers, whose activities they succeeded in paralyzing. The less reputable foreigners therefore ceased to depend on Chinese smugglers and themselves brought opium into the river. It was not until late in 1838 that the actions of the viceroy proved the emperor to be desperately in earnest. And even then barbarian merchants doubted.

The long battle, which lasted from the autumn of 1836 to the signing of the treaty of Nanking in 1842, began with an order requiring the hong merchants to investigate the opium dealings of nine members of the foreign community. This was followed by an edict commanding the nine to leave the country. The proscribed merchants, who, as the governor had intimated, were "irreclaimably sunk in folly," made no move to leave. Two years later they were still in Canton, where they were discovered by Commissioner Lin.[63] The incident produced no immediate consequences, but its implications were great. The Chi-

price of Patna opium in Canton averaged about 1000 dollars per chest. Between July and November, 1838, prices ranged from 530 to 607 dollars. Malwa experienced a less striking depreciation both because its quality was improving and because the Chinese were developing a taste for it. Much of the decline was unquestionably due to the hostile measures of the Chinese. *Canton Register Price Current*, 1831; evidence of Anthony Daniell, *Report from the Select Committee*, 1840, Q. 1294.

[63] With the exception of James Innes, who left in December, 1838. The list of names was lamentably incomplete and inaccurate, but in singling out Jardine, Innes, and Dent, the Chinese hit upon three of the largest dealers. *China Corr.*, 1840, incls. 1 and 2 in no. 91; *Chinese Repository*, Feb., 1837, pp. 463-464.

nese had now for the first time bestowed their attentions specifically upon foreign importers. Captain Elliot, the British superintendent, who held steadfastly to his view that legalization was imminent, became alarmed over the general trade, then in none too flourishing a state. If deliveries at Lintin should be seriously interrupted, the Canton market would be left without the large amounts of treasure which had financed purchases of tea and silk. Elliot found himself in the trying position of one whose official duty and ultimate beliefs were altogether at odds. Early in February, 1837, he requested the occasional visit of a man-of-war. Such a gesture, he thought, might serve as a helpful object lesson to the authorities.

But this action by no means represented his own convictions. He regarded the opium business as objectionable on both economic and ethical grounds. To Palmerston he confided his doubts. "It cannot be good that the conduct of a great trade should be so dependent upon the steady continuance of a vast and prohibited traffic in an article of vicious luxury, high in price, and liable to frequent and prodigious fluctuation. . . . I hope your Lordship will let me say that there are many reasons for regretting the extent to which the Indian income is dependent upon such a source of revenue."[64]

Throughout the spring of 1837 the trade proceeded with only minor embarrassment. Kumsingmoon was closed to foreign shipping.[65] The vessels at Lintin discreetly moved to more hospitable waters for a time, some of them going to the east coast.[66] That deliveries at the outer anchorages were not at a standstill may be gathered from the fact that more than fifteen thousand chests were landed

[64] Elliot to Palmerston, 21 Feb. 1837, *China Corr.*, 1840, no. 93.
[65] *Canton Register*, 14 March 1837.
[66] In October of 1837 about fifteen vessels were supplying that area with the drug. *Chinese Repository*, Oct., 1837, p. 304.

between April 1 and December 1. During the summer and autumn it was the native trade that felt the hand of officialdom. Some fifty or sixty smugglers and dealers were believed to have been seized in the course of a few months, while the price of connivance, it was reported, rose to seventy-five dollars a chest.[67]

Captain Elliot was by no means insensitive to the growing tenseness of his relations with the Chinese. During the autumn the authorities bombarded him with orders to send away the receiving ships. When no satisfactory answer was received, their excellencies, venturing to intimate that the superintendent must be ill suited to his position, threatened to shut off the regular trade and to expel Elliot himself.[68] The mercantile community was not inclined to take fright at this new manifestation, for hundreds of chests had been brought within the Bogue during the month in which the most stringent proclamation was published. The time had not yet arrived for extreme measures against foreign smugglers.

Apprehensive over the situation that was developing, Elliot appealed to the foreign office for the appointment of a British commissioner to deal with the smuggling problem.[69] Negotiating from some point near Peking, the envoy should emphasize the unsatisfactory character of existing arrangements and should press for early legalization. Palmerston did not see his way clear to accept the suggestion, nor did he, apparently, comprehend the problem in any adequate fashion. His reply missed the point with admirable precision: "Her Majesty's Government cannot interfere for the purpose of enabling British subjects to violate the law of the country to which they trade.

[67] *Canton General Price Current*, 12 Dec. 1837; *Chinese Repository*, March, 1839, p. 606.

[68] *China Corr.*, 1840, incl. 1 in no. 109 and incl. 1 in no. 122.

[69] Elliot to Palmerston, 19 Nov. 1837, *ibid.*, no. 110 and incl. 1.

Any loss, therefore, which such persons may suffer in consequence of the more effective execution of the Chinese laws on this subject must be borne by the parties who have brought that loss on themselves by their own acts.'"[70]

The foreign secretary, it will be seen, proposed to regard China as a nation subject to the canons of international law, as a sovereign state which could handle its foreign trade as it pleased.[71] Ideally, he was correct. British officials in China could not make it their duty to patrol the entire coast. There were only two ways to solve the smuggling problem, either to make the opium trade legal or to cut it off at its Indian source. But, though the possibility of a definitive solution was slight, Palmerston's statement seems singularly barren. To say that foreign culprits must bear the consequences of their own folly was to show a deplorable ignorance of the realities of Canton life. Both the theory and the practice of Chinese justice made it inconceivable that punishment would be visited only on the heads of those actually involved in smuggling operations. Foreigners had had enough experience with the government to know that, when once aroused, it made no subtle distinctions. All of this was ignored in Palmerston's statement of policy, which, in a word, proposed that smuggling should go on, unrestrained as well as unsupported by British authority.

Meanwhile, the mechanism of the contraband trade was undergoing a radical change. The Canton government could no longer be relied upon. Foreign importers had gone almost unscathed, but their native colleagues found the employment precarious. The impression must be conveyed to Peking at all costs that the Canton administra-

[70] Palmerston to Elliot, 15 June 1838, *ibid.*, no. 116.
[71] See A. J. Sargent, *Anglo-Chinese Commerce and Diplomacy*, p. 72.

tion had mended its ways and would show no mercy towards the drug. Hitherto, the European had left to Chinese the bribing of officials and the actual carriage of opium up the river. During 1835-1836 foreign traders had occasionally invaded the inner river with their drug, and because of the languishing state of native smuggling, the practice soon became common.[72] Since Chinese dealers were no longer able to ensure the conveyance of opium to Whampoa, the resourceful barbarians assumed that responsibility.[73]

The mantle of the native smugglers fell not only upon foreigners but upon the viceroy himself. This worthy, when his repressive measures wrought havoc with his emoluments, hit upon a new method of maintaining his income. He placed four of his own boats on the river, ostensibly to do reconnaissance work. These took a distinguished part in the contraband trade, and ultimately, as far as the Chinese were concerned, established a near monopoly of the smuggling. It seems to have been common property among the natives that the indulgent Tang was heavily interested in illicit transactions. When one of the viceroy's boats was lying at Whampoa on opium business, according to the testimony of a British merchant, "Every Chinaman would point his finger to the flag, and tell you 'That is the Viceroy's boat.'"[74] By his own subjects the covetous official was lampooned:

[72] Forbes, *China Trade*, p. 46. William Jardine, *Report from the Select Committee*, 1840, Q. 1517, stated that the viceroy's men had violated their agreement with the Chinese smugglers by seizing a vessel after her opium had been delivered. The security who had contracted with the government for the safety of all smuggling boats thereupon withdrew. The native trade thus collapsed, and the security broke up his own boats.

[73] The more substantial members of the foreign community, even those who dealt in opium, abstained from the trade in the inner river.

[74] Evidence of William Jardine, *Report from the Select Committee*, 1840, Q. 1517 ff. See also Lindsay, *Is the War Just?*, pp. 14-15.

O'er the impoverish'd, but broaden land,
Our venerable Tang holds chief command.
His favors fall on those who seizures make,
Yet in the daring game he holds a stake.
Four cruising boats his son and comrades keep
To scour the waters of the inner deep.[75]

The year 1838 saw a gradual sharpening of the issue. During the spring and summer foreign smugglers grew bolder. Their boats on the river increased from eight or ten to between thirty and forty in the course of a few months.[76] Various kinds of craft were employed, small fast-boats as well as decked and masted passage-boats, while even ocean-going vessels brought their illicit cargoes to the docks.[77] The *Chinese Repository* was led to observe that "the smuggling trade in the drug is carried on to an extent here never before witnessed. Almost every part of the river, from the Bogue on the east, to Hwátí on the west, is made the theatre of the traffic."[78] During most of 1838 the authorities showed no great disposition to interfere with foreign opium runners. A few seizures were made, and there was indubitable violence and perhaps loss of life.[79] But native dealers continued to feel the heavy hand of the government.[80] On one occasion more than twenty of them were brought into Canton city in chains, while in Macao an opium merchant was executed and over his body inscribed the significant legend:

[75] Bingham, *Expedition to China*, p. 50. A similar bit of doggerel appeared in the *Canton Register*, 21 Aug. 1839.

[76] *Chinese Repository*, Dec., 1838, p. 438.

[77] *Canton Register*, 23 Oct. 1838.   [78] March, 1838, p. 552.

[79] *Ibid.*, June, 1838, p. 112; *Canton Press*, 22 Dec. 1838; *Canton Register*, 25 Sept. 1838.

[80] Many of the more responsible members of the foreign community were apprehensive about the smuggling trade within the Bogue. Olyphant and Company, an American firm which eschewed dealing in opium as a matter of principle, in a public letter pointed out the disabilities which the practice imposed upon innocent merchants. *Canton Register*, 21 Aug. 1838.

"For traitorous intercourse with foreigners, and for smuggling opium and Sycee silver."[81] The foreign community might still doubt the viceroy's sincerity. His own boats were busily gathering the fruits of illicit trade before the blight of repression fell upon it, and there was, in truth, good reason to believe that much of the drug seized by his minions was never destroyed.[82] But by September, 1838, the trade was in a state of utter stagnation. Deliveries had practically ceased, and panic-stricken brokers were fleeing from official wrath. Foreigners might still bring their drug into the inner river, but their market had vanished.

The time in which even European smugglers could pursue their way with impunity had nearly run its course. In late November or early December the Canton government received a reprimand from the emperor, who charged it with gross negligence. The viceroy sought to vindicate himself in a fashion that was, to say the least, energetic. He struck his first blow on December 3, when, after seizing a few chests of opium, he ordered two foreigners to leave Canton. One of them was finally exculpated, but the other, under pressure from both the hong merchants and Captain Elliot, was forced to bow to his excellency's command.[83]

Three days before this controversy was settled, an-

[81] *Chinese Repository*, Oct., 1838, p. 336; *Canton Register*, 17 April 1838.

[82] Of eight chests confiscated on one occasion, four disappeared in the very act of seizure. The remaining four, while in the hands of the police, "were metamorphosed into four chests of common earth." *Chinese Repository*, June, 1838, p. 112.

[83] W. R. Talbot, who was involved through a misunderstanding, was one of the most unlikely victims that the Chinese could have selected. A member of the American firm of Olyphant and Company, he had never been connected with opium dealings. James Innes, on the other hand, had been known for years as a leader in the contraband trade at Canton and on the east coast. *Chinese Repository*, Dec., 1838, pp. 438-444; *China Corr.*, 1840, nos. 133 and 137.

other issue arose. Late in the morning foreigners noticed preparations being made in front of their factories for the execution of a Chinese opium dealer. When they protested, the official in charge, acting with a good deal of moderation, left without further ado. Crowds of Chinese began to gather, not, it appears, with any show of hostility but merely to satisfy their own curiosity. When the cry to "clear the square" was raised, some of the more tumultuous spirits among the barbarians leaped forward to the attack, belaboring the inquisitive but inoffensive Chinese with sticks. A bombardment of brickbats and stones was the reply. By early afternoon the mob was in undisputed possession of the square and seemed about to charge the foreign buildings. Grave consequences were prevented only by the arrival of a magistrate with a body of police and soldiers, who, by judicious use of the bamboo and rattan, soon dispersed the mob.[84]

Legal trade had been suspended immediately after the events of December 3. Captain Elliot was convinced that not only the prosperity but the security of foreigners in Canton was endangered by the scandalous smuggling within the Bogue and that he must interfere to stop it. When his first demand that British opium shipping leave the river produced no effect, the superintendent took an extraordinary step. Informing the Chinese that there would be no intervention on behalf of British law-breakers, he requested the commander of the preventive boats to proceed with him to the smuggling station. By December 31 the river was reported cleared, and legitimate trade, which had been under the ban for four weeks, was reopened.[85]

[84] Elliot to Palmerston, 13 Dec. 1838, *China Corr.*, 1840, no. 134; *Chinese Repository*, Dec., 1838, pp. 445 ff. All available testimony agrees upon the provocative attitude of a number of foreigners.

[85] Elliot to Palmerston, 2 Jan. 1839, *China Corr.*, 1840, no. 137 and incls. 7 and 13.

The better section of the mercantile community, one gathers, deprecated the lawless traffic within the Bogue. Foreign merchants might all—or most of them—maintain their ships at Lintin, but the bald defiance of smuggling at Whampoa was contrary to the best traditions of illicit trade. Yet they were by no means at one in approving Captain Elliot's petition "for the command of a [Chinese] government cruizer."[86] His action was interpreted as lending British support to whatever anti-opium policy the Chinese authorities chose to execute. He had, to be sure, exceeded his instructions, strictly construed, but his instructions were grossly inadequate.[87] Elliot's primary duty was to watch over the commercial relations of British subjects in China. Smuggling within the Bogue had jeopardized legal trade and might well lead to more unhappy consequences. The superintendent was literally forced to take action, for his efforts to impress upon his fellow-countrymen "the duty of conforming to the laws and usages of the Chinese Empire" had been conspicuously unsuccessful.

Her Majesty's superintendent was aware of the "novel, responsible, and undefined station" which he filled.[88] He had had no part in creating the problems which he faced, nor could they be attributed solely to the aggressiveness of foreign merchants and the obstinacy of the Chinese government. To London and Calcutta belong a share of the responsibility, the one for failing to develop a clear-cut policy in China and the other for its opium program. The instructions issued to Lord Napier, the first superintendent, have already been noticed. Orders dealing with

[86] *Canton Register*, 1 Jan. 1839.

[87] The legal issue hinged on whether the superintendent's powers warranted interference in a trade admittedly contraband in China but unmentioned in the laws of Great Britain. His instructions had never been revealed and were published only in part on December 31 of that year.

[88] Elliot to Palmerston, 2 Jan. 1839, *China Corr.*, 1840, no. 138.

the superintendent's line of conduct in special cases cast more light on his unhappy situation. When he advised that a British ship should be forbidden to proceed up the river, he was cautioned against "interfering in such a manner with the undertakings of British merchants."[89] On another occasion, when Palmerston admitted the vague jurisdiction and meager authority of the superintendents, he warned that "The assumption of powers which you have no means of enforcing . . . can only tend to impair the authority and lower the dignity of His Majesty's Commission."[90] Elliot could have drawn little comfort from the despatches that he received between 1836 and 1839. Whitehall seemed not only to be innocent of any considered policy in China, but, in general, to be indifferent to the necessity for having one. The superintendent of trade, armed only with blank cartridges, was thus left to fight his own battle and that of the foreign community.

The complicity of the Indian government scarcely requires emphasis. It would be manifestly absurd to attribute the strained situation at Canton solely or even chiefly to the eagerness of the Bengal monopolists. A multitude of influences contributed both to the spread of opium and to friction between Chinese and barbarian. Yet it can hardly be asserted that the miraculous growth of the trade represented only the natural increase in Chinese demand—that, to be specific, the demand more than trebled between 1830-1831 and 1838-1839. In 1832, for example, the Canton market was so glutted as a result of shipments from Malwa that twenty-eight firms requested a postponement of the Calcutta sales. The board of cus-

---

89 Palmerston to Elliot, 22 July 1836, *ibid.*, no. 65.

90 Palmerston to Elliot, 8 Nov. 1836, *ibid.*, no. 71. The foreign office, however, did approve the course that Elliot pursued with regard to smuggling in the river.

toms, salt, and opium, denying the appeal, observed that
the government's policy called for "the utmost possible
extension of the poppy culture and the production of
opium."[91] Competition with Malwa rather than an ap-
praisal of the Chinese market dictated the opium program in Bengal.

There is no positive evidence to show that the hostility
of the Peking government was aggravated by the prodigious quantities which reached Canton and the east
coast as a result of the opium crisis in India. Captain
Elliot, however, considered one of the most acute sources
of trouble to be "the immense, and it must be said, most
unfortunate increase in the supply during the past four
years."[92] And one of the China merchants, testifying before the House of Commons committee in 1840, charged
that "the East India Company were increasing the quantity of opium almost every year, without reference to the
demand in China."[93] At the least, one may conclude that,
when the Calcutta government chose "the only way left
of putting down the Malwa trade,"[94] that is, of offering
a large supply at a moderate price, another stick was cast
on the pile which burst into flame in 1839.

In Peking, meanwhile, the face of the Emperor Tao
Kuang, one Chinese official whose antipathy to the opium
trade was above question, had turned resolutely away
from legalization. Hsu Nai Tsi was degraded to an official
of the third rank and dismissed from public service. The
stern recommendations of his opponent—death to smokers at the expiration of a period of grace—were proclaimed, while the zeal of the Canton government showed

[91] I. O. Bengal Board of Revenue (Misc.) Proc. (opium), 9 Oct. 1832.

[92] Elliot to Palmerston, 30 Jan. 1839, *China Corr.*, 1840, no. 141.

[93] Evidence of Robert Inglis, *Report from the Select Committee*, 1840,
Q. 458, 459.

[94] Governor-general in council to the court of directors (separate revenue), 1 Aug. 1833, I. O. Letters from Bengal, CXXII.

no signs of waning. A crisis was approaching, evident even to foreigners, who tended to regard Chinese edicts with apathy born of long immunity. In January, 1839, it became known that the emperor had decided upon the almost unprecedented step of sending an imperial commissioner to exterminate the traffic.[95] At the same time, the viceroy of Canton was commanded to "scrub and wash away the filth," pending the arrival of the imperial envoy.[96]

[95] *Chinese Repository*, Sept., 1838, pp. 271-280, and Jan., 1839, pp. 498-500, 504.

[96] *Canton Register*, 29 Jan. 1839.

CHAPTER VI

THE CRISIS OF 1839

THE imperial high commissioner, Lin Tse Hsu, was a native of Fukien province and therefore—as his manifesto stated—well acquainted "with all the arts and shifts of the outer foreigners."[1] Only three times, it was reported, during the life of the Manchu dynasty had a commissioner been invested with such authority. From the Son of Heaven himself, who had determined to wipe out the opium trade, Lin received his commission to "go, examine, and act."[2] In his other posts he had been regarded as an able and resolute official, one to whom a weak but right-minded emperor, appalled at confronting the shades of his imperial ancestors with glaring evils in his administration, might naturally turn. To the Westerners Lin was to prove a revelation. At first they beheld him through eyes accustomed to corruption and vacillation in the ranks of officialdom. From skepticism the barbarians passed to amazement, from amazement to reluctant conviction. With all the warning of the

[1] *China Corr.*, 1840, incl. 1 in no. 145. In 1838, when the emperor called upon tartar-generals, viceroys, and governors to report upon a proposal for making opium smoking punishable by death, only Lin favored the suggestion unequivocally. His knowledge of the smuggling system at Canton was thorough enough, but it had been derived from a study of the memorials rather than from first-hand contact with the situation. T. F. Tsiang, "New Light on Chinese Diplomacy, 1836-49," *Journal of Modern History*, Dec., 1931, pp. 581-582; Morse, *International Relations*, I, 214; J. F. Davis, *China . . . since the Peace*, I, 309-312.

[2] *Chinese Repository*, April, 1839, p. 610.

preceding four months they were still unprepared for earnest, decisive action.[3]

Lin's opponent during the crisis was the chief superintendent of British trade, Captain Charles Elliot. His first acquaintance with China had been made five years before when he was appointed secretary to the superintendents, and in 1836 he succeeded to the position of chief. During the crisis of 1839 he proved himself to be a man of honesty and courage. Occasionally his courage got the better of his judgment, and he seemed often to lack the diplomatist's intuition in appraising a situation. Once a plan of action had been decided upon, an element of stubbornness in his nature made change difficult. But on the whole, he defended the interests of the British colony with ability and conviction. Blame, if blame is to be awarded, belongs to Whitehall rather than to the superintendent of trade, whose controversy with the imperial commissioner could be little more than a personal combat. And Lin's direct methods did not encourage diplomatic finesse on the part of his opponent.

At Canton the opium trade had shown little activity since the autumn of 1838.[4] Some of the business houses declined to act as agents for further consignments of the drug.[5] During February the commissioner was daily expected, and the city was vibrant with rumors of his probable line of conduct. The Canton government, under stress of the imperial reprimand implied in the sending of a special envoy, was not inclined to sloth. The viceroy made his position emphatically clear when the execution

[3] *Report from the Select Committee*, 1840, evidence of Robert Inglis, Q. 572, 610; Anthony Daniell, Q. 1097, 1098; William Jardine, Q. 1342.

[4] Sales were being máde, however, on the east coast. In March there were some fifty thousand chests ready for the Canton market. *Ibid.*, Q. 1352, 1353; *Chinese Repository*, March, 1839, p. 606.

[5] Many of the merchants in Canton did not own the commodities in which they dealt but merely acted as agents for houses in England or India.

of another opium dealer was successfully carried through in front of the foreign factories. While the barbarians were still protesting, Lin Tse Hsu entered Canton in state.[6]

The scene must have been a brilliant one. Absolute quiet prevailed on the river as the high commissioner and his entourage approached the city. He was seated on the deck of a large boat, the first in the procession. As he passed the factories, curious foreigners observed him to be "a large, corpulent man, with a heavy black moustache and long beard," about fifty-five years of age.[7] In his expression there was an ominous hint of firmness. Following Lin's boat were others bearing the principal officials of the Canton area. The crews were gaily dressed in red and white, with rattan hats to match, while the troops garrisoned in the forts along the river had donned new uniforms for the occasion.

For eight days the commissioner pursued his investigations, and the foreign community gave itself over to eager speculation. By the middle of March he was ready for action. After making inquiries of the compradores of the foreign factories, he tried third-degree methods on the hong merchants, so vigorous in character that one of them described the encounter, "No hav' see so fashion before."[8] Then he set about his task in earnest, issuing two edicts, one to the foreigners, the other to the hong merchants.[9] Upon the former he made two demands, after indicting them bitterly for their evil ways: first, let every particle of opium be surrendered. "There must not be the smallest atom concealed or withheld." Second, let the barbarians sign a bond to the effect that they would never

[6] *China Corr.*, 1840, incls. 1-6 in no. 146.

[7] Hunter, *Fan Kwae*, p. 137.

[8] *Ibid.*, p. 138. The compradore was the chief servant of a foreign factory, the steward and treasurer of the establishment.

[9] *China Corr.*, incls. 1 and 2 in no. 145.

again bring opium and that, if any were discovered, the guilty parties "shall suffer the extreme penalties of the law: and that such punishment shall be reasonably submitted to." Having served notice on the foreigners, Lin passed on to pay his respects to the desolate hong merchants. Their failure to obtain bonds duly signed, he threatened, would bring the death penalty to one or two of their number. "And thus will I show a lucid warning."

The commissioner had done what no other Chinese official had ever attempted. He had demanded that opium on board European vessels be surrendered to the government. Still, though the situation was regarded as grave by the foreigners, Lin thus far had only issued edicts, and edicts were an old story.[10] It was not, after all, the vigor of his diction but the energy with which he enforced his orders that produced compliance in the end. The general feeling seems to have been that to surrender opium in Chinese waters was quite out of the question, since much of it was the property of merchants in India, but that the foreign community ought to relinquish all future trade in the drug. Invoking the philosophy that had weathered previous crises, the chamber of commerce proposed to deliver something over a thousand chests to pacify the commissioner.[11] The offer was promptly rejected. Modifying his attack, Lin next sought to persuade Lancelot Dent, head of one of the largest opium firms, to enter the city for an interview. The chamber of commerce, gathered for counsel, insisted that Dent must not place himself in the power of the Chinese authorities. The latter countered with the intimation that, if Dent refused to

<hr>

[10] According to Anthony Daniell (*Report from the Select Committee,* 1840, Q. 1153, 1154), the older residents were not much disturbed. But all thought the government more in earnest than on any previous occasion. *Ibid.,* Q. 1097, 1098; Robert Inglis, Q. 610; Hunter, *Fan Kwae,* p. 138.

[11] Evidence of Robert Inglis, *Report from the Select Committee,* 1840, Q. 23; *Chinese Repository,* April, 1839, p. 622; Hunter, *Fan Kwae,* p. 139.

come voluntarily, he would be brought forcibly, for the high commissioner—"his eyes are sharp and his ears very long"—knew that he had six thousand chests of opium.[12] In the meantime, troops had begun to assemble along the river, and communications with Whampoa were cut off.

On March 22, Captain Elliot, who was at Macao, learned of the threatening turn of events at Canton.[13] His first step was to issue a notice ordering ships at the outer anchorages to proceed to Hongkong and to place themselves under Captain Blake of H. M. Sloop *Larne*. He then set out immediately for Canton and reached the foreign factories at sunset on the 24th, followed by a trail of war-junks and cruisers. With a touch of the melodramatic, he first hoisted the union jack and then inquired after the safety of Dent, whom he brought to the hall where the foreigners were assembling.

The day held further excitement for the beleaguered community. Upon the arrival of Captain Elliot, the alarm was given, the square cleared of all natives, and the doors of the factories closed and guarded by a force of soldiers armed with spears. A triple cordon of boats was formed in the river in front of the factories, while the rear was occupied by other bodies of armed men. The commissioner also issued orders requiring the departure of native servants. What devastation this produced in the hitherto well ordered *ménages* of the barbarians may be imagined. When all of the servants, "from the Compradore to the Cook," left their employers without notice, the situation became embarrassing. But the foreigners made of it all something of a lark, and "laughed rather

[12] This message was given to a delegation of four foreigners who interviewed the officials in place of Dent. As a matter of fact, Dent and Company had less than two thousand chests in its possession.

[13] One of the East India Company's agents managed to get word to him just before communications with Macao were cut off.

than groaned over the efforts to roast a capon, to boil an egg or a potato.''[14]

Their imprisonment was now a painful reality. No one was allowed to leave the square, and no messages could be sent to Whampoa or Macao save at the greatest danger to the bearer.[15] It was even forbidden to send provisions to the captives, whose plight might well have been desperate had not the resourceful hong merchants appeared with a solution. By permission of the authorities, they posted as watchmen their own coolies, whose chief duty, as it turned out, was to smuggle food to the harassed foreigners.[16]

The high commissioner also launched a direct assault upon the superintendent, blaming him for the non-delivery of the opium. For, when Elliot identified himself with the opium dealers by taking Dent under his wing, he diverted Lin's fire from the merchants to himself. And now he was ordered, in terms that left no room for ambiguity, to ''give clear commands to all foreigners to obey the orders, requiring them to take the opium on board the store ships, and speedily deliver it up.''[17] With this document Lin sent another edict urging the foreigners to make haste to obey and hinting at rich rewards if they would but capitulate. ''Polite tokens of our regard will be heaped upon you to overflowing and oh, ye foreigners, will not this be happiness indeed!''[18] The commissioner, it will be seen, possessed among his other virtues an extraordinary singleness of purpose. He had come to Canton to do one thing, to wipe out the opium trade. After that was accomplished there might be discussion and negotiation. Delivery of the drug was thus made prerequi-

14 Hunter, *Fan Kwae*, pp. 143-144.
15 *Chinese Repository*, April, 1839, p. 627.
16 Hunter, *Fan Kwae*, p. 142.
17 *China Corr.*, 1840, incl. 17 in no. 146.
18 *Chinese Repository*, April, 1839, pp. 628-633.

site to any relief of the barbarians' position. Lin Tse Hsu must first fulfill his mission.

His hand thus forced, Elliot felt compliance to be the only solution. The course of action which he proposed was apparently his own, reached without the counsel of older residents in Canton. All British opium was to be surrendered to the superintendent, together with sealed lists of all British-owned opium in the possession of British subjects. In return—this was the significant part of the announcement—Elliot assumed full responsibility, on behalf of the British government, for indemnifying those who committed opium into his hands to be delivered to the Chinese government.[19] The superintendent's decision came as a surprise to most of the foreign community. In the minds of many of the merchants there was still a strong suspicion that a compromise might be arranged with the persistent Lin. It is doubtful whether individual traders would have submitted as readily as did her Majesty's superintendent, but there was little objection when he proposed to buy the drug from its holders.[20] Elliot, after all, was as good a customer as any other, especially when the market was suffering from complete collapse.[21]

On March 27 Captain Elliot notified the imperial commissioner of his submission, requesting information on the procedure to be followed. The superintendent stated that the quantity of British-controlled opium was 20,283 chests, a figure which the Chinese accepted as correct. Lin ordered the following course of action: opium in the

[19] *China Corr.*, 1840, incl. 20 in no. 146.

[20] Evidence on the attitude of the British community comes chiefly from testimony given in 1840 before a committee of Parliament. The merchants were fighting for compensation and were interested in making their case as strong as possible. Almost unanimously they insisted that the opium would not have been surrendered if Elliot had not assumed liability.

[21] There was some suspicion in Canton that Elliot was exceeding his instructions. But these had never been published in full, and the superintendent assured the merchants that his powers were adequate.

foreign factories or on board ships at Whampoa was to be surrendered first. Receiving ships at Lintin or elsewhere were to station themselves near the Bogue to await the visit of the commissioner, while vessels on the east coast were to be recalled. With this much agreed upon, Elliot moved to restore the liberty of the foreigners. But the tone of warm approval with which Lin had greeted his original compliance was noticeably lacking in the commissioner's reply. No thought of returning the servants could be entertained until orders for delivering the opium from the storeships had been signed. Evidently the magnitude of the task of transferring more than twenty thousand chests had not impressed Lin as deeply as it had Elliot. Eventually, however, the commissioner was won over to a plan of using the deputy superintendent as transfer officer. Thereupon he agreed that, as the delivery of the opium was accomplished, the privileges of the foreigners should be progressively restored.[22]

The commissioner had now completed half his task, but he must still assure himself that the opium traffic would not appear again, once the hand of reproof was withdrawn. Foreign merchants of all nations had already signed a voluntary pledge neither to deal in the drug nor to introduce it into the Chinese Empire in the future.[23] This document did not impress Lin Tse Hsu, and he submitted his own form of bond to Captain Elliot and to the general chamber of commerce. The barbarians considered

[22] *China Corr.*, 1840, incls. 18, 19, 21-24, 26-29 in no. 146. The American, the Dutch, and the French consuls were also commanded to submit a statement of the opium in the possession of their nationals. After some negotiation with the representatives of the United States and the Netherlands, Lin accepted their word that none of the opium was owned by citizens of the two states. The American report was not strictly accurate. See note 29, *postea. Chinese Repository*, April, 1839, pp. 639-640, 641-642, 646-648, 651-652.

[23] *China Corr.*, 1840, incl. 7 in no. 148; *Chinese Repository*, April, 1839, pp. 636-637.

it a "monstrous instrument."[24] In both its sense and its patronizing phraseology it was utterly repugnant to them. Not only were the merchants in Canton ordered to withdraw from the opium trade, but they were to promise, for their governments, that the manufacture of opium and its introduction into China should be prohibited. In the future, "any merchant vessel . . . that may be found to bring opium shall be immediately and entirely confiscated . . . and the parties shall be left to suffer death at the hands of the Celestial Court; such punishment they will readily submit to."[25] Captain Elliot declined the commissioner's proposal as tactfully as possible. But to Palmerston he wrote that "if ever we are free the more practical and fit reply will be the withdrawal of all the Queen's subjects from the grasp of this Government."[26] Lin's bond required commitments for the future that Elliot had no power to give, and in any case, British merchants could not involve themselves in such an agreement, made with a capricious and inept government. The Chinese authorities thus lost their former semi-ally, the British superintendent, who had been thoroughly alienated by the commissioner's tactics.

Lin now shifted his attention to the delivery of the opium, leaving on April 10 for the Bogue, where the transfer was to take place. The English had found their original account of 20,283 chests to be inaccurate. There

[24] The words are Elliot's.

[25] The text appears as incl. 1 in no. 148 in *China Corr.*, 1840, and in the *Chinese Repository*, April, 1839, p. 650. This bond must be clearly distinguished from the relatively harmless form which the hong merchants had been compelled to give for all ships docking at Whampoa (except those of the company during its monopoly). In the first place, the wording of the new bond was much more stringent, prescribing the death penalty for offenders; and in the second place, the attitude of the authorities towards the Lintin depot in the past had been such that all opium cargoes could be left there in perfect safety before the vessel proceeded to Whampoa.

[26] Elliot to Palmerston, 6 April 1839, *China Corr.*, 1840, no. 148.

were eight more at Macao, while two Parsi firms were deficient by some five hundred chests. Elliot, to fulfill his agreement, had been obliged to purchase from Dent and Company, to whom a consignment had recently come from India, enough to make up the difference. In return he issued bills on the London treasury for more than £63,000.[27] The transfer of the main quantity of opium from private hands to those of her Majesty's representative and thence to the Chinese government was effected by an elaborate system of receipts. Those which Elliot gave to the owners of the drug specified no rate at which compensation was to be paid, but merely gave the beneficiary the right to indemnity for the number of chests he had delivered.

Of the total supply in Chinese waters about 15,000 chests were at Lintin when the surrender was demanded, and about 5000 at other ports on the coast.[28] The largest amount turned over by any one firm was 7000 chests. Russell and Company, the most important of the American houses, produced some 1500 chests, all held on British account.[29] Under the management of the deputy superintendent of trade, the business of transfer moved forward with fair harmony and despatch. When, on April 19, one-fourth of the deliveries had been completed, the servants of the foreigners were allowed to return. By May 2 more than 15,000 chests had passed into the possession of the commissioner, who then permitted licensed passage-boats to run, ships at Whampoa to open their

---

[27] Payable at twelve months' sight at the rate of 500 dollars per chest. Elliot to John Backhouse, 3 July 1839, *Additional Papers rel. to China*, 1840, no. 2 and incls.

[28] Hunter, *Fan Kwae*, p. 138.

[29] None actually owned by Americans figured in the transaction, although there was a small amount in China at the time. ''The Americans had not delivered any American-owned opium, of which we [Russell and Company] held about fifty chests of Turkey.'' *Ibid.*, p. 146.

holds for trade, and all foreigners with the exception of sixteen alleged opium dealers to leave at their pleasure.[30] Many of the barbarians left Canton as soon as the way was opened, but Captain Elliot chose to remain with the sixteen who were held as hostages for the balance of the opium.[31] At two o'clock in the morning, May 21, the last chest was placed in Chinese hands, and on the 24th the last of the British community went to Macao, leaving the foreign factories in the possession of some twenty-five Americans.[32]

Meanwhile, the destiny of the surrendered drug remained in doubt. At one time it was rumored that the whole quantity was to be sent up to Peking, a course which Elliot thought "irreconcilable with any purposes of destruction."[33] An imperial rescript ended the uncertainty, and Lin, now promoted to be viceroy of Nanking, announced that the ceremony would take place at Chunhow, where the opium had been temporarily stored. The commissioner proved as relentless in dealing with the confiscated drug as with the barbarians themselves. The opium, which had been stored in a bamboo enclosure, was closely guarded by sentinels, who admitted spectators only upon the presentation of a ticket. Some fifty officers and five hundred workmen assisted in the work of de-

[30] Elliot to Palmerston, 6 April 1839, *China Corr.*, 1840, no. 148, addendum dated 4 May and incl. 13; *Chinese Repository*, May, 1839, pp. 15-18.

[31] Public notice, 11 May 1839, *China Corr.*, 1840, incl. 1 in no. 150; *Chinese Repository*, May, 1839, pp. 20-21.

[32] Hunter, *Fan Kwae*, p. 145; *Chinese Repository*, May, 1839, p. 31.

[33] Elliot to Palmerston, 19 May 1839, *China Corr.*, 1840, no. 150, addendum dated 27 May; *Chinese Repository*, May, 1839, pp. 36-37. Elliot adhered with curious obstinacy to his belief that opium might still be legalized. He thought it possible that the twenty thousand chests would enable the Chinese authorities to establish a government monopoly, "with probably some provision for the cessation of imports for one year, and perhaps a limited and annually decreasing amount." Thus the government could make the native consumer pay such prices for his opium as would reimburse foreign claimants and leave a handsome surplus for the imperial treasury.

struction. Each ball was broken into pieces and thrown into a trench containing about two feet of water, where it was mixed with salt and lime, and, when thoroughly decomposed, the mass was sluiced off. The process was laborious and slow, averaging not more than a thousand chests daily. One of the foreign witnesses testified, "The degree of care and fidelity, with which the whole work was conducted, far exceeded our expectations."[34]

The first chapter in the struggle had now been brought to a close, but the tension among foreigners was in nowise relieved. They had congregated at Macao and other anchorages, where their future seemed at best uncertain. Notwithstanding the efforts of Captain Elliot to involve it in the controversy, the Portuguese government of Macao was preserving strict neutrality.[35] The rules which Lin had prescribed for the resumption of trade were so onerous that Elliot had replied with the only weapon at his command—a boycott of Canton by British shipping.[36] British merchants at Macao chose to regard the superintendent's injunction as a positive order, and they remained almost unanimous in their refusal to conduct trade on the terms proposed. The situation, then, as far as it concerned the imperial commissioner and her Majesty's superintendent of trade, had reached an impasse.[37]

[34] The Rev. Dr. C. E. Bridgman, *Chinese Repository*, June, 1839, pp. 70-77.

[35] *China Corr.*, 1840, incl. 2 in no. 149.

[36] *Chinese Repository*, May, 1839, pp. 22-25.

[37] In reply to an edict of Lin's urging British shipping to return to Canton, Elliot issued a document, only slightly less florid than the commissioner's, in which he reviewed the grievances of his countrymen. A good deal of Elliot's statement was sheer nonsense. The breach of faith with which he charged Lin seems unjustified. As Eames (*English in China*, p. 383) remarks, "The confinement at Canton came to an end long before the whole of the opium had been yielded up. When it is remembered how slowly things move in China, and how utterly regardless of time is the Chinese mind, the more accurate view would appear to be that, judged by Chinese

On the Chinese side, the questions still unsettled were the resumption of trade and the anti-opium bond. As for the British, Captain Elliot had convinced himself that no further relations with the Chinese could be tolerated until they made reparation for the confiscated opium and gave some guarantee of security and freedom. Both leaders were contending for the adherence of the British community, to whom enforced idleness was bound to become irksome.

Elliot had stated his attitude towards the bond in unequivocal terms, but the Americans were less apprehensive. Their willingness to do business on Chinese terms presumably raised some questions in the minds of British merchants, hitherto remarkably loyal to the superintendent.[38] Lin moved to encourage defection, and his overtures might well have resulted in the secession of at least some of the British community had not a new issue intervened. A party of foreign sailors, ashore at Hongkong, entered with roistering abandon into an affray with the Chinese, in which one of the latter was killed. The jury convened by Captain Elliot convicted five seamen of riot, but the murderer remained undiscovered.[39] With the Chinese authorities, who invoked their favorite doctrine of "a life for a life," there could be no peace until a victim had been given up. To obtain expiation for the murder of Lin Wei Hi thus became one of the commissioner's objectives. The homicide also had its effect on the status of the British community, which hitherto had found refuge

standards, the High Commissioner was unusually punctilious in the fulfilment of his pledges.''

[38] American vessels were signing an expurgated version of the bond, in which nothing was said of the death penalty. But the new regulations for foreign trade make it clear that the Chinese had not abandoned their claim. *Chinese Repository*, June, 1839, p. 82.

[39] For documents on the Lin Wei Hi affair see the *Chinese Repository*, Aug., 1839, pp. 181-194, and *China Corr.*, 1840, nos. 154, 155, and incls.

at Macao. It was soon made evident that this welcome was being sorely tried, and when, under pressure from Lin Tse Hsu, the Portuguese governor declared his inability to give further protection, the exiles were hastily transferred to Hongkong.[40] As a sanctuary the new station was less than ideal, but here they were to remain throughout most of September.

There was no doubt in the minds either of Captain Elliot or of British merchants that a prompt and fundamental change in Anglo-Chinese relations must be the outcome of the crisis. But both were willing to contemplate a temporary commercial arrangement. The indiscretion of the Chinese offered an opening. Government cruisers in Macao harbor attacked and burned the Spanish brig *Bilbaino* under the mistaken impression that she was an opium trader.[41] The *Bilbaino* affair created an opportunity which Captain Elliot was glad to seize. It was indeed possible that his excellency the imperial commissioner "would be disposed to put an end to a state of things productive of fatal mistakes."[42] The tenacious Lin was, in fact, alarmed at the protracted deadlock. In crushing the illicit trade he had brought apparent ruin to legitimate commerce, which was of much greater consequence to the Chinese state than its officials affected to believe.[43]

Weeks of dreary diplomatic sparring followed. From it all emerged a plan of carrying on trade in the outer waters, with British ships submitting to search instead of

[40] The arrival of H. M. S. *Volage* contributed a slight sense of security to the British fugitives.

[41] *Chinese Repository*, Sept., 1839, p. 271; *Additional Papers rel. to China*, IV, 1840, incl. 1 in no. 1.

[42] Elliot to Palmerston, 16 Nov. 1839, *ibid.*, no. 1.

[43] I use the word "apparent" because, although British shipping declined to come into port, British goods were being sold at Canton with the Americans acting as agents.

signing the bond. By September 22 an agreement had been reached, which left unmentioned the questions of the bond and the murder of Lin Wei Hi.[44] But even before the *modus operandi* was published, a breach in the ranks of British merchants doomed it to failure. In the middle of October, the ship *Thomas Coutts* from India entered the Canton River. Her captain deliberately proceeded to the Bogue and signed the bond in its most outrageous form— that if the smallest bit of opium were found on the ship, "I am willing to deliver up the transgressor, and he shall be punish to death according to the correctness law of Heavenly Dynasty."[45]

This incident revealed to Elliot the difficulty of holding the mercantile community longer in check and to Lin the possibility of getting British signatures to his original bond.[46] The commissioner renewed his demand for the bond and for the murderer of Lin Wei Hi in terms even more categorical than before. It was obvious to all that, as Lin asserted, "if the bond be not settled, there can by no means be any indulgence allowed."[47] The British could never accede to the form prescribed by the Chinese, nor could they give up an innocent man to be punished as a murderer. Since a large force of junks and fire-ships had collected at Hongkong, the fugitives took up a new position at Tangku.[48] And a month later the imperial commis-

[44] Elliot to Palmerston, 16 Nov. 1839, *Additional Papers rel. to China,* IV, 1840, no. 1 and incls.; Elliot to Palmerston, 21 Oct. 1839, *Additional Corr. rel. to China,* 1840, no. 1; *Chinese Repository,* Oct., 1839, pp. 324-326.

[45] *Chinese Repository,* Dec., 1839, p. 440; Oct., 1839, p. 327. Needless to indicate, the bond was of Chinese composition.

[46] *Ibid.,* p. 326. Enough points of difference had already been disclosed at a conference between the hong merchants and foreign merchants to make it doubtful whether the plan of trading in the outer waters would ever have worked.

[47] *Additional Papers rel. to China,* IV, 1840, incl. 26 in no. 1; *Chinese Repository,* Dec., 1839, pp. 430-433.

[48] *Chinese Repository,* Oct., 1839, pp. 327-328.

sioner formally excluded from trade with the Chinese Empire all British shipping save the *Thomas Coutts* and the *Royal Saxon*, which had also signed the hateful bond.[49]

While matters stood at a deadlock that could be broken only by the application of force, we may digress to examine the effect of the commissioner's measures on the opium trade in China and on the opium system in India. As far as legal commerce was concerned, Lin had succeeded only in forcing it into new channels. Conducted through the medium of the Americans, British trade in 1839 was more profitable than in any year since 1834.[50] At the outset, his severity towards native and foreign dealers produced an almost complete collapse in the opium traffic. Shipments already on their way were hastily sent on to Manila or landed at Singapore, to be sold for such nominal prices as two hundred dollars per chest or less. But despite the temporary stoppage of deliveries, a demand still remained. Even during the detention of the foreigners in Canton there were rumors that a quantity had been sold on the east coast. In June, again, reports of trade on the coast were current, whereupon the *Canton Register* remarked fervently, "We trust the controlers of these [vessels] will not hoist any flag belonging to civilized nations."[51]

Some of the drug destined for this market was bought at ridiculous prices in Singapore, whence it was carried to China both by junks and by foreign ships. On one occasion, a captain took on board several chests at a Chinese anchorage, guided only by orders to go to Singapore and deliver a sealed letter to his consignee there. No word of

49 *Ibid.*, Dec., 1839, p. 440.
50 Elliot to Palmerston, 28 Nov. 1839, *Additional Papers rel. to China*, IV, 1840, no. 4.
51 Quoted in the *Chinese Repository*, June, 1839, p. 112.

the confiscation had yet reached the Straits, and when it was learned that a vessel had brought opium from China, the inference was that imports had been effectually prohibited. The agent was thus able to buy some seven hundred chests of opium at an average of 250 dollars, which were later sold on the east coast for 2500 dollars per chest.[52]

In October, 1839, some fifteen or twenty opium vessels were visiting the island of Chusan and other points north and east of Canton.[53] In the nine months following the foreigners' capitulation, no less than eight thousand chests were delivered for consumption. Prices during the early part of the period seem to have gone well over a thousand dollars per chest, but by January, 1840, they had been stabilized at from seven to nine hundred dollars.[54] Foreign distributors were assisted by well organized bands of native smugglers. Contraband vessels now went armed to the teeth, while, in many cases, Europeans equipped their native colleagues with muskets. The smugglers took the drug in small packages, often under the cover of night. There were distressing rumors, apparently well vouched for, of violence and conflict, even to the deliberate murder of Chinese officials by foreign opium-runners.[55]

In Canton, under the immediate influence of the commissioner's presence, the trade experienced more adversity. Prices, which had been extremely low just before his arrival, now rose as high as three thousand dollars per chest.[56] But British dealers could not take such advantage

[52] Hunter, *Fan Kwae*, pp. 78-79.

[53] *Chinese Repository*, Oct., 1839, p. 328; Feb., 1840, p. 552.

[54] H. N. Clarke, agent of the East India Company, to J. C. Melvill, 30 Jan. 1840, I. O. China Corr., X.

[55] *Chinese Repository*, Jan., 1840, pp. 442, 496; *Canton Press*, 2 and 9 Nov. 1839.

[56] *Canton Register*, 29 Oct. 1839; Hunter, *Fan Kwae*, p. 77.

of the high rate as they could on the east coast. And Americans, though they enabled the British to transact their legitimate business without actually entering port, remained, for the time being at least, faithful to the commitments they had given.[57] To those who persisted in bringing opium Elliot had no intention of giving comfort. When, during the negotiations over the resumption of trade, Lin charged that newly-arrived vessels were harboring opium, the superintendent acted at once to clear himself of any shadow of complicity.[58] He instructed the commanders of British ships not carrying the drug to appear before him within forty-eight hours and to take oath to that effect. Similarly he ordered all British shipping engaged in the trade to depart "from this harbor and coast."[59] They may have departed from the harbor, but the chances are small that they left the coast. For the traffic went merrily on, with the difference that Canton had now been displaced as the principal market.[60]

Commissioner Lin failed no less dismally in his attack against Chinese dealers and smokers. Even before his arrival, addicts had been warned to mend their ways on pain of death. Three months later Lin announced omi-

[57] Morse points out that, although British merchants at Canton had bound themselves as individuals to abstain from future trade in opium, there had been no declaration of policy from British firms as a whole. *International Relations*, I, 231.

[58] Lin's suspicions were probably not unjustified. "There is much opium on board the English vessels now lying in the roads of this place [Macao], which will never be returned to the country from whence it came. A sale of it must be made here on the coast, and I shall not be surprised to hear of its being smuggled in under American colors." Captain George C. Read of U. S. frigate *Columbia* to the secretary of the navy, quoted in Dennett, *Americans in Eastern Asia*, p. 123.

[59] *China Corr.*, 1840, incl. 3 in no. 159.

[60] According to Captain Elliot, "He [Lin] found the traffic stagnant; he has made it flourish in a degree and to an extent that it has never reached before." Elliot to Palmerston, 28 Nov. 1839, *Additional Papers, No. IV*, 1840, no. 4.

nously that "the thundering wrath of the Celestial Majesty has been aroused, the axe of the executioner is whetted, and the existing laws must be enforced in all their extremity, awarding death to the guilty." The lengthy document which contains this pronouncement outlined in elaborate detail the form of correction to be applied to various classes of Chinese. Literati, subordinate officials, people of Canton, merchants of other provinces, and villagers—all were given special attention. Inquiries were to be made by local magistrates and lapses from grace to be prevented by a system of tithing-men. Smokers were allowed two months to give up the habit. Specific regulations also governed native shipping and the movements of merchants from other parts of the empire. Local officials who "decidedly fear difficulties and are fond of their ease" were urged to associate with themselves graduated scholars and other gentlemen, "who are personally pure and delight themselves in good."[61] A subsequent proclamation extended the period of grace to eighteen months beginning July 6, 1839.[62] There was no lack of picturesque quality in the warnings which issued from the commissioner's headquarters. "You, who may escape the net till that time, in the twinkling of an eye will become headless men. . . . Oh, alas!"[63]

Lin's activities were not merely prohibitory. In May, 1840, there was established an opium refuge, "outside the Yungtsing moon (or gate of eternal purity, the same gate that leads to the execution ground)," where those accused of smoking could experiment with the cure of soli-

[61] J. L. Shuck, *Portfolio Chinensis*, pp. 1-79. Lin, it may be said, had few illusions about the integrity of the average official. "If the officers are reckless of crime, their guilt ought to exceed that of the common people. If Superiors have no self-esteem it will be exceedingly difficult to execute the laws and have a name for justice."

[62] *Chinese Repository*, Jan., 1840, p. 496.

[63] *Ibid.*, Oct., 1840, pp. 404-408.

tary confinement. To persons desiring to break off the habit, medicinal pills were promised; "those who were unwilling or cannot leave off, must just wait till they die of the disease they themselves have engendered."[64]

The designs of the commissioner against native offenders, nevertheless, proved quite as futile as those directed against foreign importers. By the time the eighteen months' grace had expired, the Chinese were being worsted in the appeal to arms and the doughty Lin had passed from the scene.[65] Upon him was vented the imperial anger for having involved the state in an unprofitable war. "In fact," the Son of Heaven announced, "you have been as if your arms were tied without knowing what to do; it appears that you are no better than a wooden image; when I think to myself on all these things, I am filled with anger and melancholy."[66]

If the crisis brought about by the commissioner had but little ultimate effect upon the practices of British merchants and upon the habits of Chinese subjects, its permanent results in India were no greater. The first news from China, of course, brought anxiety to the monopolists in Calcutta. An effective prohibition of opium would hold serious consequences for the Indian revenue. The Indian drug supply consisted of some fifty thousand chests, less than half of which were in Chinese waters at the time of the confiscation. There was not only a market for the remainder to be considered, but the even more troublesome problem of the future.

At the outset, the government of India decided against any sudden change in the monopoly system.[67] But in the

[64] *Ibid.*, May, 1840, pp. 55-56.

[65] In February, 1840, he was made viceroy of Canton. He remained in that post until he was cashiered seven months later. *Ibid.*, Feb., 1840, p. 552.

[66] *Ibid.*, Oct., 1840, pp. 412-413.

[67] Governor-general in council to the court of directors, 3 July 1839 (separate revenue), I. O. Letters from Bengal and India, XXI.

summer of 1839 orders were issued for the abandonment of four of the sub-deputy agencies that had been created during the opium boom a few years before, and in the following year, the price paid to ryots was reduced.[68] Beyond that the government could only await developments, for, as the governor-general, Lord Auckland, informed the board of customs, salt, and opium, none could "pronounce upon the period when a change in the opium system might come to be considered, although I was inclined to believe in the extreme probability of such a change becoming necessary."[69] Meanwhile the demand for the drug must be met in such a way as to prevent any exceptional rise in price and to avoid giving encouragement to foreign producers.

In London, however, the board of control felt that the crisis offered an opportunity to break the intimate connection between the Indian administration and the opium business. In a letter to the court of directors the board made the rather unoriginal proposal that the monopoly be abolished and a tax imposed upon the drug.[70] Unhappily for the reformers, their arguments were a familiar story to the directors, who knew where to turn for the answer. Basing their reply upon the select committee reports of 1831 and 1832, they showed that the monopoly rested solidly upon the sanction of Parliament. They went on to assert that the monopoly was, in fact, a tax, and that the substitution of an export duty would not decrease the output. At a time of such uncertainty, to alter the system would be suicidal.[71]

---

[68] Governor-general to the court of directors, 6 May 1840 (separate revenue), *ibid.*, XXV.

[69] *Ibid.*

[70] Board of control to the court of directors, 13 Jan. 1840, I. O. Letters from the Board, XIII, no. 5008.

[71] Court of directors to the board of control, 2 April 1840, I. O. Letters from the East India Company to the Board of Control, XVI, no. 5348.

By the end of 1841 it had become apparent that the market for Indian opium would suffer no lasting damage. Exporters were still buying at the Calcutta sales and were paying, on the average, prices above those of 1837-1838. During 1840 the resident at Indore reported that "a knowledge of the decisive measures intended to be pursued by the British Government toward China appears to have had a remarkable effect in reviving the declining commerce of those who dealt in Malwa opium." And in December, 1841, the board of customs, salt, and opium suggested the removal of the restrictions on cultivation that had been in force for the preceding year. To this proposal the government of Bengal gladly agreed, being "very unwilling to continue any restrictions likely to dishearten the Poppy Cultivators."[72] While the war in China was still being fought, in fine, the opium monopoly returned to its normal basis, save that the abandoned sub-deputy agencies, unprofitable by any reckoning, were not reëstablished.

There remains the problem of whether the struggle which was to take place can be accurately described as an "opium war." Historians have repeatedly laid to rest the ghost of fighting a "war to force opium on the Chinese," but with singular persistence, it reappears in anti-opium pamphlets and undergraduate textbooks. The other point of view—that war, proceeding inevitably from Chinese exclusiveness, was the answer of the West to the contemptuous attitude affected by the East—has found ample support both at the time and subsequently. One of the statements most commonly quoted is that of John Quincy Adams, who, before the Massachusetts Historical Society, demanded that China play its commercial and diplomatic game according to western rules. For him the war was something of a missionary crusade to bring

72 I. O. Bengal Separate Consultations, 19 Jan. 1842.

light to a government in darkness. As for the opium, "This is a mere incident to the dispute; but no more the cause of the war, than the throwing overboard of the tea in Boston Harbor was the cause of the American revolution."[73]

Qualified writers, in general, have held that the struggle transcended a mere disagreement over opium, without necessarily subscribing to the Adams dogma that China was bound to order her foreign relations in accordance with western usages. At the risk of merely repeating the interpretations of Morse, Sargent, and others, it may be asserted once again that, as far as the British were concerned, only in the light of its immediate occasion can the conflict be called an opium war. The most that can be said is that incompatible views of trade and diplomatic intercourse made a war probable; the opium question and the peculiar methods that Commissioner Lin applied to it made a resort to force inevitable. And the opium dispute condemned the British government to fight its battle seemingly on the most unsavory of issues.

On the British side, three sets of interests were most intimately concerned in the events leading to the war, interests represented by the foreign office and its servant Captain Elliot, by the merchants connected with the China trade, and by the government of India. None of these would have advocated war for the sake of obtaining a placid market for Indian opium. Elliot, as we have seen, had no affection for the drug trade, and he deplored the reliance of the Indian revenue upon it. Up to the crisis of 1839, at least, he had consistently refused to give support to violators of Chinese law. And, in the previous year, he had even gone so far as to offer his assistance to the Chinese in driving smugglers from the Canton River. Commissioner Lin alienated the sympathies of the

[73] *Chinese Repository*, May, 1842, pp. 275-289.

British superintendent not by the end that he sought to gain but by the means which he adopted. Elliot freely admitted the right of the Chinese to confiscate contraband, but instead of effecting an outright seizure, the commissioner had elected to hold the entire foreign community as hostage for the delivery of the opium.

Henceforth, nothing but war would satisfy the superintendent. On April 3, 1839, he penned a despatch to Palmerston—the tone of the document suggests badly frayed nerves—arguing that the only adequate answer "to all these unjust violences should be made in the form of a swift and heavy blow unprefaced by one word of written communication."[74] Once the foreign residents were released, he shepherded the British from Canton as quickly as possible, resolved that they should not return until full reparation had been made. From this time on, his aim was to have no more dealings than necessary with Chinese officials until the foreign office had acted.

When news of the crisis in China reached Whitehall, Palmerston stated the position of her Majesty's government in terms that repeat in substance the views of Captain Elliot.[75] The Chinese, he observed, had every right to prohibit the importation of opium and to seize it when it was brought in illegally. But such laws must be enforced steadily and equitably. Her Majesty's government would have just cause for complaint if the Chinese government had suddenly pounced on the opium fleet, without first punishing its own guilty officials.[76] But the methods of Commissioner Lin were still less defensible. The only

74 Elliot to Palmerston, 3 April 1839, I. O. China Corr., I.

75 Palmerston to Elliot, 4 Nov. 1839, *ibid.*

76 Palmerston to Elliot, 4 Nov. 1839, I. O. China Corr., I. It is just as well that Palmerston did not have to deal with such a contingency. He might have protested that the Chinese action was "at least capricious, if not tainted with intentional deceipt [*sic*]." But his case would have been dubious.

answer was to act "towards the Chinese in the manner in which the Chinese are wont to proceed themselves,— that is, to begin by striking a Blow, and to give explanations afterwards." The charge of unfair means recurs time and again in foreign office despatches, from Palmerston's first declaration of policy to the treaty of Nanking. To seize contraband by direct assault upon the guilty parties was the right of a sovereign state, but to extract it by such indiscriminate pressure as Lin had applied was an outrage. The primary motive of Great Britain in taking up arms was to obtain redress for this outrage and security for the future, not to pull the chestnuts of Indian revenue from the fire.

British merchants in China shared Elliot's eagerness for a strong policy. There is no hint that they were appealing for such pressure as would legalize the drug trade itself, but they held that the home government was partly responsible for their plight. They conceived that "British subjects have carried on this trade with the sanction, implied, if not openly expressed of their own government."[77] The feeling of the Canton community was perhaps reflected by one of its veterans, when he referred to the East India Company as the "father of all smuggling and smugglers."[78] In general, however, merchants were much less concerned about the future of the opium trade than about the arrangements that were to govern legal commerce. The abolition of the company's monopoly in China had been accompanied by no new adjustment to conditions on the part of the Chinese. When, therefore,

[77] *China Corr.*, 1840, incl. 1 in no. 151.

[78] *Canton Register*, 29 Jan. 1839. "When the East India Company was growing it and selling it, and there was a declaration of the Houses of Lords and Commons, with all the bench of bishops at their back, that it was inexpedient to do it [the opium monopoly] away, I think our moral scruples need not have been so very great." Evidence of William Jardine, *Report from the Select Committee*, 1840, Q. 1498.

a possible *casus belli* arose, mercantile interests in both England and China were ready with their counsel. In the memorials which they forwarded to Whitehall, opium received little emphasis, aside from the question of compensation for that destroyed by Lin.[79] Many of the merchants would willingly have sacrificed their share in the drug trade for less limited commercial opportunities and personal liberty. The London East India and China Association stated flatly that, if Chinese objections to the trade seemed insuperable, the association would not advocate its continuance.[80] To the merchants, then, the war was to effect an opening of China rather than to assure the prosperity of the opium traffic.

Yet it was the activities of opium traders, chiefly British, that provoked the harsh measures of Commissioner Lin and thus brought to the surface the latent conflict between the two countries. For more than half a century they had defied the law of the empire, abetted by the venality of local officials. Opium vessels had pushed up the coast into ports prohibited to foreign traders, and they had even made of the Canton River a contraband thoroughfare. Opium smuggling had been allowed to go so long without effective challenge that western merchants came to regard it as an integral part of the Chinese scene. Attempts to interfere with it seemed almost to savor of impertinence.[81] It is small wonder that the

[79] See, for example, Jardine to Palmerston, 26 Oct. 1839, I. O. China Corr., I, in which one of the largest of Canton opium merchants suggests that the foreign secretary demand an ample apology, payment for the opium seized, an equitable commercial treaty, and the opening of at least three additional ports to foreign commerce.

[80] London East India and China Association to Palmerston, 2 Nov. 1839, *Memorials from British Merchants*, 1840, no. 7.

[81] There were those, for example, among the merchants who disputed the right of the Chinese to seize opium on board the storeships at Lintin, although it was freely admitted that the island was Chinese territory. In other

barbarians stood incredulous before the brusque tactics of Lin Tse Hsu. They had been given due warning, contrary to Palmerston's assertion,[82] but it is doubtful whether any verbal warning would have been effective. The Chinese had been so lavish with fearsome proclamations that one may understand, if not sympathize with, the foreigners' inability to sense the new note. Their total impression of Chinese officials had been gained from their dealings with those of the Canton area, and they failed to distinguish between a local officer and an imperial commissioner, one who stood as the emperor's *alter ego* and who represented his sovereign's resolve to have done with opium, whatever the cost. As a result, the foreign community remained, even after the seizure, a badly mystified group.

The government of India also had its stake in the opium crisis. Merchants in India whose opium had been confiscated were quick to point to the complicity of the company and to lay their misfortunes at its door. The drug trade, the Calcutta chamber of commerce alleged, "has been fostered into its recent magnitude, by every means that ingenuity could devise on the part of the British government in India . . . who have consulted on every occasion the wants and wishes of Chinese consumers, who afforded compensation when Opium, on reaching China, was found by the Chinese to be inferior to the standard guaranteed by the State,—and who even on occasions made direct consignments to their agents in China, that they might practically learn, whether con-

words, contraband could be confiscated only in the act of smuggling—a doctrine which, if generally adopted, would embarrass preventive systems far more efficient than that of the Middle Kingdom. *Report from the Select Committee*, 1840, evidence of A. Matheson, Q. 2280, 2283; William Jardine, *ibid.*, Q. 1760; Sargent, *Anglo-Chinese Commerce and Diplomacy*, p. 82.

[82] Palmerston to Elliot, 4 Nov. 1839, I. O. China Corr., I.

signments packed in new forms would be acceptable to the people of that Empire."[83]

However much or little responsibility the opium monopoly must assume for the situation that led to war, there is no evidence to show that British policy was influenced by it. The company's official interest in its narcotic product ceased with the auction sale. What happened in China was the concern of the merchants and of the foreign office.[84] This attitude the government of India preserved throughout the dispute. When, for example, Captain Elliot's secret despatch recommending immediate military action was sent to the board of control, the president made the following notation: "India, as India, appears to be only concerned in the Chinese question, inasmuch as . . . if the Chinese will not eat [sic] opium, the Indian revenue must materially suffer; but it is presumed that it is quite out of the question to suppose that the British Government would be justified in compelling the Chinese to eat opium. The question, therefore . . . seems entirely one for the consideration departmentally of the foreign office."[85] There can be no reasonable doubt that the course of action which the British government followed was charted in Canton and in London, not in Calcutta. The breach with China was intended to serve interests other than those of Indian opium.

But there were two parties to the quarrel, and, as in many conflicts, the opposing camps differed in their interpretation of causes and aims. To the Chinese it was an

[83] Memorial from the Calcutta chamber of commerce to the privy council (undated), ibid.

[84] Those responsible for the opium monopoly were, in fact, keenly interested in conditions in the China market. Not until later in the century, however, did they become involved in matters of Anglo-Chinese diplomacy.

[85] Memorandum by the president of the board of control (undated), I. O. China Corr., I.

opium war, pure and simple.[86] Commissioner Lin came to
Canton with an imperial mandate to exterminate the
trade in opium and thus to save the nation from moral
disintegration and the loss of its specie. More reckless
than he knew, he laid his axe at the root of the tree and
directed his measures against the entire foreign community. After a preliminary attempt to single out the
principal British importers, he turned to the superintendent of trade. From the latter he obtained with astonish-
ing promptness, a promise not only of the opium held on
the ships at Lintin but of the five thousand chests at ports
on the east coast.

Despite his gauche and arrogant diplomacy, one cannot help but regard Lin Tse Hsu as magnificent in his
failure. Unhappily the issue, tolerably clear at first, was
obscured by his insistence upon the preposterous form of
bond and by the homicide case. The central position
which opium occupied in his thought is rather patheti-
cally revealed in two letters which he addressed to Queen
Victoria.[87] In the first of these he proposed the measure
that was adopted in substance seventy years later—"we
in this land forbidding the use of it,—and you, in the
nations under your dominion, forbidding its manufacture." If the opium dispute could be settled, there remained, in the Chinese view, no obstacle to the resumption of normal trade relations. The canons of polite
international intercourse, the equality of sovereign
states, and the grievances of the barbarians in China
seem not to have penetrated Chinese consciousness. The
celestial empire, her officials often claimed, rules over ten
thousand states, who bring tribute to her. Years of isolation had produced an incredible case of myopia, and ignorance of other lands had bred an overweening sense of

[86] See Morse, *International Relations*, I, 253.
[87] *Chinese Repository*, May, 1839, pp. 9-12; Feb., 1840, pp. 497-503.

superiority. If Chinese statesmen had possessed more discernment, they might have been able to obtain from the British prohibition of the opium trade as a price for a commercial treaty. As it was, their policy led only to the forcible wresting of concessions, for which they received in return nothing but humiliation. Yet the actions of Commissioner Lin, however deficient in sportsmanship they may have seemed to British residents, implied a sense of public morality that might well have been envied by the East India Company.

CHAPTER VII

THE OPIUM QUESTION IN CHINA, 1840-1856

OF the developments in China the British Parliament heard nothing officially until the spring of 1840. The two states drifted into war almost imperceptibly to the ministry, to say nothing of Parliament as a whole. No papers on the subject had been laid before the House of Commons, though ominous rumors were afloat that the government of India had been instructed to prepare for active measures and that Captain Elliot, to fulfill his bargain with the Chinese, had been obliged to make purchases in the open market.[1] But of details little was known.

On March 19, 1840, a question was finally raised from the floor of the House. In reply, Lord John Russell made it quite plain that the ministry proposed to stand by Captain Elliot's diagnosis of the *malaise* and to accept his prescription of the remedy. As the leader of the House outlined British aims, her Majesty's forces were to obtain, first, reparation for the insults to the superintendent of trade and British subjects at Canton; second, indemnification for the opium surrendered to Commissioner Lin; and finally, assurance of security for the persons and property of British subjects who might choose to resort to China for trade in the future.[2]

The opposition was ready to take advantage of its op-

---

[1] 3 *Hansard*, LII, 1155-1156, 1221. In the previous August, Lord Ellenborough had asked for information. Melbourne replied that no despatches had been received. *Ibid.*, XLIX, 1052-1055.

[2] *Ibid.*, LII, 1223.

portunity. Throughout the debate the government affected to regard the opium question—excepting the actual seizure—as beside the point. The opposition, on the other hand, made much of the drug trade and of the feeble weapons with which the government had supplied its superintendent of trade. Neither side perceived in any adequate fashion the conflict between two civilizations, with their incompatible customs, laws, and theories of international intercourse. On few occasions was the debate raised above the plane of political manoeuvering.[3]

It would be footless to follow the long discussion in detail.[4] Sir James Graham, Gladstone, and Peel led the attack, while Macaulay, Palmerston, and Sir George Staunton, whose acquaintance with China surpassed that of his colleagues, were the chief defenders.[5] The speech of the young Gladstone, full of admirable quoting-material for anti-opium pamphleteers, was perhaps the most telling of the opposition statements. Sir George Staunton was the only government supporter who would admit the opium monopoly of British India to be a relevant issue. In a surprisingly objective speech he pointed out that Parliament should have hesitated before accepting it as a permanent feature of the Indian revenue system and that the select committee of 1832 should not have averted its gaze from the question of whether the best land in India should be given over to "such a pernicious article."[6] In

[3] That the debate owed a good deal to party politics is made clear by an entry in Gladstone's diary. See Morley, *Life of Gladstone*, I, 225.

[4] The debate is reported in 3 *Hansard*, LIII.

[5] Staunton had accompanied Lord Macartney's embassy to Peking in 1792 and had been a member of the company's staff at Canton from 1798 to 1817. He was the son of Sir George Leonard Staunton, who acted as secretary to the embassy.

[6] 3 *Hansard*, LIII, 743. In February, 1840, Staunton wrote to Palmerston a letter dealing with the conduct of treaty negotiations. "I have said nothing in my letter on the subject of *opium* but am bound to add that I have a strong feeling *against it* and have promised to second a motion, condemning

Anglo-Chinese coöperation lay the hope of solving the opium problem, and that could be achieved only by a treaty with the Peking government, an end to which the current struggle might lead.

After three nights of debate Palmerston offered his defense. He made it amply clear that to the government the opium question was incidental. The meager powers of the superintendents of trade he attributed, not to the ministry's policy, but to the China Act of 1833, which brought these officials into being. In any case, to have encouraged them to proceed against drug traders would have been inviting failure and ridicule. Chinese objections, he charged, were inspired by fiscal rather than by moral motives. Moreover, stopping the Bengal supply would not stop imports into China, for the profits of the company's opium trade would merely fall to Turkey, Persia, or one of the neighboring countries—an argument that was to enjoy a long and useful career in the hands of the defenders of the traffic. When the House divided, it was by the narrow majority of nine that the government was sustained. Henceforth war was an accomplished fact, never again formally challenged on the floor of the Commons.

Meanwhile, the merchants whose opium had been surrendered were having their own troubles in collecting from their government. In the autumn of 1839 certificates issued by Captain Elliot were first presented to the treasury for payment, together with the bills drawn in favor of Dent and Company for opium purchased outright.[7]

the existing practice of growing the Drug in India for the purpose of introducing it into China.'' It was apparently this motion that reached the floor of the House in April, 1843. I. O. China Corr., I.

[7] It will be recalled that Elliot, to make up the quantity of opium that he had promised to the Chinese, was obliged to buy from Dent and Company more than five hundred chests. For the opium which the merchants surrendered he merely issued certificates entitling them to ''full indemnity,'' but for Dent and Company he wrote bills on the London treasury to the amount of some £63,000.

The reply from the treasury was curt and crushing. The applicants were informed that the sanction of Parliament was necessary for such a payment and that the government had no intention of asking Parliament for authorization.[8] Unavailing were protests that the opium had not been seized by the Chinese but had been sold to her Majesty's superintendent of trade. The position of Dent and Company was perhaps even more vexatious than that of the other merchants, for the sale of Dent's opium was a purely business transaction, made under no duress from the Chinese government. The drug arrived after the surrender had been agreed upon and at the time was in perfect safety.[9]

The government's refusal to honor Elliot's certificates apparently created a miniature panic in India, especially in Bombay, where most of the confiscated opium had been owned. The certificates, known as opium scrip, were negotiated in Calcutta at the rate of about £35 per chest, while in Bombay there was little attempt to sell them even at that price. All was uncertainty. The merchants at once began to petition for a declaration of policy, praying that at least some of the money be advanced.[10] They then pinned their expectations on a meeting of Parliament. Disappointed in this resource, they could only offer the pious hope that a bill would be presented to China and that she would be obliged to pay for Commissioner Lin's expensive activities.

A number of suicides occurred among Indian merchants, "men of high spirit and ancient family [who] cannot bear the disgrace of appealing to the insolvent

[8] *Communications between the Board of Treasury, etc.*, no. 150, 1840, pp. 1-5.

[9] Palmers, Lackillop, Dent and Company to Baring, 10 Dec. 1839, *Communications between the Board of Treasury, etc.*, no. 200, 1840.

[10] Memorial from the Bombay chamber of commerce, 1 June 1839, I. O. China Corr., I.

law.'"[11] Indeed only the forbearance of creditors, it was reported, prevented an epidemic of self-destruction. The merchants did not hesitate to remind the government of its own connection with the trade and of the sanction which Parliament had given. In fact, the letters submitted to the select committee of 1840 were full of dangerous common sense. "Does it not appear ridiculous," wrote one petitioner, "that, on the one hand, Captain Elliot delivers up 20,000 chests, while, on the other, the Indian governments are bringing forward, for sale, upwards of 40,000 chests more?"[12] Opium merchants might feel themselves shabbily treated, but their pleas went unheeded at Westminster. It was late in the summer of 1843 when they were finally permitted to present their certificates for payment.

Compensation, then, was a question to be settled through the trial by battle taking place in China. The scene of the narrative must therefore be shifted to the Far East. During the winter and spring of 1839-1840, the British community remained at Tangku, having been ordered thither by Captain Elliot early in December. But even before this shift war was a fact. On November 3 an engagement took place between H. M. S. *Volage* and *Hyacinth* and twenty-nine war junks, with much damage to the latter. British military and naval forces reached China in June, and during that month Admiral George Elliot, whom the government sent out as first commissioner, procurator, and plenipotentiary, also arrived to take charge of operations.[13] Pursuant to instructions from London, action was begun in the north. The island of Chusan was occupied, and attempts were made at

[11] Evidence of James Malcolmson, *Report from the Select Committee,* 1840, Q. 1902.

[12] *Ibid.,* Q. 1892. See also the evidence of Ardasser Cursetjee, a Bombay Parsi, who was not connected with the opium trade. Q. 1984 ff.

[13] Captain Charles Elliot was to act as second commissioner.

Amoy, Ningpo, and the mouth of the Peiho River to deliver to responsible officials a despatch from Palmerston.[14] Conferences with Chinese plenipotentiaries were
begun on the Peiho and were later continued at Canton.
But the unwillingness of the Chinese to agree to the cession of Hongkong produced a renewal of hostilities. On
January 7, 1841, the Bogue forts were silenced and an
armistice agreed upon.

The instructions issued by the foreign office to the Elliots, Admiral George and Captain Charles, indicated no
purpose to press for the legalization of the opium traffic.
They were, of course, to demand full compensation for
the drug destroyed by Lin. Any treaty negotiated with
the Chinese ought to provide that contraband goods, on
sufficient proof, might be seized, "but that in no case shall
the Persons of British subjects be molested on account of
the importation or the exportation of Goods."[15] But in
February, 1841, Palmerston instructed the plenipotentiaries to arrange, if possible, for the admission of opium
as a legitimate article of commerce. The suggestion, they
were to state, did not constitute one of the demands of
England, nor was there to be any hint of compulsion. The
trade could not be stopped, Palmerston reflected, by the
lone exertions of the Chinese; neither could the British
government, even by abolishing the Bengal monopoly,
prevent the introduction of opium into China.[16]

Before this despatch was written, however, Charles Elliot and the Chinese plenipotentiary had already come to
terms.[17] Their conversations, which went on intermit-

[14] Palmerston to the plenipotentiaries, 20 Feb. 1840, Morse, *International Relations*, I, App. B.

[15] *Ibid.*

[16] Palmerston to the Elliots, 26 Feb. 1841, *Papers relating to the Opium Trade in China, 1842-1856*, 1857. Hereafter this collection will be cited as *Papers rel. Opium, 1842-56*, 1857.

[17] Admiral Elliot was forced to return to England in November, 1840, be-

tently for five months, are of no importance to the student of the opium trade, save as they offer additional evidence of the conflicting points of view. At one point in the discussion, the Chinese plenipotentiary bluntly asked whether Great Britain were prepared to stop the export of opium from British territory. Elliot replied that at all events such prohibition would make no difference in the amount that reached China. "Indeed, more than half the opium already imported into China was not grown in the Queen's dominions."[18] Arguing that the evil of extensive smuggling was more serious than that of extensive smoking, he graphically described the effects of China's sumptuary efforts. Far better, he urged, to alter the vicious tastes of the people by instruction and example, as England was doing with the liquor habit, than to try to enforce an unenforceable law.

The draft convention finally agreed upon ignored the future of the opium trade but assessed the Chinese six million dollars as indemnity for the drug seized by Lin, not, as Elliot reiterated, "because of the value of the thing taken . . . but for the principle's sake." The amount was a compromise arrived at after weeks of debate, and even then, the indemnity clauses were in the nature of a gentleman's agreement between the two plenipotentiaries.[19] Palmerston found the terms of the convention grossly unsatisfactory, "far short of what you have been instructed to obtain." There was, in truth, a grave disparity between the demands of the foreign

cause of illness. As a result, most of the negotiations were in the hands of his colleague.

[18] Memorandum of Captain Elliot's conference with Kishen, 31 Aug. 1840, I. O. China Corr., X. Elliot was referring, of course, to the native states of India.

[19] The Chinese envoy refused to assume the compensation as an obligation for the emperor but consented to accept it personally.

office and the concessions that had been wrested from the Chinese. Elliot had been ordered to obtain compensation for the opium destroyed, for the debts of the hong merchants, and for the expenses of the expeditionary forces, but he had settled for an amount no greater than that which was finally allocated to pay the opium claims alone.[20] In a word, the British plenipotentiary had allowed his own judgment to prevail over his instructions, and his convention was promptly disavowed in London.[21]

Its reception in Peking was no more favorable. Before word of British disapproval could reach China, wrath had been kindled in the imperial bosom, and the war party was again in command. The plenipotentiary was recalled and cashiered, with a sentence of death which was never executed. (The test of a Chinese official's ability, it will be seen, was wholly pragmatic.) Hostilities were resumed at Canton, and early in March, 1841, the city was at the mercy of the British. Three new commissioners were delegated to deal with the importunate barbarians.[22] But in May it became apparent that the Chinese were intending to renew the battle. As usual the imperial forces got much the worst of it. A general bombardment of the city speedily brought the commissioners to their knees. On May 27 they came to terms, agreeing to pay six million dollars in one week. Chinese forces were to leave the city within sixty days, and British

[20] If the rate at which opium was purchased from Dent and Company were taken as a standard, it would have required more than ten million dollars to indemnify the owners of the confiscated drug. But the actual value of opium at Canton at the time of the seizure was far below the price paid to Dent.

[21] Palmerston to Elliot, 21 April 1841, with ''Statement shewing what part of the Instructions to the Plenipotentiaries in China have been obeyed, and what part disregarded,'' Morse, *International Relations*, I, App. G.

[22] Two arrived in Canton on April 14. The third was on his way from Szechuan. *Chinese Repository*, April, 1841, p. 234.

troops were to withdraw beyond the Bocca Tigris as soon as the money was paid.[23]

This transaction, as it turned out, brought the opium claimants no nearer their reward. Indeed there is a good deal of uncertainty about Elliot's purpose in demanding such a sum.[24] The Chinese were under the illusion that they were settling British opium claims, and Elliot later referred to the payment as being "in diminution of the just claims of Her Majesty's Government."[25] From the proceeds, which were remitted to England and to India by Jardine, Matheson and Company and Dent and Company, he allowed the latter to deduct £63,265 18s. 4d., the price of the opium supplied by that firm during the crisis of 1839. In London the treasury board was much puzzled by the unexpected increment. After some discussion, the board declined to approve Elliot's arrangement with Dent, save as Parliament should give its sanction in the future. The balance was appropriated as a droit to the crown and as a reward to the troops who had taken part in the operations.[26]

On the day that the British forces evacuated the Can-

[23] *Papers relating to the Monies received from the Chinese Authorities,* 1842, incl. 3 in no. 3. This convention, it should be noticed, was not a general treaty of peace. It provided for little more than the exemption of Canton from British occupation.

[24] "This money has, even in official documents, been called the 'ransom' of Canton, and has been considered compensation to the military and naval forces—prize money—in lieu of the plunder of the city. This it was not. . . . Captain Elliot 'officially declared that it had reference only to the relief of this city from pressure which could not continue to be applied.' " Morse, *International Relations,* I, 286. See also *Chinese Repository,* May, 1841, p. 296; June, 1841, p. 349; Eames, *English in China,* p. 502.

[25] *Communications from Captain Elliot . . . upon the Transactions with the Chinese Authorities,* 1842, no. 9; *Chinese Repository,* Oct., 1842, pp. 571-572.

[26] Material on the "Canton ransom" will be found in *Papers relating to the Monies,* 1842. See also Aberdeen to Pottinger, 2 Dec. 1841, Morse, *International Relations,* I, App. N.

ton River, instructions were being issued to a new plenipotentiary, Sir Henry Pottinger, who was to supersede
Captain Elliot.[27] The views of the government had undergone no change, and the envoy was instructed, first of all,
to obtain compensation for the opium extorted from British subjects in 1839. Palmerston was doubtful of its
proper valuation, but by assuming each chest to have
been worth three hundred dollars, a total of slightly more
than six million was reached.[28] Pottinger was also instructed to use every opportunity to impress upon the
Chinese plenipotentiary—as a British suggestion but by
no means as a British demand—the desirability of legalizing "by a regular duty, a Trade which they cannot
prevent."[29]

The coming of the new envoy brought fresh life to a
listless war. Amoy, Ningpo, Shanghai, and Chinkiang
were captured, and Nanking was threatened so seriously
that the Chinese were forced to sue for peace. Late in the
summer of 1842, an English diplomatist again confronted
a group of Chinese plenipotentiaries, and on this occasion he dictated the terms of peace. Opium figured in the
formal treaty negotiations only in the discussion of the
indemnity. When Palmerston's bill for six million dollars
was presented, the Chinese objected, arguing that the
price of the drug had been paid by the city of Canton;
"how could payment be extorted a second time?" The
British rejoinder was disingenuous, to say the least. Instead of admitting that the "Canton ransom" had had

[27] May 31, 1841. The full text appears in Morse, *International Relations*,
I, App. K. Instructions relating to opium are also contained in *Papers rel.
Opium, 1842-56*, 1857, pp. 2-3.

[28] To be precise, 6,189,616 dollars, including the amount owed to Dent
and Company.

[29] "Her Majesty's Government make no demand in regard to this matter,
for they have no right to do so. . . . British Subjects who engage in a contraband Trade must take the consequences of doing so."

nothing whatever to do with opium claims and had been applied to other purposes, Pottinger and his aids seem to have intimated that another six million would no more than balance the account. Opium, they pointed out, was an expensive commodity, and the prime cost of the chests must have been easily twelve million dollars.[30] At Nanking the Chinese were in no position to quibble over details, and six million dollars was written into the treaty as compensation for British opium merchants.

Once the terms were agreed upon, the British plenipotentiary felt free to carry out his instructions with regard to legalization. He presented his case in a memorial of some length, enclosing a copy of his own instructions relating to opium, "so candid, so explicit, so clear." Chinese officials had heard substantially the same argument before, and during the next fifteen years it was to become an even more familiar story. They replied that no such proposal could be submitted to the emperor.[31] A better opportunity was presented when the plenipotentiaries met to sign the treaty. After the official business had been despatched, Pottinger announced his intention of making some remarks upon the opium question. The Chinese with one accord declined to enter into conversation. Upon Sir Henry's assurance that it was to be merely an informal, private chat, they exhibited lively interest, at once raising the question of why poppy cultivation should not be suppressed in India. This course, replied the Englishman, would be inconsistent with British law, and if the government chose to adopt it, would be an arbitrary exercise of power. The eradication of the evil, he unctuously informed them, "rests entirely with yourselves. If your people are virtuous, they will desist from the evil prac-

[30] *Chinese Repository*, Oct., 1842, pp. 571-572.
[31] Pottinger to the Chinese commissioners, 27 Aug. 1842, and reply, *Papers rel. Opium, 1842-56*, 1857, no. 1 and incl.

tice; and if your officers are incorruptible, and obey their orders, no opium can enter your country.''[32] But, since the reality was otherwise, it would be far better to legalize the trade at once. The Chinese plenipotentiaries seem to have been impressed by Pottinger's persuasive argument, but they were convinced that their imperial master would not listen to a word of it.

In spite of the inconclusive outcome of the discussion, Pottinger extracted one important assurance from the Chinese—that Chinese officials would confine their jurisdiction to Chinese citizens. ''Whether the Merchant Ships of the various Countries bring Opium or not, China will not need to enquire nor take any proceedings with regard thereto.''[33] Obviously this compromise was better than nothing, for it reduced the chances of collision between the subjects and officials of the two powers. But there still remained, as Aberdeen, foreign secretary in the new Tory government, informed Pottinger, the necessity for winning the Chinese government to the British solution. The motive behind opium diplomacy at this time was not the need for a profitable market in China, and Indian revenue had no place in inspiring British diplomatists to advocate legalization. As far as the profits of the monopoly were concerned, an illicit market was probably as good as a legitimate one. What disturbed the foreign office was the fear that extensive smuggling would demoralize regular commerce and would lead to strained relations between the two governments.

Notwithstanding the failure of his efforts thus far, Sir Henry Pottinger did not abandon hope that the Chinese might still adopt his view. But in commenting on the

[32] G. G. Loch, *Closing Events*, p. 172.

[33] Aberdeen to Pottinger, 4 Jan. 1843, Morse, *International Relations*, I, App. P. See also the memorandum in *Papers rel. Opium, 1842-56*, 1857, incl. no. 2.

treaty, he characterized the hope as "a very faint one."[34] To spur him to action was the odious smuggling in the Canton River, as annoying to Pottinger as it had been to Captain Elliot. A protest to the Chinese authorities yielded only sporadic efforts. In February, 1843, he drew up a memorandum stating his readiness to call "on all British subjects to conform to the demand of the Chinese Government, and warning them of the risk of disregarding it, which will lead to the confiscation of the vessel and cargo."[35] But how futile would be such an appeal with imperial officials winking at wholesale lawbreaking! At Nanking the Chinese officials had indicated that they proposed to leave British smugglers severely alone, endeavoring only to prevent the spread of opium in the interior. From this commitment they did not deviate.

Pottinger's last chance came during the discussion of the commercial treaty and tariff. When the conferences took place in the summer of 1843, there seems to have been an earnest conversation on the drug question. The British proposed that the trade be allowed at Namoa and Tsuan-chu (Chinchew). Kiying, the new commissioner for foreign affairs, countered with a curious plan of making the British plenipotentiaries securities for an annual increment of three million dollars' opium duty. In the end, Kiying, one of the most reasonable of Chinese statesmen, advised the persistent barbarian to lay the matter directly before the emperor. To a memorial congratulating the sovereign on the conclusion of peace, Pottinger therefore added a postscript requesting the "sacred Im-

[34] Pottinger to the British merchants, 28 Dec. 1842, *Chinese Repository*, Jan., 1843, p. 35.

[35] *Papers rel. Opium, 1842-56*, 1857, incl. in no. 2. This warning did not involve British officers in the suppression of smuggling. It merely reminded British smugglers that their government would lend no support to illicit practices and would raise no objection if the Chinese chose to act.

perial glance'' upon communications dealing with the opium question.[36]

The British treaties of 1842-1844, then, left the status of opium quite unaltered. Both parties tacitly agreed to ignore the facts of the trade. British smuggling was to go on, while China, with the painful object lesson of the past few years in view, was to let the question go by default. The negotiations and the various proclamations issued by her Majesty's superintendent had put the question of enforcement directly up to the Chinese authorities. England would coöperate to the extent of her power, though not, of course to the extent of prohibiting cultivation in India, since that, the Chinese were constantly informed, would only create a new problem. British consuls and naval officers could not contract to enforce the sumptuary laws of another power. That the Chinese would take decisive action again was highly improbable, especially in the light of their promise to Pottinger not to interfere with opium on foreign vessels. Their only course, if they were bent on reform, was to proceed against native smugglers and dealers. Peking must either control the traffic effectively or succumb before the British solution of legalization. In short, the British treaties could scarcely have restored ''quiet . . . to the Imperial bosom.''[37]

In England, meanwhile, the government was writing the balance sheet of the war. The indemnity assessed against the Chinese was twenty-one million dollars, six million of which was to be regarded as the value of the opium delivered to Lin. Palmerston, it will be recalled, arrived at that figure by valuing each chest, exclusive of that bought outright from Dent, at three hundred dollars.

[36] Memorandum by Morrison, 29 June 1843, *ibid.*, incl. 1 in no. 4; memorandum by Pottinger, 30 June 1843, *ibid.*, no. 2; Pottinger to Aberdeen, 25 July 1843, *ibid.*, no. 5; incl. 2 in no. 5.
[37] Imperial rescript, *Chinese Repository*, Nov., 1842, p. 630.

The government was now faced with the problem of apportioning the money equitably. There was no means of ascertaining the precise value of opium in March and April, 1839. Originally the drug that was seized had cost between 500 and 575 dollars per chest, but evidence is abundant that a chest of the best opium in the world was worth nothing like 550 dollars.[38] Even before the appearance of Lin Tse Hsu, the preliminary steps taken by the viceroy had virtually stopped deliveries. On March 5 Patna was quoted in the *Canton Price Current* at 300 dollars, Benares at 280, and Malwa at 250, and at these prices no tenders had been received. Captain Elliot, who admitted his own interest in obtaining the highest possible compensation for the merchants, estimated the value of the opium at the time of surrender as: Patna, 218; Benares, 209; Malwa, 199.

The outcome of a lawsuit in Calcutta further reënforced the view that the merchants were not entitled to the invoice price. The owner of a consignment sued his agent for the latter's failure to sell it immediately upon its arrival in Canton. Since the plaintiff was able to prove that sales were taking place at Lintin, the court was compelled to award more than nominal damages. But instead of the invoice price, it chose to allow the highest price given for Captain Elliot's opium scrip in Calcutta, Rs. 400, as the damage per chest.[39]

Whatever the market value of the drug, the essential problem was one of dividing six million dollars as fairly as possible. By the summer of 1843 a plan was formulated and in August the holders of opium certificates were invited to present them for payment. The indemnity yielded £1,281,211, after a deduction had been made in

[38] Trevelyan to Canning, 18 Dec. 1841, *Corr. rel. Actual Value*, 1843, no. 1; Pottinger to Aberdeen, 17 May 1842, *ibid.*, incl. in no. 7.

[39] Ramsabuck Mullick vs. DeSouza, *ibid.*, incl. in no. 1.

favor of Dent and Company. Quotations in the *Canton Register* and the *Canton Press* established the relative value of the different kinds of opium.[40] The amounts paid per chest were:

Patna	£66	7s	7d	2f	(303 dollars)
Benares	61	11	3	1	(274 dollars)
Malwa	64	11	2		(295 dollars)
Turkey	43	3	5	2	(208 dollars)[41]

The treatment given the merchants was the occasion for some hostile criticism. A contemporary London newspaper charged that the owners of the opium had been obliged to sacrifice more than two million sterling in direct losses, in interest charges, and in consequence of the government's decision to pay in London rather than in the East.[42] And, what was worse, the government had profited by the misfortune of the merchants. The East India revenue had gained a million sterling, while an equal amount had been transferred to the public treasury.[43] There is truth in the indictment. The experience was a costly one for the merchants and a profitable one for the government of India and her Majesty's treasury. And yet the complaints of the losers had little basis, for they received at least as much as their drug would have brought in China.[44] Fundamentally it was the preventive

[40] The computation was based on the months of September, October, and November, 1838.

[41] The quantities for which compensation was paid were as follows: Patna, 5614 chests; Benares, 1128.75; Malwa, 13,487.68; Turkey, 53.

[42] Quoted in the *Chinese Repository*, Jan., 1844, p. 56, and Forbes, *China Trade*, p. 68. At one time the government planned to make payments in Calcutta. Why the arrangements were changed is not clear. Court of directors to the board of control, 23 March 1843, I. O. Letters from the East India Company to the Board of Control, no. 6361.

[43] The latter statement has reference to the "Canton ransom" which might have been allocated to the payment of opium claims.

[44] Possibly even including interest charges for four years. The rate at

energy of the Chinese that had made the opium practically worthless. With twenty thousand chests on the coast of China, twenty more in Bengal, and nearly twelve in Bombay, the prospect of the opium market's recovering its usual scale of prices was remote, to put it mildly.[45] Elliot, a responsible officer of the British government, had promised indemnity, but he had also indicated that the value of the opium was to be appraised "in a manner hereafter to be defined by Her Majesty's Government." There was little justification for indemnifying losses produced essentially by the breakdown of the market. It is true, however, that some of the smaller merchants suffered heavily in the transaction, while some of the larger agents, speculating in Elliot's certificates, made fortunes.[46] Yet whatever their embroglio with Commissioner Lin may have cost British opium dealers, the days of plenty that followed recompensed them many times over.

For between the two Anglo-Chinese wars the opium trade attained a magnitude that it had never before approached. Receiving ships were moored at every open port in China and at some that were still in theory closed.[47] Steamers and clippers brought the drug from India in quantities that dwarfed previous imports. In the main the system worked smoothly, so smoothly indeed that little information crept into foreign newspapers in China, save for market reports, lists of receiving ships, and bulletins of arriving vessels. British officials confined their efforts to a more or less continuous, though tactful, demand for legalization. At the same time, they warned

which the merchants were paid was well above the estimated value of opium at the time of its confiscation.

[45] Elliot to Aberdeen, 19 Jan. 1842, *Corr. rel. Actual Value*, 1843, incl. in no. 5.

[46] Forbes, *Personal Reminiscences*, p. 161.

[47] By the treaty of Nanking, Shanghai, Ningpo, Foochow, and Amoy, in addition to Canton, were opened to foreign trade.

their nationals to smuggle only at the treaty ports and not to bring their opium within the limits of the port itself. As for the Chinese, they had had enough experience with contraband trade as practised by westerners and they proceeded to leave it strictly alone, although there is no evidence to show that the imperial court had abated a jot or tittle in its antipathy towards the drug. Local officials in the main continued their traditional policy of connivance, no longer under the necessity of maintaining imperial favor by spasms of activity. The attitude of both parties, British and Chinese, was one of non-interference.

Even during the war, as has been already indicated, the opium trade was prosecuted with a zeal worthy of more savory undertakings. In the spring of 1842, the commander of the American East India squadron reported that many opium vessels were at Whampoa and that the trade was carried on even more openly than before.[48] Between August, 1841, and January, 1843, forty-seven vessels giving opium as their cargo registered with the harbormaster at Hongkong.[49] On the east coast similar conditions prevailed. An officer of the British expeditionary force reported that frequently, when bothered by guard boats, Chinese dealers would leave their silver on board the opium ship until they had an opportunity to collect the drug, ultimately claiming it by means of a notched wooden tally which fitted exactly into a tally left in each bag of silver. On one occasion some fifty thousand dollars were left on board an opium vessel for more than five months.[50]

At the close of the war the contraband trade burst out

---

[48] Kearny to the secretary of the navy, 8 April 1842, *Kearny Correspondence*, no. 19, 29th Cong., 1st Sess., S. Doc. 139.

[49] *Chinese Repository*, Jan., 1843, pp. 46-55.

[50] Bingham, *Expedition to China*, p. 160.

with fresh effulgence. Hongkong, the newly acquired British colony, was the chief entrepôt for the Chinese coast. Its masters could scarcely forbid the importation of British opium into a British possession, but they could prohibit importation for the purpose of reëxport. Hongkong, as Aberdeen informed Pottinger, must not become the base for British smuggling operations. Yet that was its immediate destiny. Only a short time was required to convince Pottinger that it would be folly to interfere with the receiving ships in Hongkong harbor.[51] In 1844 little business other than in opium was transacted on the island, and its inhabitants dolefully reflected that it was "at best a second Lintin."[52] When, in the following year, Pottinger's successor sold to an opium farmer exclusive rights of retail sale on the island, it seemed as though the colony might lose even that distinction.[53] Notwithstanding a tendency on the part of some drug firms to shift their headquarters elsewhere, both as a result of the superintendents' chilly hospitality and the local opium arrangements, Hongkong remained the first port of call for vessels from India and the center from which the drug was relayed to the mainland.

At the five treaty ports and at other strategic points along the coast were moored the familiar receiving ships. Wusung (on the Hwangpu River ten miles from Shang-

[51] Aberdeen to Pottinger, 4 Jan. 1843, in Morse, *International Relations*, I, App. P; foreign office to Pottinger, 15 Nov. 1843, I. O. China Corr., III. "On a consideration . . . of your opinion so strongly expressed as to the exaggerated notion which has gone about with regard to the pernicious effects of opium, and as to the inexpediency of acting upon the authority given you to exclude opium vessels from the Harbour and Waters of Hongkong, H. M.'s Govt. are disposed to leave it to your discretion to decide whether or not it would be necessary to have recourse to that measure at least for the present."

[52] E. J. Eitel, *Europe in China*, p. 197.

[53] *China Mail*, 3 April 1845; Martin, "Report on Hongkong," *Report from the Select Committee*, 1847, App. III.

hai), Foochow, Ningpo, Amoy, Chusan, Liukung (Wei-haiwei), Chinchew, and Canton (Kumsingmoon) were favorite anchorages. In 1848 the press listed the names of some thirty-five of these ''floating citadels,'' twelve at Shanghai and eight at Kumsingmoon.[54] As a scandalized American commissioner remarked, opium stations were as well known in China as American navy yards were in the United States.[55] On the island of Namoa, long a contraband center, the smugglers made themselves thoroughly at home, building houses and roads, and even erecting a stable where riding ponies were kept for their recreation.[56] Shanghai became the most important of the opium ports, with the Yangtse Valley as the ultimate market for the drug that it received. In 1849, two years after the opening of the river to trade, Shanghai alone was importing almost half the total amount absorbed by China

[54] There was a good deal of variation both in the number of receiving ships and in their location. By 1849, for example, the number had decreased to twenty-nine, and the general tendency along the coast was towards a reduction in the size of the depot fleets. The reason for this is not clear, but two factors may have had their influence. In the first place, the larger firms tended more and more to dominate the trade, with the result that some of their less powerful rivals seem to have been squeezed out. In 1849 about half of all the receiving ships were the property of either Jardine or Dent. The facilities offered by the P & O may also have relieved some merchants of the necessity of maintaining their own storeships. In the second place, the traders at some ports, notably at Shanghai during the confusion of the Taiping rebellion, began to take the drug directly to their own factories and to sell it there. Not only were the numbers of storeships variable, but their location was also subject to occasional change. Certain markets were abandoned and others opened as the need dictated. *China Mail*, 17 Aug. 1848, 6 Nov. 1849; *North-China Herald*, 19 Jan. and 18 Aug. 1855; Morse, *International Relations*, I, 543.

[55] Marshall to Marcy, 10 July 1853, *Correspondence of Humphrey Marshall*, 33d Cong., 1st Sess., H. Ex. Doc. 123, p. 207.

[56] Davis to Kiying, 25 Feb. 1846, *Papers rel. Opium, 1842-56*, 1857, incl. in no. 17; R. Fortune, *Wanderings in China*, p. 31; *Chinese Repository*, June, 1844. In June of 1844 orders were given for the removal of British merchants from Namoa. The colony withdrew from the island, but the receiving ships remained in the neighborhood.

—in fact more than the whole empire had taken prior to
1835-1836. By 1857 the city was receiving some 31,000
chests.[57] Officialdom took very calmly the six to twelve
opium hulks perennially moored at Wusung.

At Canton, as the war drew to a close, the storeships
were comfortably established at Whampoa. From that
strategic point the foreigners did a prosperous business,
either selling opium over the side of the vessel or, what
was more to be deplored, delivering it themselves to native dealers in the city. One of the merchants wrote, "I
made deliveries of Opium at every point of the river . . .
and during the whole time I never met with molestation
from either the Chinese authorities or people."[58] It was
the foolhardiness of the drug traders themselves that cost
them the Whampoa station. When they put some twelve
small schooners on the river to run opium into the city
and when, in addition to this, they added saltpetre to
their contraband dealings, Sir John Francis Davis, the
new superintendent of trade and governor of Hongkong,
coöperating with Viceroy Kiying, evicted them from the
river. The receiving ships, representing English, Parsi,
and American firms, then took up their position at Kumsingmoon. From this anchorage they were able to supply
the needs of the Canton market, and there the fleet remained until opium ceased to be illicit.[59]

The hulks were thoroughly armed and eternally vigi-
lant. One might have thought that, as custodians of contraband, their commanders would have been apprehensive about assaults by Chinese officials. To be sure, their
armament was such as would discourage the most earnest

[57] Morse, *International Relations*, I, 358; Reed to Elgin, 13 Sept. 1858,
Correspondence of William B. Reed, incl. 1b in no. 36, 36th Cong., 1st Sess.,
S. Ex. Doc. 30.

[58] *Statements and Suggestions regarding Hong Kong*, pp. 28-29.

[59] Davis to Kiying, 11 May 1847, *Papers rel. Opium, 1842-56*, 1857, incl.
2 in no. 20; *China Mail*, 28 April, 8 and 22 May 1845.

of coast-guard officers, who appreciated, in the words of a British diplomatist, "the mockery in the invitation to assail large fleets of heavily-armed European vessels."[60] The precautions of the storeships, however, were taken not against Chinese authorities but against pirates, to use a recent analogy, the "hi-jackers" of the drug trade. One of the chief officers of the ship, a smuggler has testified, attended to the cargo, while the other did nothing but supervise the men of the fighting crew, always at their appointed stations. When opium or treasure was being transferred, an armed guard was maintained around the hatchways, forming a cordon to the gangway.[61]

The smuggling system now reached its zenith. The fury of competition possessed opium merchants, and no firm could have too elaborate a mechanism for getting the better of its rivals. Jardine, Matheson and Company was reported at one time to have had eight receiving ships stationed at the ports of China, one large depot ship of seven hundred tons moored at Hongkong, four or five clippers plying between Hongkong and the coast, and five vessels bringing opium from India.[62] Dent and Company did nearly as well, while several smaller houses, English, Indian, and American, boasted equipment that was inadequate only by comparison with the leading firms. A few hours' advantage in the China market might mean a profit of thousands of dollars, and the eastern seas became a speedway for opium vessels, all attempting to reach port with their drug and their owners' despatches ahead of rival craft. The entire mercantile community came to depend upon opium carriers for postal service, and although captains often withheld ordinary mail until

[60] Rutherford Alcock, "Note on . . . Our Relations with China," A. Michie, *Englishman in China*, I, 418.

[61] L. Anderson, *Among Typhoons*, p. 110.

[62] Martin, *China*, II, 259.

their agents in China had had time to act upon information contained in the owners' despatches, they played a
valuable part in the commercial system of the Far East.
When a ship confined its mail cargo to the despatches of
her owner, the disappointment of other merchants was
acute. In 1843 a British admiral noted in his diary:
"Anonymous opium-clipper arrived from Bombay with
only owners' despatches. Beast."[63] The reliance placed
by dealers upon market reports brought by opium vessels
—as well as the intensely speculative character of the
trade itself—is made graphic by the occasional instances
in which inaccurate reports were given. When a sleepy
P & O captain, stopping at the mouth of the Ganges on
his return from China, inadvertently misquoted Chinese
prices, protests were loud from Calcutta speculators, who
had received his news by "Electric Telegraph" and had
been led to make imprudent purchases.[64] In such a trade
as this, when every hour counted, the firm whose machinery for transmitting both drug and information was most
nearly perfect held a tremendous advantage.

Another rivalry, less apparent but no less real, was
being settled in China waters during the 'forties and
'fifties. The opium trade was one of the arenas in which
the ancient dominion of the sailing ship was challenged
by the stout competence of the steamer. At the beginning
of the period the clipper commanded the field, but in the
later 'fifties its chief use seems to have been in the coast-
wise trade, that is, in conveying the drug from Hongkong
or Kumsingmoon to its ultimate destination. The larger
British firms maintained their own fleets of steamers,
some of them fast enough to give a P & O boat a start of
two days in a run of fourteen hundred miles. There was,
for example, the old paddle-wheeler *Glengyle,* which usu-

---

[63] Michie, *Englishman in China,* I, 217.
[64] *China Mail,* 5 Oct. 1854.

ally left Calcutta a day after the mail steamer and reached Hongkong a day or two before her. Instead of entering the harbor the *Glengyle* would lie in concealment, while her despatches were carried to her owners by the first mate disguised as a Chinese. After the P & O boat had arrived and the mail had been distributed, the *Glengyle* would steam sedately into port.[65]

A number of American-built and American-owned steamships also found their way into the business. In 1858, according to the American commissioner, William B. Reed, the most active opium ship in Chinese waters was built in New York and was flying the flag of the United States.[66] During the eighteen-fifties, however, it was the P & O that appropriated an increasing share of the carrying trade. Since its boats were designed primarily for passengers, the space for freight was limited and the rates high. Only such a commodity as opium, which combined enormous value with small bulk could afford the facilities of the P & O. In 1850 a small paddle-wheel steamer, *Lady Mary Wood*, began to make regular trips from Hongkong to Shanghai, and on each voyage, opium consigned to the P & O agent was included in her cargo. Three years later no less than five P & O steamers were carrying the drug over the same route.[67] In fact, it was charged by an American commissioner that the line

65 P. H. King, *In the Chinese Customs Service*, p. 32; Michie, *Englishman in China*, I, 216.

66 Reed to Elgin, 13 Sept. 1858, *Correspondence of William B. Reed*, incl. 1b in no. 36, 36th Cong., 1st Sess., S. Ex. Doc. 30.

67 *China Mail*, 24 Aug. 1854; *North-China Herald*, 1852-1853, *passim.* These vessels were not engaged exclusively in the Hongkong-Shanghai run. In the shipping reports all were listed as having come from Hongkong, but for most of them the latter was merely a port of call on the route from Bombay or Calcutta. P & O steamers, one infers, only provided transportation for opium belonging to others. The company had its receiving ships, and the drug was consigned to its agents, but the P & O does not seem to have sold opium to the Chinese.

between India and China was maintained only by the carriage of opium.[68]

Progress, the deity of the nineteenth century, decreed that the clipper should be dethroned by the steamer. But before the doom of the sailing ship was accomplished, the builders of Boston and Cowes sent to China vessels which were masterpieces of marine construction, trim, fleet, and supremely seaworthy.[69] The first American-built clipper, the *Rose,* entered the coasting trade in 1837 for Russell and Company. Four years later, R. B. Forbes of the same firm sent out the *Anglona* and the *Ariel,* to be followed during the next two years by the *Zephyr, Mazeppa,* the bark *Coquette,* and the brig *Antelope,* "one of the prettiest little craft that was ever in the opium busness."[70] These vessels accumulated their full due of salty tradition. The *Ariel* capsized on her trial trip in Boston harbor, but later, having sacrificed eight feet from her masts, she atoned for her fault by beating the *Anglona* in a race from Macao Roads around Lintin and winning for her captain a sporting wager of a thousand dollars. The *Antelope,* under "that prince of good captains, Philip Dumaresq,"[71] was known as the only square-rigged vessel that could beat through the Formosan Channel against the northeast monsoon. "With her low, black hull, tall rakish masts, and square yards," she was a solace both to the eye of the sailor and to her owners' ledgers. These American clippers enjoyed a long and eventful career in the drug trade, some in the service of

[68] Marshall to Marcy, 10 July 1853, *Correspondence of Humphrey Marshall,* 33d Cong., 1st Sess., H. Ex. Doc. 123, p. 207.

[69] Most of the clippers engaged in the trade during the eighteen-thirties were built in India.

[70] Quoted in B. Lubbock, *China Clippers,* p. 25; A. H. Clark, *Clipper Ship Era,* p. 58.

[71] The words are R. B. Forbes' of Russell and Company, *Personal Reminiscences,* p. 152.

their original owners, others sold to English firms or American adventurers. British shipbuilders countered with the *Torrington* (1846), the property of Jardine, Matheson and Company, and during the next decade, with such well known clippers as the brig *Lanrick*, the *Eamont*, and the *Wild Dayrell*, the last two owned by Dent and Company.[72]

The yacht-like schooners and brigs, which plied up and down the coast from Hongkong or Kumsingmoon or embarked on the longer voyage to Calcutta and Bombay, deserve the aura of romance that has been cast around them. Through typhoons and through waters infested with pirates, they cut their way—even to the Gulf of Pechili, rumor had it—bearing cargoes of opium and silver.[73] The *Eamont*, one of the best known of the later clippers, was built of teak and mahogany and measured something over two hundred tons. On one occasion she was sent to open Formosa as an opium market, and in the course of her visit, had to repel the assault of hundreds of natives as well as to ride out a typhoon.[74] Everything was shipshape aboard the better clippers, the crew well paid and well fed. One of the *Eamont's* company has testified that "The officers of Her Britannic Majesty's ships on the station were very often delighted to come on board these opium-clippers and spend a pleasant evening, the more so that the table was much better than any of the hotels that were then in existence in the far-off Eastern land."[75]

Service on a clipper was regarded as a desirable appointment, and indeed the larger firms used all possible discretion in staffing their vessels. Their commanders had

---

[72] Lubbock, *China Clippers*, p. 33; Clark, *Clipper Ship Era*, p. 59.

[73] Anderson, *Among Typhoons*, p. 14.

[74] L. Anderson, *Cruise on an Opium Clipper*, pp. 53 ff.; Lubbock, *China Clippers*, pp. 33-34.

[75] Anderson, *Among Typhoons*, p. 76.

little in common with the conventional picture of the smuggling chief. For example, Captain Philip Dumaresq, who for a time paced the quarter-deck of the *Antelope* was one of the really distinguished Yankee skippers.[76] An officer of the *Falcon* described his fellow-officers on British clippers as "for the most part the younger sons of good families at home. . . . And it may be remarked that among the officers were many sons of clergymen, who, after a period of active service afloat would retire to succeed ultimately to their fathers' livings or to practise at the bar."[77]

Of the men in the fo'c'sle it is more difficult to speak. The officers of a well managed opium clipper were invariably Westerners, but the crew was ordinarily composed of Lascars and Manila men. The *Ariel*, a typical clipper, carried twelve officers, including gunners, supercargo, and quartermasters, and a crew of forty-two. In addition to these there were the boatswains and boatswains' mates, stewards, and cooks. Some precautions were necessary to avoid civil war on the vessel. Officers were armed with pistols, the magazine was directly below the captain's cabin, and great care was taken to prevent the various races and nationalities among the crew from seeing overmuch of each other.[78]

These apostles of contraband were bristling with armament. The Dent clipper *Eamont* was fitted with four eighteen-pounders on each side and two pivot guns. The *Antelope* carried two guns on a side and a Long Tom amidships, with a rack of boarding pikes around the main-mast and a large chest on the quarter-deck containing an ample supply of pistols and cutlasses. Such preparations were not intended primarily for intrusive Chi-

[76] S. E. Morison, *Maritime History of Massachusetts*, p. 340.

[77] Lubbock, *China Clippers*, p. 6.

[78] "In an Opium Smuggler," *Overland Monthly*, Jan., 1891, p. 44.

nese officials, against whom they would have been a superfluous extravagance, although there is no doubt that any competent opium skipper would have resisted forcible seizure. To the clippers, as to the stationary receiving ships, the real hazard was pirates. The years since the signing of the treaty had seen an enormous increase in piracy, never wholly absent from Chinese seas. The Chinese navy was utterly unable to cope with the violence along the coast and, in fact, had been growing noticeably weaker since the conclusion of peace.[79]

There were no more attractive cargoes in eastern waters than the opium and silver in the holds of the clippers. A brush with pirates was therefore a part of the day's work for the drug carrier, whose crew was as handy with cutlass as with holystone. An eyewitness has described an encounter in which the *Antelope* was the intended victim. As the Russell brig was passing the Ladrones, two boatloads of Chinese were seen to put out from shore. The skipper ordered a shot from Long Tom, after which a sharp watch was kept by all hands. Unfortunately the clipper was caught in the lee of the shore and lay becalmed, while the meddlesome buccaneers, now with four boats, each carrying from sixty to a hundred men, again sallied forth. This time they succeeded in boarding the clipper at both bow and stern, despite the best efforts of her defenders. Just then a squall blew up, and the *Antelope* began to move. The crew made a last gallant rush at the invaders, drove them back into their boats, and departed. On her next voyage the *Antelope* was again attacked by pirates. After running down two of their boats

[79] During the war, arms had been distributed liberally for protection against the barbarian. Privateers which had been commissioned merely continued their old occupation. When boarded, they could easily produce the old license which permitted them to practise legalized piracy. Jardine, Matheson and Co. to Woodgate, 12 Dec. 1855, *Papers rel. Opium, 1842-56*, 1857, incl. 8 in no. 26; Davis, *China . . . since the Peace*, II, 183.

and drowning their crews, Captain Watkins sailed into
Macao Roads with a Chinese suspended from each yard-
arm, as a deterrent to would-be plunderers of honest
opium craft.[80]

Steamers, clippers, and receiving ships were thus essential elements in the opium trade as it was carried on
between the two Anglo-Chinese wars. The process of sale
to Chinese dealers did not differ materially from that
pursued before treaty days.[81] It was still Chinese rather
than foreigners who did the actual smuggling into Chinese territory and who settled with the officials. The
receiving ships, in general, were within the limits of Chinese jurisdiction and were legally, as well as morally,
smugglers. But foreigners did not assume responsibility
for landing the drug.[82] Little or no secrecy was observed
in the business. Coolies bore opium through the streets
in broad daylight, and one might see as many as fifty or
sixty chests in the shops of dealers.[83]

Patently a scheme of things which depended for its

[80] From an account by a member of the *Antelope's* crew in Lubbock,
China Clippers, pp. 28-32. The writer professes to be describing a fight with
the "mandarins." At the risk of seeming to reject first-hand testimony, I
have ventured to substitute "pirates" for "mandarins." The writer, apparently on his first trip to China, was obviously unfamiliar with conditions.
The Ladrone group, the scene of the *Antelope's* skirmish, was a notorious
resort for pirates. Finally, foreigners had some difficulty in distinguishing
between official craft and predatory boats, as when the *China Mail* announced that two American cutters had been attacked by "Chinese smugglers or mandarin boats."

[81] See G. Smith, *Exploratory Visit*, pp. 130, 434-435. An anonymous writer
in the *Overland Monthly*, Jan., 1891, gives an account of robbery as practised by the clipper *Ariel*, which had apparently fallen on evil days. When
the opium had been transferred to the native craft, the *Ariel's* company
sallied over the side, reclaimed the opium, and sailed away with the silver.

[82] There are exceptions to this statement, as, for example, the smuggling
between Whampoa and Canton carried on by foreigners.

[83] Evidence of T. A. Gibb, *Report from the Select Committee*, 1847, Q.
4292. Also Crawford Kerr, *ibid.*, Q. 711; Davis to Kiying, 11 May 1847, *Papers rel. Opium, 1842-56*, 1857, incl. 2. in no. 20.

success upon the mutual apathy of Chinese and British officials left much to be desired. In his negotiations with Kiying, Pottinger had announced that British authorities could not contract to enforce the prohibitory laws of China and that the persons of British subjects were not to be disturbed by Chinese authorities, only ships and cargoes being susceptible to seizure. Kiying, for his part, had agreed that the officers of the empire would take no cognizance of opium on British vessels. Her Majesty's consuls at the five treaty ports thus found themselves in a curious position. By the treaty of Nanking they were made responsible for the discharge by British subjects of "the just dues and other dues of the Chinese government." But inasmuch as opium found no place in the Chinese tariff, there was meager ground for consular action.[84] As a rule, British opium vessels lay beyond the boundaries of the treaty ports. When this rule of the game was violated and when British traders brought their drug into port, the consul might notify the Chinese.[85]

The degree of connivance on the part of Chinese authorities varied with the port and the year. In one or two instances their hesitancy to act against opium merchants suggests that they feared consular intervention.[86] But on the whole, local officials—indifferent, covetous, or terrified by the consequences of Lin's indiscretion—showed less inclination than ever to enforce the anti-opium laws.

[84] Article XII of the supplementary treaty obligated the consuls to inform the Chinese of smuggling transactions which came to their notice. From the context it is clear that this article had reference only to evasion of regular duties, not to trade in contraband goods.

[85] It was information supplied by the British consul that led to the exclusion of opium shipping from Whampoa. In 1845 Consul Rutherford Alcock ordered Foochow merchants to refrain from bringing opium on shore. *China Mail*, 11 Dec. 1845.

[86] For an example see Thom to Davis, 5 April 1845, *Papers rel. Opium, 1842-56*, 1857, incl. 1 in no. 14.

In the end the drug was tolerated, not to say encouraged, at every station on the coast. Save for the emperor's sanction and the fact that the duties collected went into private pockets rather than into the treasury, the contraband trade was already legalized.

Chinese local authorities and British consular officials were thus committed to a policy of non-interference. In general, the Americans were equally inert, and with less reason. Cushing's treaty (1844) had specifically denounced opium as contraband, had denied to American opium traders "any countenance or protection from the government of the United States," and had obligated that government to prevent the abuse of the American flag by subjects of other nations.[87] During 1839-1840 American merchants seem to have abstained from contraband transactions, but within two years they were again taking their part.[88] When Commodore Kearny reached Hongkong in the spring of 1842, he found evidence of opium trading under American colors. His disavowal of support would have been more effective, had not the Canton government cheerfully acquitted the Americans of any complicity in drug vending.[89] From Consul Sturgis (a member of Russell and Company) Kearny also obtained a strangely unsatisfactory list of American vessels carrying on opium business in Chinese waters. Most of Russell's clippers, it appeared, had

[87] The best account of American opium policy during the period will be found in Dennett, *Americans in Eastern Asia*, pp. 124-127.

[88] The Americans, having returned to Canton, were much more vulnerable to attack than were the British who remained outside port. Furthermore, American merchants were doing handsomely by acting as agents for the legitimate trade of the English. R. B. Forbes, however, is incorrect when he says that Russell and Company abstained from dealing in opium at least until 1844. In 1842 this house was not only selling the drug on its own account but was supplying clippers to other firms. *Personal Reminiscences*, p. 161.

[89] Kearny to the secretary of the navy, 11 May 1842, *Kearny Correspondence*, no. 23, 29th Cong., 1st Sess., S. Doc. 139.

either been sold or were conveniently absent in India. Kearny suspected that both the owners and the consul had made illegal transfers. "These sham sales are well known, by which our national character is daily losing ground."[90] In fact, it was almost impossible to separate vessels that flew the American flag legally from those which merely used it as a cover for illicit operations.[91]

The commodore's efforts to prevent smuggling by Americans and thus to carry out his orders from the navy department met with little success. At Amoy he seized the *Ariel* and was persuaded not to send her to the United States only by her alleged unseaworthiness. Kearny's legal justification was not the smuggling business of her owner but the doubt about his American citizenship. As a matter of fact, the *Ariel* was not as unsafe as the commodore assumed. In 1845 she was making regular trips between India and Hongkong in the service of Dent and Company. A few months later, when Kearny's successor encountered the *Zephyr,* one of Russell's clipper fleet, taking on her cargo of Malwa at Bombay, he diligently searched for grounds which would justify his interference. He was obliged to conclude that no American law would authorize his taking action against American smugglers abroad. "The only course that appears proper for me to pursue," he wrote, "is not to interfere in their favor should they be taken by the Chinese authorities."[92] American officials in the Far East thus

90 Kearny to the secretary of the navy, 19 May 1843, *ibid.,* no. 46.

91 For a few months in 1843, after Pottinger's warning to British smugglers, the American flag seems to have been used extensively for illegal purposes. It is also true that both Americans and British often used vessels under other registries. For example, only two of the receiving ships which Russell and Company had in 1848 were American, while both of those maintained in 1854 by Augustine Heard and Company of Boston professed to be British.

92 Dennett, *Americans in Eastern Asia,* p. 126.

emerged with a policy not very far removed from that of the British consuls.

It may be said for American merchants that they seem to have reëntered the drug competition with some regret. Their memorial addressed to Congress during the crisis of 1839 expressed a desire, on both moral and commercial grounds, "to see the importation and consumption of opium in China entirely at an end." A majority of them had already pledged themselves to abstain from future dealings in opium, and it seems to have been assumed by those who signed the memorial that the trade was at an end.[93] How successfully Yankee firms conquered their scruples is indicated by the observations of the American commissioner in 1853. Humphrey Marshall was aghast at "the wholesale system of smuggling that is carried on both under the English *and American flags,* almost in view of Chinese ports, and which in my opinion amounts to a gross and abominable violation of our treaties (in their spirit) with this government."[94] There could be no room for doubt. American firms were engaged in the opium trade to the limit of their resources. Russell and Company and Augustine Heard and Company, both of Boston, seem to have been the only ones who attempted to participate in the manner of the large British houses, but smaller adventurers also found that opium had its merits as an article of commerce.[95] In 1858 William B. Reed estimated that roughly one-fifth of the opium entering Shanghai was brought by American ships.[96]

[93] *Ibid.*, pp. 122-123.

[94] Marshall to Marcy, 10 July 1853, *Correspondence of Humphrey Marshall*, 33d Cong., 1st Sess., H. Ex. Doc. 123, p. 207.

[95] I do not imply that the equipment of American firms ever approached that maintained by such a house as Jardine, Matheson and Company. But on a smaller scale their mechanism was remarkably complete.

[96] Reed to Elgin, 13 Sept. 1858, *Correspondence of William B. Reed*, incl. 1b in no. 36, 36th Cong., 1st Sess., S. Ex. Doc. 30. This statement does not necessarily mean that the opium was owned by Americans.

Under the auspices of official indifference, Chinese and foreign, and well oiled machinery, the opium trade throve. During the decade 1840-1849, the annual shipments from India averaged more than 37,000 chests, and the following ten years saw the average reach 68,000.[97] China's power of absorbing the drug was unaffected by the Taiping rebellion. After 1860, to anticipate a later chapter, exports from India declined, increased, and then remained about constant for a period of years, partly because of the expansion of poppy cultivation in China and partly because of a considered policy of the Indian government.

The position which a contraband trade of such dimensions occupied in the economy of the Far East is not easy to define. To discover whether it acted as a help or hindrance to legitimate commerce is still more difficult.[98] The fundamentals of the problem remained about what they had been before treaty days, in fact, what they had been in the days of the East India Company's monopoly. Opium was still inextricably bound up with the triangular system of trade. China was the creditor of England, England of India, and India of China, and opium was the biggest single item in enabling India to discharge her debt to England, and England hers to China.[99] If the drug had been suddenly withdrawn from the market, India would have had trouble in making her remittances to England, and London tea tables might have been innocent of tea, unless the English were willing to ship specie in enormous quantities. The editors of the *China Mail* esti-

[97] *Financial and Commercial Statistics of British India*, 1904, pp. 55-56.

[98] An admirable analysis of trade during the period is contained in Sargent, *Anglo-Chinese Commerce and Diplomacy*, pp. 126-142.

[99] The indebtedness in which India stood to Great Britain was increased by the necessity for remitting to England a part of the Indian revenue and dividends on East India Company stock. Michie, *Englishman in China*, I, 196.

mated that at least seven-eighths of the treasure used to provide cargoes for Great Britain and America was drawn from the sale of opium.[100]

During the eighteen-forties, however, the drug trade seemed an unalloyed benefaction neither to Chinese mercantilists nor to British manufacturers. For approximately the first decade after the treaty of Nanking was signed, imports of opium so far exceeded in value exports of tea and silk that the Chinese were compelled to send specie to India at the rate of about two millions sterling a year.[101] The drain of silver in payment for opium was thus a grim reality. Nor did the fact that the drug supplied money with which to buy tea and silk and a means by which remittances could be sent from India solve the problem of the British manufacturer, who was eager above all things to dispose of his textiles. The rosy expectations which had possessed British merchants in 1842 proved to be illusory. Indian opium would sell apparently in indefinite quantities, while good Lancashire cottons were mildewing in godowns at every port in China.

Manufacturers who tended to see a connection between the two phenomena found support for their views in the report of a select committee of Parliament which inquired into the state of the China trade. This committee concluded that "The payment for opium . . . absorbs the silver, to the great inconvenience of the general traffic of the Chinese."[102] The solution, as seen by the investigators, was either to expand the European market for Chinese tea and silk or to reduce the imports of opium in the hope that the silver released would be used by the Chinese to buy English goods. Opium merchants who appeared before the committee were at pains to point out

[100] 27 Oct. 1853.
[101] Sargent, *Anglo-Chinese Commerce and Diplomacy*, p. 140.
[102] *Report from the Select Committee*, 1847, p. iv.

that the absorption of Chinese purchasing power by the drug trade was no evidence that, if released, it would be diverted to the buying of Lancashire shirtings.[103] And in this conviction they were amply justified. The truth of it was that British merchants had been guilty of a grave miscalculation in forcing the China market as they had done. The Chinese did not want textiles in the quantity that English merchants proposed to supply, and possession of El Dorado itself would not have persuaded them to buy.[104]

The remedy proposed by the committee of 1847 was discredited during the next decade. The years 1845-1860 show a pronounced upward movement in Chinese exports to Europe, the silk trade registering the largest increase. By about 1851 the balance against China had disappeared, and the annual drain of silver to India was more than covered by specie shipped into Chinese ports by the English. But the greater demand for Chinese goods in Europe produced no commensurate increase in the market for British manufactures in China.[105] British merchants were therefore obliged to import into China specie at the rate of about three millions sterling a year, and the traders and tea growers of the Middle Kingdom, after paying India for its opium, merely pocketed the differ-

[103] Evidence of G. T. Braine, *ibid.*, Q. 4766: "It can hardly be supposed that the Chinese, if they were debarred from the use of opium, would use more long cloths or woollens, any more than an Englishman, if deprived of his claret, would wear more coats than he does at present." See also Alexander Matheson, Q. 4546, 4547; Alexander Williamson, Q. 1331.

[104] "The explanation lay in the fact that China herself had a vast domestic industry. There was economic and geographical justification for the neglect of foreign trade by Chinese officials, since the Empire was self-sufficing and bartered its products internally. . . . The domestic textile industry was an essential element in the rural economy of China." Sargent, *Anglo-Chinese Commerce and Diplomacy*, pp. 133-134.

[105] Imports of manufactured goods into China were increasing, but not as rapidly as exports of silk. And the growth was accompanied by heavy fluctuation from year to year. *Ibid.*, pp. 132-133.

ence. The situation may be illustrated by the figures for the trade of Shanghai in 1857. Total imports, including opium were valued at £9,379,246, while the tea and silk exported came to £11,302,834. The balance against the West was thus nearly £2,000,000. Without the imports of opium, the indebtedness would have been overwhelming.[106]

It has often been charged that trading in opium was a penny-wise policy for western merchants. The editor of the *North-China Herald* in 1855 argued that the traffic was as "essentially opposed to the interests of Foreign Merchants as it is destructive to the interests of China."[107] We may admit at once that a system of trade which placed such heavy reliance upon the imports of a vicious narcotic was not in the best of health. Opium may well have "demoralized the producing and consuming powers of China,"[108] and beyond all doubt, it hindered the establishing of amicable Anglo-Chinese relations, on which commercial prosperity was partly dependent. But the alternative was not reassuring. Either western merchants must be content to ship specie to the East until the Chinese were ready to absorb more manufactures—practically until new markets in the interior were opened —or they must discover commodities which the Chinese would accept in payment for tea and silk. Some of the consignments sent from England to China, to be sure, betrayed a certain lack of imagination on the part of their owners. A more diversified list of imports would have met perhaps with better success. But to find goods which were in demand in China was no easy matter, as the East India Company had learned years before.

[106] *North-China Herald*, 17 July 1857. The statistics given by Sargent, pp. 135-136, show a lower figure for each item, but their purport is the same.
[107] 1 Sept. 1855.
[108] Dennett, *Americans in Eastern Asia*, p. 119.

Two inferences may be drawn from what has been said. In the first place, it is not altogether correct to say that the opium trade during the eighteen-forties and eighteen-fifties, considered purely as a commercial transaction, tended in any great degree to hamper the sale of British manufactures in China. The most important element in the "sales resistance" of the Chinese was the simple fact that Lancashire textiles were ill adapted to their needs, not that payments for opium exhausted their purchasing power. On the contrary, the drug trade was the principal means by which the West reduced its unfavorable balance in China. Whether the ultimate harm done outweighed its immediate economic advantage is a speculative question which need not be opened. Secondly, the drain of silver from China to India, which had so disturbed the statesmen of the Middle Kingdom, during the early eighteen-fifties was more than offset by shipments of specie from the West.[109] Chinese prohibitionists could no longer use economic facts to reënforce their ethical argument against opium.

In the period between the two Anglo-Chinese wars our attention has been centered on the trade itself rather than on the policies of either Great Britain or China. Indian opium enjoyed sixteen relatively serene years, untroubled alike by serious competition and official interference. New markets were developed and older ones enlarged. To her Majesty's government, however, conditions were less satisfactory than to opium traders. Not only was regular commerce exposed to obvious dangers, but British policy was made to appear in a bad light. Whitehall could not be wholly comfortable about the opium traffic as long as it was even nominally contraband.

[109] Later in the century, of course, the goods balance turned against the Chinese, but by this time opium had lost its dominating position among the imports.

CHAPTER VIII

LEGALIZATION

BRITISH policy in China owed its origin to the necessities of British subjects who came to the gates of the Middle Kingdom "for traffic's sake." To obtain an honorable status for merchants and to open the Chinese Empire to their trade was the motive which inspired her Majesty's diplomatists. Between the two Anglo-Chinese wars British superintendents of trade sought to encourage peaceful commercial relations between the subjects of the two countries. To these officials the opium trade was known chiefly as an embarrassing complication. In theory it might at any time precipitate a crisis like that of 1839, and in practice it created an unhappy state of affairs.

To effect the legalization of the opium traffic was therefore a settled policy of the foreign office. The Chinese, it was argued, were impotent to enforce their own laws, and British superintendents and consuls could hardly assume that responsibility. Even the suppression of cultivation in India would not solve the problem. If her Majesty's subjects were forbidden to trade in the drug, their places would be taken by others whose sense of smuggling decorum was inferior to that of the British,[1] and China's plight would be worse rather than better. The British case, as presented by Charles Elliot and his successors,

---

[1] While consul at Shanghai, Rutherford Alcock offered his opinion that "No attempt to stop or materially diminish the consumption could possibly avail, or be otherwise than productive of aggravated mischief . . . by throwing the trade into hands less scrupulous, and relieved of all those

was a combination of truth and sophistry. The opium trade would not have been wiped out by prohibiting cultivation in British India and export from British ports, but it would have been substantially reduced.[2] Persia, Turkey, and Egypt would still have helped to supply the Chinese market. With such states there was no possibility of a mutual self-denying ordinance. At the time, however, they were producing little opium for export, and their potential output was far below that of Bengal and Malwa.

The full irony of the British contentions can be appreciated only as one recalls the opium system as it existed in India. While the superintendents of trade were solemnly assuring the Chinese that suppressing the poppy in India would do no good, the Indian government was taking lavish pains to ensure the prosperity of its opium business. It is inadequate to say that Indian administrators made terms with reality by taking what they could out of an established trade. The traffic grew not alone because of the natural expansion of the market but also because of the fostering hand of the Bengal monopolists, who saw to it that the Chinese were provided with all the opium that they could consume, and sometimes more.[3]

Yet to expect Great Britain to abolish the Bengal monopoly and to restrain exports from Malwa is to lay a

checks which under the British flag prevent the trade from taking the worst characters of smuggling.'' Alcock, it should be added, was consistently hostile to the opium traffic throughout his stay in China. Michie, *Englishman in China*, I, 197.

[2] A large preventive establishment might have been necessary to prevent clandestine shipments from ports on the west coast. Some trade through the Portuguese cities might have persisted, but since the conquest of Sind, the way was so effectively blocked that it could not have been large.

[3] The Indian government on occasion sent musters of opium to China, packed in different ways and accompanied by instructions to merchants to ascertain which best suited Chinese taste. I. O. Bengal Board of Revenue (Misc.) Proc., 24 Aug. 1821; I. O. Bengal Separate Consultations, 9 Jan. 1839.

heavy tax on the international morality of the eighteen-forties and 'fifties. A proposal to suppress the British opium trade, out of deference to a Chinese law that the Chinese themselves honored principally in the breach, would have been regarded by most Englishmen as the height of quixotism. In the words of Morse, ''The general opinion of the world was not yet so far advanced as to compel so decisive a step.''[4] Estimates of the actual harm done by the drug varied widely. Was opium a vicious narcotic or was it merely the Chinese counterpart of the Englishman's ale? There were those who protested against the policy of Britain—missionaries, Quaker reformers, and others—but often they so badly misrepresented the facts that their appeals lost all relevance.[5]

Given the premises on which the foreign office acted, legalization was the most reasonable solution. If opium were admitted to the Chinese tariff, the drug trade would be brought under control and would tend less to embitter Anglo-Chinese relationships. That the largest British import should be introduced into China by paths which were nominally contraband was an alarming spectacle to the foreign office. Hence British superintendents and plenipotentiaries, from the Elliots to Lord Elgin, were instructed to obtain for opium, if it could be done by moral suasion, the status of a legal import.

Captain Elliot and Sir Henry Pottinger, as we have seen, made conscientious attempts to carry out their in-

---

[4] *International Relations*, I, 545. Hostility towards the opium traffic seems to have been stronger in the United States than in Great Britain. American merchants regarded its apparent suppression in 1839 as a benefaction. For an ingenious attack on the trade as a device by which British merchants were enabled to appropriate the lion's share of exports from China, see Marshall to Marcy, 10 July 1853, *Correspondence of Humphrey Marshall*, 33d Cong., 1st Sess., H. Ex. Doc. 123, p. 207; also Dennett, *Americans in Eastern Asia*, pp. 122-123.

[5] The classic example of misstatement was the memorial presented by Lord Shaftesbury, which will be dealt with later on in this chapter.

structions. John Francis Davis, ex-supercargo of the East India Company at Canton, who assumed the office of superintendent in 1844, lost no time in broaching the question to the Chinese authorities. At the suggestion of Kiyıng, viceroy of Canton, he drew up a memorial which presented the case for legalization with a good deal of shrewdness.[6] In subsequent correspondence he developed with more elaborate detail the fiscal advantages that would accrue to the Chinese state. He pointed out that, if opium were to become a legitimate article of trade, the British would take precisely the same measures to protect Chinese customs revenue that they had done with respect to other commodities. The utopia sketched by the British superintendent was no less attractive to Kiying, but the great emperor, he said, would not be swayed even by the prospect of revenue, for "whilst looking to benefit the customs . . . we should certainly put a value on riches and slight men's lives.'"[7] The high moral tone of the viceroy's attitude would have been more credible had the despatch ended there. But he went on to make a curious proposal, rightly interpreted by Davis as one of mutual connivance. Henceforth, he said, the Chinese would enforce their opium laws against their own subjects, while British importers should be dealt with according to English law. To imply that British officials might enforce non-existent British laws against opium was merely a tactful way of suggesting that the matter be dropped.

Kiying's rebuff appears to have discouraged Davis for several months. But the outrageous lengths to which smuggling on the Canton River had gone and the reckless aggressiveness of foreign traders at closed ports impelled

[6] See Davis to Aberdeen, 13 June 1844, *Papers rel. Opium, 1842-56*, 1857, no. 9.

[7] Kiying to Davis, 19 Aug. 1844, *ibid.*, incl. in no. 12; see also *ibid.*, incls. 1 and 2 in no. 11.

him to further action. In the spring of 1847 he assumed a peremptory tone, threatening to send a memorial directly to Peking. Kiying begged that the memorial be postponed until he made a trip to the capital. There is no evidence that the document ever reached the imperial presence. Certainly it produced no immediate results either in Chinese policy or in the emperor's attitude towards his servant Kiying.[8]

Samuel Bonham, late governor of the Straits, who succeeded Davis in 1847, made no attempt to reopen the question of legalization. The Chinese were even less inclined to refer to it. Since 1842 a few smokers had been strangled, but against them the government seems to have had complaints other than their addiction to opium.[9] In 1849, however, there were rumors that new prohibitory measures were to be introduced. Report had it that Seu, a friend of Lin Tse Hsu, had been commissioned to suppress the trade, principally as a means of checking the flow of silver. Apparently a champion of *machtpolitik,* Seu ascribed the failure in 1839 to over-indulgent methods. He was confident that the removal of a few heads would put an end to the problem. But he profited by the unhappy experience of his friend, and he proposed to attack Chinese dealers and smokers rather than to play with the fire that was the British opium system. The rumor seemed to be confirmed in the following year, when the young Emperor Hsien Feng issued the last of the ruthless anti-opium edicts.[10]

Before deliberate and unwieldy China could carry this pronouncement into effect—if indeed it was ever in-

8 Davis to Kiying, 26 April 1845, 25 Feb. 1846, 29 April 1847, *ibid.,* incls. in nos. 13, 17, 19; Kiying to Davis, 18 May 1847, *ibid.,* incl. 3 in no. 20.

9 *China Mail,* 13 July 1848.

10 *North-China Herald,* 7 Sept. 1850, in Morse, *International Relations,* I, 549. See also Bowring to Bonham, 19 May and 24 May 1849, *Papers rel. Opium, 1842-56,* 1857, incl. 1 in no. 21 and incl. in no. 22.

tended to be more than a face-saving gesture—the Taiping rebellion intervened to create a desperate situation in imperial finances. With the revenue systems of both the affected provinces and the empire thoroughly disorganized, it was natural that the opium trade should be scrutinized as a possible source of income. British statesmen appreciated the significance of the chaos in China, and they cherished the hope, as Lord Clarendon informed Bonham, that it would lead to new concessions for western traders. Heading the list of commercial aims which Britain sought to achieve was the legalization of the opium traffic.[11]

For the first time since 1836, as far as is known, the Son of Heaven inclined his ear to a discussion of the problem. A cautious memorial from the censor Chang Wei seems to have pointed the way, and the principal officials were ordered to meet for deliberation.[12] The memorial of another censor, Wu Ting Pu, lent strength to the movement. Dismissing as inadequate the recommendations made upon Chang Wei's proposal by the boards, he plunged into the fundamentals of the question. The scarcity of silver might be attributed, he thought, primarily to the opium trade, although some of the shortage had perhaps been caused by extraordinary military expenditures. Wu Ting Pu held no brief for opium smoking, but taking a leaf from the book of Confucius and the other sages whose opinions he invoked, he argued that the lesser of the evils must be chosen. China's experiment with prohibition left little ground for optimism. There-

---

[11] Clarendon to Bonham, 7 May 1853, I. O. China Corr., IV. I do not mean to imply that a legal opium trade was the principal concession desired by the British. In the despatch referred to, it was listed in the category of "commercial aims," while more weighty matters, such as the opening of additional ports and the residence of ministers at Peking, were dealt with in another connection.

[12] *North-China Herald*, 5 Feb. 1853.

fore, let a tax of one dollar a ball—forty dollars a chest[13]
—be levied and some millions of dollars quietly reclaimed, while the barbarians naïvely thought that they
were being invited to more profitable trade relations. As
Chinese opium production was encouraged, imports from
abroad would decline and finally cease altogether. In
this way the greatness of England—which, after all,
was "merely a poor ant-hill in the ocean"—would be
sapped.[14]

The bow of Wu Ting Pu, it will be seen, had two
strings. On the one hand, to legalize the import of foreign
opium would bring direct revenue into the treasury. On
the other, to permit poppy cultivation in China, although
customs duties might be sacrificed, would stop the flow
of native silver to India. A more sophistical case for Chinese cultivation was stated a few months later by another
official. Native opium, he argued, was a different commodity from that supplied by foreigners, who adulterated their product with a poisonous drug.[15] It was the
fiscal emergency, in effect, that turned the eyes of the
Chinese again towards the solution of the opium problem
that the British had so indefatigably advocated. From
whichever side of the question the memorialists approached—foreign trade or local cultivation—their objective was to rescue the country from its financial plight.
Their arguments may have been regarded with favor in
Peking, but to bring the precedent-bound imperial court
to action required another war.

[13] As a matter of fact, the memorialist stated that thirty-three dollars
would be collected on each chest, but he was apparently misinformed as to
the contents of a chest.

[14] *Papers rel. Opium, 1842-56*, 1857, incl. in no. 25. This was about the
time that the balance of trade began to favor China, but the shift was not
yet recognized by the Chinese. For other factors which produced a shortage
of silver see Morse, *International Relations*, I, 469 ff.

[15] *China Mail*, 17 Nov. 1853.

The Arrow War (1856-1858), sometimes described as the "Second Opium War," forms no part of the story of the drug trade save in its consequences. It can hardly be pictured as "chasing away the darkness of heathenism, and substituting for its iron rule the benignant sway and gentle influence of Christianity," but it was not a conflict to force the legalization of the opium traffic.[16] The treaty of Nanking, at best, had left the opening of China half effected. Equality in diplomatic intercourse was not yet achieved, and traders from the West still felt themselves unnecessarily hampered. The immediate occasion for the war, "that wretched question of the 'Arrow,' which is a scandal to us," went unemphasized, if not unmentioned, in the peace negotiations.[17] The latter were conducted on the larger issues of Anglo-Chinese relationships. In the conferences between the British plenipotentiary, Lord Elgin, and the Chinese commissioners, the opium question was also passed by without discussion.

To the British foreign office, however, legalization had seemed for years the only rational solution, while the financial exigencies of the rebellion created a strong presumption in its favor on the part of the Chinese. Opium was already a legitimate import in everything but name. Since 1842, the trade had encountered few obstacles, and officials had enjoyed to the full the fruits of connivance. During the years 1856-1858, when the financial strain became intolerable, they came into the open and announced

[16] *Fraser's Magazine*, Feb., 1857, quoted in J. Rowntree, *Imperial Drug Trade*, p. 90.

[17] T. Walrond, *Letters and Journals of Lord Elgin*, p. 209. The lorcha *Arrow*, whose British registry had expired some days previously, was boarded by Chinese officers on a charge of piracy. The crew, consisting almost wholly of Chinese, was seized. At the demand of Consul Parkes, the men were released but an apology for the act was refused. The Canton officials also promised to refrain from further demonstrations of the kind. The British fleet replied with a bombardment of Canton.

frankly that a duty would be collected for military purposes. At Shanghai a tax at the rate of twelve taels per
chest was finally imposed.[18] Twelve boats stationed near
the receiving ships at Wusung, flying flags which bore
the inscription "Public Committee for Patriotic Collections," reported sales to the customs house. Duty was
then collected from native dealers. The whole procedure
radiated such an official atmosphere that the *North-China
Herald* informed its readers that "an Imperial duty upon
opium has at last been imposed at this port."[19] The pre-
fect of Foochow proposed to the American consul that
opium be reported at the customs house and that foreign
merchants charge enough to allow the payment of duty
at the rate of twenty-four taels per chest. The consul of
course refused to give his sanction, and the tax was collected by means of spies near the foreign godowns, who
noted the names of Chinese purchasers.[20] The Ningpo

[18] In 1857 the tael was made the unit of trade at Shanghai. It was a
modification of the Chinese ounce, containing 525 grains of fine silver. Its
rate of exchange on London during 1857 varied from 6s. 6d. to 7s. 10d.
Morse, *International Relations*, I, 471; C. F. Remer, *Foreign Trade of China*,
p. 31.

[19] 21 March 1857. It is possible that the duty was actually an imperial
one, imposed by order of Peking. The *Herald* stated that ten of the twelve
taels were to be remitted to the capital, the two remaining to go for the expenses of collection. The emperor, it was reported, desired that no publicity
be given to the new policy and had promised that it would be abandoned if
foreigners objected. If the emperor really decided to raise revenue from
opium—as he had no legal right to do without foreign consent—it would do
much to explain the conduct of the Chinese delegates at the subsequent tariff
negotiations. The taotai of Shanghai apparently raised the tax from twelve
to twenty-four taels during 1857-1858. Glover to Reed, 31 Aug. 1858, *Correspondence of William B. Reed*, incl. 1a in no. 36, 36th Cong., 1st Sess., S. Ex.
Doc. 30; G. W. Cooke, *China*, p. 180.

[20] *North-China Herald*, 27 June 1857; U. S. consul at Foochow to Parker,
5 May 1857, *Correspondence of Peter Parker*, exhibit 2d in no. 22, 35th
Cong., 2d Sess., S. Ex. Doc. 22, pp. 1353-1354; Dunn to Reed, 21 Jan. 1858,
Correspondence of William B. Reed (cited hereafter as *Reed Corr.*), incl. 1s
in no. 10, 36th Cong., 1st Sess., S. Ex. Doc. 30. During the confusion caused
by the rebellion foreign merchants often stored opium in their own godowns.

authorities, unable to reach an agreement with native dealers, farmed the right of collection to a local speculator. In 1858 the Amoy officials, who for some time had been levying two dollars per chest for military expenses, raised the impost to fifty dollars. Thus the logic of events was pushing the Chinese government inexorably towards legalization.[21]

Lord Elgin was instructed by Clarendon "to ascertain whether the Government of China would revoke its prohibition of the opium trade."[22] The British plenipotentiary held few illusions about the character of the traffic or indeed about many of the contacts between Westerner and Chinese. While stopping in Calcutta he confided to paper his indignation at the attitude assumed by his compatriots in the East towards "inferior races." At Tientsin he reverted to the same theme. "I have seen more to disgust me with my fellow-countrymen than I saw during the whole course of my previous life, since I have found them in the East among populations too weak to resist and too ignorant to complain." On another occasion he referred to "the horrid opium-shops, which we are supposed to do so much to encourage."[23]

The American commissioner, William B. Reed, is usually credited with having fortified the determination of Lord Elgin to apply "the only remedy which appeared to him practicable."[24] Reed had come to China thoroughly

21 *North-China Herald*, 28 May 1857, 13 March and 9 Oct. 1858; Doty to Reed, 22 Jan. 1858, *Reed Corr.*, incl. 2m in no. 10.

22 Clarendon to Elgin, 20 April 1857, *Correspondence relating to the Earl of Elgin's Special Missions to China and Japan, 1857-59*, 1859 (cited hereafter as *Elgin Corr.*, 1859) no. 2. The formal instructions are silent on the subject of opium.

23 Walrond, *Letters and Journals of Lord Elgin*, pp. 199-200, 252-253, 189-190. See also the evidence of Sir Thomas Wade, *Report of the Royal Commission*, I, 1894, Q. 1291.

24 L. Oliphant, *Narrative of the Earl of Elgin's Mission*, p. 484. As will be indicated presently, there is reason to think that Reed had less to do

hostile to the opium trade and under instructions to indicate to the Chinese authorities that the United States neither sought the legalization of the traffic nor would uphold its citizens in their violation of Chinese law. In the American treaty drafted at the Taku forts, the drug was specifically declared contraband, in accordance with the precedent set by the treaty of Wanghia (1844). But even at Taku the Chinese seem to have been rather indifferent, perhaps recalling the unedifying part played in the opium trade by Americans.[25] In the American treaty of Tientsin, however, no anti-opium clause appeared, because, as the plenipotentiary explained to Washington, it would have made American exploits in the drug trade seem all the more scandalous. Furthermore, Lord Elgin had requested the omission on the ground that an article condemning the opium traffic would seem a gratuitous slap at British policy.[26]

with bringing about the legalization of the opium trade than has been assumed.

[25] Cass to Reed, 30 May 1857, *Reed Corr.*, pp. 8-9.

[26] W. A. P. Martin, a missionary who accompanied Reed as interpreter, roundly attacks him for his change of heart. (Martin, *Cycle of Cathay*, p. 184.) And Morse (*International Relations*, I, 554) classes him "among those who have betrayed great causes." Dennett's opinion (*Americans in Eastern Asia*, pp. 325-326) seems on the whole a fairer one: "The American Commissioner was debating, as related to a drug, the old and also modern question of the relative merits of ineffective prohibition as compared with high license and regulation. If Mr. Reed was on the wrong side of the argument there is no reason whatever to suppose that his error was any other than that of judgment, and with him stood many foreigners of long experience in China who could be charged with no friendliness towards the opium trade."

The Russian treaty also omitted specific reference to opium. The original draft was altered to "please the English by erasing the special mention of opium from the contraband articles of import. It is a useless clause, to be sure, but the Count is strong in his views as to the bad policy and results of the trade in the drug." "Journal of S. Wells Williams. Reed and Ward Missions," *Journal of the North China Branch of the Royal Asiatic Society*, XLII, 51.

The treaties of Tientsin were signed in June of 1858. During that summer Reed's ideas became more firmly set, and he determined to present them in all candor to Lord Elgin.[27] While in Shanghai he took occasion to consult various shades of opinion—official, missionary, and mercantile—only to learn that they were almost unanimous in preferring any arrangement to the existing one. Even the missionaries, who were implacably hostile to the trade itself, were driven to favor legalization as the only alternative to the outrageous farce of prohibition.[28] In a much-quoted letter Reed outlined the situation for the benefit of the British plenipotentiary. He tactfully reminded Elgin that, by the new American treaty, opium would be contraband or not, according to the law of China. And then he went on to urge the need for a definitive solution. "I appeal to your Excellency's high sense of duty, so often expressed to this helpless though perverse people, whether we, the Representatives of Western and Christian nations, ought to consider our work done without some attempt to induce or compel an adjustment of this pernicious difficulty."[29] To Reed the practical issue was legalization or nothing. Opium ought to be admitted upon the payment of a duty sufficiently high to restrict the supply but low enough to keep the trade from illicit channels.

[27] In return for the omission of the anti-opium clause from the American treaty, Lord Elgin had agreed not to press the demand for legalization at the time. The American thought that "Lord Elgin's half-expressed reluctance to comply with his instructions was very creditable to him, believing as I do that he feels a strong repugnance to this infamous traffic and the connection of his government with it." Reed to Cass, 30 June 1858, *Reed Corr.*, no. 23, p. 357.

[28] Reed to Cass, 9 Nov. 1858, *ibid.*, no. 36, pp. 493 ff. The only exceptions, it was stated, were a few English and Parsis who found smuggling more profitable than a legal trade could ever become.

[29] Reed to Elgin, 13 Sept. 1858, *Elgin Corr.*, 1859, incl. 1 in no. 212; *Reed Corr.*, incl. 1b in no. 36; Oliphant, *Narrative of the Earl of Elgin's Mission*, pp. 484-485.

The suggestion found a receptive spirit in Lord Elgin, who had refrained from raising the question at Tientsin, not from any lack of conviction but because it seemed unfair "to urge the Imperial Government to abandon its traditional policy in this respect, under the kind of pressure which we were bringing to bear."[30] At Shanghai, where discussions on the tariff were then taking place, it was thought that conditions might be more favorable for broaching the delicate issue. After much annoying delay the Chinese commissioners were finally appointed. But before formal sessions of the tariff conference began, and before Lord Elgin, who was in Japan, had had time to act upon Reed's suggestion, the Chinese appear to have reached their decision. Conversations were held between the two commissioners and H. N. Lay, chief of the imperial maritime customs.[31] When the question of opium was raised, according to Lay's account, the Chinese replied, "We have resolved to put it into the tariff as . . . foreign medicine."[32] This preliminary meeting is credible enough despite the fact that no record of it was published in the official report and that Lay's story came out some twenty years later. Subsequently his version was corroborated by Laurence Oliphant and Sir Thomas Wade, who acted as secretary and interpreter respectively to Elgin's mission.[33] When one recalls that duty on opium

[30] Elgin to Reed, 19 Oct. 1858, *Elgin Corr.*, 1859, incl. 3 in no. 212.

[31] During the Taiping rebellion, when the Chinese city of Shanghai was in the hands of the insurgents, the foreign merchants organized a commission to collect duties on behalf of the Chinese government. The plan which this commission foreshadowed—of collecting duties on foreign trade through the agency of foreigners themselves—was realized in the imperial maritime customs. Although employees of the Chinese government, the principal officials of the service were foreigners. China owed the development of the system to the genius of Sir Robert Hart. Morse, *Trade and Administration*, Chapter XII.

[32] *The Times*, 22 Oct. 1880.

[33] "There is one most important incident left out [of the official report],

was already being collected in the name of the government at three or four of the treaty ports, it is not difficult to believe that the Chinese voluntarily resolved to make the drug a legal import.

The formal meetings of the tariff commission began in the middle of October, 1858. The major part of the work fell, for the British on Wade and Oliphant, and for the Chinese on two officials of Kiangsu province. With the four also sat H. N. Lay. Wade and Oliphant informed the Chinese of their instructions "not to insist on the insertion of the drug in the tariff, should the Chinese Government wish to omit it."[34] The Chinese commissioners at once admitted the necessity of a change. The government, they said, had not relinquished its moral objections, "but the present generation of smokers, at all events, must and will have opium."[35] Having made their concession, Sieh and Wang now bent all their diplomatic efforts towards isolating the drug from the other items in the tariff. They refused to admit it at the regular five per cent *ad valorem* provided by the treaty of Tientsin. Foreigners should not carry it into the interior, nor should it be included in the regular tariff. In effect, opium was to be a matter for special negotiation.

Agreement on a rate of duty was reached only after some debate. The Chinese declined to consider fifteen or

probably because I did not think it sufficiently serious; and that is that the whole thing having been well thought out between Mr. Lay and the Superintendent of Customs, when we met for our first conference, inasmuch as it was a proposal affecting opium . . . both Mr. Oliphant and myself came to it with a certain amount of formality, when the Superintendent . . . asked, "What is the use of talking about that when Mr. Lay and myself have settled the whole thing?" In this account the conduct of the Chinese commissioners was a little less decorous than in the official version. But the important fact is clear, that there had been preliminary discussions, during the course of which the Chinese had consented to legalize opium. Evidence of Sir Thomas Wade, *Report of the Royal Commission*, I, 1894, Q. 1329.

[34] *Times*, 25 Oct. 1880.   [35] *Elgin Corr.*, 1859, incl. in no. 213.

twenty taels per chest—about the regular five per cent *ad valorem* which applied to articles not enumerated in the tariff. After all, China's moral scruples must not be sacrificed too cheaply. The British, for their part, argued that the rate must not be set so high as to drive the trade into illicit channels, making it more profitable to smuggle than to pay the impost. The duty, a compromise between extreme claims made by both sides, finally came to rest at thirty taels per chest.

The opium provisions, it should be noticed, were not introduced into the ordinary tariff but formed the subject of a special article.[36] In the future, the drug would be handled at the port of entry precisely as any other article of trade, paying the prescribed duty to the imperial maritime customs. But after it passed into the hands of the Chinese purchaser the imperial government was at liberty to tax as it chose.[37] Foreigners were not permitted to carry opium beyond the treaty ports. On this point the Chinese had been firm, foreseeing a long train of unpleasant complications. Lord Elgin admitted their objection, for he was quite aware of the trouble that might arise, "if foreigners were entitled under the sanction of treaties, to force this article into all the districts of the interior of China."[38]

However deplorable that a narcotic should become an item of free and legal commerce, it must be said that Elgin's plan was superior to the system that it supplanted. With the government of India standing firm against any alteration in its monopoly policy and with the Chinese government impoverished and disintegrat-

[36] Article V in the rules of trade, *Hertslet's China Treaties*, no. 7.

[37] Lord Elgin agreed that the usual interior transit duty of two and one-half per cent need not be applied to opium. His "formula was, let them tax it as high as they please, only regularize it." Evidence of Sir Thomas Wade, *Report of the Royal Commission*, I, 1894, Q. 1327, 1329.

[38] Elgin to Malmesbury, 8 Nov. 1858, *Elgin Corr.*, 1859, no. 222.

ing, no other course appears to have been possible. Throughout the negotiations Lord Elgin's objective was clear and his motives above reproach. To the Shanghai merchants he described the new status of opium in indubitable language. "It must be distinctly understood that the modifications introduced into the Chinese Tariff do not in any degree fetter or restrict the discretion of Great Britain as regards the traffic in that article. If the British people and the British Government see fit to do so, they may still make it penal for a British subject to engage in it. . . . In my recent discussions with the Chinese Imperial Commissioners, I have merely sought to induce them to bring the trade in opium from the region of fiction to that of fact."[39] Nothing was farther from his intention than that the way should be eased for British opium merchants. The only possible verdict is that of a missionary-diplomatist, whose antipathy to the opium trade and whose devotion to the best interests of China were alike unimpeachable: "Bad as the triumph is, I am convinced that it was the best disposition that could be made of this perplexing question; legalization is preferable to the evils attending the farce now played."[40]

The opium question in China was thus settled on a basis which, far from ideal, was the best that could be compounded from such discordant elements. In England, meanwhile, a protest against the government's connection with the trade had been gathering force. Initiative was taken by a group of evangelicals and Quakers, whose unconquerable reformism penetrated so many dark areas in nineteenth-century life. The question presented itself to them not only as a matter of public morality, but in a narrower sense as a religious issue. As an obstacle to the

[39] *Ibid.*, incl. in no. 236.
[40] "Journal of S. Wells Williams. Reed and Ward Missions," *Journal of the North China Branch of the Royal Asiatic Society*, XLII, 96.

progress of Christianity in China, opium bulked large in
the reports sent home by foreign missionaries. During
the first Anglo-Chinese war a memorial was addressed to
Palmerston by a group calling itself the "Society for the
Suppression of the Contraband Trade in Opium." Among
the signatures such names as Gurney, Fry, and Fox were
conspicuous. In addition to offering the hope that her
Majesty's plenipotentiaries would be given appropriate
instructions, the memorialists called upon the government "to discourage the cultivation of opium in the Indian Peninsula."[41]

In 1843 Lord Ashley (later Lord Shaftesbury) added
the opium trade to his multitudinous reform interests,
"as the cause of Christianity and of God."[42] At the request of Samuel Gurney and William Fry, son of Eliza-
beth Fry, he consented to challenge the monopoly on the
floor of the House of Commons. It had been intimated
that the government would not be averse to its abolition
and that the board of trade was actually favorable.[43]
Inspired by this assurance, Ashley launched his attack.
Petitions were also presented from committees of the
Wesleyan, Baptist, and London Missionary Societies.[44]
Ashley's indictment of British opium policy was scath-
ing enough, bristling with statistics and quotations from
first-hand observers. Unfortunately either his righteous
indignation or his unfamiliarity with conditions in China
led him into lamentable over-statement and a use of
authorities that was less than critical.[45] He was sup-

[41] I. O. China Corr., II.

[42] E. Hodder, *Life of Shaftesbury*, I, 466.

[43] As it later transpired, this information was not altogether correct. It is
true, however, that English statesmen were often embarrassed at having to
defend the opium policy of their Anglo-Indian colleagues.

[44] 3 *Hansard*, LXVIII, 362 ff.

[45] He asserted, for example, that the Chinese were eager for British manufactures, but that the opium trade constituted an insuperable barrier. He

ported, with reservations, by Sir George Staunton, whose long stay in China lent weight to his words. It is undeniable that they made, as Ashley set down in his diary, "a sensible impression on the House."

The government was disturbed by the strength of the anti-opium group, which during the course of the debate proved sufficiently powerful to overwhelm a motion to adjourn. The speeches for the defense, including that of Sir Robert Peel, were not impressive. There is something in Ashley's charge that "he [Peel] . . . assumed the tone of a low, mercantile, financial soul, which . . . placed him in my mind much below the Christian level, and not any higher than the heathen."[46] The government was unprepared for the encounter and would have preferred to avoid it, for tariff negotiations were then taking place in China. When Peel asked that the motion be withdrawn, lest it prejudice these negotiations and that the matter be left in the hands of the government, Ashley, of course, complied. There is no evidence that the question ever received consideration from a ministry already burdened with more immediately pressing concerns. But in the passage-at-arms the anti-opiumists had scored a moral victory. *The Times* found the "grave, temperate, and practical" argument of Ashley "far more statesmanlike in its ultimate and general views than those by which it was opposed."[47]

The withdrawal of Ashley's motion marked a lull in anti-opium agitation, while the reformer busied himself with the ten-hours bill and other projects. But in 1855, indomitable in his well-doing, he again raised the ques-

also stated that the traffic was carried on by depraved and desperate fellows, a charge that was only partly correct.

46 Hodder, *Life of Shaftesbury*, I, 476.

47 6 April 1843. *The Times* was not in complete agreement with Ashley's motion, but the editor was much impressed by some of his arguments, especially his claim that opium preëmpted the market for British manufactures.

tion, this time in the form of a memorial to the government.[48] Convincing as may have been his main argument, that the opium trade was a blot upon the British name and that the complicity of the government in it should cease, his case was once more weakened by appalling exaggeration. The government, on this occasion, took pains to obtain from its plenipotentiary in China, Sir John Bowring, a critical judgment upon Ashley's assertions. Bowring returned, along with his own views, memoranda by some of the better informed missionaries, physicians, and merchants.

With many of Ashley's arguments the reports from China took issue. That the trade was "with scarce an exception, carried on under English colors, and by British subjects," was at best only a half truth. The economic assumptions on which the memorialist based his case were also considered invalid. For the opium trade, far from stealing the market from British manufactures, was the principal means by which specie was supplied for the purchase of Chinese products. Ashley, in adducing the old drain-of-silver argument, had betrayed the antiquity of his knowledge. During the two previous years P & O steamers had brought into China over 28,000,000 dollars more than they had carried out.[49]

Two of the documents submitted by Sir John Bowring are worthy of special attention, for they came from witnesses who may be properly called unwilling. Both missionaries, Dr. Hobson and the Rev. Dr. W. H. Medhurst, although they deplored the opium trade, regarded the Ashley memorial, at least in part, as an unfortunate series of over-statements. In contrast to the twenty million smokers in China assumed by Ashley, neither Hobson nor Medhurst was inclined to place the figure much

[48] *Papers rel. Opium, 1842-56*, 1857, pp. 77-80.
[49] Bowring to Clarendon, 8 Jan. 1856, *ibid.*, no. 26.

above two million.[50] Both, however, disagreed emphatically with the policy of the Indian government, and both urged that cultivation be stopped. "Why, Sir John, should not the . . . quantity be diminished every year, and the fertile plains of Hindostan grown with cotton and other useful products?"

Despite the chilly reception which his memorial received, Ashley had no intention of letting an evil pass unrebuked. Having evidently abandoned all hope of appealing to the government on the ground of morality, he resolved to attack from the legal angle. In March of 1857, Ashley—now Earl of Shaftesbury—moved in the House of Lords to refer to the judges the twofold question, whether it were lawful, first, for the East India Company to derive a revenue from the monopoly of opium, and secondly, to manufacture it for export to China.[51] The monopoly, he argued, was really a commercial enterprise and as such prohibited by the Act of 1833, and the trade to China an unfriendly act and a violation of treaty obligations. When the opinion of the law officers of the crown was handed down some five months later—for Shaftesbury had withdrawn his motion to refer to the judges on condition that the law officers be consulted—it proved, on the first count, to be favorable to the monopoly.[52] On the second, they held that, although the trade in opium was no direct infraction of the treaty of Nanking, it was "at variance with its spirit and intention, and with the conduct due . . . as a friendly power, bound by a treaty

[50] Hobson thought that four million was a maximum but that two million would be a fairer estimate. Hobson to Bowring, 6 Nov. 1855, *ibid.*, incl. 1. Medhurst's "Remarks on the Opium Trade" (*ibid.*, incl. 5) is a valuable monograph on the opium question.

[51] 3 *Hansard*, CXLIV, 2027-2033.

[52] The legal advisers of the board of control for India were also invited to submit their case to the law officers.

which implies that all smuggling will be discountenanced by Great Britain.''[53] This opinion was robbed of whatever force it might otherwise have had by the fact that the second Anglo-Chinese war was then in progress. From that encounter emerged a temporary settlement of the opium question, one that guaranteed by treaty the right of foreigners to import the drug.

In England, then, British opium policy was increasingly to be subjected to criticism, while in China during the decade following legalization the trade in the Indian drug pursued a fairly even course. But a formidable competitor was arising in the form of native opium, which hitherto had been a negligible factor. Although reports and memorials submitted in the eighteen-thirties indicate that cultivation was in progress, the total production seems not to have been great and the quality was certainly inferior.[54] The memorialists of 1852-1853 also refer to Chinese opium as a fact and urge that its manufacture be officially sanctioned.

Not until after the Arrow War are we put in possession of even approximate data. In 1864 Robert Hart, inspector-general of the imperial maritime customs, requested from his commissioners information on the use of native opium at the various open ports. Five replied that native opium had been brought into their cities, but, excepting Canton, in quantities of less than five hundred piculs.[55] In no case had native opium appreciably dimin-

[53] Quoted in Rowntree, *Imperial Drug Trade*, p. 112.

[54] In 1849 two specimens of Chinese opium were analyzed by the government physician in Hongkong. The results, duly reported to the government of India, showed that, while one was hopelessly bad, the other variety might in time approach Indian opium in quality. I. O. Abstracts of Separate Revenue Letters, V.

[55] *Native Opium, Customs Special Series*, no. 1. A picul, 133⅓ pounds, was nearly equivalent to a chest of Malwa opium and somewhat less than that of Bengal (160 pounds).

ished the demand for the Indian drug.[56] One of the chief uses of the former, whose purchasers were among the poorer classes, was as an adulterant for the more costly foreign narcotic.[57]

The meager shipments of the drug into treaty ports, as reported by customs commissioners, form no very good index of the volume of Chinese cultivation. For the ports, particularly those along the seaboard, where consumers had long been accustomed to the Indian variety, showed more reluctance to adopt native opium than did the remote provinces.[58] Four years before the customs inquiry, it was stated that all of the opium consumed in West China was of local origin.[59] Assuredly the seventh decade of the century saw native cultivation distinctly on the increase. Restrictive efforts of officials—for the law still remained on the statute books—were sporadic and ineffectual. When a conscientious governor complained that poppy growing in Shansi interfered with the production of grain and inflated food prices, the emperor commanded all governors to issue proclamations against the budding industry. Although the imperial edict stimulated foreign trade in certain sections, its chief consequence

[56] It was thought that some 1500 piculs had been shipped into Canton during the year, more than half from Yunnan, the remainder from Kweichow and Szechuan. The price averaged about two-thirds that of Malwa and four-fifths that of Patna.

[57] The Chinese dealer would bore a hole in a ball of Bengal opium, extract part of the juice, and introduce a quantity of the native drug. The ball was then sealed and sold as pure Indian opium. With Malwa, the outer skin was peeled off, and a mixture made of the Indian and Chinese drugs. The skin was then replaced and the adulterated product sold to country dealers. *Consular Reports*, 1876, *Shanghai*, p. 10.

[58] By the treaty of Tientsin a number of new ports were opened to foreign trade. Some, such as Nanking, Hankow, and Chinkiang, were in the interior.

[59] *Papers relating to the Opium Question*, 1870, *Supplement*, 1872, p. 16. This collection, published by the government of India, will be cited hereafter as *Calcutta Papers*, 1870.

was to enable officials to lay a high tax on poppy land.[60] In 1869 and 1872 the prohibition was reiterated, with results that were equally ephemeral.[61]

Reports from her Majesty's consuls during the eighteen-sixties reveal a growing apprehension for the future of British opium. The year 1869-1870 saw the first chest of Chinese opium brought to Foochow, while at Tientsin the native drug was excluding the foreign from inland markets. In the same year the consul at Canton reported gloomily on the prospects of Bengal and Malwa. Yunnan and Szechuan opium was coming regularly to Shanghai, where preferential taxation guaranteed a sale for it. Chinese in the treaty ports may not have been satisfied with its flavor, "but, should the quality improve, and the demand constantly increase, Indian opium must inevitably lose ground unless a heavy reduction be made in the enormous duty imposed in India."[62] Newchwang reported cultivation to be extending into Eastern Mongolia and Manchuria, though foreign imports seem to have held their own.[63] A missionary in the same vicinity wrote, "A few years ago opium was a stranger to this quarter of the world, but now it is rising with great rapidity into ominous and terrible significance."[64]

About 1870 Baron Richtofen, dean of European geographers of China, visited most of the opium regions. In Honan and Shansi he found cultivation extensive. The best fields were reserved for the poppy, which was grown as publicly as wheat. Effects of excessive consumption

[60] *Consular Reports*, 1866, *Tientsin*, p. 149; *Foochow*, p. 41; *Chefoo*, p. 63; *Shanghai*, p. 100.

[61] *Ibid.*, 1869, *Tientsin*, pp. 146-147; 1872, *Tientsin*, p. 112; *Calcutta Papers*, 1870, pp. 222, 239.

[62] *Consular Reports*, 1869, *Canton*, p. 43; *Foochow*, p. 64; *Tientsin*, pp. 146-147; *Shanghai*, p. 19.

[63] *Ibid.*, 1867, *Newchwang*, p. 205.

[64] *Calcutta Papers*, 1870, *Supplement*, 1872, p. 20.

were also apparent to the learned German, who observed "the population of whole towns . . . disfigured by the haggard faces and staring eyes, consequent upon the use of opium."[65] In Shensi the fertile loess offered admirable ground for the poppy, an opportunity which the thrifty Chinese peasant had utilized. Its terraced slopes abounded in the brilliantly colored flowers. Szechuan, later to become the largest opium-producing province in China, was yielding huge quantities but of an inferior grade.[66] Yunnan, the other great opium region, was not described by Richtofen in detail, but all observers agreed that it was contributing heavily to the supply of the native drug.[67]

Those who had held that legalization would not necessarily mean an increase in the imports of Indian opium were vindicated in their opinion. From 1855 to 1870 the figure remained about stationary. But the primary reason was one that the advocates of legalization had scarcely reckoned on, the enormous growth in Chinese production.[68] The opium habit was probably spreading, but new smokers, in a large measure, were being supplied with the native drug. In some areas the prosperity of the import trade depended principally on the success of the

[65] Richtofen, *Chihli, Shansi, Shensi*, p. 39; *Honan and Shansi*, p. 23.

[66] The difficulty of obtaining a credible estimate of the Chinese output is illustrated by the conflicting reports on the production of Szechuan. Richtofen stated that in the eastern part of Szechuan not more than one-fiftieth of the arable land was given over to the poppy, but by a series of elaborate computations he concluded that the province produced a hundred thousand piculs. About the same time Rutherford Alcock reported that two-thirds of the arable land was under poppy cultivation, while the Hankow chamber of commerce anticipated that 7500 chests, less than one-tenth of Richtofen's estimate, would be yielded. *Calcutta Papers*, 1870, *Supplement*, 1872, p. 18.

[67] For Yunnan, also, estimates of cultivation varied from 68,000 acres to one-third of the province.

[68] During the eighteen-fifties and early 'sixties the policy of the Indian government called for a fairly small provision.

local crop.[69] The competition was felt most keenly at the newly-opened ports in the north and in the interior. For in markets served by such cities as Newchwang, Tientsin, and Hankow, where the foreign drug had never been as solidly established as in the older treaty ports and which were within reach of the great producing regions of North and West China, Indian opium was condemned to wage a losing battle.

The course of the British opium trade in China was affected by influences other than native competition. With the achieving of legal status the traffic lost the picturesque appeal of its earlier days, and in the decade following legalization the points to be noticed are not clipper ships and smuggling technique, but earthy details of taxation and the like. First of all, there was a shift in the relative importance of certain ports, notably Shanghai, which felt keenly the opening of new cities on the Yangtse and in North China. Formerly all the supplies for districts farther up the coast had been purchased in Shanghai by native dealers and distributed to the consuming areas by them. After the new system went into operation, the city tended to become a depot for receiving and trans-shipping, while the real trade was carried on by foreign merchants at the new treaty ports. The opium business of Shanghai, flourishing since 1843, was thus severely crippled.[70]

Chinese taxation also affected the division of trade among the various ports. By the new commercial regulations, it will be recalled, opium paid import duty at the rate of thirty taels a picul, but once in the hands of the Chinese buyer, the government's power to tax was unrestricted. During the Taiping rebellion a new impost called *likin* was introduced by the beleaguered imperial govern-

---

[69] *Consular Reports*, 1862-1864, especially *Tientsin*, 1863, p. 133.
[70] *Ibid.*, 1864, *Shanghai*, p. 66.

ment and was first collected in the early 'sixties. This tax, to be levied at the rate of one-tenth of one per cent on goods in transit, was to apply universally throughout the empire.[71] Likin arrangements, however, varied with the different provinces, some, such as Hunan, boasting only one station for the entire province, while Kwangtung, within a radius of two hundred miles from Canton, maintained six likin barriers.[72] Both the system itself and the method of collection were regarded as oppressive by foreign opium dealers. At Shanghai, for example, 35.72 (Shanghai) taels were collected immediately after the chest was landed, whereas Canton levied about half as much and Swatow officials only ten taels.[73]

This inequality in likin tended to drive the trade away from some ports and to concentrate it at others. Two chests of opium, having entered China by different ports, might compete for the same interior market, one having paid taxes of more than a hundred taels, the other of only thirty.[74] Merchants protested sharply at the high rates assessed at some of the treaty ports in contrast to the leniency shown at those frequented only by natives. Thus the junks which brought opium from Hongkong to one of the ports near Canton paid less than half as much as the Canton custom house collected.[75] At Amoy the peculiar

[71] Likin was an extraordinary tax which must be distinguished from the regular transit dues. ''The Likin was a forced contribution or 'benevolence' extracted from the mercantile community; it was elastic in character and might take the form of dues in transit or a terminal tax on goods which had passed into native hands.'' Sargent, *Anglo-Chinese Commerce and Diplomacy*, pp. 159-160.

[72] Morse, *Trade and Administration*, p. 107.

[73] *Consular Reports*, 1873, *Shanghai*, p. 162; *Canton*, p. 10; *Report on Consular Establishments*, 1869, *Swatow*, p. 109.

[74] ''We may mention a case that has come to our knowledge, of opium sold at Shau-wu-foo, which from Foo-chow paid 130 taels; while opium brought from Swatow paid only 30 taels per chest.'' *Corr. resp. the Revision of the Treaty of Tientsin* (China, no. 5), 1871, incl. 2 in no. 31.

[75] *Consular Reports*, 1868-1869, *Canton*, p. 37.

method of raising likin worked to the disadvantage of foreigners. The tax was farmed out to privileged associations, whose control over the local market was semi-monopolistic. Foreign opium was subjected to likin, but the Chinese dealer—at the same time the tax collector—could not be expected to impose a high rate of duty on himself.[76]

The likin tax also helped to convert some part of the opium trade into a smuggling operation. For example, from Hongkong quantities were taken directly to Hankow on the Yangtse. The cost of transportation was about twenty taels, or ten less than the legal import duty at Shanghai, its normal entrepôt, to say nothing of the likin that would have been assessed there.[77] At some ports evasion of likin was an organized business. Foochow reported that a gang of Chinese cutthroats specialized in smuggling opium from the foreign hongs. For a regular fee they would defy the likin collectors, who were "often afraid to make resistance to men of this turbulent class who generally secrete knives about their persons," or they would employ the horseboys of foreigners to carry the drug from the hong furtively, ball by ball.[78]

A further feature of the likin system which annoyed foreign merchants was the method by which the tax was normally collected at the treaty ports. Stations were established within the foreign concessions, almost at the doors of European warehouses, and Chinese purchasers were carefully shadowed. This technique was applied not only to opium but to other goods as well. British officials took the position that such levies were legal as regards opium, for it had been Lord Elgin's intention to allow taxation of the Indian drug as soon as it passed into Chinese hands. But they also held that the collection of likin

---

[76] Report on Consular Establishments, 1869, Amoy, p. 62.
[77] Consular Reports, 1870, Hankow, p. 80.
[78] Memorials of Chambers of Commerce in China, 1867-1868, p. 37.

upon other merchandise within the port settlements did violence to the treaty of Tientsin.

British merchants, in fine, discovered that legalization had not remedied all of the untoward conditions in the opium trade. The specter of Chinese production was sufficiently disturbing. But there was the further fact that the traffic, though it had attained legality, was yet to be regularized. As a result of differential likin rates, dealers at some ports were under an undoubted handicap, which was imposed neither upon their fellow-countrymen at other ports nor upon their native competitors. The next step was to be the creation of a uniform system of opium taxation which would obtain throughout the empire. As for the Chinese, whether reconciled to legalization or not, they found that the new régime was not without its compensations. And the imperial government was soon to learn that it could demand and receive a larger share of the proceeds of the trade than it had been awarded in 1858.

CHAPTER IX

OPIUM AND TREATY REVISION

THE privileges granted to British merchants by the treaty of Tientsin remedied some of their perennial grievances, but as always, they found much to criticize in the new order of things. Their most insistent complaints had to do with matters other than opium. Yet in the two attempts at treaty revision—Sir Rutherford Alcock's unsuccessful convention of 1869 and Sir Thomas Wade's Chefoo convention of 1876—the drug question took a more prominent part than its real importance justified. In the first instance, the Chinese government, realizing that it possessed a formidable bargaining weapon in its threat to encourage local cultivation, sought to claim a higher duty on opium as compensation for relaxing the tariff in other respects. This attempt came to nothing, but in 1876, Sir Thomas Wade was obliged to concede to the Chinese better arrangements for levying likin on opium in order to obtain exemption within the port area for other commodities. Owing, in part, to the provision made for opium, the Chefoo convention was not formally ratified by Great Britain until 1885 and then only after a new opium clause had been introduced. Finally, it may be observed that, during the nine years when ratification was hanging fire, the Indian government for the first time made its influence explicitly felt in Anglo-Chinese opium diplomacy.

The tariff and commercial regulations which accompanied the treaty of Tientsin were to run for ten years without change. As the time for revision approached, both sides were clarifying their views as to the direction which alteration should take. Sir Rutherford Alcock, British minister at Peking,[1] took counsel with the various chambers of commerce in China and the United Kingdom. The Tientsin opium dealers, for example, felt that foreigners should be allowed to carry the drug into the interior, while the community at Amoy complained of the differential duties paid by native junks and foreign vessels upon imported goods. The Chinkiang chamber was annoyed at the preferential treatment given Chinese traders in the collection of likin on opium.[2] From Hongkong arrived a curious memorial stating the views of the "princely house," Jardine, Matheson and Company, who took the bull by the horns by demanding that the fifth rule of the commercial regulations be relaxed.[3] "We enter upon the subject with none of the delicacy or hesitation which, out of deference to the preconceived ideas of many well-meaning people, we should have experienced eight years ago . . . for since 1860 it has been rendered abundantly clear that the use of opium is not a curse, but a comfort and a benefit to the hard-working Chinese. As well say that malt is a curse to the English labourer, or tobacco one to the world at large. . . . After the evidence of the past we feel justified in claiming that those who deal in opium shall be permitted to supply the

[1] By the treaty of Tientsin ministers from the treaty powers were permitted to reside in Peking.

[2] *Memorials of Chambers of Commerce in China*, 1867-1868; British merchants at Amoy to Swinhoe, 18 Oct. 1867, *Corr. resp. the Revision of the Treaty of Tientsin* (China no. 5), 1871 (cited hereafter as *Corr. resp. Revision*, 1871), incl. 6 in no. 31; British merchants at Chinkiang to Alcock, 30 May 1867, *ibid.*, incl. 3 in no. 1.

[3] Rule V, it will be recalled, prohibited foreigners from carrying the drug into the interior, and in general prescribed less lenient treatment for opium than for other imports.

inland Chinese with the drug as freely as they are the dwellers at the ports."[4]

Alcock was convinced that to press the demands of the more aggressive merchants, as regarded either opium or other imports, would be to invite disaster. For he discerned correctly the sorry state of the Chinese administration. The ultimate solution for Anglo-Chinese relationships, he felt, could lie only in a sweeping reform of the Chinese political system, a hope that could not be realized during the minority of the emperor. But meanwhile some of the outstanding difficulties might be compounded in conferences with the Chinese authorities. In other words, the principle of mutual concession without the application of western force was to be given a trial. To follow the negotiations in detail would be irrelevant to the purpose of this study. Since the convention of 1869 never became operative, it requires emphasis only as it serves to throw into relief, first, the policy of Peking towards the drug trade, and secondly, the anxiety of Calcutta to maintain the position of Indian opium in China.

During the course of the negotiations Sir Rutherford Alcock met with three of the higher officials of the *tsungli yamen*[5] in an informal conversation. No subordinates were present, and the confidential character of the interview allowed the Chinese to speak freely upon two delicate subjects—missionaries and opium. Allusion was made to the hostility which the literati bore towards foreigners, when one of the Chinese queried, "How could it be otherwise? They had often seen foreigners making war on the country, and then again, how irreparable was the injury they had inflicted on the whole empire by the

[4] Jardine, Matheson and Company to MacDonnell, 28 Nov. 1867, *Corr. resp. Revision*, 1871, incl. 2 in no. 32.

[5] The Chinese foreign office, established after the Arrow War.

foreign importation of opium.'"[6] If only the drug trade were abandoned, there might be a prospect of more amicable relations. Alcock replied with the speech that seems to have formed the stock equipment of British diplomatists in China. Not the Indian system but the Chinese passion for opium was the root of the trouble. Closing the interview, the Chinese expressed a desire to see the dual experiment—prohibition in both India and China—given a trial.

In the following month, June, 1869, Prince Kung[7] presented to the British minister a memorial in which was embodied the proposal foreshadowed in the earlier conversation. It contained also a veiled threat that the Chinese government might feel obliged, as a temporary measure, to use the native drug to drive the foreign from the market. But to obtain revenue by allowing the people "to go on to destruction," the writers piously observed, would be unworthy of "the beneficence of Heaven." Far better for both countries to forbid the growing of the poppy.[8] Sir Rutherford Alcock was deeply impressed by the Chinese argument, both by its apparent honesty and by its menacing references to native cultivation. The latter seemed especially alarming to him when he learned that Li Hung Chang had actually encouraged poppy culture in the provinces of which he was viceroy and that his brother had done likewise in a neighboring province.[9]

[6] Alcock to Clarendon, 20 May 1869, *Corr. resp. Revision*, 1871, no. 138; evidence of Sir Rutherford Alcock, *Report of the Select Committee on East Indian Finance*, 1871, Q. 5694. See also Alcock's interview with the Indian council, 4 Feb. 1870, *Calcutta Papers*, 1870, addendum to App. IV, p. 19.

[7] Brother of the late Emperor Hsien Feng and president of the *tsungli yamen*.

[8] Evidence of Sir Rutherford Alcock, *Report on East Indian Finance*, 1871, Q. 5694.

[9] *Ibid.*, Q. 5696; Alcock to the government of India, 11 Oct. 1869, *Cal-*

Had Alcock been of a cynical turn of mind, he might have seen in the Chinese insistence upon prohibition merely a device to exclude Indian opium from the field for the benefit of the native product. It is, in truth, a little difficult to reconcile the eloquence with which Chinese statesmen pleaded for prohibition in 1869 with their passivity towards legalization a decade before. But conditions in Peking had changed. A new group of statesmen was now in command, while those who introduced opium into the tariff had passed from the scene. The financial pressure, which had been directly responsible for Chinese consent to a legalized trade, had been slightly relaxed. And, perhaps most important of all, here for the first time the Chinese were negotiating a treaty as equals of the foreigner, not as his defeated opponents. There may have been—and probably was—an element of bargaining in the position taken by Prince Kung. Announcing complete prohibition as China's policy, he could demand a price for whatever compromise he was obliged to make. But there was also an element of sincerity that carried conviction in Alcock's mind. At one time he was seriously tempted to abandon the negotiations.[10]

In the end, the Chinese were brought around to a compromise. By the convention that was signed on October 23, 1869, additional duties were to be paid on imported opium and exported silk, while the British were to receive, in return, certain commercial concessions.[11] Opium was to pay duty at the rate of fifty taels per picul instead of the thirty that had been levied since 1858. By the Brit-

cutta Papers, 1870, pp. 262-264. Li Hung Chang was viceroy of Hupeh and Hunan, while his brother presided over Szechuan.

[10] Memorandum of Alcock's conference with the Indian council, 4 Feb. 1870, Calcutta Papers, 1870, addendum to App. IV, p. 9.

[11] Text, Corr. resp. Revision, 1871, incl. 1 in no. 152. The British obtained the right to trade at closed ports in native boats. Bonded warehouses were to be set up, and coal mines in the south were to be opened.

ish minister this clause was regarded as a distinct triumph. In notifying Clarendon of the convention, he pointed out that the added tax would give the imperial government a stake in the foreign trade—an argument that was a bit forced—and a motive for suppressing native cultivation, in other words, "a retaining fee in our cause."[12] To persuade the *yamen* to accept even this retaining fee Alcock seems to have made some vague commitments for the future.[13] Whatever their motives, the Chinese had taken their stand upon total prohibition and to dislodge them had required skilful manoeuvering.

The British ministry found the terms of the convention unobjectionable, but to the merchants it was anathema. The foreign office was deluged with a flood of memorials, a few of which related to the new opium duty. Sassoon and Company of Bombay, the largest dealers in the Malwa drug, protested against the impost as encouraging opium production in China. The chairman of the Hongkong chamber of commerce wrote in a similar vein.[14] But opium was only one item in the convention, every term of which was abhorrent to mercantile interests. British traders who had looked for a commercial millennium found that mutual concession was proposed. Before such pressure as they brought to bear the government was obliged to give way. The convention was therefore rejected.[15]

---

[12] Alcock to Clarendon, 28 Oct. 1869, *ibid.*, no. 152; evidence of Sir Rutherford Alcock, *Report on East Indian Finance*, 1871, Q. 5870.

[13] Memorandum of Alcock's conference with the Indian council, 4 Feb. 1870, *Calcutta Papers*, 1870, addendum to App. IV, p. 10.

[14] *Further Memorials respecting the China Treaty Revision Convention* (China no. 6), 1870, nos. 3-5.

[15] Granville to Alcock, 25 July 1870, *Corr. resp. Revision*, 1871, no. 153. Morse concludes that two provisions—permission for a Chinese consul to reside at Hongkong and the imposition of fifty per cent additional duty on foreign woven fabrics—were the major grounds of opposition. *International Relations*, II, 218.

Responsibility for having wrecked Alcock's revision has been laid by some at the door of the Indian government.[16] That the addition of twenty taels to the duty on Indian opium should be received with little enthusiasm in Calcutta was natural enough, but to say that the government of India played obstructionist is quite untrue. In London the India office promptly concluded that the convention offered no just ground for complaint.[17] More illuminating, however, are the deliberations of the council in Calcutta. Early in 1870 Sir Rutherford Alcock, visiting the Indian capital on his way to England, presented his agreement to the council. He reviewed the course of his negotiations with the Chinese government and reaffirmed his conviction that the responsible statesmen of imperial China were as unequivocally opposed as ever to the opium trade. Alcock was at no pains to minimize the danger implicit in Chinese cultivation. And he was thoroughly persuaded that the imperial government, if India would forego her opium revenue, could suppress poppy growing in China "more or less effectually."[18] Writing from Bombay a month later after talking with the Sassoons and other opium merchants, Sir Rutherford put the case still more incisively. India, he asserted, must choose one of two policies. Either she must enter into an agreement with the Peking government to check the poppy in China or "by doubling the quantity and largely diminishing the cost of the Indian drug, accept the strug-

16 See Rowntree, *Imperial Drug Trade*, p. 101. Sir Thomas Wade stated in 1894 that opium "was one of the two causes which broke down" the agreement. "There were two conditions, one affecting silk and one affecting opium. The Indian Government objected to that affecting opium." *Report of the Royal Commission*, I, 1894, Q. 1301.

17 Foreign office to the India office, 3 Jan. 1870, and India office to foreign office, 31 Jan. 1870, I. O. Home Corr., LXV.

18 Memorandum of Alcock's conference with the Indian council, 4 Feb. 1870, *Calcutta Papers*, 1870, addendum to App. IV, p. 10.

gle of competition.'' To bring the Chinese authorities to terms would involve not only accepting the added duty proposed by the convention but also laying some restriction upon exports from India. ''Will you remember me,'' he added with a touch of malice, ''to Sir Richard Temple [one of his cross-examiners on the council], and give him this my last word before I leave the Land of Opium.''[19]

The council realized that the opium revenue was approaching a crisis, as serious, perhaps, as that brought on by Malwa half a century before. With the immediate question of accepting or protesting against Alcock's convention was indissolubly connected the larger issue of how to meet the competition of the Chinese drug. The Peking government, it was admitted, was hostile to the opium traffic and would probably go to the length of encouraging native cultivation in order to kill the import trade. But, if India accepted the additional duty, would the Chinese government apply an effective brake to the local industry? And, if a joint agreement to limit both Indian exports and Chinese production were arranged, would not the loss of Calcutta and Bombay be merely the gain of Peking and the provinces? Within the council there was some slight sentiment in favor of mutual restriction, but the majority held that such a policy would be inviting the Chinese to develop their own industry, while the Indian trade was bound by self-imposed fetters. As the commander-in-chief of the army remarked, ''We must not on any account allow ourselves to be led astray by Chinese proclivities, or any considerations deviating from the line of commercial and financial expediency.'' If a commercial war were inevitable, the advantage would lie with him who was best prepared.[20]

This point of view was eloquently reflected in the reso-

19 Alcock to R. B. Chapman, 11 March 1870 (demi-official), *ibid.*, p. 19.
20 6 Feb. 1870, *ibid.*, p. 12.

lution which the council adopted.[21] India, its officers acknowledged, was in no position to protest against the proposed import duty on opium. Having reached that conclusion, the council passed on to the really basic question—what to do about Chinese competition. If Peking was about to make an onslaught on Indian opium, there was only one reply to make. The output of the Bengal agencies must be increased, if possible, to sixty thousand chests a year. To ensure an adequate provision it might even be necessary to reverse the ancient policy of British India and permit cultivation in the Bombay and Madras presidencies. A week later the path seemed even more unmistakable, and the supreme government formally resolved to spare neither effort nor expense in order to raise the production of Bihar and Benares opium to sixty thousand chests.[22]

In summary, then, the Indian government had no part in killing Alcock's treaty revision. Partly because they felt they had no right to do so and partly because they cherished a faint hope that twenty taels additional duty per chest—about a million and a half annually—might restrain the Chinese government from fostering the native industry, the Calcutta authorities lodged no protest. The most significant result of Alcock's visit, however, was to lend strength to the arguments of those who had already launched the British opium system upon a new career of expansion.[23] In the eighteen-twenties and 'thirties, Malwa was the enemy; in the 'sixties and 'seventies, it was Chinese opium. But both were fought by similar methods and in both instances control of the China market was at stake.

As for the ill-starred convention of 1869, its rejection

[21] 18 March 1870, *ibid.*, p. 21.   [22] 25 March 1870, no. 2090, *ibid.*
[23] Previous reports from China had aroused grave apprehensions in India, and expansion was already under way.

by Great Britain made plain the fact that British merchants would never be satisfied by a treaty revision that
grew out of mutual concession. Only when a situation
should arise in which the English felt justified in applying pressure could the desired privileges be obtained.
This condition was created in February, 1875, when a
British exploring party from Burma was ambushed in
Yunnan and a young interpreter murdered. With magnificent irrelevance, Sir Thomas Wade, British minister
at Peking, at once made six demands upon the imperial
government, only three of which had any connection with
the Yunnan episode. After a long period of negotiation,
punctuated by fits of irritable diplomacy on the part of
the British envoy, Li Hung Chang was finally sent to
Chefoo to treat with him.[24]

With most of the questions at issue we are not concerned. The only problem which bore directly upon the
opium trade was the taxation of foreign goods at the
treaty ports. As we have seen, likin collectorates had
been set up almost at the door of the foreign hongs, and
the tax was levied not only upon opium but upon other
imports as well. The British government contended that
this practice, as applied to goods other than opium was
an infraction of the treaty of Tientsin. Opium, according
to Sir Thomas Wade, stood in a separate category. Lord
Elgin had intended to let the Chinese deal with the drug
as they chose, once it had been removed from the importer's premises.[25] In other words, for Chinese revenue officers to collect likin on general imports at the foreign set-

[24] During the year and a half that intervened between the murder and the
meeting at Chefoo, the three irrelevant demands were once withdrawn and
were again preferred. See Morse, *International Relations*, II, 297-299.

[25] This interpretation rested more upon Sir Thomas Wade's recollection
of Elgin's purpose than upon anything explicitly stated in the treaty. Rule
V permitted the Chinese to levy transit dues at will, but the point at which
they might legally begin to tax was not specifically indicated. Wade's view,

tlements was illegal but to levy it on opium was quite within their rights.

It was not merely a case of insisting that the Chinese abandon the one and permitting them to continue the other. For, theoretically allowable or not, the methods by which revenue officers collected likin on opium were thoroughly abhorrent to foreigners. They complained of the uneven rates assessed at the different ports and of the surveillance maintained over their places of business. They argued that the arrests which Chinese officials made just outside their warehouses were injurious to trade. To such claims the Chinese retorted that the practice was made necessary by the close bonds of sympathy between foreign importer and native smuggler and by the fact that Europeans acted as convoys for Chinese-owned opium.

To evolve a system which would meet the objections of foreigners without depriving the Chinese of their lawful revenue was the stubborn obstacle. From the British point of view, it would be an enormous advantage to move all likin collectorates from the foreign settlements. But this, Sir Thomas Wade was aware, would open large loopholes for smuggling opium and would mean a substantial loss to the Chinese treasury. The most desirable of all arrangements would be to evict likin collectorates from the port settlements and to allow the imperial maritime customs to handle the likin levy on opium, at a uniform rate for all ports. This solution, indeed, had been already foreshadowed in a memorandum by Robert Hart, the trusted adviser of the imperial government.[26]

which he reiterated time and again, was never questioned by the foreign office, but British opium merchants were not persuaded that it was the correct one. See Wade to Derby, 14 July 1877, *Margary Corr.* (China no. 3), 1877, no. 39; Wade to the viceroy of India, 16 Feb. 1879, *Corr. resp. Chefoo Convention* (China no. 3), 1882, incl. in no. 10.

[26] Memorandum by Robert Hart, *Margary Corr.* (China no. 3), 1877, incl.

In the conversations at Chefoo, Sir Thomas Wade offered the idea to Li Hung Chang. Li was interested in the suggestion, but when it came to setting a uniform rate, Chinese and English views diverged hopelessly.[27] By failing to reach an agreement the two negotiators prevented a complete regularization of the opium trade. For it was a halfway measure that they determined to put into effect. British opium was to pay likin to the imperial maritime customs but at a rate prescribed by each provincial government.[28] In return the Chinese conceded that the ground rented by foreigners (the concessions) should be the area of exemption on other imports. The new treaty ports, for which the convention also provided, were to be opened immediately, while the clauses affecting likin and opium were to become operative as soon as the British government had come to an understanding with the other treaty powers.[29]

The convention was damned by its likin and opium provisions. To foreigners, who had repeatedly protested against likin stations barely off their premises, the new scheme would have meant some relief. But it was much less than the other treaty powers were seeking. They demanded that (non-opium) imports be exempt from likin not only within the foreign concessions but up to the second likin barrier. The convention's "one unfortunate feature," reported the American minister, "is the pro-

in no. 2. This document also appears in R. Hart, *These from the Land of Sinim*, appendix, and in Morse, *International Relations*, II, App. D. Drawn up at the request of the Chinese government, Hart's report forms one of the ablest analyses ever written of the points of difference, commercial and otherwise, between China and the foreigner. Hart proposed that 120 taels per picul be collected by the imperial maritime customs and that the drug be allowed free circulation within a radius of thirty *li* of the port.

[27] Wade to Kung, 10 Nov. 1879, *Corr. resp. Chefoo Convention* (China no. 2), 1880, incl. 1.

[28] Article III, section iii, *Hertslet's China Treaties*, no. 12.

[29] Article VI, section iii, *ibid.*

posed settlement of the likin question.''[30] Rather than accept the British solution, the other members of the diplomatic body chose to open separate discussions with the Chinese, meanwhile urging their respective government to refuse ratification.[31]

Of more direct importance here is the change contemplated in the opium trade. This was an issue of no more than academic concern to the other treaty powers. The question was British, pure and simple, and one on which the government of India might well express an opinion.[32] In October, 1876, Lord Derby informed Sir Thomas Wade that the convention was satisfactory from an imperial point of view, but that the opinion of the viceroy of India must be obtained before her Majesty's position could be stated finally.[33] The year 1877 passed and no action was taken. The Chinese executed their part of the agreement by opening the new ports, without disturbing Whitehall's painful silence. During 1878 the government bestirred itself to announce that ratification had already taken place, with the exception of the likin and opium provisions and that a modification of those terms was being sought.[34]

The failure of Great Britain to ratify the opium clause was the result as much of mismanagement on the part of that genial and scholarly Irishman, Sir Thomas Wade, as of Indian obstructionism. It seems to have taken him a year to realize that Calcutta, not London, was the strate-

30 Seward to Fish, 3 Oct. 1876, *U. S. Foreign Relations*, 1877, p. 73. Relevant French documents will be found in Cordier, *Histoire des Rélations de la Chine*, II, 188-193.

31 Wade to Granville, 3 June 1882, *Corr. resp. Chefoo Convention* (China no. 3), 1882, no. 11.

32 By the eighteen-seventies the subjects of no other treaty power were taking a significant part in the opium trade.

33 Derby to Wade, 19 Oct. 1876, *Margary Corr.* (China no. 3), 1877, no. 10.

34 3 *Hansard*, CCXLII, 36-37.

gic point. Not until late in 1877 was his draft brought
officially to the attention of the Indian government, and
by that time much of the earlier momentum was lost. In
October, 1876, the India office telegraphed the purport of
the opium article to the Calcutta authorities, who in turn
cabled to Wade in Peking.[35] No reply was forthcoming,
and the Indian government was obliged to wait nearly a
year for the authentic text.

The viceroy and his council were a bit nettled that the
opium clause "should have received even the conditional
assent of Her Majesty's Plenipotentiary at Pekin, without previous consultation with us," and they were justi-
fiably annoyed that so much time had passed before Indian interests were considered.[36] They had, however, only
one genuine objection to the convention. That had to do
with the undefined character of the rates at which likin
was to be collected. The convention, it will be recalled,
had left the rate to the need or whim of each provincial
governor. Collection by the imperial maritime customs,
the Indian authorities pointed out, would make the tax
much more certain and would obviate, in a large measure,
the fear of smuggling which hitherto had restrained the
fiscal excesses of local officials. Patna and Malwa might
thus be saddled with outrageous imposts. Sir Thomas
Wade had tried to anticipate this objection by suggesting
that the Chinese would not tax opium beyond what it
could bear, but for the Indian government, the effect was
ruined by his further remark that "the drug will bear
heavier taxation than that now imposed upon it, and
heavier taxation will probably be laid upon it." What
Calcutta demanded, before subscribing to Wade's settle-

[35] Government of India to the India office, 5 Oct. 1876, I. O. Separate
Revenue Letters Received from India, no. 19 of 1876.
[36] Government of India to the India office, 11 Jan. 1878, I. O. Letters
from India (political dept.), no. 1 of 1878.

ment, was an explicit definition of the amount of likin to be assessed at each treaty port—and, preferably, assurance that the scale would not exceed the current one.

Sir Thomas Wade had sailed for England shortly after the signing of the convention, and on his return voyage to China in 1878-1879 he paid a visit to Calcutta. In a long letter to Lord Lytton, the viceroy, he sought to make amends for his apparent disregard of Indian interests. He explained that the opium clause had entered the convention only because it was necessary to banish likin stations from the foreign concessions and at the same time to compensate the Chinese for their loss on opium. With respect to Chinese policy, Sir Thomas spoke comfortable words to the viceroy. The possibility of prohibition on moral grounds, he declared, was remote, for Indian opium was as much a necessity to Chinese taste as was the revenue derived from it to the Peking exchequer. Delay was embarrassing. "We cannot say to the Chinese, 'Take back your four ports of residence that you have opened . . . and take your *li-kin*, as before, off opium as you may.' "[37] The Indian authorities declined to enter into a discussion and merely forwarded the despatch to London.[38]

Having attempted to soothe the viceroy, Wade returned to Peking to save what he could out of the wreckage. Profiting by the criticism of the Calcutta authorities, he again sought to hit upon a uniform rate which would be acceptable to the *tsungli yamen.* Conferences with Li Hung Chang again proved inconclusive, while a plan to apply the old convention experimentally at Shanghai only died of inanition.[39] In the following year, when the Grand

[37] Wade to the viceroy of India, 16 Feb. 1879, *Corr. resp. Chefoo Convention* (China no. 3), 1882, incl. in no. 10.

[38] Government of India to the India office, 22 May 1879, I. O. Separate Revenue Letters Received from India, no. 10 of 1879.

[39] Notes between Kung and Wade, 10 Nov. 1879—30 Jan. 1880, *Corr.*

Secretary Tso Tsung Tang, who as viceroy of Shensi and Kansu had been a vigorous and successful anti-opium crusader, arrived in Peking, a fresh start was made. Li Hung Chang also visited the capital, and again the discussion revolved around a uniform rate, which not only would exempt foreign opium from further taxation within the first likin area, as had been contemplated in previous discussions, but would commute all transit dues in the interior of China. Tso Tsung Tang's offer of 120 taels likin plus the regular thirty taels import duty naturally failed to evoke sympathetic response from the British minister. Li's demands were more moderate than those of his old-school colleague. On the new basis, Wade was prepared to go as high as sixty or even seventy taels, but he balked at eighty.[40]

With direct negotiations at an impasse, the way was opened for a number of curious and rather impracticable schemes. Li Hung Chang suggested the chartering of a Chinese company to be given a monopoly of all the opium produced in India for export to China. A similar proposal was made by a group of Cantonese. An extraordinary plan emanated from one Samuel, a financier, who had visited India to investigate what he regarded as a faulty system of remitting opium proceeds. On the completion of his study, he pushed on to China, where he obtained an audience with Li Hung Chang. To Li he suggested that Great Britain declare a monopoly of the

resp. Chefoo Convention (China no. 2), 1880, incls. 1-5; Wade to Granville, 3 June 1882, *Corr. resp. Chefoo Convention* (China no. 3), 1882, no. 11. Wade also held a series of conversations with the ministers of the other treaty powers on the taxation of inland trade. It must be emphasized again that before the convention could become operative it had to be ratified by all treaty powers. The other ministers were still insisting that foreign goods other than opium must be exempted from likin not only within the foreign concessions but up to the second likin barrier.

40 Wade to Granville, 3 June 1882, *Corr. resp. Chefoo Convention* (China no. 3), no. 11.

world's opium supply and of the trade to China and other markets, thus minimizing smuggling and securing the revenue of both China and India. On a later occasion this financial knight-errant made an even more singular proposal—that he, as a business man, should become monopolist of all the opium output of India, guaranteeing at the same time a net revenue of one hundred taels per chest to the Chinese government. Robert Hart was inclined to favor the plan, but the *yamen*, holding that the "object in raising the tax is not for the producing of more revenue but for the discouraging of the trade," memorialized against it.[41]

After their conferences with Samuel, whom they incorrectly inferred to have official status, the Chinese determined to reply with an unofficial mission to India. Ma Kieh Chung, formerly a member of the legation staff at Paris, was despatched to Calcutta, where he sounded out the authorities on a new plan by which the Chinese government would itself become the consignee of all opium exported to China. For this concession a fixed sum would be paid to the government of India for perhaps thirty to fifty years, the amount diminishing *pari passu* with shipments to China. At the expiration of the period the opium trade from India to China should cease altogether.[42]

There were now at least a half dozen possible solutions to the muddled problem.[43] Of these the most hopeful from

[41] *Ibid.; London and China Telegraph*, 5 Dec. 1881, cited in Morse, *International Relations*, II, 385; D. C. Boulger, *Halliday Macartney*, pp. 404-405.

[42] Memorandum by Major Baring, *Report of the Royal Commission*, II, 1894, App. XV.

[43] While Anglo-Chinese diplomacy was making but feeble progress, the United States took occasion to state its attitude towards the opium trade. In 1880 the American commission which effected a settlement of the immigration question also negotiated a commercial treaty. Included in the latter at the request of the Chinese was an article which rigidly prohibited Americans from dealing in the drug. This interdict was little more than a gesture,

the point of view of future developments was Li Hung Chang's offer of 110 taels per chest. However preposterous the rate seemed to Sir Thomas Wade, there was much to be said for a scheme which would regularize the opium trade not only at the ports but throughout the empire. For, in the first place, the duty would be collected uniformly at every treaty port, and in the second place, payment to the customs would carry with it exemption from all further imposts in the interior. Wade had come within ten taels of meeting Li's demand, but the *yamen* refused to compromise, threatening, if a settlement were not soon reached, to take matters into its own hands, ''raise the rate of likin to 150 taels . . . or . . . devise some other measure. . . . There is no telling.''[44]

Negotiations in China had thus reached a deadlock. The final settlement was to take place in London. At the risk of entering upon a long digression, we may take advantage of the change in locale to examine the position taken by the various interests involved—the merchants, the Indian government, the British foreign office, and, most inscrutable of all, the Chinese authorities—and incidentally to obtain a panoramic view of the opium issue in the eighteen-seventies and early 'eighties.

During the last quarter of the century, the better Eng-

for in the main American citizens had withdrawn from the traffic, although American ships occasionally carried opium on British account. The commission's interpretation of Chinese policy is not without interest. Peking, it virtuously reported, was attempting ''to isolate the British Government from the other Christian powers, and to compel that Government to take the odium of forcing this wicked and demoralizing traffic for the avowed purpose of financial advantage.'' Dennett, *Americans in Eastern Asia*, p. 543. (This sentence was omitted from the despatch as printed in *U. S. Foreign Relations*, 1881, p. 200.) See also Pethick to the commissioners, 22 Nov. 1880, *U. S. Foreign Relations*, 1881, p. 217; *Hertslet's China Treaties*, no. 98.

[44] Kung to Wade, 25 Jan. 1882, *Corr. resp. Chefoo Convention* (China no. 3), 1882, incl. 4 in no. 11.

lish houses tended to withdraw from the opium trade, which fell increasingly into the hands of a few large Jewish firms of Bombay. The ordinary British merchant knew little and cared less about developments in the drug traffic. But since remittances were still heavy—in some months over £500,000 from Shanghai alone—London bankers found the opium trade a potent factor in settling the rates of exchange.[45] The day of the great merchant princes, each of whom maintained his full panoply of ships and agents, was passing, and, especially at the secondary treaty ports, the actual importing was done more and more by Chinese dealers and brokers.[46] A consignment of drug might be purchased in Calcutta or Bombay by one firm, shipped to China in a vessel belonging to another, and marketed at the port by a third. But despite their changing personnel, the newer opium merchants were no less decided in their stand on Anglo-Chinese relationships than their predecessors had been. During Wade's negotiations they followed the expected formula of taking as much and giving as little as they could. After the confidential mission of Ma Kieh Chung, the opium magnates of both Calcutta and Bombay registered emphatic protests, devoutly trusting that no "proposal of the Chinese government for British assistance in levying and realizing fresh taxes should find favor."[47] Contrary to Wade's opinion, they held that the Chinese had no right to levy likin, even on opium, at the port. From merchants in Kwangtung came a similar declaration.[48] The London committee of the Shanghai chamber of commerce

[45] Pethick to the commissioners, 22 Nov. 1880, *U. S. Foreign Relations*, 1881, p. 217; *The Times*, quoted in *Friend of China*, Feb., 1880, p. 71.

[46] *Decennial Reports of the Imperial Maritime Customs*, 1882-1891, p. 323.

[47] *Corr. resp. Chefoo Convention* (China no. 3), 1882, incls. 3 and 4 in no. 4.

[48] Herton and Company to the chairman of the chamber of commerce, Calcutta, 31 July 1881, *ibid.*, incl. 8.

deplored the prospect of the government's making itself indirectly responsible for the collection of an indefinite amount of likin at the various treaty ports. Altogether it may be inferred that the proposal to raise the duties was not finding favor with the opium fraternity.

The initial attitude of the Indian government, as we have seen, was to question the vague likin arrangements of the Chefoo convention and to deprecate any additional charges upon the foreign drug. By 1881 the Calcutta authorities had mellowed, and all objection to the original draft of the convention had been withdrawn.[49] They had ceased to demand that China content herself in the future with what she had been able to collect in the past. In the House of Commons, under fire from the anti-opium group, Lord Hartington declared that "If China should ask to have greater fiscal liberty than she enjoys at present, I should certainly not, in the interests of the Indian revenue, feel justified in imposing any unreasonable resistance to such a demand."[50] To the secretary's statement of Indian policy the council in Calcutta subscribed.

The Indian authorities indicted Peking not with insincerity but with impotence either to suppress cultivation within, or, if the rates of duty were substantially raised, to prevent smuggling from without. They were naturally alarmed lest their drug should be too heavily weighted down in its race with Chinese opium. But to insist that Malwa and Patna must be placed on a parity with the native product would have exposed them to much justifiable criticism. Of Chinese prohibitory legislation the Indian council had no fear, save as it might lead to a revival of contraband trading. The Chinese people had developed

[49] India office to the government of India, 16 June 1881, *Corr. with the Government of India*, 1882.

[50] Government of India to the India office, 19 Dec. 1881, *ibid.*, p. 15; 3 *Hansard*, CCLX, 1508.

a taste for the drug, and to suppose that a moribund dynasty could root out the vice by a law, only half enforced, was sheer nonsense. "We venture to think that the idea that the habits of the Chinese people can be changed by any other means than the slow process of education and moral training . . . is illusory and chimerical."[51]

No defender of Indian policy could be altogether at ease, for anti-opium sentiment in England was becoming both organized and articulate. In 1874 there was created a committee, which with the financial support of a Yorkshire Quaker, Edward Pease, grew into the Anglo-Oriental Society for the Suppression of the Opium Trade.[52] One of the prime objectives for which the society fought was the removal of the diplomatic pressure by which, it conceived, the opium traffic had been maintained. Consequently its weight was thrown wholeheartedly for ratifying the Chefoo convention as the first step in freeing China from her ignominious position. Memorials were presented, meetings held, and an official organ, the *Friend of China,* issued. In the spring of 1877 a deputation from the society visited the new Chinese legation in an effort to discover the official Chinese attitude. The minister had learned his lesson well, and his evasive answers were not all that his earnest questioners had hoped for.[53]

A meeting held at Mansion House in the autumn of 1881, at which the lord mayor presided, demanded that the government support Chinese efforts to suppress the

[51] Government of India to the India office, 19 Dec. 1881, *Corr. with the Government of India,* 1882, p. 13.

[52] Hodder, *Life of Shaftesbury,* III, 429-430; *Friend of China,* Aug., 1880, pp. 141-142; evidence of J. G. Alexander, *Report of the Royal Commission,* I, 1894, Q. 468. In 1880 Shaftesbury was elected president. The society drew its support from the same groups that had formed the backbone of ephemeral anti-opium bodies in the past—Quaker reformers, evangelicals, and missionary interests.

[53] *Friend of China,* April, 1877, pp. 151-156.

traffic and withdraw all encouragement from poppy growing in India. On the platform, among others, were the Archbishop of Canterbury, Cardinal Manning, and Lord Shaftesbury, who presented the resolution—a triumvirate which might well overawe evil itself.[54] The attack was also pushed in the House of Commons, where debates occurred in 1880, 1881, and 1883.[55] On all three occasions the leading champion of the anti-opium cause was Sir Joseph Pease, a Quaker baronet, who was later to become president of the society.[56]

Such a bombardment could scarcely pass unnoticed by the government of India or by Chinese statesmen, at least one of whom—Li Hung Chang—had his ear to the ground of English opinion. Its effect upon the former was revealed by a despatch from Lord Hartington to the Indian council, in which he pointed out that the anti-opium movement, though founded upon prejudice and misapprehension, must inevitably gain strength, "so long as the position of the Indian Government is not perfectly unassailable."[57] To the Chinese the agitation disclosed allies in an unexpected quarter. In 1877, when the society addressed a manifesto to the Chinese people, many saw in it only a hoax or possibly a testimony to the alarm felt by European merchants at the increasing opium output of China. A few years later, the astute Li Hung Chang, in a letter to the society, used the occasion to strike an

[54] *The Times*, 22 Oct. 1881. The government of India referred to this gathering as an "influential meeting."

[55] 3 *Hansard*, CCLII, 1227; CCLX, 1451; CCLXXVII, 1333.

[56] Only in 1883 was a motion put to vote. On the question that "in any negotiations on the subject of opium the Government of China would be met as that of an independent state, having full right to arrange its own import duties," the noes had it, 182 to 126. Parliamentary criticism of the Bengal monopoly will be discussed in the following chapter. The debates here mentioned concerned British opium policy towards China.

[57] India office to the government of India, 16 June 1881, *Corr. with the Government of India*, 1882.

attitude of lofty morality. "Opium is a subject in the discussion of which England and China can never meet on
common ground. China views the whole question from a
moral standpoint: England from a fiscal. . . . The ruling
motive of China is to repress opium by heavy taxation
everywhere . . . never the desire to gain revenue from
such a source."[58] Li's indictment would have been more
convincing were it not for his own devious policy towards
the drug. His suspicious biographer has remarked that
on the opium issue Li was no better and no worse than
his colleagues. He was willing to take advantage of western idealists to obtain a monopoly for the native trade
by extinguishing the Indian. Li above all was a practical
statesman, concerned more with immediate necessity
than ultimate end. On the one hand, he solemnly assured
the anti-opium society of China's inexorable resolve to
wipe out the evil, while, on the other, he was cultivating
the poppy on his ancestral estates in Anhwei and in the
province of Chihli, which he governed.[59]

The chameleon-like attitude of Li Hung Chang only
epitomizes that of the Chinese government.[60] Innumer-
able advocates, pro- and anti-opium, have studied Chinese policy, and each has come away confirmed in his
prejudices. Good evidence may be found to support any
preconceived opinion. The whole course of the imperial
government towards opium is a maze in which only the
most elusive clues appear. At one time a high-minded
British diplomatist would assert that the government's
hostility to opium had in nowise abated. A few years
later another would intimate that its primary concern
was revenue.

[58] *The Times*, 29 July 1881.

[59] J. O. P. Bland, *Li Hung Chang*, p. 123.

[60] I do not imply that the motives of the Chinese government were as open
to question as were Li's. But its policy was no more consistent.

The key to this confusion seems to lie in the disinte-grating state of the Manchu dynasty, a process acceler-ated by the impact of the West. It was a sadly befuddled China that was negotiating with Sir Thomas Wade. There was anarchy at the capital and far more in the provincial administrations. The British minister re-ported one of his conversations with officials of the *tsungli yamen,* during the course of which he referred to the diverse practices of local officials and inquired which represented the policy of the central government. The reply might quite as well have come from the financial secretary of the Indian government. "They said, so long as the habit exists, opium will be procured, either from India or elsewhere. Any serious attempt to check the evil must originate with the people themselves."[61] This state-ment, placed beside the letter of Li Hung Chang to the anti-opium society, Tso Tsung Tang's to Sir Thomas Wade, and the *yamen's* reply to Samuels, will indicate the chaotic mental state of Chinese leadership. China did not know its own mind.

But certain facts are irrefutable. In the first place, the cultivation of the poppy in China, as revealed by British consular reports and those of the imperial maritime cus-toms, was growing by leaps and bounds. During the dec-ade 1875-1885, opium shipments from India remained the largest single item in Chinese imports and showed an average annual gain of about five thousand chests over the previous ten years.[62] By the end of the period a grad-ual decline in the Indian trade had set in. From some sec-tions Patna and Malwa had been completely excluded, while in others they were used in combination with the

---

[61] *Corr. with the Government of India,* 1882, p. 11.

[62] The average annual imports for the decades 1865-1875 and 1875-1885 were about 77,000 and 82,000 chests respectively. *Financial and Commercial Statistics of British India,* 1904, p. 55.

native product. Consumption was plainly increasing, but Chinese, not foreign, opium was profiting by the trend.[63]

To attempt an estimate of the total output would be a useless exercise. Qualified observers varied in their conclusions all the way from an amount equal to the imports from India to four or five times that.[64] One traveler placed the Szechuan production at 50,000 chests, while the consul at Chengtu, six years later, thought it to be over 170,000, or more than twice as much as was being shipped from India.[65] To put it conservatively, by 1885 China was probably producing twice as much opium as she was importing.

The testimony of travelers and missionaries colors the picture of widespread cultivation. In Yunnan Alexander Hosie walked five miles without seeing a crop other than the poppy.[66] Two missionaries who passed through West China reported that three-quarters of all the land seen by them was devoted to poppy growing, and that no Indian opium, as far as they could learn, was imported into

[63] The prices which foreign opium brought in China markets showed a tendency, still more marked in the following decade, to decline. See, for example, *Decennial Reports* (Customs), 1882-1891, pp. 326, 414, 503.

[64] The consul at Ichang estimated the output of Yunnan, Szechuan, and Southwest China at 224,000 piculs. Sir Robert Hart, writing two years earlier on the basis of reports from his commissioners (who varied from 25,000 to 265,000 chests for the total production of the empire), held that, ''As far as we know to-day, the Native Opium produced does not exceed the Foreign import in quantity.'' *Consular Reports*, 1881, *Ichang*, p. 38; *Opium, Customs Special Series*, no. 4, 1881, pp. 2-3.

[65] Davenport, *Report on Yunnan*, 1877; *Consular Reports*, 1883, *Chengtu*, reprinted in the *Report of the Royal Commission*, II, 1894, App. XII. This document gives a detailed picture of poppy cultivation as practised in Szechuan in the 1880's. Since the visit of Baron Richtofen in 1872, the crop had expanded enormously. The consul's calculations were criticized with some measure of justice by a missionary writing in the *Friend of China*, Jan., 1884, pp. 3-4.

[66] *Report of a Journey through . . . Kweichow and Yunnan* (China no. 1), 1883, p. 6.

Yunnan and very little, if any, into Szechuan.[67] Among British consular officials there was great apprehension over the future of the Indian drug in China. The consul at Newchwang was forced to admit that ''The import of opium is dying a natural death.''[68] Throughout North China cultivation had expanded phenomenally. ''All over . . . Liao-tung . . . the poppy may now be seen,'' and passing northwards to Kirin, the traveler would find only about twenty per cent of the available land devoted to other crops.[69] In some of the older treaty ports, although Indian opium still controlled the market, the native drug was assuming large proportions. Several thousand piculs were brought each year from distant Szechuan to Shanghai where, despite heavy transportation charges, they were able to undersell Patna and Malwa.[70] In general, the latter still held their preëminence only along the coast south of Shanghai.

The amazing growth of the native industry evoked from officialdom a typical variety of response. On the whole, attempts to check cultivation were unimpressive, though by no means always insincere. In the autumn of 1876 and again in 1877, the *Peking Gazette* contained edicts forbidding the crop.[71] Both, in a large measure, were inoperative. Officials continued to tax the prohibited flower, and indeed one officer was degraded for misappropriating revenue from this source.[72] In 1880 the opium

[67] *Rangoon Times*, quoted in *Corr. with the Government of India*, 1882, pp. 29-30.

[68] *Consular Reports*, 1884, Part I, p. 133.

[69] Report by the commissioner of customs, *Consular Reports*, 1875, pp. 11-12.

[70] *Decennial Reports* (Customs), 1882-1891, p. 327. The commissioner at Chefoo reported that of the 132 smoking saloons in the city only five sold pure foreign opium, thirty sold mixtures of native and foreign, and ninety-five sold nothing but native. *Ibid.*, p. 51.

[71] *Friend of China*, Jan., 1878, p. 94.

[72] *Ibid.*, Feb., 1878, p. 98.

likin office at Chungking in Szechuan, which employed a staff of some thirty-one persons, reported monthly collections of between fourteen and seventeen hundred taels.[73] In his journey through Szechuan, Hosie observed on one side of the road a prohibitory proclamation from the viceroy, while on the other were blooming fields of gorgeous poppies.[74] From Ichang the British consul reported that ''The proclamations against it . . . are a well-understood signal to all that the proportion of smuggled opium to duty paid opium is getting too large.''[75]

There were, to be sure, periods and provinces of enforcement. In Chihli and Manchuria a series of floods, drought, and bad harvests was interpreted by the devout as punishment for their disobedience. During the next two years their superstitious zeal resulted in a diminution in both the local yield and imports. But it soon appeared that the vials of heaven's wrath had been emptied, and the peasants resumed their profitable husbandry.[76]

In at least two instances, Chinese officials attained distinguished, if temporary, success. Tso Tsung Tang, as viceroy of Kansu and Shensi, two of the largest opium areas, was able to reduce cultivation to negligible proportions.[77] The province of Kiangsu was the scene of one of the most sensational reforming crusades. Here the moving spirit was one Tan Chun Pei, the acting governor, who as a subordinate official had shown such zeal that armed forces were required to protect him from the

---

[73] *Decennial Reports (Customs)*, 1882-1891, pp. 89, 91. To credit the likin office with thirty-one employees in 1880 may not be strictly accurate, for this report was written in 1892. But the staff could not have been much smaller a decade before.

[74] *Report of a Journey through Szechuan, Yunnan, and Kweichow*, cited in *Report of the Royal Commission*, I, 1894, App. I, p. 138.

[75] *Consular Reports*, 1880, *Ichang*, p. 44.

[76] *Ibid.*, 1884, Part I, *Newchwang*, p. 158.

[77] *Corr. with the Government of India*, 1882, p. 39; *Friend of China*, July, 1884, pp. 134-136.

anger of the peasants. When the remarkable Tan became governor of the province, he issued stringent rules, which were enforced with ruthless impartiality. He also brought pressure on the literati to give up the vice and by ingenious publicity methods sought to create sentiment on the question. Not only was the poppy utterly suppressed, but, with the exception of those in the foreign settlement of Shanghai, practically no opium divans remained in the province.[78] It would be pleasant to point to other viceroys and governors who followed the example set by Tso Tsung Tang and Tan Chun Pei. But these two stand as luminous exceptions to the almost universal practice of provincial officials.[79] And two earnest Mrs. Partingtons could scarcely withstand the flood of opium that deluged China in the eighteen-eighties.

The position of the Chinese government may be briefly summarized. Its leading officers still professed a moral objection to the use of opium, perhaps not so implacable as that of Lin Tse Hsu, but for all that a conviction to be reckoned with. Their hostile demonstrations against the drug had met with nothing but failure. The Indian trade had steadily increased, and Chinese cultivation—in some parts of the empire three and one-half times as profitable as cereal crops—was flourishing as never before. Since the chaos of the Taiping rebellion, local officials had been more headstrong than ever.[80] And to all the other prob-

---

[78] *Consular Reports*, 1882, *Chinkiang*, p. 3; *Corr. with the Government of India*, 1882, pp. 38-41. It is instructive to notice that the closing of the opium dens did not reduce the business done by retailers. The conclusion seems to be that addicts transferred their smoking to their own homes. The British consul at Chinkiang observed that an increase in crime followed the shutting of the divans.

[79] There were others, such as Chang Chih Tung, who did effective work in Shansi.

[80] Peking, however, could still act. In the autumn of 1877, five officials, who had been denounced as opium smokers, were stripped of their rank. It was assumed by the British consul at Shanghai ''that they are extreme in-

lems of managing a medieval state in a modern world was added a chronic shortage of funds. As a British consul put the case, China might as well consume opium of her own production—since Indian opium could be excluded by no other means—and thus save the six or eight million sterling which she contributed annually to the Calcutta exchequer.[81]

There was nothing essentially inconsistent about the Chinese demand for a high duty on the Indian drug. Such a tax would serve two purposes—discourage the use of foreign opium and replenish a depleted treasury. With some of the Chinese statesmen, such as Li Hung Chang, the main issue was probably revenue; with others, the moral aspect apparently predominated. At any rate, the stone might be aimed at two birds, either one of which deserved slaughter. If imports were not cut off by heavy taxation, at least the revenue would be benefited. If the trade were killed, then attention might be directed to the local industry. Since the Indian government was not inclined to consider a mutual self-denying ordinance, let the highest possible tax be imposed upon Indian opium and both the moralists and financiers be satisfied.

However confused Chinese diplomatists may have been as to their ultimate aim, there was complete unanimity on the question of immediate steps. Chinese policy, in a word, was to obtain British consent to the highest possible rate of import duty and likin, an impost which would be collected by the imperial maritime customs uniformly at all treaty ports. This objective is emphasized by the final chapter in the Chefoo negotiations. In 1879 Marquis Tseng was accredited to London and Paris. To the new minister the anti-opium society addressed a let-

stances of the vice, or that there are other charges, in addition to that upon which they are punished, against them.'' *Ibid.*, p. 42.

[81] *Consular Reports*, 1881, *Tientsin*, p. 126.

ter, seeking from him a statement which would guide the
society in its appeals to the British government. Tseng
was much disposed to recognize unpleasant facts. The unseemly phenomenon of bloodthirsty edicts accompanied
by the cultivation and taxation of the poppy had lent currency to the opinion that China's antagonism was only
assumed. "No," he reminded the society, "statesmen
must be practical men, and not merely *doctrinaires.*" To
suppress the trade immediately would doubtless be heroic, "but beautiful as is the heroic, unfortunately, it can
seldom find a place in politics and economics." Vested
interests, fiscal arrangements, and, most serious of all,
confirmed smokers had created a Gordian knot which required patient unraveling, not the swift stroke of a
knight-errant's blade. Gradual suppression was therefore recommended to the anti-opiumists. China, without
abandoning her inveterate hostility towards the drug
trade, had determined to appropriate a larger share of
the spoils until the time was ripe for its complete exter-
mination.[82]

Tseng's instructions ordered him to demand eighty
taels likin or a total of 110 taels duty, but if necessary to
accept Sir Thomas Wade's offer of one hundred.[83] Late
in 1882 it appeared that England, no less than China, was
eager to reach an understanding, and unofficial conferences were held between the Chinese legation, the foreign
office, and the India office.[84] The British began by badly
underestimating Chinese expectations. The *tsungli yamen* had profited by six years of meditation on the ways
of western countries and knew that the British could

[82] Boulger, *Halliday Macartney*, pp. 397-402.

[83] The Chinese demand of 110 taels will be recognized as that which Li
Hung Chang had made upon Sir Thomas Wade in Peking.

[84] Boulger, *Halliday Macartney*, pp. 403-404; 408-409; communications
between Granville and Tseng, 31 Jan.-3 March 1883, *Corr. resp. Duties on
Opium*, 1885, nos. 1-4.

be forced to pay heavily for their delay. When Lord Granville proposed that likin should be collected by the maritime customs at the old rate, the Chinese negotiators proved unresponsive and held out for a uniform rate of 110 taels (eighty likin and thirty import duty) which would commute all further taxation until the package of opium had been opened by the retailer.[85] The British had two important criticisms of the Chinese plan. One was that the rate of likin was too high by ten taels, and the other that foreigners ought to be permitted to carry opium into the interior.[86] Both were refused by Tseng, who pointed out that, after all, the treaty of Tientsin gave the Chinese the right to tax the drug as they chose. Eighty taels, he insisted, was something of a concession, but by reducing the cost of collection the imperial government could afford to practise this self-denial.[87]

Before a final decision could be reached, it was necessary to consult the Calcutta government. In December, 1884, Lord Kimberley, secretary of state for India, sought the viceroy's counsel. "Chinese . . . insist on 80 taels. For political reasons I propose to agree. Have you any objection?"[88] The viceroy had objections, to be precise, two in number. He was inclined to doubt the wisdom of a

[85] Boulger, *Halliday Macartney*, pp. 410-411; *Corr. resp. Duties on Opium*, 1885, annex to no. 5.

[86] Granville to Grosvenor, 27 April 1883, *Corr. resp. Duties on Opium*, 1885, no. 8 and incl. Tseng left for Russia on May 4, and the negotiations lapsed for more than a year.

[87] This was a concession only for purposes of effective diplomacy. The eagerness of the Chinese to establish a uniform rate of likin, to be levied by the maritime customs, indicates that the old system was not successful. Collection had been in the hands of provincial officials, with the result that a considerable fraction of the tax never reached the capital. Under the new scheme, however, the tax would be imperial revenue and would be paid into the treasury by the customs.

[88] India office to the government of India, 3 Jan. 1885, *Report of the Royal Commission*, VII, 1895, App. D.

uniform rate of likin for all ports,[89] and he felt, with the foreign office, that seventy taels per picul would be quite sufficient. Kimberley, in reply, put with some emphasis the argument for capitulating to the Chinese demands. He reminded the Indian government of the advantages which would lie in a completely regularized opium trade, and since other powers were urging the change, "it is not desirable that Her Majesty's Government should be represented as preventing it for the sake of the Indian opium revenue." Moreover, the clamor of the anti-opium group in the House of Commons, who demanded that China be permitted to tax the Indian drug as she pleased, was becoming ominous. "I need not remind your Excellency that the adoption of a resolution . . . condemnatory of your opium revenue, would prove embarrassing to your government."[90]

Regardless of Calcutta's attitude, Kimberley determined to sanction the terms proposed by Tseng, and on February 9, 1885, the foreign office agreed to 80 taels likin—110 including the import duty.[91] The additional article to the Chefoo convention, signed on July 18, 1885, represented a minor diplomatic triumph for the Chinese. All of their principal demands had been incorporated. Henceforth when opium was imported into China, it

[89] The Indian government was evidently cherishing the hope that provincial authorities would be allowed to establish the rates and would enter upon a price war to attract trade.

[90] India office to the government of India, 22 Jan. 1885, *Report of the Royal Commission*, VII, 1895, App. D.

[91] Granville to Tseng, 21 March 1885; *Corr. resp. Duties on Opium*, 1885, no. 11, and incl. 1 in no. 18; *Hertslet's China Treaties*, no. 14. Having gained his chief end, Tseng gladly assented to the conditions which Granville imposed. The Chinese, he promised, would give guarantees that all internal taxes on opium would be abolished, that foreign opium offered at retail would not be taxed at a higher rate than the native drug, and that the agreement might be abrogated whenever it appeared that transit certificates —which covered the drug after it had left the treaty ports—were being dishonored.

would be deposited in bonded warehouses or hulks approved by the customs service and removed only after the tariff and likin duties had been paid. Then the drug might be repacked in bond for shipment to the interior. Customs officials would issue transit certificates, valid only in the hands of Chinese subjects, which would exempt the article from additional taxation until it was sold at retail. On February 1, 1887, the new system went into operation.[92]

One other issue remained to be ironed out. The additional article provided that a commission be appointed "to inquire into the question of the prevention of smuggling into China from Hongkong." Illicit trade from Hongkong to the mainland had flourished ever since the annexation of the island by the British. Fleets of junks, which specialized in carrying opium, were accustomed to wait at both Hongkong and Macao, and when the none too watchful preventive eye was turned, to slip unostentatiously to the mainland.[93] This traffic did not come under the surveillance of the maritime customs, for it was carried on altogether in native junks, which landed their cargoes not at the treaty port of Canton but at smaller anchorages in the Canton estuary and elsewhere. An overwhelming proportion of the opium which reached the Canton district—much of it foreign-owned—came by this clandestine route.[94] In 1868 Chinese customhouses, re-

[92] Salisbury to Tseng, 18 July 1885, and Tseng to Salisbury, 18 July 1885, *Corr. resp. Duties on Opium*, 1885, incls. 2 and 3 in no. 18. The article was not to go into effect until the Chinese government had obtained the assent of the other treaty powers. The British had indiscreetly notified Germany of its provisions before the Chinese had had time to act, and the Berlin foreign office then attempted to obstruct the opium agreement until the question of internal taxation on other goods was settled to its taste. Boulger, *Halliday Macartney*, pp. 413-414.

[93] Salt was another important item in the cargoes of the junks.

[94] During the decade 1875-1884 the inspector of customs at Canton re-

enforced by patrol boats, were established near Hongkong and Macao and were placed under the authority of
the Canton hoppo.[95] Obviously the right of the Chinese
to take this action was unimpeachable, but to foreign
merchants in Hongkong, who referred to the revenue
cruisers as "the blockade," it was an incredible nuisance.
The island lay so close to the mainland that what was
regarded as undue interference with the trade of a free
British port was almost inevitable. Even with these precautions, the loss to the Chinese government was heavy,
for much smuggling still took place, and when duties
were collected, the native revenue farmers took pains to
underbid the maritime customs. It was estimated that the
loss on opium alone from Hongkong in 1885 totaled a half
million taels.[96] To place this junk trade under the control
of the maritime customs would at once mean increased
receipts for the Peking treasury and relieve Hongkong
of the odious blockade.

As early as 1871, Sir Thomas Wade had sought an understanding with the *tsungli yamen*. But the Chinese,
irked by the rejection of Alcock's convention, refused to
open more ports as a price for British aid in bringing the
Hongkong opium trade under effective control. Not until
the *yamen* had received what it was bargaining for in the

ported annual imports averaging less than a thousand chests, while the consumption of the Canton area in 1874-1875 was estimated at about fifteen
thousand chests. Because of this unreported junk traffic, the returns of the
imperial maritime customs do not give an accurate picture of the amount of
opium actually imported into China. Statistics showing exports to China
from India supply a more reliable index. *Decennial Reports* (Customs),
1882-1891, p. 558. See also *Report from the Commissioners . . . to Inquire
into . . . Alleged Smuggling*, 1884.

[95] At first, opium passing these stations paid likin only, but later they
collected import duty as well. In practice the rate of duty actually levied
was lower than that collected by the maritime customs. *Ibid.*, pp. 558, 582-
583.

[96] Morse, *International Relations*, II, 381.

additional article could it be beguiled into negotiations.[97] From the deliberations of a joint commission emerged a plan to place the junk trade under the jurisdiction of the maritime customs, while Hongkong was to take suitable precautions against the use of the colony as a smuggling base. The coöperation of the Macao government was essential, and the Portuguese, seeing an opportunity to realize their ancient ambition, demanded the cession of the island to them in full sovereignty and a treaty which should include a most-favored-nation clause. An envoy was sent to Peking, the agreement signed, and the opium arrangement made effective.[98]

Two new collectorates were established by the customs, one for Hongkong located at Kowloon and one for Macao at Lappa, with six principal sub-stations. The inspector general acted with energy to intimidate smugglers. At one point one hundred and fifty men armed with Winchester rifles patrolled a land border day and night, and a bamboo latticework, eight feet high, was erected along the entire land frontier. The water boundary, more difficult to control, was guarded by three revenue steamers and ten launches.[99] The innovation more than justified itself. Native opium shipping was now taxed at the same rate and in the same manner as foreign. As a consequence, foreign bottoms reclaimed a large share of the trade, and Canton, the natural distributing center, again received huge imports of opium. The amount which paid

[97] Wade to Granville, 6 May 1871, *Calcutta Papers*, 1870, *Supplement*, 1872, p. 49. The financial secretary of the Indian government noted on this despatch: ''If the opium trade were altogether unobjectionable, it would probably be feasible for us to come to some arrangement with the Chinese Government to give them a *percentage* of our revenue on condition of their leaving the article absolutely free.''

[98] *Hertslet's China Treaties*, no. 73. Macao could not be alienated by its new owners without Chinese consent.

[99] *Decennial Reports* (Customs), 1882-1891, pp. 581-582, 682-683. Macao, though usually thought of as an island, forms the tip of a peninsula.

duty at Canton during the first year of the new system was nearly ten times as much as was collected in the preceding year.[100] Revenue was salvaged both for Peking and for the colony of Hongkong.[101]

The salutary effects of the additional article itself were no less striking. Foreign opium merchants naturally viewed the projected system with something akin to horror. They argued, of course, that the rate of 110 taels was too high and that it would place their goods under an intolerable handicap in China. There was an element of truth in their claim, for the Indian drug was well taxed before it reached China. But the decline of foreign opium in price and value was more intimately connected with Chinese production than with Chinese taxation. Foreigners also cherished doubts whether the transit passes that guaranteed imported opium free circulation in the interior would be duly honored by local officials. Here their fears were absolutely groundless. Consuls and customs officials alike testify that the system worked with almost unbelievable smoothness. In Kwangtung, when the authorities proposed an additional impost, it was promptly vetoed by Peking.[102] At Kiukiang an attempt was made to levy a "voluntary contribution" of four taels a chest for the relief of famine sufferers. After a fleeting existence of four days, the practice was killed by a peremptory telegram from the *tsungli yamen*.[103] These deviations were exceptions to the rule. On the whole, China fulfilled her part of the agreement in good faith.

One of the most important economic consequences of

---

100 *Ibid.*, pp. 558-559.

101 The revenue of Hongkong gained chiefly because of the fact that opium consumption in the colony was more effectively controlled and because of the "practical monopoly of smuggling into China which was now secured by the [Hongkong] opium farmer." Morse, *International Relations*, II, 386.

102 *Decennial Reports* (Customs), 1882-1891, p. 559.

103 *Consular Reports*, 1890, *Kiukiang*, no. 880, p. 2.

the additional article was to alter the balance between the various treaty ports. Formerly the opium traffic had tended to gravitate to cities where the rate of likin was low. But with a uniform rate in force, the trade was thrown back into its natural channels, so that the port nearest the consuming district became the entrepôt. Foochow, for example, gained at the expense of Amoy, Swatow, and other ports, while Wuhu lost to Chinkiang.[104] Shanghai, farther from the ultimate market but possessing superior credit facilities, appropriated some of the trade that in the past had paid duty at Wuhu, Chinkiang, and Ningpo.[105] In other words, differential taxation no longer influenced the route by which foreign opium entered the Middle Kingdom.

China, for the first time in her years of contact with the West, was thus placed in possession of an agreement of her own seeking. The eagerness betrayed by Chinese statesmen for the ratification of the Chefoo convention opium clause leaves no room for doubt. The longer ratification was postponed, the stronger appeared the case of the Chinese, and in the end they dictated the terms of settlement. On the other hand, the British were a little less than justified when they prided themselves that at last China had no further cause for complaint over the opium question. This comfortable reflection leaves out of account the melancholy history of the drug trade. The harm, in a large measure, had already been done. By the additional article the imperial government was allowed a larger share in the proceeds. But suppression was apparently as far away as ever.

The status of China under the additional article be-

[104] *Decennial Reports* (Customs), 1882-1891, p. 412; *Consular Reports*, 1888, *Wuhu*, no. 519, p. 3.

[105] *Consular Reports*, 1888, *Chinkiang*, no. 592, pp. 1-2; *Ningpo*, no. 523, p. 4.

comes less impressive when the alternative is considered. Although she might abrogate the agreement after four years, she would not then be a free agent with respect to foreign opium. The statement made by a spokesman for the government on the floor of the House of Commons was palpably false. ''The Chinese at any time may terminate the treaty on giving twelve months' notice, and to protect themselves they may increase the duty to any extent they please, or they may exclude it altogether.''[106] On the contrary, the text of the article stated explicitly that, in the event of the termination ''of the present additional Article the arrangement with regard to Opium now in force under the Regulations attached to the Treaty of Tientsin shall revive.''[107] China was still bound to admit foreign opium, which, by the treaty of Tientsin, she could tax out of existence only after it had left the hands of the importer. Clearly, unequal treaties continued to govern the relations of the Middle Kingdom with the West.

[106] 3 *Hansard*, CCCLII, 316.

[107] Sir Joseph Pease, who had precipitated the debate, accepted this as an official statement of the government's policy and abstained from pressing the matter further. The position of China under the additional article was aired in the hearings of the royal commission in 1894. Several anti-opium witnesses pointed to the speech of Sir James Fergusson (quoted above), April 10, 1891, and challenged its accuracy. Information from the foreign office made it quite clear that, if China saw fit to abrogate the additional article, the opium clause in the regulations of 1858 would come into operation again, and the drug would be handled as it had been between 1858 and 1885. *Report of the Royal Commission*, I, 1894, App. IV; see also evidence of Dr. Maxwell, Q. 252-256; Sir Thomas Wade, Q. 1302; Sir Joseph Pease, Q. 21-23.

CHAPTER X

THE INDIAN OPIUM SYSTEM
UNDER THE CROWN

LONG before the "Act for the Better Government of India" transferred the reins of sovereignty from the hands of the East India Company to those of the crown, the main features of the opium system had been accepted as final.[1] The changes made during the next half century were those of detail rather than of broad outline. Just prior to the relinquishing of control by the company, the various regulations which had been passed from time to time were consolidated into a single opium law.[2] This statement was approved by the new government of India and became the legal basis of the monopoly. Ultimate authority was vested in the government of India in its financial department, but, except on larger questions of policy, most of the decisions were made by the Bengal board of revenue, whose work was subject to review by the government of Bengal.[3] This division of powers was neither logical nor especially effective, for the Bengal administration had no immediate interest in the opium revenue, and its activities were confined chiefly to rubber-stamping the recommendations of the board of

[1] Actual political power had been surrendered to the crown years previously. The Act of 1858 did little more than to abolish the fiction of the company's sovereignty.

[2] Act XIII of 1857. Text, *Report of the Royal Commission*, II, 1894, App. XLVIII.

[3] The Bengal board of revenue consisted of two members, one of whom was in charge of the opium department.

revenue. Furthermore, the Benares agency, where about half of the drug was produced, lay beyond the legal jurisdiction of the Bengal government. In practice, the heads of the opium department were the agents in Bihar and Benares, whose posts were regarded as two of the most attractive plums in the Indian civil service.[4] These, with their corps of sub-deputy agents and subordinates, guided the destinies of the monopoly. Monthly auction sales in Calcutta continued to be the means by which the opium provision was made available for the export trade.[5]

Although statistics would seem to prove the contrary, the latter half of the century saw the monopoly increasingly on the defensive. Both revenue and exports to China, it is true, showed a phenomenal growth until about 1880, when the peak was reached.[6] But even before this time, there were forces making for decline. In the development of the opium system under the crown, three questions merit emphasis. First of all must be examined the actual policy which the government of India followed towards its revenue and towards the provision from which the revenue was drawn. Here the opium administrators vacillated between the two principles which had been debated in the earlier days of the monopoly—whether to draw a high percentage of profit from a small

[4] The ''appointment is, indeed, apt to be treated as a suitable provision for a moderately meritorious officer, who is thought not quite good enough to be made a Commissioner.'' *Report of a Commission . . . to Enquire into the Working of the Opium Department*, 1883, pp. 235-236.

[5] Originally there were only two auctions each year. The number gradually rose until, from 1848-1849 on, monthly sales became the rule. Mac-Kenzie, Lyall and Company handled the business on commission until 1870-1871, when the board of revenue itself assumed charge.

[6] Exports of the Bengal drug to China attained their highest point in 1879-1880 (48,722 chests from Calcutta, together with 46,114½ of Malwa), and the opium revenue (Rs. 5,92,68,360, and Rs. 8,45,12,940 including Malwa) reached its maximum in 1880-1881.

provision or a lower profit per unit from a larger output.[7] During the eighteen-sixties and 'seventies, when Chinese and Persian opium began to dispute the position of the Indian drug in China, the die was cast in favor of another era of mad expansion. The weapon which had been used against Malwa was now turned against a new and, in the end, a more formidable competitor. To solve the further problem of fluctuating yields and provisions of uncertain size, the government inaugurated the plan of putting up for sale a fixed quantity of opium annually and of accumulating a reserve supply, with which the produce of lean years might be supplemented.

Secondly, the monopoly was obliged not only to fight the competition of Chinese and Persian opium, but also to defend itself from attacks within the Indian administration itself. The years 1858-1881 saw four different onslaughts directed against the drug system of British India, led in each case by servants of the government. Impelled both by economic and moral considerations, they demanded that the monopoly give way to a plan similar to that which obtained in Malwa. Although the only tangible result of this agitation was to add a number of bulky documents to the Indian archives, it was not without prophetic significance. In the third place, there was the Malwa trade, which contributed nearly half of the total exports to China. The evolution of the opium system in the west of India is not an eventful story. In days of prosperity the price of transit passes was raised by the Bombay government, despite inevitable protests from opium merchants, and lowered again when the trade itself fell upon evil days.

When the crown assumed full control of India, the opium revenue, next to that from land and salt, was the largest single increment to the Indian treasury, aggre-

[7] The term ''small provision'' is used, of course, only in a relative sense.

gating something over one-seventh of its total income.
During the years between the first Anglo-Chinese war
and the end of the company's tenure, the revenue mounted
rapidly, though erratically. By 1846 the system was not
only running at full blast, but the directors were being
asked to approve an extension of cultivation. This they
refused to do, "adverting to the principle which we have
always maintained, of obtaining our revenue by procur-
ing high prices for a limited provision rather than reduced prices for an extended one."[8] Even with no special
efforts to encourage cultivation, the produce of the monopoly was doubled within the next two years, but both
prices and revenue fell off, in part because of uncertain
conditions in the Chinese market.[9] It soon appeared that
a provision limited to 36,000 chests would not accomplish
its purpose of raising prices. Therefore, in 1851-1852 and
again in 1855-1856, the rate at which the drug was purchased from the peasants was reduced.[10] Within a few
seasons the output fell from nearly 50,000 chests to
21,000, but the revenue, on the contrary, revived mag-
nificently.

The wearisome oscillations of the opium monopoly between small and large provisions will be meaningless
without a statement of the principles on which the Indian
government acted. Any feeling that, for the benefit of
Chinese morals, the supply ought to be restricted had
long since disappeared, and the question was decided
solely on economic grounds. The aim of the government
was so to adjust the provision that the largest possible

8 Governor-general in council to the court of directors (separate revenue),
22 Jan. 1846, no. 2 of 1846, I. O. Letters from India and Bengal, XLIX;
court of directors to the governor-general in council (separate revenue), 17
June 1846, no. 4 of 1846, I. O. Despatches to Bengal and India, XLIX.

9 I. O. Bengal Separate Consultations, 6 Sept. 1848.

10 *Ibid.*, 18 Sept. 1850; minute by Sir Cecil Beadon, 21 Feb. 1865, *Calcutta Papers*, 1870, p. 41.

net revenue would be gained. Let it be assumed, for the present, that Bengal and Malwa enjoyed control of the China market. Under these conditions, two factors still served to limit the volume of production in Bengal. In the first place, the output of opium must not be so great, in proportion to the Chinese demand, as to depress prices unduly. In the second place, the provision must be held below the point at which overhead charges would eat up the additional profits. The government's duty was to see that production was kept at as high a pitch as possible without falling victim to the law of diminishing returns. A further complication was the Malwa trade, which was less remunerative than the monopoly drug to the public treasury and which would expand, if the provision in Bengal were excessively curtailed. Such reasoning was valid only as long as there was no serious competition in China. If opium from another source invaded the market, then the principle of large provisions must be invoked, whether profits suffered or not. As early as 1850, the Indian government was faintly uneasy about reports of Chinese cultivation. Before many years passed, the call to battle with the Chinese drug was to dictate the size of the output and was to do it on a grand scale.

In 1858, as the East India Company relinquished the last vestige of its sovereignty, the opium revenue was highly satisfactory. But as much could not be said for the general state of Indian finance. The mutiny and the years following increased the deficit until it was nearly equal to the annual income of the government.[11] The situation demanded heroic remedies, and the India office selected as member of the council a financier who did not hesitate to prescribe them. After presenting his taxation program, James Wilson was led to reflect upon the opium revenue—"one of the most unique facts that the history

[11] Sir R. Temple, *Men and Events*, p. 192.

of finance affords, that a government, without calling upon its people to make any sacrifice whatever . . . should be able to derive a revenue . . . of so large a sum. But what security have we that this will always continue?"[12] The policy of restricting the supply as a means of raising prices, he held, was suicidal, for high prices must stimulate competition and set the stage for fiscal tragedy.[13] The council gave heed to Wilson's prudent words. Cultivation unquestionably had fallen to a dangerous level. The obvious remedy was to raise the price paid to ryots for their opium. The first increase failed to interest the peasants, who had discovered that, in a period of rising agricultural prices, other crops were profitable, and there was nothing to do but to advance the rate another notch.[14]

This measure bore reassuring fruit. The financial statement of Samuel Laing in 1862 proclaimed new confidence in the security of the opium revenue, which, he declared, was no more precarious than that accruing to Great Britain from gin and tobacco. Opium was *sans pareil* for the stolid celestial—and here an awakened poetic sense got the better of the sober financier: "The Chinese, whose greatest deficiency . . . is in the imaginative faculties, resorts to that which stimulates the imagination and makes his sluggish brain see visions and dream dreams."[15] Upheld by the natural instincts of millions of Chinese, the monopoly had little to fear.

Laing's faith in the new policy was justified, in one

[12] *Corr. between the Government of India and the Government of Madras*, no. 339, 1860, p. 79.

[13] See Strachey, *Finances and Public Works of India*, p. 244, and evidence of Sir Cecil Beadon, *Report on East Indian Finance*, 1871, Q. 3239.

[14] India office to the government of India, 9 Dec. 1861, I. O. Separate Revenue Despatches to India, no. 41 of 1861.

[15] Proc. Legislative Council, 16 April 1862, *Copies of Corr. between the Secretary of State for India and the Governor-General of India in Council*, no. 354, 1862; also I. T. Prichard, *Administration of India*, II, 205-206.

respect, by its results. In 1863-1864 there was harvested a crop of bumper proportions, one that proved both gratifying and embarrassing. With some 64,000 chests thrust on the market and all bought from the ryots at high rates, the cost of production increased and sale prices declined.[16] As a result, the net return by no means reflected the apparent prosperity of the monopoly. In seeking to avoid the peril of a small provision, the Indian government had gone to the other extreme. Excessive fluctuation had been the lot of the revenue during the preceding decade, and there was little evidence that conditions would change for the better under the new dispensation. Patently the opium system required stabilization. It was Sir Cecil Beadon, lieutenant governor of Bengal, who brought forward a plan.[17] The obvious means was to place a fixed amount of drug on sale each year and to accumulate a reserve supply with which to augment the provision of lean seasons. Beadon proposed that 45,000 chests be regarded as the normal provision. Two years later, after Jardine, Matheson and Company had begged for at least 50,000 chests, the ideal provision was set at 48,000, with a reserve supply of 10,000.[18] That this promising scheme could not be put into effect for some years was owing, in part, to a succession of indifferent crops and, in part, to ominous reports of Chinese production, which with each year of delay tended to make the Indian government demand a heavier output in Bengal.

For after 1860 the future of the Indian trade was

[16] *Financial and Commercial Statistics of British India*, 1904, Opium, no. 7.

[17] Minute by Sir Cecil Beadon, 21 Feb. 1865, *Calcutta Papers*, 1870, p. 41.

[18] Board of revenue to the government of Bengal, 8 April 1867, no. 945, and minute by Sir Cecil Beadon, 18 April 1867, *ibid.*, pp. 56 ff. See also Strachey, *Finances and Public Works of India*, pp. 245-247, and evidence of Sir Cecil Beadon, *Report on East Indian Finance*, 1871, Q. 3240, 3241.

clouded by the uncertainties of large-scale competition. Both Persian and Chinese opium gave the Calcutta monopolists uneasy moments. In the former case their anxiety was wasted, for the Persian drug never seriously threatened the preëminence of Indian opium and competed with it at only a few Chinese ports. For some years apparently opium from Persia had been finding its way to West China by the overland route through Bokhara.[19] This avenue of approach was so obscure and tedious that the trade seems to have passed almost unnoticed. But when direct maritime contact with China was established, there was more cause for worry. No possible check could be applied, since Persian opium vessels touched at no British ports.[20] The journey from the Near East to China was made both in the ships of the Messageries Impériales and, more commonly, in vessels owned by Persian merchants.[21]

Throughout the eighteen-seventies imports of Persian opium into China were on the increase. Growers took pains to improve the quality of their drug, while the low taxes imposed by their government enabled it to undersell Indian opium by a substantial margin.[22] And yet in no year did the imports from Persia total as much as ten per cent of the shipments from India. By about 1885 an annual average of something less than six thousand chests had been struck.[23] While this quantity may have diverted some purchasers from buying Malwa, the effect upon India could not have been great. It was only on the

[19] Memorandum on Persian opium, *Calcutta Papers*, 1870, pp. 194-195.

[20] Dealers in Persian opium begged permission to land their drug at Bombay for trans-shipment on the payment of Rs. 50 per chest. The privilege was refused.

[21] W. Nicol and Company to the government of Bombay, 12 Jan. 1869, *Calcutta Papers*, 1870, p. 183.

[22] *Corr. with the Government of India*, 1882, p. 25.

[23] *Decennial Reports* (Customs), 1882-1891, Appendix, p. xxiii.

island of Formosa that Persian opium succeeded in expelling the dearer drug from the market. Among the poor islanders, who had no cheap native opium near at hand, the Persian variety enjoyed wide popularity, for it was easy to adulterate, and although defective in flavor, it had a pure opium content higher than that of the best Indian product.[24]

The real danger, however, lay not in the relatively insignificant shipments from the Persian Gulf but in the fields of waving poppies sown by Chinese peasants. This condition explains the touchy atmosphere which pervaded the British opium system in the eighteen-seventies and the frantic expansionism of its managers. As early as 1860, when deciding to call for a larger poppy crop, the Indian authorities were deliberately aiming "to check its extension in China." The ensuing decade merely supplied additional evidence that Patna and Malwa were facing more critical opposition than they had yet encountered. Sir Rutherford Alcock's negotiations with the Chinese in 1868-1869 served to bring new facts into the open and to transmute the vague fears of the Indian government into a demand for courageous action. At the outset there was needed authoritative and up-to-date information. The Bengal board of revenue urged the sending of a special deputy to study the opium situation in China—a proposal which was vetoed by the supreme government.[25] Not content with the annual consular reports from China, the Indian council requested quarterly bulletins of the opium trade. The arrangement lasted only a year, for Calcutta

[24] *Decennial Reports* (Customs), 1882-1891, p. 483. "The great cause of the popularity of Persian opium is its mildness and comparative cheapness, as the residue, or ashes, can be used, mixed with fresh drug, for as many as five or six smokings."

[25] Board of revenue to the government of Bengal, 16 Feb. 1869, no. 695C, and government of India to the government of Bengal, 6 July 1869, no. 1936A, *Calcutta Papers*, 1870, pp. 217-219.

found the "perfunctory" reports of little assistance.[26] From the consul at Shanghai was received by each mail a statement of the daily prices at that port.[27] If, in the past, the government of India had been attentive to reports from the China market, in the future it was to be doubly so. It is no exaggeration to say that the opium policy of British India between 1860 and 1885 was born in the poppy fields of Szechuan and Yunnan.

The task of the monopoly was therefore twofold: first, to produce enough opium to compete with the indigenous drug in China;[28] secondly, to stabilize prices and revenue by auctioning a fixed quantity each year. The objective of 48,000 chests proved unexpectedly difficult of attainment. After the huge yield of 1863-1864, crops were bad and peasants lukewarm about poppy culture.[29] But the government was undaunted. The financial secretary called upon his colleagues to extend "production in Upper India, and possibly in Madras: it may be even in the Bombay Presidency itself! Wherever, in fact, opium can be profitably grown and delivered to us at Rs. 5 per seer.'"[30] The Bengal government, on which the work devolved, was not clear that the "very jaunty instruction" to provide 48,000 chests for 1870 and future years could be carried out. Reports indicated that many of the best lands

[26] *Ibid.*, pp. 38, 44.

[27] Government of India to the India office (separate revenue), 28 July 1871, no. 15 of 1871, I. O. Separate Revenue Letters from India.

[28] Bengal opium, of course, could not compete with Chinese on an absolute basis. It must always sell at a higher price than the native drug, but superior quality gave it an important initial advantage.

[29] The introduction of the plan of fixed provisions was completed by a notification dated March 8, 1879, some fourteen years after Beadon's first minute, and it was not until 1880-1881 (and then for only three years) that a uniform number of chests was auctioned. J. Strachey, *Finances and Public Works of India*, p. 247. See also *Report on the Administration of Bengal, 1867-68*, p. 84.

[30] Note by R. B. Chapman, *Calcutta Papers*, 1870, p. 19.

had been withdrawn from the poppy and given over to more lucrative crops.[31]

Under pressure from the viceroy, the Bengal government and the opium agents did their best. Two new depots were opened in the Bihar agency and additional districts in the Benares area.[32] Even a blight, which damaged a part of the poppy crop did not prevent the government, now playing for high stakes, from displaying an excess of goodwill towards the ryots. Balances due from cultivators whose fields had been ruined were remitted, "in order that their losses this season might not deter them from poppy cultivation in future years."[33] But the yield still proved disappointing. Whatever the obstacles, the Indian administrators were not inclined to stop with a modest 48,000 or 50,000 chests. The frenzy of expansion touched them. In the Calcutta council John Strachey declared for a provision of 54,500 chests. Sir Richard Temple, who was something of a skeptic about the future of the revenue, supported him: "I am clear for extending the cultivation and insuring a plentiful supply. . . . They [the Chinese] had better have our good opium than their

[31] Grey to Chapman (semi-official), 29 April 1869, *Calcutta Papers*, 1870, p. 89; letters from sub-deputy opium agents, *ibid.*, pp. 93 ff.

[32] Government of Bengal to the government of India, 23 Jan. 1869, no. 287, *Calcutta Papers*, 1870, pp. 81-82; government of India to the government of Bengal, 30 Jan. 1869, *ibid.*, p. 85. The temper of the opium administration during this period is revealed by the following, from the lieutenant governor of Bengal to C. H. Campbell, 22 April 1869:

"I have a telegraphic message from Simla, urging 'that every possible expedient that you (I) approve should be used even now to extend the opium cultivation next season to the utmost practicable extent.' From all accounts it is not practicable to do anything more in the Behar agency. . . . But are you quite satisfied that the fullest possible extension (that is, of course, under the existing circumstances, and without an increase of price) is being pushed in the Benares agency? . . . If Carnac [the Benares agent] should see his way to doing anything more than he has done already to extend the cultivation for next season, you need not hesitate to sanction it at once." *Calcutta Papers*, 1870, p. 88.

[33] *Report on the Administration of Bengal, 1870-71*, p. 186.

own indifferent opium.'"[34] The climax to the performance came in the spring of 1870 when, after interviewing Sir Rutherford Alcock, the supreme government resolved to increase the provision for the Chinese market to 60,000 chests. If Bihar and Benares could not supply the difference, the Punjab, Sind, Oudh, and perhaps even Bombay would have to be called to the rescue.[35]

The vicissitudes of the monopoly during the eighteen-seventies illustrate the difficulty of maintaining a constant supply of opium, as well as the intensely speculative character of the industry itself. A year of drought plus a reduction in price of a few annas per seer might mean a difference of thousands of acres. Conversely, one or two seasons of plenty would fill the government go-downs to overflowing and win discouraged ryots back to the poppy. The first two crops harvested after the government had declared for 60,000 chests were utter failures, and the enormous revenue of 1872—nearly £2,000,-000 more than had been anticipated—was realized by marketing at high prices a quantity held over from the previous year's reserve.[36] The next few yields were all that could be desired. By 1875 the government was debating whether the pendulum had not been allowed to swing too far, and during the two years following the opium agents sought only to hold production steady.[37]

[34] Minutes by J. Strachey and Sir R. Temple, 20 and 27 April 1869, *Calcutta Papers*, 1870, pp. 85-87, 88-89.

[35] Resolution no. 2673 (separate revenue), 8 Sept. 1876, I. O. Separate Revenue Collections, XIII, 1876. An emissary was despatched to the Punjab to study the field. His recommendation that poppy culture on government account be introduced into twelve districts was negatived by the governor general, who preferred the Malwa system of pass duties. Resolution no. 1167 (separate revenue), 21 Feb. 1873, *ibid.*, X, 1872-1873.

[36] Government of Bengal to the government of India (separate revenue), 2 Aug. 1872, no. 3336, *ibid.;* Sir Richard Temple's financial statement for 1872-1873, *Proc. Legislative Council, 1872-73*, pp. 262-263.

[37] Resolution no. 2673 (separate revenue), 8 Sept. 1876, I. O. Separate

But the Indian authorities soon became aware that 56,400 chests, which had meanwhile been set as the standard provision, could not be sustained without further extension of cultivation. By 1882 the reserve supply had reached a precarious level, and again the cry for more acreage was raised. Unhappily for the immediate welfare of the revenue, the obstacles were more serious than in previous decades. From both Bihar and Benares came counsels of despair. Recent attempts to introduce the poppy into Allahabad and Mirzapur, by the Benares agent's admission, had met with flat failure. The ryots charged that they had been "badly treated in the old days, that they did not understand the cultivation, and that they had other crops that paid well and wanted no change."[38]

The government of India was thus brought to a candid scrutiny of the facts. In its conclusions one misses the easy optimism of Samuel Laing. That the opium revenue "may undergo a considerable diminution" was not in itself a novel opinion. Since the report of the famous committee of 1832 it had been pointed to as a feeble reed, but it had always managed to survive. What was new was the evidence that the authorities adduced—the improvement, both qualitative and quantitative, of Chinese and Persian opium and the progressive difficulty of extending cultivation in India.[39] Fifty years before, the Chinese drug had been no peril, while in Bengal only the most superficial possibilities of opium production had been explored. But by the eighteen-eighties, there was not only

Revenue Collections, XIII, 1876. Also no. 1090, 6 June 1877, *ibid.*, XIII, 1877-1878.

[38] *Corr. with the Government of India*, 1882, pp. 5-6.

[39] A sample of Shansi opium analyzed by order of the Indian government in 1881 proved to be better than any samples of Patna or Benares submitted from the production of the previous year. Amoy opium was also found to be of good quality, but Szechuan was still inferior. *Ibid.*, p. 30.

competition with native opium in China, but competition with other crops in Bengal. Potatoes, sugarcane, and tobacco in particular were reported to be luring peasants from the poppy.[40] The problem received attention from a commission of the Indian government, whose report, though less than flattering to the opium department, minimized the danger from this source.[41]

As if to confirm the council's melancholy premonitions, the crop of 1882-1883 was a dismal failure. Then, to confute these same premonitions, there followed a series of extraordinary yields and with them a renewed enthusiasm for poppy culture on the part of the ryots. So large became the reserve supply that in 1886-1887 a process of weeding out unprofitable peasants and districts was begun, during the course of which the acreage was reduced by nearly twenty per cent.[42] The object of these operations—to reduce the quantity of opium in stock—was attained with embarrassing promptitude. The season was a bad one, the first of several adverse years, and the ruin of the next year's crop forced upon the government the necessity of decreasing the standard provision to 54,000 chests.[43] One misfortune succeeded another, until it ap-

[40] *Moral and Material Progress of India, 1881-82*, 1883, p. 33. A collection of evidence on this point will be found in the testimony of Sir Joseph Pease, *Report of the Royal Commission*, I, 1894, Q. 100.

[41] *Report of a Commission . . . to Enquire into the Working of the Opium Department*, 1883, p. 219; *Report on the Administration of Bengal, 1885-86*, p. 37; *Moral and Material Progress of India, 1885-86*, 1887, p. 37. It should be noticed that, although the commission concluded that there was no occasion to fear other crops, its own statistics (p. 215) show that in most districts the poppy yielded a smaller net profit than potatoes, sugarcane, or tobacco.

[42] Evidence of J. F. Finlay, *Report of the Royal Commission*, II, 1894, Q. 5100; *Report on the Administration of Bengal, 1889-90*, p. 332.

[43] Government of India to the government of Bengal, 13 July 1891, no. 2953, cited in Baines, ''The Government Policy with regard to the Supply of Bengal Opium,'' *Report of the Royal Commission*, VI, 1895, memorandum VII, p. 173.

peared that the fates themselves had intervened to relieve India of her opium problem. The year 1891-1892
brought the most discouraging results in twenty years,
and the quantity offered for sale, even including the reserve stock, was less than in any season since 1874. In
1897-1898 the monopoly returned a net revenue lower
than at any time during the previous fifty years.

It was a tortuous path that the government had pursued since 1858. During almost the entire period, the
opium agents had been under orders either to expand or
contract the area of cultivation. Between 1861 and 1881,
for example, the price paid to peasants for their opium
was raised three times and lowered twice. To relate, as
has been done in the preceding pages, a story so repeti-
tious is pardonable only insofar as it serves to reveal
some of the complexities of the British opium system.
The twisting and turning of the Indian administration
becomes significant only as its ends are kept in view. Obviously the driving motive behind British policy was to
insure a profitable sale for the Indian drug notwithstanding the inroads made by Chinese opium. Thus provisions
of excessive size became the rule. But also, the output
must be controlled, lest prices fall needlessly low. To
reconcile these two aims—a large but constant provision
—was thus the government's problem. That it was solved
only in part helps to explain the apparent caprice of the
Indian authorities.

During the late eighteen-eighties, as we have seen, a
series of bad seasons involved the Bengal government in
a new campaign to swell the acreage. In 1891-1892 the
government of India stepped in to veto this expansionist
program, announcing that henceforth the area under cultivation should not be increased by deliberate effort.[44]
There was no intention of proclaiming a policy of genu-

[44] *Ibid.*, p. 175.

ine reduction. The government's intervention merely indicated that it was becoming sensitive to criticism and had determined, in the future, to give as little offense as possible.[45] But in the House of Commons the decision was the occasion for misdirected rejoicing on the part of the anti-opiumists. In April, 1891, during the course of a debate condemning the opium revenue as morally indefensible, Sir James Fergusson, undersecretary for foreign affairs, asserted, "I freely admit that the Government of India have never denied that it would be very desirable that this source of revenue should be altered. They have taken means to reduce it, and they have diminished the area on which the poppy is grown."[46] The floor leader of the House stated the same position even more categorically.

These declarations, misleading as they were, temporarily stilled the anti-opium tumult in the House of Commons. Sir Joseph Pease agreed to rest content with the assurance given. And yet, if the statements of its official spokesmen represented the view of the ministry, the government was laboring under a curious misapprehension.[47] The decision of the Indian administration in favor of the *status quo* had been officially interpreted as a definite policy of reduction. In reality, no great and permanent diminution was contemplated. The Calcutta government had merely forsworn the feverish expansion of the past, but it had no intention of abandoning what it was pleased to term "normal expansion." Confirmation of this inference is to be found in the statistics for the next decade,

[45] Evidence of Sir David Barbour, *Report of the Royal Commission*, II, 1894, Q. 2098.

[46] 3 *Hansard*, CCCLII, 323.

[47] Two weeks later the undersecretary of state for India issued a statement denying the assertions of Smith and Fergusson, but this seems to have made little impression on the anti-opium members of the House. *Ibid.*, p. 1152.

during which a hundred thousand acres were added to the area licensed for poppy cultivation.[48]

While the monopoly was valiantly striving to maintain itself against Chinese and Persian opium, opposition emanating from within the Indian government itself had to be dealt with. On four occasions between 1858 and 1881, proposals were made to abolish the monopoly and to substitute an export tax on the drug. In two of these instances the champion of the insurgents was Sir William Muir, famous as an Arabic scholar and an authority on the caliphate. No question of prohibition was involved in any of the suggested changes. The attack sprang solely from objections, first, to the monopoly as an economic device, and secondly, to the humiliating rôle of the government as a drug merchant. A tax on opium grown under a system of free cultivation, it was argued, would both preserve the revenue and close the door against hostile criticism.

During the years 1858-1860, a serious effort—the first since the days of Philip Francis—was made to introduce a fundamental change into the Bengal monopoly. Papers were submitted to the government of India by Sir Robert Hamilton, agent to the governor-general for Central India, and by William Muir, a member of the Allahabad board of revenue. Specifically Muir proposed that licenses to cultivate the poppy be issued on payment of an acreage tax and that opium intended for export should pay duty at the rate of Rs. 400 a chest.[49] The question was referred to the government of Bengal, which replied with

[48] *Moral and Material Progress of India, 1901-1902*, 1903, p. 172.

[49] Note by Sir R. Hamilton, I. O. India Separate Revenue Proc., 21 Jan. 1859; minute by W. Muir and supplementary minute, *ibid*. Material dealing with attempts to introduce the Malwa system into Bengal is summarized, with ample quotations from the sources, in Finlay, ''Account of Previous Proposals for Abolishing the Government Monopoly in Bengal,'' *Report of the Royal Commission*, II, 1894, App. XI.

a sturdy glorification of the drug arrangements as they existed. "All the evils imputed to the opium monopoly," it declared, "whether direct or indirect, and whether affecting India, England, or China, are without exception imaginary."[50] This ringing diapason was enough to dissuade the supreme government from debating the proposals at length. The issue was thus buried, only to be exhumed four years later, when allies were discovered in Sir Charles Trevelyan, financial member of the council, and the Bombay government. Although little was accomplished, Trevelyan was able to point to errors in Bengal opium accounting which made the fiscal superiority of the monopoly seem a little less pronounced.[51]

In 1868 a new onslaught was launched by the persistent Sir William Muir, now a member of the viceroy's council. On this occasion he was inclined to be more attentive to statistical evidence. Assuming an export duty of Rs. 700 per chest and shipments from both Bombay and Calcutta of 83,000 chests, the net revenue, he estimated, would exceed six millions sterling, considerably more than had been derived during the last few years. Muir's statement on the ethics of the monopoly merits quotation because, in substance, it is an accurate indictment of British opium policy. *"Prima facie* the change proposed would remove a blemish from the Administration without imperilling the finances. That cannot be an edifying position for the Government to occupy, in which it has to determine year by year the quantity of opium which it

[50] Government of Bengal to the government of India, 14 April 1860, no. 1780, I. O. India Separate Revenue Proc., 27 July 1860. For the opinions of the two opium agents and their sub-deputies see *ibid.*, and also *Report on East Indian Finance*, 1871, App. II.

[51] Government of Bombay to the government of India, 28 Sept. 1864, no. 3727, I. O. Bombay Revenue (Misc.) Proc. Trevelyan criticized the board of revenue for not adding the interest on advances to the cost per chest. He also pointed to the inconvenience of tying up something like two million sterling at a time when cash was needed for public expenditures.

will bring to sale, in which there is a constant inducement
for it to trim the market, and in which its haste to secure
wider harvests and larger returns has repeatedly recoiled
upon the trade, stimulated baneful speculation, and gam-
bling in Central and Western India, and ended in much
misery. . . . The change would relieve the British Government from the odious imputation of pandering to the
vice of China by over-stimulating production, over-stock-
ing the market, and flooding China with the drug, in order
to raise a wider and more secure revenue to itself.''[52]

The apparent strength but the real weakness of Muir's
formula lay in the fact that it sought to reconcile self-
interest with social duty. His financial meditations make
it clear that no sacrifice of revenue was being suggested.
''China wants our opium; our traders and merchants are
ready to supply it. The license duty will support the revenue, and thus the action of the Government will be that of
check, and no longer of stimulus.'' In theory, the argument was legitimate enough. Administered without regard to financial return, a tax would probably have had a
restrictive effect. But in practice, to maintain a revenue
of normal proportions would have required a crop so
large that any idea of checking output by means of taxation was illusory. And the Indian government, it may be
added, would have seen to it that the rate was sufficiently
low not to discourage cultivation.

Muir's proposal fell upon unreceptive ears in the viceroy's council, where his colleagues were either antagonis-
tic or frankly contemptuous. Sir Henry Maine recorded
a minute in which he bluntly reduced the moral argument
to reality. After dismissing the fiscal contentions as a

[52] Minute by Sir W. Muir, 22 Nov. 1868, *Calcutta Papers*, 1870, p. 6. This
document was also reprinted by the Society for the Suppression of the
Opium Trade, and it is summarized, with copious quotations, by Finlay in
the *Report of the Royal Commission*, II, 1894, App. XI.

blind to conceal the ethical objective, he put the case candidly and in part accurately. "If it be right to raise a revenue out of opium at all, it is quite immaterial in what way we raise it. . . . The true moral wrong, if wrong there be, consists in selling opium to the Chinese, and the only way to abate it would be absolutely to prohibit the cultivation of the poppy in British India, and to prevent the exportation of opium from the native states."[53] As a result of the opposition within the council and adverse reports from the Bengal administration, the papers were filed away with the non-committal notation, "No orders."[54]

The last of the suggestions looking towards the adoption of the Malwa system in Bengal came from the India office itself. The years 1880 and 1881 saw anti-opium demonstrations in the House of Commons directed, first, against the Indian government's connection with the trade, and secondly, its policy towards China.[55] In both instances the attack was sufficiently formidable to give the government pause. Moved by the dangerously heretical tendency of a section of the House, Lord Hartington, secretary of state for India, thought it best to bolster up his stand by reference to Calcutta. Prohibition, he pointed out, was quite inconceivable, but it would be more whole-

[53] *Calcutta Papers*, 1870, p. 9. The governor-general, Lord Lawrence, afterwards stated that it would be desirable to get rid of the monopoly but that he himself was disinclined to be the agent of change. "If it was a question of moderate loss, or a loss even that we could afford, I would not hesitate to undertake it." *Report on East Indian Finance*, 1873, Q. 4512-4514.

[54] The Bengal government criticized Muir's figures in that they made no allowance for the cost of a preventive service, for loss through smuggling, or for probable decline in excise revenue. Furthermore, they assumed that the pass rate could be kept at Rs. 700 per chest. Government of Bengal to the government of India (finance), 13 Sept. 1869, no. 3355, *Calcutta Papers*, 1870, pp. 21-25.

[55] 3 *Hansard*, CCLII, 1227 ff.; CCLX, 1451 ff.

some all around if the government's connection with the opium industry were a little less intimate.[56]

The reply came in the form of a lengthy despatch, largely the work of Sir Evelyn Baring. To those who favored the Malwa system for economic reasons it offered an unanswerable argument, while, from the point of view of ethics, at least it swept away some of the non-essentials. The Indian government held, legitimately enough, that the ultimate object of the anti-opiumists was to stop the trade altogether. Cardinal Manning, for example, rejoiced in the existence of the monopoly. "Nero," he remarked at the Mansion House meeting in 1881, "had wished the Roman people had only one neck, and it was in the same sense that he [the Cardinal] desired that the opium trade should remain a monopoly, for the sword was impending over it, and he would rejoice at the time when it finally descended."[57] If the chief criticism of the trade was that it debauched the Chinese, then the only answer, asserted Baring, was prohibition. Whether it were more unethical to raise a revenue by monopoly than by taxation could be left to the schoolmen. An export tax would bring slight comfort to demoralized Chinese.

The financial section of the despatch was a carefully reasoned document, in which it was proved beyond a doubt that, judged by the norm of revenue, the Malwa plan was inferior to the monopoly. The council dealt not only with the question of substituting quasi-free cultivation but also with that of total prohibition or great restriction. Needless to remark, the consequences foreseen would be wholly disastrous.[58] On the specific issue of

[56] India office to the government of India (revenue), 16 June 1881, no. 59, *Corr. with the Government of India*, 1882, p. 4.

[57] *The Times*, 22 Oct. 1881, cited *ibid.*, p. 9.

[58] The council again emphasized the part played by opium in the neat triangular system under which British trade in the Far East was conducted. The

superseding the monopoly by an export tax, Baring's case was unassailable. For the previous twenty years the Indian treasury had cleared an average of Rs. 858½ on each chest of opium. The highest export tax that could be levied was Rs. 600, leaving a difference of over Rs. 250 per chest. The only way by which the government could secure its revenue would be to impose a low rate, which, in turn, might stimulate cultivation. And thus the last state of the anti-opiumists would be worse than the first.

The council's assertion that the monopoly, in reality, had been a blessing to both India and China—to the latter because it had raised the price and limited the supply—need not be taken seriously. It was perilously close to the indiscreet doctrine of Sir George Campbell—"If the Chinese must be poisoned, he would rather they were poisoned for the benefit of our Indian subjects than for the benefit of any other exchequer."[59] But in one respect the continuance of the monopoly might yet prove a blessing to the Chinese, in that suppression could be more easily accomplished. Baring's argument on this point contained an element of truth and should have weighed more heavily with the anti-opiumists than it did, averse as they were to basing the policy of a Christian nation on the exigencies of colonial finance.[60] Reducing the price paid for crude opium would at once divert the ryots to other

drug traffic was still helping to balance the commerce of Great Britain, India, and China. *Ibid.*, p. 17.

[59] 3 *Hansard*, CCLII, 1249.

[60] Sir Arthur Cotton, the great advocate of internal improvements in India and a confirmed opponent of the opium trade, once declared, "My position is this, that there is not the slightest excuse for our having recourse to such abominable means of balancing our finances." He cited as an example the state of Godavari, whose revenue, raised with difficulty, was less than half of what it later became as a result of improvements only in part completed. If each district of India were to do only one-ninth as well, the opium revenue would be compensated for. Lady Hope, *Sir Arthur Cotton*, pp. 480-481.

crops, whereas, under a system of free production, private vested interests would make the task infinitely more difficult.[61] As Cardinal Manning pointed out, there were certain advantages in an opium system that possessed only one neck.

This despatch, unanswered by the home government, marked the end of the agitation for adopting the Malwa system in Bengal. In England the anti-opium party was no longer demanding merely the abandonment of the monopoly, but many of its members at least were clamoring for complete suppression. Although the earlier proposals of Sir William Muir were regarded with sympathetic interest by the anti-opium group, no emphasis whatever was placed upon the merits of the Malwa plan in the House of Commons debates of the eighteen-eighties. The awakened conscience of Great Britain, as represented by Sir Joseph Pease and his colleagues, was not to be satisfied by such timid steps.[62]

The whole controversy, extending over a period of twenty-five years, is significant as an attempt not only to alter existing machinery but also to render the opium revenue less susceptible to moral objection. On the side of finance, the official spokesmen had all the best of the discussion. The government would certainly have lost money by introducing an export tax system into Bengal.

[61] It is interesting to compare this frank statement of the ease of suppression with the multitudinous difficulties which occurred to the government of India during the royal commission's inquiry in 1894.

[62] Evidence of development in the program of the anti-opiumists is suggested by a comparison of F. S. Turner's British Opium Policy, published in 1876, with the speeches made in Parliament during the early eighteen-nineties. Turner, who was secretary of the Anglo-Oriental Society for the Suppression of the Opium Trade, held that Sir William Muir's proposal did not go far enough, but he also declined to be "shut up to Sir R. Temple's reductio ad absurdum of total prohibition." The government should withdraw from the monopoly, "and, if it takes revenue at all, take only that which accrues from taxation honestly meant to have a restrictive force." British Opium Policy, p. 205.

To be sure, success or failure depended on certain conjectural items, but even here the government made a rather better case than Sir William Muir and his associates.[63] Admittedly the Malwa revenue was extracted at less cost to the government, but the huge monopoly profit netted in Bengal more than outweighed the saving. In only one respect were the economic arguments of the opposition tenable. Under a system of free cultivation, the ryot might have received something like the full value of his opium, although middlemen and zamindars would probably have absorbed a part of the old monopoly profit.

Few ethical laurels were garnered by either side. To one jealous of the good name of the British raj, it might, in truth, have appeared less scandalous had the government drawn its revenue from an export tax. But the change would have been an ethical advance only if the duty had been set high enough to have a restrictive effect. That solution neither party cared to contemplate. In the main, Sir William Muir and his allies were tilting at moral windmills, for they were trying to obtain for India credit for a moral reform without sacrificing any advantages.[64] When, on the other hand, the Indian government professed solicitude for Chinese welfare, one might well be skeptical. By and large, Sir Cecil Beadon was entirely correct when he stated before the committee on East Indian finance that the government regarded

[63] These unknowns were: whether the pass duty could be maintained at more than Rs. 600 or even at that figure; whether the loss from smuggling and in excise revenue would have been appreciable; and whether a preventive service would have been as costly as was anticipated. Rs. 700, the rate on which success depended, was clearly the limit that could be imposed.

[64] Sir William Muir may have been led to emphasize the financial aspect in order to strengthen his moral argument, as the only means by which the change could be made even remotely acceptable to his colleagues in the council. Beyond doubt, he felt deeply about the ethical question. He may well have realized that unless he could offer the equivalent of the monopoly revenue, his proposal would be laughed out of court.

opium only "as a means of obtaining revenue." Consideration for Chinese consumers, he went on to say, would probably not deter the administration from doubling the cultivation, if the financial return seemed sufficiently attractive.[65] This being true, the official view of the Indian government—that the monopoly was really a benefaction to China—becomes disingenuous, to say the least. Incidentally, Sir Evelyn Baring enunciated this curious doctrine just as a new program of expansion was being launched in the Ganges Valley.

Whether introducing an export tax into Bengal would have added to or diminished the total production is an open question, on which even those most intimately connected with the opium industry disagreed. One sub-deputy opium agent asserted that "It is quite an erroneous idea . . . to suppose that the cultivation of Opium stands in such high favor with the Assamees that, on throwing open the monopoly, the poppy would be sown broadcast throughout the land.'"[66] And the Bengal board of revenue itself conceded at one time that cultivation might decrease and the export trade decline.[67] In the end, the answer would depend upon such imponderables as the rate at which the ryots were paid and the amount of transit duty assessed, both of which would be governed by conditions in China. Exceptionally good years would probably have resulted in a larger output, but excessive production would soon have reacted against the Bengal dealers and speculators. There is little reason to assume that, with a reasonably high export duty, the opium trade would have expanded materially.

[65] *Report on East Indian Finance*, 1871, Q. 3329, 3330.

[66] Sub-deputy opium agent at Allynge to the Bihar agent, 10 March 1859, no. 19, I. O. India Separate Revenue Proc., 15 Sept. 1860. The word "assamees" refers to a class of Indian cultivators.

[67] Board of revenue to the government of Bengal, 20 Nov. 1859, no. 405, *ibid.*, 27 July 1860. See also *Report on East Indian Finance*, 1871, App. II.

.But the British opium system had its other side, the pass duties on Malwa, which were furnishing roughly one-third of the opium revenue. The production of the drug in Central India and Rajputana differed in important respects from the Bengal industry, especially in its financial structure. Lacking the stabilizing influence of the British monopoly, the native-state trade was even more highly speculative than was its counterpart in the east of India. In Bengal the government itself made cash advances to cultivators, purchased their product, carried on the manufacturing process, and made the final sale to exporters. In Malwa these various functions were discharged, to a much greater degree, by separate agencies. Peasants might receive advances from local *sahookars,* from agents of larger native capitalists at Indore or Rutlam, or from representatives of Bombay firms. The sahookars, native money-lenders, were often unscrupulous sharpers, always alert for an opportunity to get the ryot under their control. Sometimes these worthies manufactured the drug themselves, but frequently they sold it to other merchants in Indore or Bombay. In all of these transactions, time bargains played a large part. A good deal of opium also reached the hands of zamindars in payment for rent.

As the drug approached the coast, speculative factors were multiplied. When telegraphic news of a rise in China prices reached Bombay, the warehouses were at once turned inside out and all available opium shipped eastward. Merchants in Malwa, averse to paying heavy storage charges in Bombay, moved their drug only when favorable word was received. But by the time it reached the coast, earlier shipments might already have glutted the market and turned prospective profit into loss. As a rule, the dealers in Central India had no concern with the exporting business. A consignment might change hands two or three times in Bombay before it finally came to rest in the hold of a China-bound vessel.

The British government took its toll on the route to the coast. At government scales, located at Indore, Ajmir, Ahmedabad, and some minor points, the drug was weighed and transit passes were issued.[68] Merchants paid for their passes in *hundis,* bills payable in Bombay on six days' sight. Shipment was then made—in the latter part of the century by rail—to the seaport, where the consignment was detained until the bills had been safely cashed. Meanwhile, government inspectors examined the drug, and, if no adulteration was discovered, affixed the official seal to the package. But often the duplicity of Malwa sahookars was not to be revealed by superficial inspection. Chinese buyers therefore continued to purchase the native-state drug with their eyes open.[69]

The career of the Malwa opium system under the British crown was relatively uneventful, save for its commercial crises. Only two phases of its evolution demand emphasis. In the first place, there was a further attempt on the part of the British to prohibit illicit growth and export. The old agreements prohibiting poppy cultivation in native states under the immediate authority of Bombay had long since fallen into desuetude, and the inhabitants were manufacturing drug for their own use. Indeed, it was charged that licit consumption in the west of India had almost ceased.[70] Most of the opium smuggled into British territory was intended for local use, though a small fraction may have found its way to China. The opium act of 1878 provided a spur for a closer definition

[68] By far the largest proportion was weighed at Indore.

[69] *Calcutta Papers,* 1870, pp. 3-4, 118, 138.

[70] Finlay, ''Account of Previous Proposals,'' *Report of the Royal Commission,* II, 1894, App. XI; *Moral and Material Progress of India, 1886-87,* 1888, p. 71.

of the rights of these states.[71] New engagements were negotiated, which bound local chiefs to stop cultivation and to prevent transit through their territories of any opium other than that which had complied with British regulations.[72] The government also directed its attention to Central India and Rajputana, the great producing fields of Malwa opium. In 1878-1879, while arranging for a uniform salt tax throughout India and abolishing the inland customs line, the British introduced into the new agreements a prohibition against the export of opium "by all routes and in all directions heretofore barred by the Inland Customs Line."[73]

Of greater relevance to this study, however, is the prosaic story of transit passes. Unable to control production in the native states directly, the British had contented themselves by restraining the trade through pass duties, thus salvaging what revenue they could. Originally, therefore, the Malwa drug had been regarded as the ugly stepdaughter of the British régime. But when, in some years, it brought larger returns to the Indian treasury than did the Bengal monopoly, it took its rightful place in the opium family. Yet the monopoly always remained the favorite child, whose welfare was a first consideration in setting the price of passes. On the one hand, the rate must not be so low as to react adversely on Bengal prices, nor on the other, so high as to kill the Malwa trade or lead to large-scale smuggling. Within these limits, it was British policy to impose as heavy transit duty as could be collected.

[71] Act I of 1878, §5, *Report of the Royal Commission*, II, 1894, App. XLVIII.

[72] *Ibid.*, App. X, pp. 363-370; Aitchison, *Treaties*, VI, 188-189; *Report on the Administration of Bombay, 1882-83*, p. 240. For the unique arrangements made with Baroda see *Report of the Royal Commission*, II, 1894, App. X, especially pp. 358-359.

[73] Text of the clauses relating to opium, *ibid.*, pp. 354 ff.

The annexation of Sind so played into the hands of the government that within five years the price of transit passes was raised from Rs. 125 to Rs. 400. This latter rate, exorbitant as it appeared at first, conferred an important advantage on Malwa dealers in China during the late eighteen-fifties, when the Bengal provision, held to an abnormally low level, was yielding excessive prices at the Calcutta auctions. The Bombay trade flourished as never before, and in 1859 the government of India saw fit to add another Rs. 100 to the transit duty.[74] When in the early 'sixties the monopoly embarked on one of its most brilliantly successful campaigns of expansion, the pass rate was again raised in order to equalize the market value of the two varieties. In imposing Rs. 700 per chest the government overreached itself. A panic ensued in Malwa, caused partly by the new rate and partly by the larger provision in Bengal and the resulting fall in prices. Six Indore opium firms went bankrupt, and a score of brokers absconded. Petitions poured in from Bombay merchants.[75] In consequence, the British raj was obliged to beat a quick retreat and lower the price of passes to Rs. 600. Under the stimulus of this concession the traffic from Malwa reached new heights, in 1862-1863 more than fifty thousand chests paying duty to the British government.[76]

The necessity for supporting Calcutta prices at a time when enormous provisions were being auctioned dictated further additions to the pass rate in 1877 and 1879. But

[74] The government of Bombay often found itself taking exception to the supreme government's Malwa policy, especially to Calcutta's habit of manipulating Malwa pass rates to satisfy the needs of the monopoly. See, for example, government of Bombay to the government of India, 7 March 1859, *Calcutta Papers*, 1870, p. 114.

[75] *Ibid.*, pp. 120, 123-126, 129-130.

[76] This year also saw the revenue from Malwa opium at its highest point, Rs. 3,23,94,090.

it was found impossible to maintain a duty of Rs. 750 or
even Rs. 700 per chest. Competition with Persian and
Chinese opium was an uncongenial reality, felt no less in
Malwa than in Bengal. As a result of their improvement
in quality, these drugs were providing excellent adulter-
ants as well as passable substitutes for the more expensive varieties. A reduction from Rs. 700 to Rs. 650 found
the trade still depressed, for production had been over-
stimulated at a time when prices in China were on the
ebb. The additional article to the Chefoo convention also
took its toll. During the year 1885-1886, the principal
opium merchants in Bombay memorialized the government of India, praying that the rate be lowered to
Rs. 500.[77] This petition was of no avail, but five years
later the continued adversities of the Malwa trade forced
a reduction to Rs. 600.

During the last decade of the century the decline persisted—with some encouraging fluctuations—until in
1896-1897 fewer than 23,000 chests passed the government scales. As if the normal burdens of the trade were
not enough, there was the fall in the gold value of silver,
which reacted unfavorably upon the exchange in China
and further crippled the activities of opium dealers.[78] In
1897 the price of transit passes was established at
Rs. 450, lower than at any time since 1859. This reduction
administered a slight check to the decline, though scarcely
enough to give confidence to an anxious government. By
the end of the century the sun of Malwa was gradually
but indubitably sinking.

To repeat an observation made on an earlier page, the
British opium system, as the new century approached,
found itself increasingly on the defensive. Resisting the
proposals of Sir William Muir and his associates had

[77] *Moral and Material Progress of India, 1885-86*, 1887, p. 38.
[78] *Bombay Opium Report, 1896-97*, p. 6.

been simple enough. But there were other signs, far more ominous than mere suggestions that monopoly give way to export tax. There was some reason to think, for example, that the ryots of Bengal were not altogether satisfied with their lot and that many of them continued to grow the poppy mainly in order to receive advances from the government. Far more dangerous to the monopoly, however, was the competition of native Chinese opium. New Chinese consumers were legion, but the Indian government gathered little of the increase. Until the eighteen-nineties British imports of opium managed to hold their own in an absolute, though not in a relative sense, but during that decade they declined perceptibly. Would the Chinese drug be able, in the end, to drive its competitor from the market? This was the question which oppressed the Indian monopolists but one that was never put to the test of experience. For, before the two varieties could fight it out commercially, the anti-opium movement in England revealed itself as an enemy even more implacable than Chinese competition.

CHAPTER XI

THE ANTI-OPIUM MOVEMENT AND THE ROYAL COMMISSION

THE Society for the Suppression of the Opium Trade, it will be recalled, took its rise from a committee organized in 1874 under the auspices chiefly of Birmingham and North Country Quakers. It was the injustice done to China by the "forcible importation" of opium that gave the society its early rallying point. The Chinese, argued the anti-opiumists, must not be held to the treaty of Tientsin, but must be allowed to determine their own policy towards the drug. And on this platform the society carried on an effective campaign.

When, by the additional article to the Chefoo convention, China attained its immediate objective, the anti-opium movement waned palpably. Coercion of the Chinese had now ceased, and internal dissension, lack of funds, and above all, the absence of any clear-cut purpose nearly ended its usefulness. Largely through the indefatigable energy and broad tolerance of Joseph Gundry Alexander, a Quaker barrister who became secretary of the reorganized society, the scattered forces were rallied for an attack on a new salient. The old drive was directed against British policy in China, the new against the opium policy of the Indian government. With a growing confidence in its ultimate triumph, the society committed itself to nothing less than total suppression of cultivation in Bengal.[1] In the statement of principles drawn up in

[1] *Friend of China*, March, 1886, pp. 4-9. Included in the society's new

1886, the Malwa trade was passed over, but within a few years, it too was laid out for eventual slaughter. At the same time, the society moved to quicken the apparently dormant conscience of China, for it was frankly recognized in England that Peking officials had assumed a heavy burden of proof.

In Parliament the anti-opium group found itself gradually gathering strength. Most of its leaders were Conservatives or Liberal Unionists, but the movement sought to avoid taking on a party complexion. Resolutions against poppy growing in British India were easily downed in 1886 and 1889, but the obstinate question arose once more in 1891.[2] Sir Joseph Pease, now president of the revivified society, moved a resolution condemning the opium trade as morally indefensible and urging the Indian government to give up its own drug business and to stop the transit of Malwa through British territory.[3] His argument was powerful enough, though disfigured by excessive reliance upon proof texts. He pointed significantly to the mass of petitions which had been presented—from the convocations of Canterbury and York, the Wesleyan conference, the Roman Catholic bishops, and from virtually every other important church body in the British Isles. Not satisfied with generalities, he charged the government of India with over-calculating the opium revenue and criticized the large increase in the military budget.[4] His resolution was supported by Mark Stewart,

aims were the prohibition of retail trade in opium throughout British India and the exclusion of the licensing system from Upper Burma.

[2] 3 *Hansard*, CCCV, 278; CCCXXXV, 1143.

[3] *Ibid.*, CCCLII, 285 ff. Material dealing with the anti-opium movement in Parliament is summarized in Baines, ''Note on the History of the Movement in England against the Opium Trade,'' *Report of the Royal Commission*, VI, 1895, Memorandum VI.

[4] The government, he declared, had failed to include in its statement of costs interest on capital tied up in stock and equipment and on advances to cultivators. He concluded that the opium revenue should be estimated at no

another old anti-opium campaigner, who dealt principally with consumption in India.

It was at this point that the spokesmen for the government, Sir James Fergusson and W. H. Smith, alluded to the decreasing cultivation as evidence of Calcutta's change of heart. The true state of affairs has already been suggested—that cultivation was reduced mainly by natural forces within the industry and that the government's new policy was opposed merely to *artificial* expansion. Smith manoeuvered the anti-opiumists into agreeing that deficiencies in the Indian budget might be made good by grants from the imperial treasury, stating that the government would oppose the motion unless such a provision were added. Notwithstanding criticism from the treasury bench, the House supported Pease's resolution, which had been offered as an amendment to the customary motion for going into committee, by a vote of 160 to 130.[5] The debate, begun at nine o'clock, continued for nearly four hours, and the hour for adjournment intervened before a division was taken. Sir Joseph Pease later declined to press for a vote, expressing himself as well satisfied with the government's declaration.

The near-success of this demonstration inspired the anti-opiumists to enthusiastic activity. The movement not only felt fresh momentum from the vote of 1891, but its leaders took encouragement from the composition of Gladstone's new government, three of whose members belonged to the society, while several others had voted for Sir Joseph Pease's motions at one time or another.[6]

more than £3,500,000 instead of the £4,000,000 budgeted by the Indian government.

[5] 3 *Hansard*, CCCLII, 314 ff., 342-344.

[6] In 1892 a memorial from the society was presented to Lord Kimberley, secretary of state for India. His reply, a reiteration of the Indian government's traditional stand, showed that there would be ample opposition within the cabinet. *Report of the Royal Commission*, I, 1894, App. III.

The anti-opiumists were tireless in their efforts to organize sentiment outside Parliament. A huge meeting was held in Exeter Hall, the evangelical forum, and preparations were made to deluge the House of Commons with petitions. In the end, these totalled nearly twenty-five hundred, bearing some 205,000 signatures.[7] When the opium motion was given a place on the order of business for May 26, the society marshalled its resources for a definitive effort.

The strategy of the anti-opium leaders was to press for the appointment of a royal commission, whose duty should be to investigate means of implementing the vote of April 10, 1891. Alfred Webb, a new member of the House, made the motion, which Sir Joseph Pease seconded. Webb took as his premise the resolution of two years before, which condemned the opium revenue as morally indefensible. Assuming that only fiscal obstacles stood in the way, he moved the appointment of a royal commission to study three related questions: reforms and retrenchments in Indian expenditures, methods of developing Indian resources, and the amount of temporary assistance from the British treasury which might be required to meet a deficit in the revenue.[8]

The government had no intention of allowing the motion to be carried in this form. The venerable Gladstone, who in this instance chose to relax his vigilance on moral issues, appeared as the champion of the ministry. That the young man whose bitter denunciation of the first Anglo-Chinese war had evoked the salvos of the anti-opium party should now emerge as a defender of the traffic may be explained, perhaps, by the tension within his cabinet and the precarious state of his Irish bill.[9]

[7] *Friend of China*, July, 1893, p. 113.

[8] 4 *Parliamentary Debates*, XIV, 591.

[9] The anti-opiumists interpreted Gladstone's action as due to pressure

There was some justice in his argument that Parliament should not bind itself to a specific program without an extensive inquiry into the problem. But the tone of the "G.O.M.'s" speech was not that of one who was eager to solve it. He recalled all sorts of barriers to stopping the trade. Relations with China, he reminded the House, were not as they had been in the past. The Middle Kingdom was her own master and could prohibit or tax opium as she chose.[10]

A commission should be therefore appointed to inquire *whether,* not *how,* the opium traffic should be suppressed. After parliamentary technicalities had been put out of the way, the prime minister moved to amend the order of reference so that it became a pallid reflection of Webb's original demand. According to the new version, the House of Commons merely urged "the Government of India to continue their policy of greatly diminishing the cultivation of the poppy and the production and sale of opium," and prayed for the appointment of a royal commission. This body was to report on six different subjects, the most important of which were whether the growth and manufacture of opium should be prohibited in British India and the native states, and whether the transit arrangements with the latter could be justly terminated. Beyond these matters, the commission was instructed to study the probable financial consequences of prohibition, the possibility of reform short of complete prohibition, and the practices and attitudes of the Indian peoples with regard to opium.[11]

from "the Secretary of State for India, the Earl of Kimberley, who declared that he would resign his office rather than consent to a resolution implying that the Indian Opium Revenue was to be surrendered." H. G. Alexander, *Joseph Gundry Alexander,* pp. 63-64.

[10] This interpretation of the additional article of 1885 was, as we have seen, quite false.

[11] 4 *Parliamentary Debates,* XIV, 634.

The committee of the society held several feverish meetings and ended by rejecting the government's proposals.[12] But the House accepted Gladstone's amendment, transforming the commission into something radically different from what the anti-opiumists had contemplated.[13] The opium trade had been condemned as morally indefensible, and Webb's motion had looked to ways and means of executing this judgment. The order of reference, however, gave to the commission a wholly new character. Yet the temper of the anti-opium leaders was not one of despair. J. G. Alexander, always hopeful, considered the action of the House to be "the greatest and most solid forward step that the movement for the suppression of the opium trade has yet made."[14] Unhappily, when the commission's hearings in India began and, still more, when the bulky report was finally published, the triumph of victory gave way to disillusionment.

It was as well for the anti-opiumists that their faith in the royal commission was tempered by the equivocal order of reference which Parliament had given to it. But they could hardly anticipate that a body of inquiry would succeed in unearthing as little adverse evidence as did eight of the nine gentlemen who toured India on behalf of the British government, or, perhaps more accurately, that so little adverse testimony would find place in the final report. There was little criticism when the personnel of the commission was announced, the *Friend of China*,

[12] *Friend of China*, July, 1893, pp. 117-118.

[13] The division was 184 to 105, the members of the anti-opium society voting against the government. It was suspected that Gladstone, because of his Irish bill, was anxious to avoid a division. "When the House met that day, the anti-opiumists had grounds for thinking that the Government resolution No. 1 would commence with the word 'when' instead of 'whether.' As the afternoon wore on, they were informed that a colleague of Mr. Gladstone's [presumably Lord Kimberley] absolutely refused to assent to this." Rowntree, *Imperial Drug Trade*, p. 116.

[14] *Friend of China*, July, 1893, p. 109.

indeed, hailing it with positive satisfaction.[15] Lord Brassey was appointed chairman. Indian interests were represented by Sir James Lyall, formerly lieutenant governor of the Punjab, and Arthur Fanshawe, director general of the Indian post office. Since none of the principal anti-opium leaders was able to serve, the cause was committed to the care of Arthur Pease and Henry Wilson. Pease, a brother of Sir Joseph, offered no difficulties to the defenders of the revenue, and it was Wilson, a Yorkshire M. P., not hitherto conspicuous as one of the opposition leaders, who submitted the minority report and generally stood out as the one vigorously anti-opium member of the commission. To speak for the natives of India the Maharaja of Darbhanga and the Dewar of Junargarh were selected. The roll of the commission was completed by Sir William Roberts, a medical man, and R. G. C. Mowbray, a Conservative member of Parliament.

The commission began to take evidence in London, where proceedings were conducted in a fashion unobjectionable to the anti-opiumists. After a week of it, hearings were adjourned, to be resumed in Calcutta two months later. Wilson, accompanied by J. G. Alexander as secretary, preceded his colleagues to India in order to familiarize himself with the field and to marshal evidence favorable to the anti-opium cause. A few days in Bombay convinced them that the obstacles were greater than they had suspected. Rumors began to reach them that the Indian government was making elaborate preparations for the commission's reception. Substantial natives, from whom much had been expected, showed a "strong disposition to take their cue from the officials in this bureaucratic country."[16] From the beginning the commission

---

[15] *Friend of China,* Oct., 1893, pp. 145-146.

[16] Alexander, *Joseph Gundry Alexander,* p. 46; *Friend of China,* Jan., 1894, pp. 195, 200-201.

was viewed with a suspicious eye in many quarters, as a meddling inquiry into Indian affairs imposed upon the government by faddists. From Bombay, Wilson and Alexander proceeded to the Ganges opium field and thence to Calcutta, where the commission was to reassemble.

The industry of the investigators was unexceptionable. Not only did they listen to testimony in Calcutta, Patna, Benares, and the main centers of British India, but they also pushed their way into Burma and the native states of Rajputana, Central India, and Gujarat.[17] In all, some 723 witnesses were examined. The result was more than 2500 pages of closely printed testimony—containing about 29,000 questions—appendices, report, memoranda, and annexures, a document as baffling as the opium problem itself. A study of the evidence contained in the seven volumes merely emphasizes what has been implicit at many points in this study, that one may see in the opium trade whatever he is looking for. The testimony offers an unsurpassed field to the historian for a critical study of historical evidence, and to the psychologist for data on the fallibility of human observation. Physicians, for example, whose experience had been similar, presented diametrically opposing testimony.[18] Missionaries and government officials, in general, took the positions that would be expected of them. In short, one may find good authority for whatever point of view suits his fancy.

The achievements of the inquiry were wholly quantitative. The report was an impressive document, but the changes which it produced in British opium policy were so trivial as to be unworthy of record. Yet by rubber-stamping the system as it stood, the commission provided

[17] Because of its demanding itinerary, the commission was obliged to divide its forces. Burma and Central India, for example, were visited by one section, while the other pursued its inquiries elsewhere.

[18] Cf. the evidence of Dr. William Huntly with that of Surgeon-Captain W. H. Neilson, *Report of the Royal Commission*, IV, 1894, pp. 58-64, 66-67.

a parliamentary rationale for the government of India and its revenue. In summary, the conclusions reached were as follows: No considerable demand existed for prohibiting the growth of the poppy in British India. To extend such prohibition to the native states would be an unjustified interference with the rights of chiefs and people. As a means of regulating the production of opium, "the Bengal monopoly seems to us to be the best system," though certain changes might be made in the minutiae of administration.[19] The finances of India, the commission held, were in no position to bear the cost of prohibitive measures, while the people of India were unwilling to do it. The two Indian members added annexures differing slightly from the recommendations of the majority. The Dewar of Junargarh, for example, urged that the Chinese government be informed "that any action on their part towards the stoppage of the importation of Indian opium into China, would be unhampered by the treaty obligations entered into by them with the British Government."[20]

The majority report was signed by Arthur Pease, whose complaisance remained an unsolved mystery to his anti-opium friends.[21] But Henry Wilson, the belligerent non-conformist of the commission, registered a minute of vigorous dissent, in which he charged that the report was more "an elaborate defence of the East India Company and of the present Government of India than . . . a judicial pronouncement on the immediate questions submitted to us."[22] During the course of the investigation, Wilson had complained of the conduct of the Indian government.[23] And again in his minute of dissent he returned

[19] *Report of the Royal Commission*, VI, 1895, p. 96.
[20] *Ibid.*, p. 135.   [21] *Friend of China*, Oct., 1898, p. 89.
[22] *Report of the Royal Commission*, VI, 1895, p. 151.
[23] Wilson to Brassey, 17 Jan. 1894, *ibid.*, V, 1894, pp. 368-369.

to the attack, alleging both that the government had taken an undue part in arranging the evidence and that his colleagues, in their report, misrepresented the testimony that had been laid before them.

The historian's interest in the royal commission lies less in its pallid report than in its procedure. Rarely has an investigating body worked under more ambiguous conditions, and rarely has one been less careful to preserve itself from the suspicion of bias. It is unnecessary to accept all of the detailed criticisms which, even before the inquiry was completed, arose from the anti-opium camp. What remains is the fact that the hearings of the commission radiated the tumult of battle rather than the calm of the laboratory. The proceedings developed into a tournament between two points of view, with both sides determined to state their case in as extreme a form as possible.[24] The government of India was apparently convinced that the hosts of evangelical righteousness were descending upon the opium revenue. And the anti-opiumists were equally persuaded that the government was using all of its resources to resist a thorough investigation.

Neither the commission nor the Indian government behaved with the prudence that the situation should have imposed. At the outset, Lord Brassey, with a naïveté that the Calcutta authorities could scarcely credit, invited them to arrange "the course of inquiry, places to be visited, and witnesses."[25] The Indian government, in reply, offered to suggest witnesses who would give independent evidence, as well as to hold itself responsible for evidence on certain technical questions. It naturally declined to search for those who would testify against the

[24] The tendency towards exaggerated statement was commented upon by the Dewar of Junargarh in his annexure, *ibid.*, VI, 1895, p. 134.

[25] *Ibid.*, V, 1894, p. 362.

drug, leaving that task to the anti-opium society. On matters of itinerary and witnesses the commission was, of course, to be the final authority, but an important advantage had already been conferred upon the government.

Inevitably the inquiry took on an official complexion. Scarcely had the commission set foot in India when a letter from the viceroy, Lord Lansdowne, was circulated among its members, strongly supporting the opium system and prophesying dire results if it should be interfered with. Incidentally, this document was not printed in the report and was mentioned only by Wilson in the appendix to his minute.[26] During their stay in Calcutta, all of the commissioners, except Wilson, lived at the residency.[27] The staff of the commission was made up wholly of Indian government officials. The secretary returned to London with the other members, where at the India office he began the drafting of the commission's report, a task that was completed by his successor, another Indian official. Still another civil servant accompanied the commission on tour to arrange for the appearance of official witnesses. This official also returned to London and assisted in preparing the final report, contributing two historical appendices.[28]

Precisely what part the government of India took in the guidance of witnesses remains a question. Certain heads of evidence were left to the local governments, and

[26] *Ibid.*, VI, 1895, p. 161.

[27] 4 *Parliamentary Debates*, XXXIV, 296.

[28] R. M. Dane, whose monographs evoked more criticism from anti-opiumists than they deserved. His ''Historical Memorandum,'' VII, 1895, App. B, is a useful account of the Bengal monopoly and the Malwa trade to 1832. In a large measure, the sources are allowed to speak for themselves. Dane's ''Narrative of the Events . . . preceding the First Anglo-Chinese War,'' *ibid.*, App. C, was written to prove that the opium trade was not the chief cause of the war. Its value derives chiefly from material quoted from India office manuscripts.

from these Calcutta required lists of witnesses with abstracts of their evidence.[29] Indeed, one local administration ordered that none of its officers communicate directly with the commission.[30] This filtering of evidence through the government offices in Calcutta, though perhaps intended merely to facilitate the inquiry, was liable to misinterpretation. Had the procedure been followed only with respect to questions of fact, there would have been little cause for complaint. But some of the heads of evidence were highly controversial, and here the precautions taken by the government of India seem to have exceeded the limits of propriety.

One of the most extraordinary bits of preparation had to do with the production of evidence from the native states of Rajputana. Here the British resident was instructed to invite the durbars to appoint witnesses and to suggest a British official to act as Rajputana's representative. The appointment fell upon Lieutenant Colonel Abbott, who laid his plans with more than due care. He first sent to the durbars a note containing his interpretation of the points on which evidence was sought. Accompanying this document was a series of questions based upon the views he had stated. But even this was not enough. "I propose," the colonel wrote, "that all witnesses be examined at the headquarters by the Durbars, with the aid of Political Officers, and that the written replies of the Durbars to the questions asked of them [by Abbott himself] be based on the information which these witnesses supply. These same witnesses should, of course, be sent to appear before the Commission, and should reach Ajmere a week in advance of it, in order that I may

[29] *Correspondence regarding the Report of the Royal Commission*, 1896, p. 53.

[30] 4 *Parliamentary Debates*, XXXIV, 296.

become acquainted with all, and see if each one understands on what points he is required to give evidence."[31]

Many of the points on which native-state witnesses were examined were controversial, to say the least, and on these such elaborate coaching as Colonel Abbott gave was utterly at variance with the judicial character of a royal commission. How much compensation, for example, were the native states entitled to in the event of total prohibition? Here the colonel offered an infinite variety of headings under which the durbars could claim damage, many of them so subtle as to be merely fantastic.[32] On such questions, the self-interest of the native states, in the congenial atmosphere of official encouragement, produced astounding figures.[33] The drilling of witnesses seems to have been accomplished with military efficiency. The commissioners, in fact, must have been bored by the precision with which substantially the same story was repeated, sometimes in identical language.[34]

It is of less importance to make other detailed criticisms than to reëmphasize the fact that the inquiry assumed the character of a trial of strength between the Indian government and the anti-opium society. And the fault lay as much with the commission as with the government. Lord Brassey himself made the crucial error, when he gave over the commission into the keeping of the Indian government and its officials. Not only the investigators but the Calcutta authorities themselves were placed in an indefensible position. The government might protest that it was not refuting anti-opium charges but was merely assisting the commission, as, in fact, it had been

[31] *Report of the Royal Commission*, IV, 1894, p. 386.
[32] *Ibid.*, pp. 386-387.
[33] See Rowntree, *Imperial Drug Trade*, pp. 126-127.
[34] *Report of the Royal Commission*, IV, 1894, Q. 21,150 and 21,156.

requested to do.[35] But such disclaimers could hardly carry conviction with the anti-opium group, who recalled Brassey's remark to Alexander, "We all appreciate that in this encounter in which you are engaged with the Government of India upon its own ground you are placed in circumstances of no ordinary difficulty."[36] Some of the charges of the opposition were doubtless overdrawn. If the Indian government presented its side of the case with all the effectiveness it could muster, nothing could surpass the zeal with which Wilson and Alexander sought to ferret out evidence against the drug. Yet the fact remains that the commission, in a large measure, allowed itself to be managed by the Indian authorities, and that the auspices under which its inquiry was conducted prejudiced the acceptance of its conclusions.[37]

On still another score the commission's report was open to grave criticism. China, which with the Straits consumed more than nine-tenths of the opium exported from British India received much less attention than it merited. Here, to be sure, the blame belongs to Parliament, which had supplied the investigators with an order of reference in which China was utterly unmentioned. In

[35] *Correspondence regarding the Report of the Royal Commission*, 1896, p. 50. One of the most fruitful sources of controversy arose from the fact that the limited time of the commission permitted the examination of fewer witnesses than had been anticipated. When the Indian government reduced the size of the list, anti-opiumists were loud in their protests that opposition witnesses had been excluded. As a result of this episode the commission resolved to make its own selection, a decision for which the government expressed its gratitude. *Ibid.*, p. 52.

[36] Alexander, *Joseph Gundry Alexander*, pp. 69-70.

[37] Technical assistance such as only the Indian government could give was obviously required by the commissioners, some of whom were quite unfamiliar with the opium question. But there was no good reason why the staff of the commission should have been composed of government officials. At the least, if only for the sake of appearances, the secretary should have been without professional interest in the opium revenue and the report should have been drafted by non-official hands.

point of fact, the commission rather exceeded its instructions when it hesitated to judge "the moral objections raised against the Indian opium revenue without considering the effects of that trade abroad."[38] By studying only India at first hand, the commissioners saw a country whose opium problem was trivial by comparison with China's and whose vested interests, governmental and private, tended to quash ethical objections, admittedly less urgent in the case of India than of China. If the opium habit was pernicious, China was the place to study its effects, not Calcutta and Patna. If the drug were a benefaction to mankind, its merits should have been more apparent in China than elsewhere.

Neither the method by which the commission collected its China evidence nor the way in which the returns were handled was reassuring. The governors of the Straits and of Hongkong and the British minister at Peking were requested to obtain evidence from competent witnesses, according to a form prescribed by the commissioners. In addition to the replies sent from China testimony was also taken from missionaries and diplomatists who were in London during the hearings. The majority of missionaries in China, admitted the commission in its report proper, strongly condemned the use of opium, although a minority (three out of fifty-two) took a less pronounced view. Whereupon the writers of the report proceeded to cite two of the three semi-favorable testimonies, seriously garbling the evidence and badly misrepresenting the intentions of the writers.[39] Opinion among the consular group was that opium smoking in moderation was not harmful, though a minority condemned it as injurious. Here again violence was done to the evidence, for the majority was much narrower than would be gathered

[38] *Report of the Royal Commission*, VI, 1895, p. 1.
[39] *Ibid.*, p. 50.

from the report. One official, for example, who was listed with those believing that "moderation was not harmful and that moderation was the rule," said actually, "Perhaps thirty per cent use it [opium] without any injury, forty per cent with but slight injury, and thirty per cent with great injury."[40] Another, whom the commission quoted as stating that the majority of smokers went unscathed, offered it as his opinion that about fifty per cent were injured.[41]

On the political side the commissioners emphasized the additional article to the Chefoo convention.[42] China had sought the agreement, and the text had been drafted in accordance with her demands. There was nothing, they concluded, to justify the assumption that Indian opium was being forced upon the Chinese, especially when the latter had made no move to denounce the article as they might legally have done in 1892. The commission failed to mention, however, the alternative, which, as we have seen, was a return to the less favorable provisions of the treaty of Tientsin. There was no good reason, the report observed with truth, to believe the rulers of China dissatisfied with the status of the opium question. This discouraging conclusion was confirmed by the experience of J. G. Alexander himself, who visited China on his way home from India. Three representative Chinese statesmen whom he interviewed protested their eternal hostility to the drug, but, pointing to treaty obligations, declined to take action. Li Hung Chang flatly refused to consider Alexander's scheme of concurrent suppression of the poppy in India and China.[43] The Chinese, the com-

[40] Ibid., V, 1894, p. 309. See also Arnold Foster, "The Report of the Opium Commission," Contemporary Review, July, 1898, pp. 121-138, and Rowntree, Imperial Drug Trade, pp. 182-183.

[41] Report of the Royal Commission, V, 1894, p. 316.

[42] Ibid., VI, 1895, pp. 51-52.

[43] Friend of China, Aug., 1894, pp. 13-15.

mission recalled, were producing a large share of the opium that they consumed. Altogether there was no occasion to interfere with the drug trade to China, unless the latter should specifically request a change of policy. If this ever occurred, the question would require fresh consideration.

The shortcomings of the royal commission become the more glaring when its work is placed beside that of the less pretentious Philippine committee, which in 1903 was appointed to study the opium habit in the East. Whereas the British seemed befogged by a cloud of witnesses and pressed for time, the Americans pursued their inquiry in a fashion leisurely enough to enable them to assimilate the evidence as it was received. The Philippine committee spent some five months touring the Orient, where its members took infinite pains to interview as many different shades of opinion as possible and to see at first hand that on which they were to pass judgment. Their conclusions were not those of anti-opium zealots, whose critical sense was sacrificed to ethical motive. Many smokers, the report admitted, continued to use the drug throughout their lives without apparent injury. Chinese denunciations of opium, the committee suggested, were sometimes to be regarded with skeptical eye.[44]

One of the most illuminating experiences of the American investigators was their visit to Japan, the one oriental country whose attitude towards the drug habit was indubitable and whose law was enforced with an effectiveness unknown elsewhere in the Far East. From Japanese authorities, who pointed out that "China's curse has been Japan's warning," the committee learned of the horror with which the vice was regarded.[45] The Philip-

[44] *Report of the Philippine Commission*, 59th Cong., 1st Sess., S. Ex. Doc. 265, VI, 30.
[45] *Ibid.*, pp. 21-22.

pine report, a molehill beside the mountain submitted by the royal commission, influenced opinion on the drug question in a way that its bulky predecessor failed to approach. It led not only to the prohibition of opium in the Philippine Islands but also to the first attempt to deal internationally with the problem.

To anti-opiumists the royal commission's report was a disaster; to the ordinary M. P., bored by a fifty-year-old issue, it promised some relief; but to the Indian government it came almost as a stay of execution. Such triumph was rarely achieved, and the government was quite justified in exulting over the "vindication of the past action of the Government of India . . . and of the views which have guided us."[46] The cabinet decided to accept the report without change, though one suspects that its enthusiasm was not extravagant. In any case, the government was anxious to avoid a violent debate and division. No little pressure was put upon the anti-opium group to stay its fire, but neither Sir Joseph Pease nor John Ellis was inclined to yield.[47] The debate in the House of Commons, precipitated when the report had been barely presented, was notable only for the slashing attacks of Pease and Ellis.[48] Ellis' speech, had his fellow-members been prescient enough, might have seemed an augury of what would befall the opium revenue, when, a little over a decade later, he was to appear as undersecretary for India. But the House was not reluctant to shelve the drug question and expressed itself satisfied with the commission's verdict.

[46] Government of India to the India office, 19 Oct. 1895, *Correspondence regarding the Report of the Royal Commission*, 1896, no. 2.

[47] A. T. Bassett, *Life of Ellis*, p. 125.

[48] 4 *Parliamentary Debates*, XXXIV, 278-321.

CHAPTER XII

THE ENDING OF THE TRADE

THE last thirty years of the Indo-British opium trade to China were not the least remarkable of its history. In 1895, when the royal commission presented its report, all was gloom in the anti-opium camp. The Indian government received the vindication it had sought, while opposition in the House of Commons, for the time being, was effectively quieted. And in China there was little evidence of discontent with existing opium arrangements. The movement against the drug traffic had been given what was meant to be a decisive check. Only a prophet of more courage than prudence would have predicted that, a little more than a decade later, negotiations would be under way for a definitive ending of the trade. The conclusion came with a suddenness that must have startled even the anti-opium leaders. A nationalist reform in China, a change of front in Parliament, and a new spirit of accommodation in India created an atmosphere in which agreement was a relatively easy matter. That the salutary results of the compact have been largely nullified by conditions in China is no fault of British policy.

The ten years following the royal commission's report were devoid of significant incident. In India, the government, secure in its acquittal, once more allowed poppy acreage to increase. The standard provision was set, in 1901, at 48,000 chests, and the administration professed its intention of regulating cultivation accordingly.[1] De-

[1] When the anti-opium society attacked the Indian government for in-

spite an outlook which, in the main, seemed discouraging, anti-opiumists might have found satisfaction in some elements of the Indian situation. For one thing, the opium revenue was declining, both in absolute figures and in the proportion of the total revenue which it represented. As John Morley pointed out, the average for the fourteen years ending in 1894 was five million sterling, while the average between 1894 and 1905 was only three million.[2] Moreover, owing in part to the increase in the general income of the Indian government, the opium revenue no longer appeared to be the bulwark against bankruptcy that it had seemed in the past.[3] The fortunes of the trade were not improved by the closing of Indian mints to the free coinage of silver and the consequent appreciation in the value of the rupee. To maintain their profits in terms of rupees at the old level, Indian merchants would have had to raise opium prices in China by about twenty per cent.[4]

On the whole, there was perhaps less obvious ground for optimism in China than in India. While opium was becoming a less essential support of the Indian financial structure, with Chinese revenue the tendency seems to have been otherwise. Certainly the income which authorities in China derived both from foreign imports and from transit duties and other taxes on the native drug was nothing to be lightly relinquished. There was no longer

creasing cultivation, the India office replied that the extension was natural, not forced. It pointed out, also, that the report of the royal commission relieved the government of any obligation to reduce the poppy area. *Correspondence as to a Memorial from the Society*, 1902.

[2] 4 *Parliamentary Debates*, CLVIII, 507.

[3] In 1880 opium represented about fourteen per cent of the total of Indian revenues, while by 1905 it had shrunk to only seven per cent. A few years before it had fallen to five per cent. *Ibid.*, p. 508; *Friend of China*, Oct., 1897, p. 97.

[4] Sargent, *Anglo-Chinese Commerce and Diplomacy*, p. 262; Remer, *Foreign Trade of China*, pp. 89-90.

the specter of a drain of silver to shock Chinese statesmen into ethical endeavor. With the enormous increase
in imports from the West, China's balance of trade in
goods was adverse, but opium represented in 1894, for
example, only about fourteen per cent of the total imports.[5] Moreover, remittances from Chinese emigrants
overseas seem not only to have paid for the goods surplus
but to have provided a net import of silver. Chinese
statesmen, though always ready to excoriate Indian policy, showed singularly little concern about ridding China
of its curse. Let India cease to send the drug, they replied
when questioned, and the Middle Kingdom would deal
with its own problem. The anti-opium fervor of the old
China was played out. Only as new forces were invoked,
guided by new hands, would a serious attempt be made to
root out the evil.

A new force was, in fact, stirring the waters. For almost the first time in their history, Chinese coveted the
ways of other nations, if only to save the tottering empire from such humiliation as was brought by the war
with the despised Japanese. The reform movement,
checked by the *coup d'etat* of 1898, drew fresh strength
from the failure of the Boxer demonstration. China, beyond doubt, had embarked upon the path of change. But
a strong nation, the ideal of the reformers, was incompatible with widespread opium addiction. Japan, from
whom the Chinese had learned a painful object lesson,
had dealt with the danger early and decisively. It was
clear that the reformers' program must be directed
towards the opium menace. Chang Chih Tung, a distinguished official of the old school trying to learn the ways
of the new, whose book *China's Only Hope* was a manifesto of the reform movement, pointed eloquently to the
drug habit as one of the evils which must be obliterated,

[5] Remer, *Foreign Trade of China*, p. 90.

if China were to take its place on equal terms with the West.[6] In short, the spirit of change which revivified Chinese life early in the twentieth century, lifted the opium question once more into the domain of live issues.

The chain of events which led to the suppression of the trade from India was started almost fortuitously. A treaty between Great Britain and Tibet was negotiated at Lhassa in September, 1904, but inasmuch as it had not been signed by the Chinese resident, it could not be put into operation. Tang Shao Yi, an American-educated Chinese, who had been a professed anti-opiumist since his student days, was appointed special commissioner to Tibet and sent to India to negotiate. A by-product of his discussions with the Calcutta government was an intimation that India might listen to a proposal to end the opium trade. The finance member of the council, indeed, went so far as to state that the government could manage without the opium revenue. It was apparent that a joint agreement might be in prospect. To the Chinese envoy, aware of the historic attitude of the Indian administration, the news must have seemed almost incredible.

Tang was persuaded that the opportunity, so long sought, must be seized with vigor. Returning to China, he announced to his surprised countrymen that "It was the Chinese craving for the drug, and not England's desire to force it on China, which was responsible for the continuance of the traffic in Indian opium." The Middle Kingdom thus found itself launched upon another anti-opium crusade, not, unfortunately, its last. To his colleagues in Peking Tang proposed three years as the period during which the opium habit and poppy cultivation were to be stamped out. The government found him too precipitant, and ten years was finally agreed upon.[7]

[6] *China's Only Hope*, Chapter IX.
[7] Letter from Tang Shao Yi, *Friend of China*, Jan., 1909, p. 13; Jordan

An imperial decree, issued on September 20, 1906, commanded that "within a period of ten years, the evils arising from foreign and native opium be equally and completely eradicated."[8] To devise measures for implementing the imperial decision fell to the lot of the government council, whose recommendations, submitted some two months later, were all that could be desired, providing they could be translated from paper into effective action. The council suggested that certificates be issued for all land under poppy and that the quantity be reduced by one-ninth each year.[9] Opium dens were to be closed within six months, and shops for the sale of appliances within a year. Addicts were to be handled by means of a complicated scheme of licenses, with appropriate distinction between young and old smokers, and between scholars and ordinary citizens. For nobles and officials the council demanded especially stringent treatment. Finally, Peking announced its intention of negotiating with foreign governments "in order to close the sources of supply."

This declaration, in reality, was not as reckless as it seemed, for an intimation had come not merely from the government of India but from Parliament itself, that such a proposal would be smiled upon. Happily the change of heart in China synchronized with a new demonstration of strength on the part of the anti-opiumists in Westminster. In 1906 the atmosphere of England was much more receptive to the gospel of reform than it had been a decade before, and the anti-opium group took full

to Grey, 20 Sept. 1906, *Correspondence respecting the Opium Question* (China no. 1), 1908, no. 1.

8 Sir John Jordan, British minister at Peking, was at first inclined to view the movement with pardonable skepticism. He recalled the fact that foreign opium brought to the Chinese treasury £859,136, while native opium yielded some £6,768,750.

9 *Correspondence respecting the Opium Question* (China no. 1), 1908, incl. in no. 5.

advantage of the new mood. The society no longer lacked champions, for 250 members who took their seats in Parliament after the general election of 1906 were committed to the support of its cause. At the same time, with the coming of John Morley to the India office as secretary of state, and John Ellis, for years a leader of the society, as undersecretary, the opponents of the trade could well take heart.

Once more, in May of 1906, the familiar motion was introduced, condemning the traffic as morally indefensible and requesting the government to bring it to a speedy close.[10] Morley, to whom the cabinet had given a free hand and who was well aware of the "extraordinary amount of steam up both in England and Scotland against our share in the opium business," replied with a speech that for fair mindedness had never been approached by an Indian secretary. As he himself recognized, it was not easy to state the case honestly "without hurting the feelings either of the [India] office or of my good friends the philanthropists."[11] After tactfully deprecating the note of exaggeration on both sides, he passed on to explain the opium revenue in detail to the new Parliament. He emphasized also the fact that it was a declining branch of revenue, over whose shrinkage there were few regrets. His dismissal of the royal commission's report was delicately accomplished. "He did not wish to speak in disparagement of that Commission, but somehow or other its findings had failed to satisfy public opinion in this country and to ease the conscience of those who had taken up the matter." But would it be fair to saddle the overtaxed Indian people with an additional burden of three millions sterling? There were obstacles, Morley reminded his hearers, but any plan for restricting the consumption

[10] *Parliamentary Debates*, CLVIII, 494-500.
[11] Morley, *Recollections*, I, 172.

of opium, if brought forward in good faith, would be agreed to by the Indian and British governments, ''even though it might cost us some sacrifice.''[12] The resolution was agreed to without division, and the crusaders, having at last reached their goal, ''linked each other's arms and marched down from the lobby to the street singing the doxology.''[13]

This demonstration took place some four months before the imperial anti-opium decree was issued in Peking. By the time the Chinese government submitted its proposals for the reduction and ultimate extinction of foreign imports, there was ample assurance that they would be favorably received. Concretely, Peking suggested that the amount of Indian opium imported by China be reduced by one-tenth annually, beginning in 1907. The Chinese urged also that, along with a heavy increase in the taxes levied on native opium, the consolidated tariff and likin charged on the foreign drug be doubled, not as a revenue but as a restrictive measure. Furthermore, both prepared and raw opium from Hongkong had been finding its way to the mainland. Could the British government discourage this practice? Opium dens and shops in the foreign concessions were another sore point, for, if suppression were successfully carried out elsewhere, they could easily act as bases for drug distribution in Chinese cities. Here the coöperation of foreign powers was obviously required. Finally, it was desired that the exportation of morphia to China be forbidden.[14]

To the Indian government this program came as no great surprise. E. N. Baker, the finance member of the

---

[12] 4 *Parliamentary Debates,* CLVIII, 505-515.

[13] Alexander, *Joseph Gundry Alexander,* p. 130. According to Morley, if a division had been taken, the resolution would have been carried by a majority of two hundred.

[14] *Correspondence respecting the Opium Question* (China no. 1), 1908, incl. in no. 6.

council, in his financial statement for 1907-1908, took the prospective loss with admirable calm. Indian revenues, he remarked in a burst of fiscal optimism, had been showing remarkable elasticity, and if the extinction of the trade were brought about gradually, there was no cause for anxiety.[15] He was supported by Lord Minto, whose words must have sounded strange in the mouth of a viceroy of India. "There is no doubt throughout the civilized world a feeling of disgust at the demoralizing effect of the opium habit in excess. It is a feeling which we cannot but share. We could not with any self-respect refuse to assist China on the grounds of loss of revenue to India."[16]

But the Indian government, face to face with the inevitable, found the Chinese proposals too sweeping to be accepted without discussion. As the authorities in Calcutta pointed out, it would be much more satisfactory to limit exports from India rather than to accept responsibility for the quantities that entered Chinese ports. And for 1908 they professed themselves willing to reduce shipments of Indian opium to 60,000 chests, including consignments to other points in the East as well as to China. Peking, it was felt, ought to be satisfied with such a gesture until the success of its new internal policy could be appraised. To demand a doubled tax on foreign opium, however, was presuming too much on the newly demonstrated good nature of the Indian government.

It was the task of the India office to work out a compromise between the Indian and Chinese points of view. The Chinese, it was admitted, were entitled to something

[15] *Indian Financial Statement for 1907-1908*, p. 10. By recent reductions in taxation the government had sacrificed more income by twenty per cent than was represented by the entire opium revenue.

[16] *Proceedings of the Legislative Council on the Financial Statement for 1907-1908*, p. 240. Two Indian members of the council at once rose to demand a subsidy from the imperial treasury, one charging that India was about to be sacrificed to English faddists.

more definite than the Indian government had offered, while India could not make commitments as irrevocable as Peking desired. The India office therefore urged a tentative agreement for three years during which period the amount of opium exported from India would be reduced annually by one-tenth of the average exports to China. During the years 1901-1905 total shipments from India averaged about 67,000 chests, of which the Chinese received about 51,000. Consequently, the Indian government would reduce its annual exports by 5100 chests a year for three years. At the end of this time, if the Chinese program of suppression were keeping pace, the arrangement would be extended until the destruction of the Indian opium trade to China was accomplished. This compromise, duly accepted by the Chinese, governed the trade during the next three years.[17]

Doubtful though foreign observers may have been as to its permanence, there was an unmistakably earnest note in the new Chinese offensive. Barrages of decrees rained down, as in the past, but behind them was all the force that a reinvigorated government could summon, inspired by what was aptly described as "an ill-defined moral and patriotic motive."[18] In the autumn of 1907 a number of dignitaries were removed from their stations for having failed to give up the habit, and in the spring of 1908 a fresh set of decrees made their appearance, designed to stir laggard officials into action. To enforce the new regulations upon the higher officers, Prince Kung, impeccably aristocratic, was created one of a group of imperial commissioners, who within a few months denounced and cash-

[17] India office to the foreign office, 25 May 1907, *Correspondence respecting the Opium Question* (China no. 1), 1908, no. 13. Morley had already given orders to reduce cultivation in India to the level of 1901. 5 *Parliamentary Debates*, CLXVI, 287.

[18] *Correspondence respecting the Opium Question* (China no. 1), 1908, incl. in no. 28, p. 31.

iered several, including two Manchu sub-chancellors of the grand secretariat. These had falsely reported their triumph over the opium habit.[19]

The provinces, as a whole, by no means reflected the enthusiasm that shook the capital. In general, it was reported, smokers were not taking out the required licenses, and opium shops were inspected only spasmodically, while anti-opium societies in many places were dying a natural death. Perhaps the most hopeful sign was the evidence of a new-born public opinion, hesitating but sufficiently powerful to lend strength to the hands of provincial officials who chose to act. Yet the evidences of progress were not unimpressive. As the British minister said in a despatch sent in November, 1908, the inference "which I derive from a study of all the available evidence is that, considering the magnitude of the task, the success which has so far attended the movement is as great as could reasonably be expected."[20]

It soon appeared that Chinese opium reform was proceeding unevenly with regard both to the various provinces and to the different phases of the program. Late in 1908 and throughout 1909 provincial governors began to take a more active interest in the movement. In Peking, for example, opium smoking appeared to have been almost obliterated by the autumn of 1909, while in Szechuan, the crucial province from the point of view of poppy cultivation, the viceroy was moving intelligently and energetically towards suppression, experimenting meanwhile with cereal crops as substitutes. On the other hand, in Kweichow, described as probably the most opium-sodden province of the empire, little seems to have been accomplished. In all save the most depraved provinces, the closing of opium dens was enforced uniformly

[19] *Despatch from H. M. Minister in China* (China no. 1), 1909, p. 2.
[20] *Ibid.*, p. 1.

and rigidly.[21] But, with the meager statistical arrangements of the empire, the elaborate machinery for registering poppy lands broke down, and the Chinese authorities themselves were coming to the conclusion that nothing would do but total prohibition of poppy growing after an announced date. Despite these inconsistencies, the British legation, in the autumn of 1909, was inclined to believe that "China has more than fulfilled her share of the bargain."[22]

Apart from the major questions of Indian imports and Chinese cultivation, the joint agreement involved a number of minor issues. First of all was the matter of opium shipped to China from non-treaty powers, chiefly Turkey and Persia. With these Peking dealt by fiat. After January 1, 1909, drug from the Near East could be imported only under special permits, the number issued to be reduced by one-ninth annually until shipments ceased.[23] As to opium dens in the foreign settlements, the crux of the problem lay in the international concession at Shanghai, where some sixteen hundred divans flourished. After demurring for months and demanding indubitable proofs of Chinese success, the municipal council began to restrict the number of licenses granted, a process that was to require two years for completion.[24] Hongkong agreed to close its own opium dens and to prohibit the export of the prepared drug to China, while the consent of the Japanese government brought into operation the old

[21] Report by Max Müller, *Despatches from H. M. Minister at Peking* (China no. 3, 1909), 1910, p. 27.

[22] *Ibid.*, p. 29.

[23] *Despatch from H. M. Minister in China* (China no. 2), 1908, p. 4. The government set 1125 piculs as the annual import figure. In 1911 Peking altered its plans and announced that, after January 1, 1912, no more Persian opium would be admitted. *The Times*, 23 Aug. 1911.

[24] *Despatch from H. M. Minister in China* (China no. 1), 1909, p. 6. The last of the opium shops, as distinguished from opium divans, were not closed until March, 1917. *North-China Herald*, 7 April 1917.

commercial treaty of 1902 interdicting the import of morphia into China.[25]

The beginnings of international action against the drug traffic form no essential part of Anglo-Chinese opium relations. In 1909, an international opium commission met at Shanghai, called largely through American initiative. From the point of view of the Chinese, the gathering was useful chiefly for the way in which it focussed international eyes upon their efforts. At the same time, it revealed the fact that the central government had little idea what was happening in the provinces and that its statistical mechanism was faulty beyond all conception.[26] The Shanghai commission also directed attention to an aspect of the opium habit infinitely more threatening than the traditional methods of consumption. Partly as a result of the movement against poppy cultivation and opium smoking, the subtler vice of morphia pills and injections was making alarming inroads. It was reported that in Manchuria a dollar's worth of morphia would go as far as three dollars' worth of opium. The prevalence of anti-opium medicines containing morphia enabled the habit to gain a foothold almost imperceptibly.[27]

There was nothing radical in the resolutions of the commission. To the Chinese, however, it gave the accolade of international approval, recognizing "the unswerving sincerity of the Government of China in their efforts to eradicate the production and consumption of opium." As for the other states, they were urged to close the opium dens in their concessions, to prohibit the manufacture of and trade in anti-opium remedies containing

[25] Jordan to Grey, 2 Oct. 1907, *Correspondence respecting the Opium Question* (China no. 1), 1908, no. 23; *Despatch from H. M. Minister in China* (China no. 2), 1908, p. 5; *Despatch from H. M. Minister in China* (China no. 1), 1909, p. 6; *China Year Book*, 1913, pp. 651-652.

[26] See the *Report of the International Opium Commission*, I, 27-30.

[27] *Ibid.*, II, 67.

the drug, and to apply their own pharmacy laws to their nationals in China.[28]

While the powers were debating the international status of opium, China and Great Britain hewed to the line of their agreement. With the end of the three-year probationary period in sight and with Chinese figures so unreliable, the British felt obliged to take systematic steps to assure themselves that China was fulfilling her part of the bargain. Sir Alexander Hosie, consul-general at Tientsin, whose China experience covered many years, was assigned to the task. Visiting as many of the large producing areas as possible and appraising the others through qualified observers sent on tour, he returned with a report that, on the whole, was immensely favorable to Chinese efforts. As in the past, progress was moving at an uneven pace in the different provinces. In Kansu, for example, Hosie informed the viceroy, to the latter's embarrassment, that no less than eighty fields of poppies lay within ten miles of the provincial capital. On the other hand, Szechuan and Shansi were pronounced entirely free of cultivation, while in Yunnan and Kweichow poppy acreage had been reduced by seventy-five and seventy per cent respectively, as compared with 1907. But Shensi and Kansu could be credited with declines of only thirty and twenty-five per cent.[29]

With Hosie's confirmation of Chinese claims, there was little doubt that the tentative arrangement would be

[28] The negotiation of a treaty was not within the competence of the commission, and an international conference was called to complete the work of the Shanghai body. An account of this gathering, which met at the Hague in January, 1912, would be irrelevant to this study, since the British delegates were forbidden to discuss the Anglo-Chinese agreement. Chapter IV of the resulting convention dealt with the opium question in China, in general validating the recommendations of the Shanghai commission. The reluctance with which many of the nations ratified the convention forms a melancholy epilogue.

[29] A. Hosie, *On the Trail of the Opium Poppy*, II, 287-288.

transformed into a definitive agreement. The points at issue had to do not so much with essentials as with troublesome details. The British, for their part, were irritated by the obstacles which had been placed in the way of the Indian drug. A most flagrant breach of the agreement was committed by the Canton viceroy, who, taking advantage of his fleeting opportunities, imposed a heavy tax on Indian raw opium, on the pretext of supplying a packet of anti-opium medicine with each purchase of the drug.[30] At other ports the Indian product found itself placed under a handicap in its competition with native opium. Such infractions could be met by diplomatic protest. But there was another element of difficulty—the refusal of the Chinese people, moved either by fear or by virtue, to buy Indian opium in the quantities which dealers were entitled to import. Opium merchants, cynical as ever about Chinese policy and their speculative habits quite unconquered, paid enormous prices for the drug in India. The Chinese showed no great enthusiasm to pay for their enterprise, and in 1910, for instance, accepted some six thousand chests less than had been anticipated. These were merely added to the already heavy stocks in bond at Hongkong and the treaty ports, patiently awaiting profitable sale. In the spring of 1911 the accumulated quantity was estimated at between 18,000 and 21,000 chests.[31]

The Chinese also had their objectives in the negotiations. Some of the drug that had been exported from India, in theory to Singapore and elsewhere, had been reaching the coasts of China. To discourage this practice, the British, even before the new agreement was put into force, began to issue export permits for each chest of opium legally shipped to China, the certificates to be

[30] *Indian Financial Statement for 1911-12*, p. 2.
[31] *The Times*, 18 April 1911; 5 *Parliamentary Debates*, XXV, 1042.

turned over to the Chinese customs authorities.[32] The Chinese negotiators were even more interested in conserving the victories already won, and they demanded that, as each province was pronounced free of cultivation, the Indian drug should be denied admission. Although inclined to balk at the seven coast provinces—which consumed perhaps ten times as much foreign opium as all the rest of the country—the British ultimately yielded on condition that the ports of Shanghai and Canton remained open to foreign shipments until the last. Peking also made good its claim to impose on foreign opium tariff and likin duty at the staggering rate of 350 taels per chest, contracting to levy an equivalent excise tax on the native drug. There was much criticism of the new agreement, both by anti-opiumists and by the new national assembly of China, a body that was unwilling to make haste slowly, but signatures were finally added on May 8, 1911. The Indian opium trade to China was thus doomed, by process of annual reduction, to extinction not later than 1917.[33]

In India, meanwhile, the opium system was adapting itself to changing conditions. The revenue from the China trade might be on the wane, but its sunset was glorious. Into the treasury, year after year, came huge increments, created both by the soaring of prices at the Calcutta sales and by the enormous quantities which were rushed from Malwa to the coast. In 1908-1909, for example, some 15,000 chests were expected to pay transit duty. None was more surprised than the Indian treasury when well over twice as many reached Bombay. Even though such surpluses could not be used for current expenses, the budget seems to have been placed under no undue strain.[34] In

[32] Uncertificated stocks at Hongkong were to be granted permits and the quantity exported from India reduced proportionately.

[33] *Treaty Series*, 1911, no. 13.

[34] *Indian Financial Statement for 1909-10*, p. 7. Income from opium,

1910-1911, to be sure, additional taxes were imposed, but there is some reason to think that the increase in governmental expenditure was as much responsible as the anticipation of falling opium receipts.[35] By the following year, the situation was considerably relaxed.

To reduce the opium establishment in Bengal was a fairly simple matter. During 1910 the Bihar agency was closed down, and arrangements made for curtailing the remaining staff.[36] Even with the smaller area, some difficulty was experienced in preventing the ryots from throwing up cultivation, owing to the rise in agricultural prices. Bengal growers, in fact, took to other crops with an alacrity that was almost embarrassing.[37] Malwa was a more delicate problem, for the British raj felt obliged to soften the blow that was about to fall upon the revenues of the native states. After all, were not the durbars of central India asked to pay for England's virtuous satisfaction by surrendering income to which they could see no ethical objection?[38] It was inevitable that they should lose in the end, if the China trade were effectively closed. But, in the meantime, the Indian government would do all it could. In order to clear away the large stocks of Malwa and to release capital for other undertakings, Bombay was assigned a disproportionately large share of the permitted exports. Early in 1912 the government of India intervened to still more beneficent ends by doubling the pass duty and by putting export certificates up

above the budget estimate, was allocated to capital expenditure for educational and sanitary purposes and to the reduction of the temporary debt in England.

[35] *Indian Financial Statement for 1910-11*, pp. 8-9; *Proceedings*, pp. 316, 322-323.

[36] *Moral and Material Progress of India, 1911-12*, 1913, p. 190; *Indian Financial Statement for 1912-13*, p. 7.

[37] *Indian Financial Statements for 1910-1911*, p. 14, and *1914-1915*, p. 14.

[38] See Asiaticus, ''The Black Gold of Malwa,'' *National Review*, June, 1911, p. 715.

at auction. Of the proceeds one-half went to the durbars. British advisers also sought to put Malwa producers in contact with non-Chinese markets, which they had hitherto made no attempt to exploit.[39]

The methodical procedure of the Indian government was not duplicated in China, where the revolution immensely complicated the work of suppression. Poppy cultivation, it soon became evident, had been merely scotched, and the gaudy flowers appeared as promptly as the processes of nature would allow. Not all of the earlier gains, however, were lost. Of the five provinces that had been declared free of cultivation—Szechuan, Shansi, and the three provinces of Manchuria—there was some relapse in Shansi and Szechuan.[40] The new republican government, beset by problems more staggering than either Peking or London realized, seemed in no haste to declare itself, still less to call provincial governments to time. In June, 1912, the first anti-opium mandate was issued from the capital, but it was not until later in that year that the new régime proclaimed itself in action.[41]

To vindicate its good faith, the government launched forth with more vigor than prudence. Any lingering ideas of gradual suppression seem to have been incontinently abandoned, and the issue, in some districts, resolved itself into a trial of strength between the military and the peasants. Severe fighting occurred in Fukien, where the cultivators placed themselves under the protection of a rebel chief, a self-styled descendant of the Mings.[42] Re-

[39] *Indian Financial Statements for 1910-1911*, p. 14, and *1912-1913*, p. 5; 5 *Parliamentary Debates*, XXVI, 1660.

[40] Jordan to Grey, 26 May 1913, *Reports from H. M. Minister at Peking* (China no. 2), 1913, pp. 5-6; *China Year Book*, 1914, p. 700.

[41] *The Times*, 19 Aug. 1913.

[42] Jordan to Grey, 26 May 1913, *Reports from H. M. Minister at Peking* (China no. 2), 1913 p. 1; *China Year Book*, 1913, p. 539.

ports from Kweichow pictured two thousand soldiers loosed upon the country, uprooting plants and beheading peasants. In other sections the program was carried out by less sensational methods. The cost was heavy, but the authorities could point to whole provinces in which poppy cultivation had been utterly extinguished. Early in 1913, Chihli and Kiangsi were declared closed to Indian imports, followed a few months later by Anhwei, Shantung, and Hunan.[43] British investigators, as they made their way past fields covered with freshly pulled poppy plants, may have had doubts about the permanence of the achievement. But they had no legal ground for expressing their suspicions.

To the Indian trade the new campaign was disastrous, for it was by no means limited to indigenous cultivation. The agreement of 1911 had defined somewhat ambiguously the rights of Chinese officers with regard to the Indian drug. On the one hand, they were forbidden to interfere with wholesale transactions in imported opium, but, on the other, the central government was entitled to discourage consumption and retail trade as it thought best. In other words, if the Chinese could manage to crush the demand for Indian opium, there was no valid basis for appeal.[44] The new criminal code of the republic charged headlong into the problem by declaring the entire opium trade illegal. As the *Times* correspondent pointed out, the system set up by the Anglo-Chinese agreement could operate only if Chinese subjects violated the law, and, if they did, the British government would become an accessory to the crime;[45]

To decide when officials were deliberately harassing foreign trade and when they were merely campaigning

[43] Jordan to Grey, 26 May and 2 June 1913, *Reports from H. M. Minister at Peking* (China no. 2), 1913, pp. 7 ff.

[44] 5 *Parliamentary Debates*, XLV, 1932 ff.

[45] *The Times*, 19 Aug. 1913.

against the opium habit in general required a nice discrimination. Some were plainly acting in violation of the agreement, as when the Anhwei *tutuh* seized and burned seven chests of Malwa.[46] Others were so successful in intimidating purchasers that deliveries were stopped. In a measure, the merchants were responsible for their own plight. They had bought at outrageous prices in India and had declined to sell in China at a reasonable profit.[47] And demonstrations against the foreign drug, justified or not, made it no easier for them to dispose of their stocks.

A crisis in the Indian trade was reached late in 1912. Business at both Shanghai and Hongkong was at a standstill, while the auction price of Malwa export permits dropped from Rs. 2443 in August to Rs. 722 in December.[48] Something over twenty thousand chests, which were valued at about ten millions sterling and on which foreign banks had loaned three or four millions, were marooned at the treaty ports.[49] To prevent utter demoralization the Indian government was obliged to respond to the appeals that came from Bombay merchants. Auction sales of opium were stopped at once, and an arrangement made to purchase drug from the Malwa states on government account.[50] This prompt action quieted the situation for the time being. Accumulated stocks ap-

[46] As a result of his temerity, the Peking government received a bill for 25,000 taels. *China Year Book*, 1913, p. 532.

[47] One firm paid 2500 taels per chest but refused to accept 4000 taels, anticipating that the market price would go to at least 5000 and perhaps 8000. *North-China Herald*, 25 May 1912.

[48] *Indian Financial Statement for 1913-14*, p. 3.

[49] 5 *Parliamentary Debates*, LII, 2152. Estimates as to the exact number varied. The *North-China Herald* (17 May 1913) put the figure at 25,300 chests, including those certificated in India.

[50] Sales were actually suspended on three months' notice, but the upset price imposed was so high as practically to stop all transactions at once. The government agreed to purchase from the native states the difference between their actual exports and the quantity assigned to them in the Indian schedule of reduction. *Indian Financial Statement for 1913-14*, p. 3.

peared to be passing into consumption at the rate of about two thousand chests a month.[51] It was doubtful, however, whether a temporary suspension of Indian exports would meet the need, given the savage speed with which Chinese cultivation was being suppressed. If only the opium in China waters and that in India already certificated for export could be sold, the British might consider themselves well out of it. This conclusion was reflected by the undersecretary of state for India, when, on May 7, 1913, he announced that Great Britain would never sell another chest of opium for shipment to China, if persuaded that the Chinese were in earnest about their indigenous cultivation. Though phrased with some care, the secretary's statement in reality meant that the Indo-Chinese opium trade had come to an end.[52]

There remained the problem of the stocks at Hongkong and Shanghai, in whose destiny Chinese anti-opiumists were hardly less concerned than Indian merchants. To prevent this opium from passing into the hands of consumers became as much their object as to exterminate the rest of the native crop. How futile, they reasoned, to preach to Chinese peasants, with thousands of chests of foreign opium awaiting the famine prices that would soon prevail! In March of 1913, the National Opium Prohibition Union of China appealed for a worldwide subscription with which to buy and destroy the accumulated stocks. During the summer the Peking foreign office offered, without success, to pay the cost of sending the lot back to India, and the president of the Prohibition Union visited England in an effort to persuade the government not to press for its sale. Throughout 1914 the business of suppression went merrily on, accompanied by public cere-

[51] This figure, as given by the undersecretary for India, was challenged by the *North-China Herald,* which asserted (17 May 1913) that the average was nearer 1200 a month.

[52] 5 *Parliamentary Debates,* LII, 2190.

monies of opium and opium instrument burning. In the following year some fifteen provinces were held to be closed to the traffic.[53] Yet a residue of foreign opium was still held in Shanghai.

It was not an edifying situation. The British were unquestionably within their treaty rights, and the Chinese perhaps unduly exercised over the mote in their neighbor's eye. As a matter of fact, the British legation seems tactfully to have withdrawn from the controversy, its place taken by a "combine" of opium merchants in China and India. This combine, formed early in 1913 to maintain prices in a falling market, took upon itself the task of finding an outlet for its stocks.[54] It was obviously in the provinces still open to foreign trade that the fortunes of foreign importers might be saved. In the spring of 1915, an agreement was reached between the Peking government and the combine, by which the latter was permitted to sell its drug, free of all interference, in Kiangsu, Kiangsi, and Kwangtung, paying to the government 3500 dollars a chest for the privilege. Even here, however, things did not go smoothly. Owing, the combine charged, to smuggling from other provinces and certainly to the confusion resulting from the Cantonese revolution, sales in the South were seriously compromised. The expiration of the agreement in 1917 found the combine still in possession of over 1500 chests, which might perhaps have been disposed of in safety, had not their owners been at such pains to keep prices high.[55]

In Peking affairs had been going from bad to worse.

[53] *China Year Book*, 1914, p. 700; 1916, p. 673.

[54] *North-China Herald*, 16 May 1914, 12 May 1917. There was a combine at Hongkong, as well as at Shanghai, but the latter seems to have been the more active body.

[55] *North-China Herald*, 17 Feb. 1917. The dollar referred to in this paragraph is the Mexican dollar, which had, at the time, a gold exchange value of about forty-five cents.

Of genuine anti-opium opinion there was still an ample
volume in the country, but to the ruling clique now in
command at the capital, the declining days of the trade
merely represented an opportunity for personal profit.
When the combine demanded an extension of the agreement, Peking refused to listen. Instead, a special envoy
was sent to Shanghai to negotiate. From his conversations with the combine emerged an arrangement by which
the Chinese government contracted to buy the balance of
the opium at 8000 taels per chest.[56] Notwithstanding the
fantastic claims which reached China from Indian members of the combine, the latter was satisfied with its bargain. But in Peking the reception was otherwise. With
well grounded suspicion of its executive and backed by
the independent section of the native press, the Chinese
parliament raised such a volume of protest that the
agreement was pigeon-holed.[57] Chinese opinion refused
to be convinced either that it was necessary to buy the
stocks or that, as the government professed, they would
be used for medical purposes. The fact that, six months
after reports of the deal were published, the last provinces were inspected and pronounced free of poppy cultivation, could scarcely have allayed the fears of Chinese
anti-opiumists, now profoundly doubtful of their government's good faith.

[56] Payment was to be made in six per cent bonds secured by the land tax
and stamp duty. One clause in the agreement provided that a copy be sent to
the British legation in Peking. This was sheer bluff on the part of the combine, for the legation neither expected nor received any official announcement of the engagement. *Ibid.*, 15 June 1918.

[57] A good deal of uncertainty surrounds the negotiation of the agreement.
Feng Kuo Chang seems to have been the principal agent, although he
charged that all the arrangements had been made by Tang Shao Yi, who, in
turn, publicly denied the charge at an anti-opium meeting. In Peking it was
asserted that both Feng and Tang were bribed to manage the affair. Feng
also announced that he had been under pressure from the British legation—
a palpable falsehood. *North-China Herald,* 17 Feb. 1917, 15 June 1918.

The last chapter of the Indian opium trade to China, then, was to be as grotesque as its previous history. An outraged parliament had quashed the old agreement with the opium combine, but by the summer of 1918 another was signed. This document called for the transfer of 1576 chests of opium to the Chinese government and the resale of the same amount to a Chinese syndicate at 8000 taels per chest.[58] When it appeared that the syndicate was nothing but a ring of officials, apparently including most of the cabinet, the elements of scandal were complete. Popular feeling, aroused by this flagrant breach of trust, became vociferous. Petitions rained down from organizations and individuals, conscientious officials, whose years of labor thus stood to be nullified, lending their indignant voices to the outcry.[59] A committee of the Kiangsu provincial assembly demanded that the purchased drug be burned in order to complete China's successful campaign and to keep faith with the world.[60] To patriotic Chinese, in short, the shameless deal signified the moral collapse of their government.

The Peking clique wilted under the attack. As long as possible it temporized—long enough, in fact, to sell three hundred chests to the syndicate—and then gave way, announcing that the remainder would be burned.[61] But, even with its formal intentions proclaimed, the government showed no disposition to execute its program. Not until the end of the year was it clear that Peking had surrendered. The final burning of the opium was accomplished with becoming ceremony. Not only were three new furnaces constructed in Shanghai for the occasion, but repre-

---

[58] *Ibid.*, 15 June 1918. The government was also to receive from the combine a loan of five million dollars.

[59] *Ibid.*, 15 and 29 June 1918; *The Times*, 4 July and 29 Aug. 1918. There was some reason to think that the Indian stocks were to form the basis for a huge monopoly of opium in China.

[60] *North-China Herald*, 23 Nov. 1918.   [61] *The Times*, 26 Nov. 1918.

sentatives of welfare and civic organizations were invited to witness the proceedings. The task of destruction occupied eight days, and on January 25, 1919, the last chest of Indian opium was given to the flames.[62]

The few hundred chests destroyed in Shanghai were of no more than symbolic significance. In reality, Chinese anti-opiumists should have reserved more of their anxiety for the cultivation that reappeared during the latter part of 1918. It was as melancholy a symptom as the behavior of the freebooters in Peking, and there was little reason to be reassured about the future. The last fifteen years have seen the reëstablishment of the Chinese opium industry on a vast scale. Both voluntarily and under compulsion from their masters, the war lords, Chinese peasants are again busily harvesting the narcotic juice in quantities that cannot be accurately estimated.[63] This local cultivation, together with the fact that China has become one of the world's best markets for high-tension drugs, has spun a web far more intricate than that of the old Indian trade.

The history of opium in China since 1918 thus seems to have confirmed the doubters in their attitude towards the prohibition experiment. Yet to charge that the joint agreement was merely another example of realistic Chinese imposing on English idealism does less than justice.[64] It is impossible to regard the agreement, as originally put into effect, as other than a program accepted in good faith by both parties—by the Chinese as a means of ridding themselves of their historic incubus, by the British as a way out of an unsavory enterprise. Whitehall could not have been perfectly convinced that the Chinese

[62] North-China Herald, 25 Jan. 1919.

[63] For reports of production in various parts of the country, see China Year Book, 1931, pp. 590 ff.

[64] See J. O. P. Bland, " 'For Ways That Are Dark,' " English Review, reprinted in Living Age, April, 1931, pp. 156-160.

had mastered their opium problem, although it never published its suspicions. In too many instances, suppression, carried through by hands that were ruthless rather than firm, was bound to be temporary. Often the object was to prepare for the British investigator rather than to deal fundamentally with the problem of opium production.

Why, then, did the British government allow itself to be persuaded?[65] It is important to recall, first of all, that the confusion of the Chinese revolution and the war years was thought by many to be merely temporary in character and that a central government would soon reassert itself. Few, even among students of the Far East, could foresee that confusion would lengthen into semi-permanent chaos. The world badly overestimated the ease with which Chinese society could pass from the Middle Ages into the twentieth century. Furthermore, during the years 1914-1918, opium in China was the least of the concerns of the British foreign office, and, politically, there were excellent reasons for doing nothing that would alienate the Chinese. But the essential fact is probably that the British government, once India altered its point of view, determined to abolish the trade, regardless of what China might achieve. To Whitehall the *pari passu* agreement was as much a device for holding China to her own resolves as it was a legal contract. At the least, there was never any intention of allowing the traffic to regain its foothold, whether the Chinese chose to grow poppy or not. The editor of the *North-China Herald*, at a time when the Peking government was behaving its worst, voiced what seems to have been the attitude of enlightened foreigners, and perhaps that of the British gov-

[65] In the agreement of 1911 there was no provision requiring the Chinese to keep cultivation *permanently* suppressed. It may be doubted, therefore, whether the British had a legal right to demand further evidence about native production in a province that had been once closed to Indian opium.

ernment. After noticing the discouraging outlook, he observed that "any attempt to take advantage of a Chinese lapse from grace by suggesting a revival of the trade would be greeted with as little favour as a prospective revival of the slave trade."[66] British India has not only remained loyal to the letter of its commitments, but, in the care taken to prevent monopoly opium from reaching Chinese shores, it has gone well beyond its legal obligations.[67]

The original sincerity of the Chinese government is not easy to disprove. Despite breaches of the agreement in various provinces, foreign observers were almost unanimous in concluding that Peking in 1911, for example, was in deadly earnest.[68] Chinese officials were probably inspired by a variety of motives, ill-defined and confused. With many creditable exceptions and with some justification, their hostility was less implacable to native opium than to the Indian drug. Yet there was a large residue of genuine anti-opium sentiment, connected vaguely with the broader reform movement. The reformers, attempting to remodel an already weakened Chinese society, succeeded only in shattering it, and in the wreckage lay the high hopes of the anti-opiumists. That the Chinese have not lived up to their responsibilities under the joint agreement cannot be explained solely by the derelictions of individual politicians. These may be given what condemnation they deserve, but beyond, there lies the essential fact of an ancient civilization in chaos. And without political stability, effective control of the drug habit would be illusory. To solve the opium problem in the Far East is to guess the riddle of contemporary China.

[66] *North-China Herald*, 15 June 1918.

[67] See Gavit, "*Opium*," pp. 94-95. The Indian government has required import certificates from the countries to which its opium was shipped. In 1925 announcement was made that no more drug would be sold to Macao.

[68] *The Times*, 18 April 1911.

BIBLIOGRAPHICAL NOTE

MANUSCRIPT SOURCES.

The bulk of the material used in the preparation of this study is available in print. Unpublished sources have therefore served a supplementary rather than a primary purpose. The manuscripts consulted are all preserved in the India Office, London, most of them in the record department and a few in the political. Sir William Foster, *Guide to the India Office Records, 1600-1858* (London, 1919), enables the student to find his way about in the masses of documents, the more confusing because of the frequent reorganizations of the East India Company's service and the consequent changes in the classification of records. If the investigator seeks material after 1858, he must depend upon the India Office *Press Lists*. My selection of documents to be studied was determined solely by two objects: first, to fill in gaps left by the published material; and second, to corroborate or to correct inferences suggested by printed documents. In the paragraphs which follow no attempt will be made to describe in detail the various classes of records nor to explain their relationship one to another. For the answer to such questions the reader may be referred to Foster's *Guide*. I have prefaced citations of India Office manuscripts with the initials ''I. O.''

The more important matters affecting the opium system were dealt with in correspondence which passed between London and India. Chief among these series are, on the one hand, Letters Received from Bengal, continued by Letters Received from Bengal and India, and Separate Revenue Letters Received from Bengal and India; on the other, Despatches to Bengal, Despatches to Bengal and India, and Separate Revenue Despatches to Bengal and India. (During most of the period covered by this study, the income from opium, along with that from customs and salt, was known as ''separate revenue.'') Similar series cover relations between London and Bombay. Another set of letters, preserved in the political department and cited in this volume as ''I. O. Letters from India, political dept.,'' yielded evidence on the Indian government's attitude towards the Chefoo convention. Letters from the Board of Control and Letters to the Board of Control contribute some material on opium policy during the first Anglo-Chinese war, while a miscellaneous series of ten volumes of China correspondence (1833-1843), kept in the political department, contains a few documents not included in the published *Correspondence relating to China, 1834-39* (*Parliamentary Papers,* 1840). Letters between the foreign office and India Office are found in the Home Correspondence series.

The consultations and proceedings of the various governmental bodies in India represent another general class of material. These deal with the minutiae of administration as well as matters of broad policy. Opium transactions at different stages in the history of the monopoly, were recorded in the Bengal Revenue Consultations, Bengal Board of Revenue (Miscellaneous) Proceedings, Bengal Separate Consultations (salt and opium), Bengal Public Consultations, and India Separate Revenue Proceedings. Odd volumes of other series—such as the Canton Factory Diary, Bengal Political Consultations, Separate Revenue Collections, and Home Miscellaneous—were also examined.

PRINTED SOURCES: PARLIAMENTARY.

In citing documents presented to Parliament, I have not, in most instances referred to the *Parliamentary Papers* by name. My usual form of citation includes the title of the individual document and the year of the sessional papers in which it appeared. For example, *Papers relating to the Opium Trade in China, 1842-56,* 1857, indicates that the item appeared in the *Parliamentary Papers* for 1857.

The investigator of the opium trade owes some of his most essential material to the vigilance of Parliament. The affairs of the East India Company were examined with great frequency, and the bulky reports which appeared comprise important collections of material on the opium question. The establishment and the early years of the Bengal monopoly are described in the

Ninth Report, one of *Eleven Reports from the Select Committee on . . . the Administration of Justice in Bengal,* 1782-1783. The appendices are of especial value. Indian opium history during the next twenty-five years is related, though less adequately, in the *Second Report,* 1810, and the *Fifth Report,* 1812 (*Five Reports from the Select Committee on the Affairs of the East India Company,* 1808-1813). Opium receives some, but not a great deal of attention in a *Report from the Select Committee of the House of Lords on . . . the Foreign Trade of the Country,* 1821. The outlines of the China trade are sketched in the minutes of evidence in *Two Reports from the Select Committee on the Affairs of the East India Company, etc.,* 1830. (I have given citations only to the first report, using the formula, *Report from the Select Committee* [Commons] 1830.) This may be supplemented by a report from the Lords' committee of the same title and date. Appendix IV of the *Third Report,* 1831, is the best printed source for the East India Company's Malwa policy, while still another *Report . . . on the Affairs of the East India Company,* in six parts, 1831-1832, supplies further data on the Indian opium system and the China trade.

The case of the merchants involved in the crisis of 1839 is presented in the *Report from the Select Committee on the . . . Surrender of Opium, etc.,* 1840. Along with their pleas for compensation, the witnesses managed to throw a good deal of light on the crisis and its background. The *Report from the Select Committee on the State of Our Commercial Relations with China,* 1847, expresses the disappointment of British mercantile interests over the commercial results of the treaties. Of greatest value for the history of the monopoly during the eighteen-sixties are the *Reports of the Select Committee on the Finance and Financial Administration of India,* in eight parts, 1871-1874. The most important is that presented in 1871 (cited as *Report on East Indian Finance,* 1871), which includes testimony on both the policies of the Indian government and the situation in China. The smuggling trade from Hongkong to the mainland is examined in a *Report from the Commissioners . . . to Inquire into . . . Alleged Smuggling,* 1884.

The *Report of the Royal Commission on Opium,* 7 vols., 1894-1895, has already been treated at length (Chap. XI). It remains only to mention some of the more important appendices. These fall naturally into two groups, the one comprising documentary sources and the other monographs contributed by various writers. In the first category may be mentioned without comment, "Correspondence with the Foreign Office concerning the Operation of Existing Treaties with China" (I, App. IV); J. F. Finlay, "Arrangements with Native States regarding Opium" (II, App. XV); "Papers regarding the Visit of Mah Kie Tchong to India in 1881" (II, App. XLVIII); "Despatch from the Secretary of State . . . on the Chefoo Convention" (VII, App. D). The special studies included in the report are fairly numerous and unequal in value. Two historical notes contributed by Sir James Lyall (VI, Annex. III; VII, App. A), though frank rationales of the opium system, are suggestive. J. A. Baines wrote a history of the anti-opium movement in England (VI, Annex. VI), compiled chiefly from *Hansard,* and a note on the government's action in regulating poppy cultivation in the early eighteen-nineties (VI, Annex. VII). R. M. Dane's historical memoranda have already been noticed. (See Chapter XI, n. 28.) Two royal commissions which investigated Indian finance in 1896-1900 and 1914 offer little assistance to the student of the opium system, although the *Report of the Royal Commission on Indian Finance and Currency,* 1914, has some material on the adjustment of the Indian budget to losses occasioned by the Anglo-Chinese opium agreements.

The opium crisis of 1839 led to the publication of the correspondence which had passed between the superintendents of trade and the foreign office, as well as one collection which antedated the period of the superintendents: *A Copy of All Papers . . . on the Subject of Hostilities between the Chinese and British Subjects Engaged in the Opium Trade, 1830-33,* 1840, the chief source for the riot at Kumsingmoon. The standard source for occurrences in China between 1834 and 1839 is *Correspondence relating to China, 1834-39,* 1840, some 458 pages of despatches, letters to and from Chinese officials, and translations of Chinese public documents. Supplementing and continuing this collection are *Additional Correspondence*, 1840, *Additional Papers*, 1840, and *Additional Papers*, No. IV, 1840. Between 1840 and 1845 various papers dealing with compensation for the confiscated opium were also presented to Parliament. These hardly merit individual mention.

For the period between the two Anglo-Chinese wars the essential source is *Papers relating to the Opium Trade in China, 1842-56*, 1857, in which are recorded some of the early legalization discussions, replies to Shaftesbury's memorial, etc. The tariff negotiations which resulted in a legalized opium trade are covered in *Correspondence relating to the Earl of Elgin's Special Mission to China and Japan, 1857-59*, 1859. The most important material bearing on Sir Rutherford Alcock's convention of 1869 is published in *Correspondence respecting the Revision of the Treaty of Tientsin* (China no. 5), 1871. Documents dealing with Sir Thomas Wade's Chefoo convention appear in *Correspondence respecting the . . . Murder of Mr. Margary* (China no. 1), 1876, in *Further Correspondence* (China no. 4), 1876, and in *Further Correspondence* (China no. 3), 1877. The last named (cited as *Margary Corr.* [China no. 3], 1877) is the most valuable. Subsequent attempts to reach a solution of the opium and likin questions are outlined in *Correspondence respecting the Agreement between . . . the Governments of Great Britain and China* (China no. 2), 1880, and its sequel of the same title (China no. 3), 1882. *Correspondence with the Government of India, etc.*, 1882, elaborates the attitude of that government, and *Correspondence respecting the Duties on Opium in China* (China no. 5), 1885, describes the formulation of the additional article to the Chefoo convention.

The Anglo-Chinese agreements of 1908 and 1911 are covered in exchanges of correspondence between the Peking legation and the foreign office. These documents, whose character may be inferred from the citations in Chapter XII, need not be mentioned specifically. In the same connection we may note the *Correspondence relative to the International Opium Commission at Shanghai* (China no. 2), 1909.

A mass of material on opium is embodied in the reports of British consuls. Some of these are genuinely valuable monographs, while others are merely perfunctory chronicles. Between 1862 and 1886 the reports of consular officials were published in two series: *Commercial Reports from Her Majesty's Consuls in China, 1854-61,* in eight parts, 1855-1863, and *Commercial Reports from Her Majesty's Consuls in China, 1862-86,* in sixty-two parts. After 1886 the report of each consul was published separately with its own command number. In some years the entire body of reports was summarized by the secretary of the legation, and the précis appeared under the title, *Report on the Foreign Trade of China.* Besides these routine returns, particular areas and subjects were often dealt with in special reports, as, for example, the journeys of consular officials through unfamiliar sections of China.

Miscellaneous returns dealing directly or indirectly with opium would include a wide variety of documents, if all were to be listed. Some of the *Financial Statements of the Government of India* appear in the *Parliamentary Papers* (all of them after 1881-1882), together with the *Proceedings of the Legislative Council* on the *Financial Statement.* Of use also are the *Annual Statements showing the Moral and Material Progress of British India,* a series begun in 1859-1860. Statistical returns are fairly numerous, but figures on opium are usually to be found in a more available form elsewhere. Two papers of special character may also be mentioned: *Observations on Some Questions of Indian Finance,* by Sir John Strachey, 1874, and a *Return of an Article on Opium,* by Dr. Watt, 1890-1891 (later published in *A Dictionary of the Economic Products of India*), an able study of the drug in India, though its tone is distinctly official. The comments of the Indian government on the royal commission's report appear in *Correspondence regarding the Report, etc.,* 1896. Controversial exchanges of letters between the anti-opium society and the India office were presented to Parliament as a *Return of Correspondence as to a Memorial from the Society,* 1902, and a *Return of Further Correspondence,* 1902.

Hansard's Parliamentary Debates contribute little factual matter not available elsewhere in rather more trustworthy form. For the history of the opium question in Parliament, *Hansard* is, of course, the essential source.

PRINTED SOURCES: INDIA, THE EAST INDIA COMPANY, AND CHINA.

Most of the early published records of the East India Company, such as the volumes admirably edited by Sir William Foster and E. B. Sainsbury, have to do with a period before the opium trade was well established. The same may be said of Sir George Birdwood, *Report on the Old Records of the India Office* (2d reprint, London, 1891), Birdwood and Foster, *First Letter Book of the East India Company* (London, 1893), and F. C. Danvers, *Report . . . on the Portuguese Records* (London, 1892). G. W. Forrest, *Selections from the State Papers, 1772-1785,* 3 vols. (London, 1890), contains a few items. Of much greater importance is A. Shakespear, *Selections from the Duncan Records,* 2 vols. (Benares, 1873), which includes material dealing with the establishment of the Benares agency and the first opium contract in Bengal. Sir J. E. Colebrooke, *A Digest of the Regulations . . . of Bengal,* 3 vols. (Calcutta, 1807), reproduces the advertisement for the contract of 1793.

The miscellaneous sources for the Warren Hastings trial do not fall readily into a bibliographical classification. For the sake of convenience, they may be mentioned at this point. One account, nearly contemporary with the trial, is the anonymous *History of the Trial of Warren Hastings* (Debrett, London, 1796), written by one whose sympathies were clearly with the defense. A later record is E. A. Bond, *Speeches of the Managers and Counsel in the Trial of Warren Hastings,* 4 vols. (London, 1863). In the sixth volume of the *India Courier Extraordinary . . . Appendix . . . relative to W. Hastings,* 9 vols. (London, 1786-1787), appear the most valuable documents on the monopoly in the years immediately following the Hastings administration and on the *Betsy-Nonsuch* voyage to China. This collection has been cited as *Warren Hastings Documents.*

Most serviceable of all the publications of the Indian government is the rare *Papers relating to the Opium Question* (Calcutta, 1870), together with the *Supplement,* 1872. Here are recorded opium deliberations of the council, reports from various officials in India and China, and, in short, most of what is needed to reconstruct the history of the monopoly in the 'sixties and early 'seventies. A *Report of a Commission . . . to Enquire into*

the Working of the Opium Department (Calcutta, 1883) pro-
vides a detailed criticism of the opium establishment as well as
some historical material. Of the routine reports of Indian governments the most helpful is perhaps the series of *Annual Reports on the Administration of the Bengal Presidency.* The *Reports of the Opium Administration of Bengal* and those of Bombay are concerned chiefly with the minutiae of each year's work.
The standard collection of Indian treaties is Sir Charles U.
Aitchison, *A Collection of Treaties . . . relating to India,* 11
vols. (3d edit. rev., Calcutta, 1892), and the most comprehensive
statistical source is *Financial and Commercial Statistics of British India* (1894–), which, after 1907, was merged into the annual
Statistics of British India.

Difficult to classify but infinitely valuable to the student of
the opium trade is H. B. Morse, *The Chronicles of the East India Company Trading to China, 1635-1834,* 5 vols. (Oxford and
Cambridge, Mass., 1926, 1929). These volumes, whose character
entitles them to be considered both as a documentary source and
as a secondary work, are a year-by-year narrative of events at
Canton. From the records of the China factory Morse has extracted a mass of material illuminating not only the commercial
activity of Westerners in China but also the relations of the
company with Chinese officials. Copious quotations from the records and a generous number of statistical tables make the work
an admirable and reliable substitute for the manuscripts themselves. Eight official papers relating to Chinese opium policy
appear in J. Lewis Shuck, *Portfolio Chinensis* (Macao, 1840),
and Sir Robert Hart's important memorandum to the Chinese
government is published as an appendix to *These from the Land
of Sinim* (London, 1901).

The most useful official publications of the Chinese government are the reports of the imperial maritime customs. Both the
Decennial Reports (the first was issued in 1893 covering the
decade 1882-1891) and the special series provide authoritative,
impartial information. In the special series the most important
opium titles are *Native Opium,* special series, no. 1 (Shanghai,
1864) ; *Opium,* no. 4 (Shanghai, 1881) ; *Native Opium,* 1887, no.
10 (Shanghai, 1888) ; Joseph Edkins, *Opium: Historical Note or*

the Poppy in China, no. 13 (Shanghai, 1889), which was also reprinted in the *Report of the Royal Commission,* I, 1894, App. II; *The Opium Trade: March Quarter,* 1889, no. 14 (Shanghai, 1889). The standard collection of treaties is, of course, *Hertslet's China Treaties,* 2 vols. (3d edit. rev., London, 1908).

PRINTED SOURCES: MISCELLANEOUS.

To supplement British sources certain collections of American public documents have also been consulted. Chief among these are the *Kearny Correspondence,* 29th Cong., 1st Sess., S. Doc. 139; *Correspondence of Humphrey Marshall,* 33d Cong., 1st Sess., H. Ex. Doc. 123; *Correspondence of Peter Parker,* 35th Cong., 2d Sess., S. Ex. Doc. 22; *Correspondence of William B. Reed,* 36th Cong., 1st Sess., S. Ex. Doc. 30. The volume of *Foreign Relations* for 1876 contains despatches revealing the American attitude towards the likin provisions of the Chefoo convention and that for 1881 explains the anti-opium clause in the American treaty of 1881. The American correspondence on the Shanghai commission appears in the volumes for 1907-1909. International action against opium owed a good deal to a *Report of a Committee Appointed by the Philippine Commission to Investigate the Use of Opium, etc.,* 59th Cong., 1st Sess., S. Ex. Doc. 265.

The proceedings of the Shanghai commission are described in the *Report of the International Opium Commission,* 2 vols. (Shanghai, 1909), and those of the Hague conferences in *Actes et documents* (La Haye, 1912-1914).

LETTERS, MEMOIRS, AND ACCOUNTS OF TRAVELERS.

The multitude of books that grew out of travels and residences in the East—in a fair proportion of them opium is noticed—impose a duty of selection upon the bibliographer. Any list must seem captious to one familiar with the field. Edited correspondence may be readily disposed of, for despite the volumes of letters of Indian administrators and others which have appeared, references to opium are meager and generally without significance. The one essential work of this kind is Theodore Walrond, *The Letters and Journals of James, Eighth Earl of Elgin* (London, 1872). Less important bits of evidence are to be found in Charles Ross, *The Correspondence of Charles, First Marquis Cornwallis*, 3 vols. (London, 1859); H. H. Dodwell, *Warren Hastings' Letters to Sir John Macpherson* (London, 1927); Holden Furber, *An Indian Governor-Generalship* (Cambridge, Mass., 1933), the correspondence between Sir John Shore and Henry Dundas, 1793-1798.

In the paragraphs which follow I have, in general, restricted myself to works in which opium is more than a matter of casual reference and whose authors, by reason of their position or experience, are entitled to speak with some degree of authority. The writings of sixteenth and seventeenth-century travelers— Barbosa, Bernier, Fitch, Van Linschoten, and others, who have been, or might have been, cited in Chapter I—are omitted, because their importance derives chiefly from the meagerness of other sources and because their principal value to a student of the opium trade is indicated by the use made of them in the text. I have also abstained from mentioning a number of individuals who visited China in the late nineteenth or early twentieth centuries and who observed, briefly or at length, poppy cultivation in China but who add little to what is available in official sources.

A vivid account of the early China trade is that of the American, William C. Hunter, *The Fan Kwae at Canton before Treaty Days, 1825-44* (London, 1882). Robert B. Forbes, *Personal Reminiscences* (Boston, 1878), gives a less detailed report. Some interesting observations on the opium trade during the war are made in J. E. Bingham, *A Narrative of the Expedition to China* (London, 1842), while Granville G. Loch, *The Closing Events of the Campaign in China* (London, 1843), is a source for Pottinger's opium discussions with the Chinese plenipotentiaries. The realities of the trade between the Anglo-Chinese wars are described by an ex-opium smuggler, Lindsay Anderson, *A Cruise on an Opium Clipper* (London, 1891), and *Among Typhoons and Pirate Craft* (London, 1892), while an anonymous writer, "In an Opium Smuggler," *Overland Monthly*, Jan., 1891, contributes similar details. Some mention of the trade is made by the Rev. George Smith, *A Narrative of an Exploratory Visit to . . . China* (New York, 1847), and by Robert Fortune, *Three*

Years' Wanderings in China (2d edit., London, 1847). Abbé Huc, *A Journey through the Chinese Empire* (Am. edit., New York, 1855), is at no pains to conceal his hostility to opium and British opium policy. Valuable sources for Elgin's negotiations are Laurence Oliphant, *Narrative of the Earl of Elgin's Mission to China and Japan* (Am. edit., New York, 1860) ; F. Wells Williams, "The Journal of S. Wells Williams, etc.," *Jour. North China Branch of the Royal Asiatic Soc.*, XLII, 1911; W. A. P. Martin, *A Cycle of Cathay* (New York, 1896). The special correspondent for the *Times* in 1857-1858, George Wingrove Cooke, *China* (London, 1858), has contributed entertaining comments on events in China.

Baron K. Richtofen, in his *Letter on the Provinces of Honan and Shensi* (Shanghai, 1871), and his *Letter on the Provinces of Chihli, Shansi, etc.* (Shanghai, 1872) offers data on Chinese cultivation, and Alexander Hosie, *On the Trail of the Opium Poppy*, 2 vols. (London, 1914), gives his semi-official conclusions on the same subject.

Indian memoirs are both fewer in number and less helpful in content. Henry St. George Tucker's criticism of the company's Malwa policy appears in his *Memorials of Indian Government*, edited by Sir J. W. Kaye (London, 1853). Sir Richard Temple, *Men and Events of My Time in India* (London, 1882), contains little on opium specifically but a good deal on Indian budgetary problems, while the Benares opium agent, J. H. Rivett-Carnac, *Many Memories of Life in India* (London, 1910), throws but feeble light on his professional responsibilities. The great Indian pro-consuls, one gathers from their memoirs, were not particularly interested in opium questions. Viscount Morley, *Recollections*, 2 vols. (London and New York, 1917), comments sympathetically on the anti-opium group in Parliament.

MISCELLANEOUS SOURCES.

Some of the early commercial guides are not without interest to the student of the opium trade. Two standard manuals, John Phipps, *A Practical Treatise on the China and Eastern Trade* (Calcutta, 1835), and Robert B. Forbes, *Remarks on China and the China Trade* (Boston, 1844), are especially valuable. The section on opium in Phipps includes statistics, quotations from documents, and general information for the drug merchant. William Milburn, *Oriental Commerce*, 2 vols. (1st edit., London, 1813), is of use statistically, while J. R. Morrison, *Chinese Commercial Guide* (1st edit., Canton, 1834), contributes an assortment of commercial facts. *Dalrymple's Oriental Repertory*, 2 vols. (London, 1797), a miscellaneous collection of papers, contains one item of importance in opium history.

For contemporary information on the details of opium production reference may be had to H. T. Colebrooke, *Remarks on the Husbandry and Internal Commerce of Bengal* (Calcutta, 1804); Elijah Impey, *A Report on the Cultivation, Preparation and Adulteration of Malwa Opium* (Bombay, 1848); D. Butter, "On the Preparation of Opium for the China Market," *Journal of the Asiatic Society of Bengal*, March, 1836 (V, 171-179); W. S. Sherwill, *Illustrations of the Mode of Preparing Indian Opium for the Chinese Market* (London, 1851); W. C. B. Eatwell, *On the Poppy Cultivation and the Benares Agency* (Government of Bengal, *Selections from the Records*, no. 1, 1851).

There is no dearth of controversial pamphlets dating from the late eighteenth and first half of the nineteenth centuries. But, in general, neither the facts nor the arguments which they adduce are sufficiently novel to warrant emphasis here. As examples, mention may be made of the following: T. H. Bullock, *The Chinese Vindicated* (London, 1840); An American Merchant (C. W. King), *Remarks on British Relations and Intercourse with China* (London, 1834); A Resident in China (H. Hamilton Lindsay), *Is the War with China a Just One?* (London, 1840); R. Palmer, *Statement of Claims of the British Subjects Interested in Opium* (London, 1840); Sir George T. Staunton, *Observations on our Chinese Commerce . . . and the Opium Trade* (London, 1850), and *Remarks on British Relations with China* (London, 1836). The Warren Hastings controversy produced the following, among others: Joseph Price, *A Short Commercial and Political Letter . . . to the Right Honourable Charles James Fox* (London, 1783); Major John Scott, *A Narrative of the Transactions in Bengal* (London, 1784); Warren Hastings, *Memoir relative to the State of India* (London, 1787) ; Philip Francis, *Letter to the Rt. Hon. Lord North* (London, 1793 ?).

NEWSPAPERS AND PERIODICALS.

Three of the most important sources for the situation in China before treaty days are the *Canton Register,* which appeared from 1827 to 1844, after which (to 1859) it was known as the *Hongkong late Canton Register,* the *Canton Press,* and the *Chinese Repository* (1832-1851). Complete files of the *Register* and the *Press* were not available, but the *Repository,* edited by the Americans E. C. Bridgman and S. Wells Williams, covers the ground admirably. Editorially it was hostile to the opium trade and somewhat more sympathetic towards the Chinese than were the other Canton publications. Both the *China Mail* and the *North-China Herald* supply additional details for the mid-nineteenth century. I have leaned heavily on the latter for material on the twentieth-century opium question in China. Relevant numbers of *The Times* were also consulted.

As the organ of British anti-opium sentiment, the *Friend of China* (1875-1917) proved indispensable for the progress of the movement in England and valuable for items reprinted from the Far Eastern press.

SECONDARY WORKS : A SELECTED LIST.

Before passing to modern authorities, notice may be taken of several older volumes, which, by reason of their authors' positions, may be classified as quasi-source material. These are Peter Auber, *China* (London, 1834), a chronicle written by the secretary to the court of directors, who had access to the company's papers; S. Wells Williams, *The Middle Kingdom,* 2 vols. (1st edit., New York and London, 1848), which describes some of the events in which the author was an actor; the Rev. Charles Gutzlaff, *A Sketch of Chinese History,* 2 vols. (New York, 1834) ; Sir J. F. Davis, *The Chinese* (London, 1836), and *China: during the War and Since the Peace,* 2 vols. (London, 1852). R. M. Martin, *China,* 2 vols. (London, 1847), which supplied a good deal of ammunition for anti-opium pamphlets, is hopelessly unreliable on the drug question.

The most authoritative account of Anglo-Chinese relations is, of course, H. B. Morse, *The International Relations of the Chinese Empire, 1834-1911,* 3 vols. (London and New York, 1911, 1918). Some aspects of British opium policy have been treated definitively, particularly periods in which the drug trade was a diplomatic issue of major importance. What is lacking, from the point of view of this study, is a discussion of the Indian phase and of the decades in which the opium trade had little influence upon British policy in China. In *The Trade and Administration of China* (rev. edit., London, 1921) Morse includes a good deal of historical material. A. J. Sargent's excellent volume, *Anglo-Chinese Commerce and Diplomacy* (Oxford, 1907), is less detailed on political questions than is Morse, but the author has an unerring touch in dealing with commercial matters. C. S. See, *The Foreign Trade of China (Columbia University Studies,* LXXXVII, New York, 1919), surveys the subject historically in a volume that is strongly Chinese in tone, while C. F. Remer, *The Foreign Trade of China* (Shanghai, 1926), is concerned chiefly with the period after 1871. The years 1600-1843, especially diplomatic developments during the latter part of the period, have been covered by J. Bromley Eames, *The English in China* (London, 1909), with generous quotations from manuscript sources. E. H. Pritchard, *Anglo-Chinese Relations during the Seventeenth and Eighteenth Centuries, University of Illinois Studies in the Social Sciences,* XVII (Urbana, 1929), is the first writer to have made extensive use of the material in Morse's *Chronicles.* Henri Cordier, *Histoire générale de la Chine,* 4 vols. (Paris, 1920), is the standard history of China in a western language. His *Histoire des rélations de la Chine avec les puissances occidentales, 1860-1900,* 3 vols. (Paris, 1901-1902), is less satisfying in its treatment of British policies than of those of Continental powers. American relations with the Orient are best described in Tyler Dennett, *Americans in Eastern Asia* (New York, 1922), although for non-political contacts especially, K. S. Latourette, *Early Relations between the United States and China, 1784-1844* (New Haven, 1917), remains an important authority.

Indian studies, in general, are less directly helpful. The opium system was taken so much for granted that references to it are usually trivial, if they appear at all, both in the standard histories and in more specialized studies. The *Cambridge History of India* (Cambridge, 1922-32), especially the fifth and sixth volumes, is useful for purposes of reference. F. C. Danvers, *The Portuguese in India,* 2 vols. (London, 1894), contains Albuquerque's letter on the early trade, and Sir W. W. Hunter, *History of British India,* 2 vols. (London, 1899-1900), incomplete because of the author's death, makes some observations on the subject, but does not progress far enough in time to be of much assistance. Two able studies, Sophia Weitzman, *Warren Hastings and Philip Francis* (Manchester, 1929), and M. E. Monckton Jones, *Warren Hastings in Bengal, 1772-74* (Oxford, 1918), contribute minor items. Sir Richard Temple, *India in 1880* (London, 1880), gives a good semi-official statement of the company's opium policy, while Chapter XIV of Sir John and Lieutenant General Richard Strachey, *The Finances and Public Works of India* (London, 1882), is a defense of the opium revenue. In two subsequent volumes Sir John Strachey repeats what is substantially the same case. I. T. Prichard, *The Administration of India from 1859 to 1868* summarizes the problems and achievements of British rule, and the *Imperial Gazetteer of India,* 26 vols. (new edit., London, 1909), is, of course, a standard work of reference.

Two works which throw light upon a picturesque aspect of the trade are Arthur H. Clark, *The Clipper Ship Era* (New York, 1910), and the occasionally inaccurate but entertaining Basil Lubbock, *The China Clippers* (4th edit., Glasgow, 1919). Lubbock's most recent volume, *The Opium Clippers* (Boston, 1933), was not received until the present study was in proof. Within its covers will be found a good deal of hitherto unassembled material on both clippers and opium merchants, some of it based on private manuscripts. But the book, as a whole, suffers from the inclusion of irrelevant matter, a lack of documentation, and faulty organization.

Biographical studies of British nineteenth-century statesmen are proverbially numerous, but few of them hold essential material, though many refer to the opium question in passing. For the purpose of this study, one of the most valuable is Demetrius

C. Boulger, *The Life of Sir Halliday Macartney* (London, 1908).
Macartney, who was English secretary to the Chinese legation in
London, took a leading part in the negotiations from which
emerged the additional article to the Chefoo convention. Alexander Michie, *The Englishman in China,* 2 vols. (Edinburgh and
London, 1900), has told the story of Sir Rutherford Alcock's
career. No biographer has appeared for Sir Thomas Wade, Sir
Henry Pottinger, and other diplomatists whose duties involved
them in opium questions. Important sources for the anti-opium
movement in England are Edwin Hodder, *The Life and Work of
the Seventh Earl of Shaftesbury,* 3 vols. (London, 1887), and
Horace G. Alexander, *Joseph Gundry Alexander* (London,
1921). J. Wesley Bready, *Lord Shaftesbury and Social-Indus-
trial Progress* (London, 1926), in a chapter on Shaftesbury's
anti-opium activities, accepts the "good earl's" pronouncements
uncritically and, in consequence, falls into errors of fact. Minor,
though useful, references appear in the Rev. G. R. Gleig, *Memoirs of the Life of Warren Hastings,* 3 vols. (London, 1841);
Lady E. R. Hope, *General Sir Arthur Cotton* (London, 1900);
J. O. P. Bland, *Li Hung-Chang* (New York, 1917); John Morley, *The Life of William Ewart Gladstone,* 3 vols. (London,
1903); Sir J. W. Kaye, *The Life and Correspondence of Henry
St. George Tucker* (London, 1854); A. T. Bassett, *The Life of
the Rt. Hon. J. E. Ellis* (London, 1914).

SECONDARY WORKS: ON THE OPIUM QUESTION SPECIFICALLY.

The opium trade has accumulated in its own right a considerable bibliography. Some of the titles represent academic studies,
others are popular, controversial statements of the question, but
almost none of them deal with the subject historically. Concerned
chiefly with the contemporary opium problem but paying some
attention to the immediate background are Michel Liais, *La
question des stupéfiants manufacturés* (Paris, 1928); Jean Gas-
tinel, *Le trafic des stupéfiants* (Aix-en-Provence, 1927); Olof
Hojer, *Le trafic d'opium* (Paris, 1925); Albert Wissler, *Die
Opiumfrage* (Jena, 1931); Wie T. Dunn, *The Opium Trade in
Its International Aspects* (New York, 1920).

Of controversial writings, by far the most noteworthy, both

BIBLIOGRAPHICAL NOTE 371

in its content and in its historical importance, is Joshua Rowntree, *The Imperial Drug Trade* (London, 1906). This volume, partly because of its devastating analysis of the *Report of the Royal Commission*, did much to arouse English sentiment against the trade. John Palmer Gavit, *"Opium"* (New York, 1925), is an excellent popular statement of the case by an American journalist. Ellen LaMotte, *The Opium Monopoly* (New York, 1920), and *The Ethics of Opium* (New York, 1924), writes of opium in an emphatically polemic tone.

The nineteenth century also produced its share of controversial works, most of them drawing on familiar sources. F. Storrs Turner, *British Opium Policy and Its Results to India and China* (London, 1876), has the merit of quoting extensively from printed sources that are not available on this side of the Atlantic. J. B. Tinling, *The Poppy Plague and England's Crime* (London, 1876), is based upon more study than its title suggests, and J. Spencer Hill, *The Indo-Chinese Opium Trade* (London, 1884), proves himself to be an able advocate.

ARTICLES AND PAMPHLETS.

Among scholarly articles, by far the most important for this study is H. B. Morse, "The Provision of Funds for the East India Company's Trade at Canton in the Eighteenth Century," *Journal of the Royal Asiatic Society*, April, 1922 (pp. 227-255), a by-product of the author's researches in the Canton factory records. Friedrich Hirth, "The Hoppo Book of 1753," *Journal of the North China Branch of the Royal Asiatic Society*, 1882 (New Series, XVII, 221-235), records the fact that opium was listed in the Chinese tariff. Articles dealing with opium as a current question appeared frequently during the nineteenth century. The following may be cited as examples: Sir Rutherford Alcock, "Opium and Common Sense," *Nineteenth Century*, Dec., 1881 (X, 854-868); B. Fossett Lock, "The Opium Trade and Sir Rutherford Alcock," *Contemporary Review*, April, 1882 (XLI, 676-693); Sir Edward Fry, "England, China, and Opium," *ibid.*, Feb., 1876; June, 1877; Jan., 1878 (XXVII, 447-459; XXX, 1-10; XXI, 313-321). In "The Report of the Opium Commission," *ibid.*, July, 1898 (LXXIV, 121-138), Arnold Foster published a damaging attack upon the China conclusions of the royal commission. H. F. MacNair, "An Analogy in Stimulants," *China's New Nationalism and Other Essays* (Shanghai, 1925), contains some interesting suggestions on legal aspects of the opium trade. The anti-opium movement in China and the Anglo-Chinese agreements of 1908 and 1911 evoked a considerable number of articles, few of which constitute essential material. In one publication (*The Asiatic Quarterly Review*), for example, appeared Marshall Broomhall, "The Present Position of the Anti-Opium Movement," Jan., 1909 (XXVII, 85-99) ; Donald N. Reid, "A Behar Planter on the Opium Question," July, 1906 (XXII, 42-51) ; Major J. F. A. MacNair, "The Opium Question," July, 1909 (XXVIII, 147-157). An anonymous writer, Asiaticus, "The Black Gold of Malwa," *National Review,* June, 1911 (LVII, 710-718), analyzes the probable effects of the Anglo-Chinese agreements in the native states. C. F. Tsiang, "New Light on Chinese Diplomacy, 1836-49," *Journal of Modern History,* Dec., 1931 (III, 582-591), is based on recently published Chinese documents.

A formidable mass of controversial pamphlets was published under the auspices of the anti-opium society, some of them representing polemics of a rather high order. Examples of the better sort of pamphleteering are J. G. Alexander, *India's Opium Revenue* (London, 1890) ; J. G. Alexander, *Substitutes for the Opium Revenue* (2d edit., London, 1892) ; Theodor Christlieb, *Der indo-britische Opiumhandel und seine Wirkungen,* translated as *The Indo-British Opium Trade* (London, 1879) ; Joshua Rowntree, *The Opium Habit in the East,* London, 1895; Arnold Foster, *Municipal Ethics* (Shanghai, undated).

A NOTE ON CURRENCY, WEIGHTS, AND STATISTICS

THE chief currencies by which the nineteenth-century opium trade was measured were, of course, the Spanish dollar, the tael, and the rupee. The Spanish (Carolus) dollar, which had an intrinsic value of 4s. 2d. was invoiced by the East India Company from 1619 to 1814 at 5s., and at its actual cost thereafter (Morse, *Chronicles*). Its exchange value in China was always in excess of 4s. 6d. The Chinese tael is not a coin but a weight of silver, its gold price being determined as that of any other commodity. Statistics of foreign trade are given in Haikwan or customs taels, a fictitious currency unit that existed only on the books of the maritime customs. Between 1864 and 1917 the average sterling value of the Haikwan tael was a little over 4s. 6d. This figure, however, has little meaning, for the value of the tael actually varied from a high point of 6s. 8d. in 1864-1865 to a low of 2s. 7d. ½f. in 1915, its general course, despite fluctuations year by year, being steadily downward. The equivalent of 100 Haikwan taels was 111.4 Shanghai taels. Until 1872-1873 the sterling value of the rupee was 2s. But the decline in the price of silver forced the rupee down until, at one time, it reached a level of 1s. 1d. In 1899 the rupee was made legal tender at the rate of 1s. 4d.

Western equivalents of oriental weights have been indicated in footnotes in the text. For convenience of reference, they may be recapitulated here. A Bengal opium maund contains slightly more than 80 pounds; a seer, about 2 pounds. A Chinese catty is equal to about 1⅓ pounds, and a picul contains 100 catties, or 133⅓ pounds. A chest of Bengal opium, therefore, weighs about two maunds, 120 catties, or 160 pounds.

Owing to the cost of printing statistical matter and to the fact that published figures are comparatively accessible, no detailed tables have been given. The following may, however, be taken as a guide to some of the better sources:

1. For the annual production of monopoly opium and its average price per chest from 1787-1788 to the present, together with the number of Malwa chests which paid transit duties, see the *Report of the Royal Commission*, VII, 1895, App. B, pp. 61-62; *Financial and Commercial Statistics of British India*, which covers about two-thirds of the nineteenth century; and, for more recent years, *Statistics of British India*. Earlier issues of this publication (1911-1912, for example) also contain material dealing with the nineteenth century.

2. For the net opium revenue (from 1811-1812), see the *Report from the Select Committee*, 1832, *Parliamentary Papers*, XI, 320-321; *Return of Opium, etc., Parliamentary Papers*, 1865; *Statistics of British India*.

3. For shipments from Calcutta to China and the Straits (from 1795-1796), see the *Chinese Repository*, Aug., 1837, pp. 195-196, and *Statistics of British India;* for shipments from Bombay, see the *Chinese Repository*, Phipps, *China Trade*, p. 235, and *Statistics of British India*. Estimates of exports from Daman to China also appear in Phipps and the *Chinese Repository*.

4. Imports into China present a more difficult problem. Save for the years 1817-1833, when estimated imports appear in the records of the Canton factory as summarized by Morse, the safest figures for the early period are those giving shipments from India. From 1864 on, the reports of the imperial maritime customs supply a record of imports into the treaty ports. These are reproduced in *Financial and Commercial Statistics of British India* and in the earlier issues of *Statistics of British India*. Care should be taken to include with the shipments into treaty ports the quantities imported into Hongkong, most of which eventually reached the mainland, either by smuggling or by paying duty at a native port.

INDEX

Abbott, Lieutenant Colonel H. B., arranges for witnesses from Rajputana, 322-323.

Aberdeen, Earl of, foreign minister, urges legalization, 187; statement of, on Hongkong opium trade, 194.

Abkari opium, defined, 41 n.

Acts, parliamentary: Lord North's Regulating Act, 28; China Act of 1833, 125, 178; Act for the Better Government of India, 280.

Adams, John Quincy, quoted, 167-168.

Additional article, see Chefoo convention.

Aden, opium from, 2; visited by Chinese, 13.

Adulteration, danger of, 34, 37, 40; practised, 43-44; method of, 235 n.; of Malwa opium, 306.

Advances, to poppy cultivators, 5, 19-20, 26-27, 305, 310; interest on, 297 n., 312 n.

Afyun, 11.

A-fu-yung, 14.

Ahmedabad, opium revenue of, 5; weighment at, 306.

Ain-I-Akbari, 5, 10 n.

Ajmir, weighment at, 306.

Albuquerque, Affonso de, quoted, 2, 5 n.

Alcock, Sir Rutherford, British minister to China, quoted, 197, 214 n.; cited, 237 n.; disciplines Foochow merchants, 205 n.; negotiates convention of 1869, 242-250; discusses convention with Indian government, 248-250; negotiations of,

stimulate increase of cultivation in India, 288.

Alexander, J. G., secretary of the Society for the Suppression of the Opium Trade, 311; hopeful of the royal commission, 316; accompanies Henry Wilson to India, 317-318; visits China, 326-327.

Allahabad, cultivation encouraged in, 107; failure of attempts to introduce poppy into, 292.

American clippers, 200 ff.

Americans, in China, import specie, 67; bring bills of exchange, 67 n., 131 n.; import Turkey opium, 68-69; use Lintin anchorage, 114 n.; consul reports to Lin, 153 n.; no opium owned by, surrendered, 155 n.; remain in Canton, 156; sign anti-opium bonds, 158 n.; handle legal trade of British, 159 n., 163, 206 n.; faithful to anti-opium commitments, 163; participate in opium trade, 206-208; memorialize Congress, 208; violate treaty of Wanghia, 224; prohibited from trading in opium, 258 n. See also United States.

Amoy, base for operations in Formosa, 16; visited by *Merope*, 122; in Anglo-Chinese war, 181, 185; opened to foreign trade, 192 n.; *Ariel* seized at, 206; opium taxed at, 223; likin at 239-240; chamber of commerce on treaty revision, 243; loses in opium trade, 278; good quality of opium from, 292 n.